Masters

of

Jazz

Gérald Arnaud

and

Jacques Chesnel

Chambers

EDINBURGH   NEW YORK   TORONTO

Published 1991 by W & R Chambers Ltd,
43–45 Annandale Street, Edinburgh EH7 4AZ
95 Madison Avenue, New York N.Y. 10016

First published in France as *Les grands créateurs de jazz*
© Bordas, Paris, 1989
© English text edition W & R Chambers 1991

Library of Congress Cataloging-in-Publication Data applied for

ISBN 0550 17007 3

Other titles in
Chambers Compact Reference

To be published in 1993

Cover design Blue Peach Design Consultants Ltd
Typeset by Alphaset Graphics Limited, Edinburgh
Printed in England by Clays Ltd, St Ives, plc

Acknowledgements

Translated from the French by Louis Marcellin-Rice

Adapted for the English edition by Alan Dury
Kenny Mathieson

Entries provided for the English edition by Anthony Troon:

The Euro-jazz decades	Humphrey Lyttelton	Stan Tracey
Sandy Brown	Tommy Smith	Eberhard Weber
Jan Garbarek	John Surman	

Chambers Compact Reference Series Editor   Min Lee

Illustration credits

Contents

Wind in the wings

Tongue-tip jazzmen

The 'bizarre brigade'

Jazz goes electric

Swing machines

Into the melting-pot

Jazz and other art forms

Foreword

The authors dedicate this book to
Yvonne and Maurice Cullaz

Let's not cheat: forewords are always written afterwards, as a coda or final chord. Feel free, therefore, to 'listen' to it only at the end, because these words are neither 'warnings' nor instructions ... On the contrary, we would like this book to read like an adventure, in the same way as it was written by us: a walk and an exploration, a pilgrimage and a rambling in a universe where the most familiar sounds prove to be the most mysterious.

Jazz is at the same time the most bare-faced and the most secret music: the more one loves it, the less one 'possesses' it. It is the art which most freely but also most inwardly expresses the genius of this century. Born with the century, it assumed all its contradictions, all its accelerations, it proclaimed its rebellions and rhapsodized its hopes. 'It tells us about pain, and we couldn't care less: that's why it's beautiful, real', said Erik Satie.

But, just like life, jazz resists the simplifications of history. A chronological approach does not teach us any more than dissecting a dead body does about its life. Jazz is alive and well and that is why we have preferred to fling jazz open through a lively interview, using its own language which is that of its own voices and instruments : each part of this book weaves in and out of the total experience, taking big strides through its styles and periods.

For jazz is an eternal reiteration of the same themes, always renewed, the intoxication of a daily routine lived dangerously, day in day out. It is called the music of the night; in fact, it is also the music of dreams and of insomnia. Each page of this book reminds us that its great artists all lived 'around midnight'. That was the death of some of them, but most of them found a new dimension o happiness which is available for us all to share.

Duke Ellington

She named him 'the President', he christened her 'Lady Day'. Their love was like a song and its music.
Billie Holiday and **Lester Young**

Dizzy Gillespie

Jazz prehistory

The idea of a piece in this essentially spontaneous art, jazz, is obviously not the same as in the written music of the European tradition. And yet it is stricter and more clearly defined than in purely ethnic and traditional improvised music. A 'jazz work' is the creation, or the re-creation of a basic theme — which can be of extremely varied complexity — in a specific context as regards the date, place and performer. What distinguishes it from a 'classical' work is its definitive nature, being non-reproduceable and impossible to fix by simple musical notation. It is above all a performance, and only the recording can reproduce, to a large extent at least, the thousands of nuances which contribute to its 'historic' value.

This is why one can say without too much exaggeration that the history of jazz started on February 26 1917. On that day the Original Dixieland Jazz Band, a white quintet from New Orleans, recorded the first jazz record at the Victor Studios in New York. One should perhaps say 'jass', because the spelling of the word was then as imprecise as its meaning and its etymology. Countless theories exist to explain its origin, from 'chasse beau' (a Louisiana dance figure) to the 'jass-belles' (from Jezabel, a prostitute in Cajun slang), or 'jass' (a slang word for sexual intercourse), not to forget the French verb 'jaser'.

The ODJB, led by the cornet player James La Rocca, was certainly not one of the jazz 'greats', even if it was immensely popular around 1920. Its importance is mostly symbolic, because its 'Livery Jass Blues', the first jazz track as such ever to be recorded, puts everything that went before it in the shade. Henceforth the history of jazz was to be primarily that of jazz records, and its true beginnings seem therefore all the more enigmatic, and remain the object of endless speculation and research for musicologists.

The great Afro-American mystery

Much more systematically than in the Caribbean or Latin America, the African slaves brought to the United States were uprooted and deprived of their cultural traditions. Ethnic groups were mercilessly dispersed, languages and religious cults were outlawed, and the few musical instruments that had been brought across the ocean were confiscated and destroyed. All this explains why there is no trace, not even in the evidence from the last century, of any African traditions like the Brazilian candomblé, the Argentinian candombé or the Cuban santeria. But it was also probably this cultural genocide which enabled all the more vital forms of music to develop, because they were not based only on nostalgia for a lost continent. By being silenced, the African traditions became in some way subliminal, and these have constantly been coming to the surface even in the more elaborate forms of the musical heritage of Black America. Ethno-musicologists are in fact not very surprised to find in this music clear though inexplicable similarities to music still played in West Africa, which is where most Afro-Americans originally came from. In a population estimated at 700 000 in the first generation, it would seem incredible that no minority could have conserved at least a part of their clandestine heritage. There is plenty of

1

evidence from the end of the 18th century of musical events whose origin was distinctly African. Pinkster Festivals (celebrations related to Pentecost) brought hundreds of slaves together all over the country to the sound of improvised drums, particularly in the famous Congo Square in New Orleans, which was to become a tourist attraction. Alongside the banjo, which was considered a replica of certain African string instruments, a few European instruments were to be heard, notably the flute and the violin or fiddle. But it is really in everyday life that the common fund of Afro-American tradition has built up, in the *work songs* and *field hollers*, whose original 'response' system gradually integrated itself in the liturgical chants of the first exclusively black churches which were founded at the beginning of the 19th century.

At the time of the Civil War these *spirituals* were so much richer and more powerfully expressive than the hymns sung by the whites that the latter reacted with the 'second awakening' movement, organizing huge religious rallies in the countryside. These *camp meetings* were led by pastors who were to some extent the fore-runners of the modern 'TV evangelists'. But it was in the black churches that a model of expressionist practice directly inspired by African cults first appeared. Spirituals are punctuated by the *ring shout*, a frantic dance accompanied by shouts that lead the participants to an individual and collective state of trance. It was probably around that time that the blues was born. This type of profane solitary chant with its poetic dimension seems to have been originally a discreet, or even clandestine form of expression, since the name itself does not appear in white texts until the beginning of this century. The curious thing is that this art, which is the most authentic Black-American art form, was made popular by its integration with a white tradition, perhaps the most racist one of all, the *minstrel show*.

This kind of road show, which appeared around 1840, consists of white actors with boot-blacked faces performing grotesque parodies of the life of Blacks in Southern plantations. Yet it was in the North that the minstrels achieved their greatest popularity, and for a long time New York was their capital. For the most part their music bore no resemblance to their 'model', but from 1855 some Blacks followed their example by putting on shows portraying the prehistory of Afro-American show-business. This masquerade was to continue for a long time, since in 1927 the white minstrel Al Jolson starred in *The Jazz Singer*, the first film with a sound track. The archaic minstrel show has long since disappeared, and been replaced by the *variety show* or 'vaudeville' which is much more dignified, and where many famous singers and dancers (like Sammy Davis Jr) started their careers.

The small 'Creole' world

Amongst the different styles of genuine negro music which developed around the middle of the 19th century in the United States, there exists a basic common denominator which was to become the very essence of jazz. That is the relativity, the sort of 'off-set' nature of the high pitch of the sound and the accentuation of the rhythm. The first developments were the discovery of the *blue notes* which are minute and selective alterations in the third, seventh and sometimes fifth notes of the octave. The second was the then very tentative use of syncopation, which was to become general and systematic in *ragtime*, and then find its ideal expression in jazz as such.

Ragtime, which appeared in the second half of the last century, was an integral part of jazz history, if only because so much of it was written down, but these were not so much musical scores, rather transcriptions of a musical form for which even recordings on piano-rolls for mechanical pianos do not give a perfect interpretation. In any case, the name 'ragtime' expresses perfectly the highly syncopated nature of this style, which was the first universally popular music played by American Blacks. Its interpreters were essentially accomplished pianists, more or less trained in the European school, generally with a thorough knowledge of Romantic works, from which they drew original inspiration. It was on the rebound, by discovering some of their scores (especially those of Scott Joplin, see p. 26) that composers at the beginning of this century (Debussy, Satie, Stravinsky and Ravel) became passionate about jazz, to which genre they wrongly considered that ragtime belonged. Ragtime, though, was not yet jazz, accenting as it did the strong beats (1 and 3) in 4/4 time in the European manner. But it was already very close to jazz due to its dynamism and its 'spring' or 'bounciness'.

The origins of ragtime include the *cake-walk*, a burlesque dance of the plantation slaves which, in contrast with the minstrel show, consisted of a sort of fascinated parody of the master's dances, quadrilles, polkas, mazurkas, etc. There were some masters who encouraged the playing of European instruments (especially brass), and this even became a way to increase the 'value' of slaves on the market, opening the way to freedom for some. The reputation of some Afro-American musicians had already crossed the Atlantic, as is witnessed by the singer Elizabeth Taylor Greenfield (born in 1808) and the horn player Frank Johnson (born in 1793), who were invited to play before Queen Victoria. After the Civil War, there was a proliferation of military bands of repute, composed entirely of black musicians.

It was above all in the 'Creole' community that a real professional musical activity developed: this word 'Creole' does not have the same meaning in Louisana as in the other ex-French colonies, it simply indicates the urban half-castes forming a cultural group with a pronounced difference from the black community, even after the abolition of slavery. Often educated and even sophisticated, and attached to their French origins through their 'patois' or dialect, their patronyms, and their customs as a whole, they gradually came to lose their identity and were absorbed into the Afro-American community under the effect of the 'Jim Crow' laws, enacted in the Southern States after the Civil War. This ambiguous situation encouraged them to consider music, and the piano in particular, as a sort of aristocratic tradition. Ragtime then became a heritage for them, which increased their standing all the more because white American composers like Gottschalk adopted it, and in Europe, tunes like that of the Republican Guard entered their repertory. At the end of the 19th century a distinction could be made between four flourishing 'schools': Joplin's in Sedalia (Missouri); one in St. Louis, clearly interracial; in Harlem, where the *stride* style was to be born (see page 29); and of course, in New Orleans.

At that time the great port of Louisiana was the capital of all that was lively and creative in this Creole society. The ragtime pianists, nicknamed *professors*, enlivened countless *honky-tonks* and pleasure houses, mostly concentrated in the *French Quarter*, and especially in the exclusive neighbourhood of Storyville. They never rubbed shoulders with the black orchestras, stationed in the west of the 'Crescent City'. But nevertheless the importance of ragtime in New Orleans was to be decisive in the transition which transformed the primitive forms of Afro-American music into proper jazz. Besides, ragtime was adapted to the banjo and the accordion, and survived up to the 1930s in the virtuoso and sophisticated form of the *novelty*. As popular as the waltz in the preceding period, ragtime first appeared as the Black version of the 'prelude', a form of improvisation dear to romantic pianists. It was therefore natural that it should also become the brilliant prelude which heralded the arrival of jazz.

Vocal jazz

From the fields to scat

The history of instrumental jazz is characterized by a constant dynamic thrust, a dizzy ascent where surpassing oneself is a sort of asceticism, where the technical limits and the conceptual a prioris are always overtaken and questioned by each generation. Singing, which is the origin of all the melodic and rhythmic expression of jazz, appears by contrast as a property where the same landscapes are revisited ad infinitum, landscapes which constitute the common soil of all Afro-American music. Thus instrumental jazz always appears as a 'studied' form, elaborated as though it had been refined from this popular basis, while vocal jazz is only artificially distinguishable from the ethnic forms from which it draws its authenticity. Its bases remain forever the blues, gospel songs, *preaching* and *jive*, this language of the ghetto coded at the same time by its slang usage, its syncopated diction and the humorous translation of a marginal way of life. From the working songs and the *field hollers* to *rap*, which resuscitates jive as an autonomous musical style, this fidelity to the spoken language, to the natural inflections of the word, has always distinguished the Afro-American vocal style. It is certainly a matter of style rather than repertoire, since from the turn of the century, jazz singers have had the intelligence to adopt and adapt the magnificent repertoire of the great composers of Broadway or Tin Pan Alley.

The rules for interpretation — which are very flexible — have often been fixed by men who were also great instrumentalists, like Louis Armstrong, Fats Waller, then Dizzy Gillespie and Ray Charles. But it was the women who reached the highest peaks of emotion and invention, dominated by the unequalled trinity of Billie Holiday, Ella Fitzgerald and Sarah Vaughan. The jazz singers tended to pass as amazons in a more or less macho world glad to reduce them to an embodiment of charm.

As for the male singers, their role evolved during the passing of decades. Originally *entertainers* and their close relations, the minstrels in the 1920s and 1930s, they became *crooners* in the 1940s. Then Bebop wanted them as 'oral virtuosos' capable of interpreting *vocalese*, in other words the 'setting to words' of the most complex instrumental solos. This joyful verbal delirium opened the voice to a generation of geniuses, of whom Al Jarreau and Bobby McFerrin are the best known.

The 'entertainers'

Inseparable from instrumental jazz, the role of the 'jazz singer', the heir of the
'minstrel', has always been to make us laugh through our tears.

Louis Armstrong (see page 79) was obviously the archetype and the most imitated model of vocal jazz. His first recorded song, 'Heebie Jeebies', (1926), became legendary as the invention of *scat*. This manner of vocalizing by onomatopaeia had existed for some time, but 'Satchmo' made it a major art. His style was influenced by male and female blues singers (he accompanied about twenty, including Bessie Smith when she was making her debut), and remained inseparable from his own phrasing and cornet vibratos. From the middle of the 1930s, he concentrated more on singing than trumpet, and in spite of a certain laxity in his choice of repertoire, he changed all mud to gold, transforming even the most hackneyed tunes, like 'Ramona' and 'Hello Dolly!' They made Armstrong the first jazz 'superstar'.

Fats Waller (see page 30) whose songs, like 'Ain't Misbehavin'', Armstrong popularized was also primarily a great instrumentalist who 'moved on' to singing, but with the appreciable advantage of being a pianist, and thus able to accompany himself. Associated with Andy Razaf, the famous song writer of Madagascan origins, he created a singing style that was full of both irony and complicity, blending in a somewhat sticky American middle-class sentimentalism.

With his natural cheeky diction he helped to rid popular singing of any emphasis inherited from the operetta or bel canto.

The four **Mills Brothers** (born between 1912 and 1914) met in New York in 1931 to form the most famous pre-war vocal quartet. Accompanied by a simple rhythmic guitar, they popularized jazz or musical comedy themes, harmonizing them in an unprecedented way and substituting the words with an astonishing imitation of wind instruments. They recorded with Armstrong, Ellington, Basie and Calloway.

Cab Calloway (1907) achieved his first success at the same time with 'Minnie the Moocher', the song that became a fetish, which he included in all his shows and which featured in one of the best 'clips' of the pre-war cinema. His big band replaced that of Ellington at the Cotton Club, and became a nursery for young soloists, including Dizzie Gillespie. Hi-scat singing, his talent as a comedian and dancer, his flashy elegance and his inimitable jiving made him the model for all those in Europe who were to call themselves the 'zazous' after one of his favourite onomatopaeias.

Slim Gaillard (1916–1991) could have been just another Calloway. But from his début, his personality transcended the burlesque to heave itself to the level of dada, and a nonsense which was evidently full of sense! A jazz equivalent of the Marx Brothers all rolled into one, the inventor of *vout*, a language he alone could understand, tap-dancer, percussionist, pianist and guitarist, he was able to create an absurd universe, at the same time hermetic and hilarious. His duo with the double-bass player Slam Stewart (*Slim and Slam*) became instantly famous in 1937 thanks to *Flat Foot Floogie* which was immediately adopted by Fats Waller.

Gaillard went to live in Hollywood, and had a part in the film *Helzapoppin'*. He recorded with Dizzy Gillespie and Charlie Parker. His career was to be somewhat episodic, in spite of a comeback he made in France in the 1980s.

Billie Holiday

1915, Baltimore — New York, 1959

A whole life in a voice

A tragic destiny whose painful stages were revealed in her singing.

Although she did not possess obvious vocal resources — her range was limited, her voice lacked resonance, and could be harsh and grating at will — Billie Holiday must be considered as the most touching of jazz singers. More than anyone else she used her voice as an instrument, disregarding the conventions, transforming (and giving herself totally to) the most banal songs, creating the emotional climate found in the blues (which she actually seldom sang — ten times out of the approximately 270 pieces she recorded). Her pronunciation and her phrasing, her voice oozing with sensuality, her controlled vibrato and the way she had of amplifying the sustained notes, her fine use of rhythmic intervals, all

these features resemble the style of Lester Young, who was a faithful friend (he called her 'Lady Day') and who shared a similar destiny.

During their brief existence (she died at 44 and he at 50, with four months between them), they revealed a pain (and a thirst) to live, a daily inescapable and desperate struggle, an overwhelming drama of self-destruction, not looking for pity but rather haughtily resigned, in an inevitable disintegration caused by alcohol and sedatives, taken to forget unaccepted vexation and constant failure.

After an unhappy childhood (rape, correction house, prostitution), Billie Holiday sang in cabaret and attracted the attention of the critic John Hammond, who enabled her to make her first record with Benny Goodman. She became famous (records with Teddy Wilson and with her own orchestra, an engagement with Count Basie where she made friends with Lester Young, tours with the Artie Shaw Orchestra, the success of her interpretations of 'Strange Fruit', 'Lover Man', 'God Bless the Child', a film, *New Orleans* opposite Louis Armstrong) but in about 1941, she became addicted to drugs. Her health failed, her voice was coarsened by drug abuse and sickness. It became cracked and broken, poignant with an emotion made more intense by her sorrows and distress, the vanished hopes left in the ghettos of Baltimore and elsewhere.

Shortly before her death, she published her autobiography, *Lady sings the Blues*, of which a film was made in 1972 with Diana Ross in the title role.

In Billie Holiday's own words:

'You can dress yourself up to the hilt in white satin, put gardenias in your hair without seeing a sugar cane on the horizon, and nevertheless, you feel like a slave in a plantation.' 'Drugs never helped anyone to sing better nor to do anything better. It's Lady who is telling you so. She has taken enough to know a lot about it. If anyone tries to contradict me, ask him if he thinks he knows something about drugs that Lady Day doesn't.' (Extracts from *Lady sings the Blues*)

Ella Fitzgerald

1918, Newport News

A naturally infectious joy to sing

She charms as much as she sings thanks to her extraordinary presence and charisma.

Her immediate impact conveys the pleasure she gets from singing, which she wants to share freely. For the general public she is unrivalled as the best known jazz singer, because she knows how to detach herself naturally from petty realities and give the best of herself, to bring her listeners the 'little moments of happiness' everybody needs in their life. She sings for herself in order to sing better for her audience, which explains the endless feast of her impressive recording successes, which have never been equalled by any other woman jazz singer. While Sarah Vaughan's interest in the words often seems only relative, Ella enjoys them and plays to the full with even the silliest of them, before launching into crazy improvisations, mixing scat singing with funny quotes in a torrent of exuberant humour. Hardly any singer has achieved such vocal control or mastery of rhythms and tempos, allowing her to perform with so much innovation, swing and vitality.

It is true that everything went well for her right from the start. After getting a first prize at a talent contest at the Harlem Opera House in 1934, when she was sixteen, she became the star of drummer Chick Webb's Orchestra (1935–1939), and became the leader of the band when he died. She then sang with a number of vocal groups, and participated in the *Jazz at the Philharmonic* concerts organized by Norman Granz, who had become her manager. She went on countless tours, accompanied by subtle pianists such as Oscar Peterson and Tommy Flanagan, or by great orchestras like Duke Ellington's or Count Basie's. She recorded the great classics, and in particular performed a sublime *Porgy and Bess* alongside Louis Armstrong.

Sophisticated Ladies
Dinah Washington (1924–1963). The 'Queen of the Blues', with her metallic, insistant vibrato voice, expressed all the aspirations and disappointments of the Black community with a pinch of sardonic humour, and with considerable commercial success.
Anita O'Day (1919), whose style was very pure, improvized with amazing ease and gusto. She was the lead singer in the bands of Gene Krupa (alongside Roy Eldridge), Woody Herman and Stan Kenton in the forties.
Helen Merrill (1930), gave jazz great dramatic impact with her talent for giving confidential warmth to emotionally powerful phrases.
Carmen McRae (1922) was an excellent pianist and a remarkable stylist whose richly nuanced voice gave a theatrical dimension to her songs. Her art was at its best when she sang ballads.

Antibes Festival — Juan les Pins, 1964
Accompanied by Tommy Flanagan on the piano and with Roy Eldridge on the trumpet, Ella was interrupted in the song *Mack the Knife* by the 'cigales' in the Gould pine forest. On the spot, she improvised a blues to the rhythm of their strident chirpings which she dedicated to them calling it 'The Cricket Song'.

Sarah Vaughan

1924, Newark — New York, 1990

From Muse to Diva

The most accomplished of the vocalists is also the singer with the best musical technique.

The 'divine' Sarah Vaughan possessed immense talents, notably her harmonic creativity and keen sense of improvisation which have earned her the admiration of jazz musicians as well as the adoration of the general public. With as wide a range as an opera singer, she made the most difficult pieces sound both easy and fun. She flitted cheekily from bass register to soprano with a rare elegance and surprising sophistication.

After studying piano and singing, she won a talent competition at the Apollo in Harlem. Ella Fitzgerald encouraged her and she started her career as second pianist and singer in Earl Hines's band, then joined singer Billy Eckstine. She started to work in the New York night clubs, where she was soon attracted by the new sounds of Bebop, and made recordings with some of its inventors including Dizzy Gillespie and Charlie Parker.

'Sassy' soon became a star, and extended her repertoire to include 'jazzy' pop numbers in order to reach a larger audience. Whether she sang with a trio or with Count Basie's big band, or even with a symphony orchestra, Sarah became known as *the* singer of modern jazz, bringing her consummate skill to a blend of scat singing, in which she was a past master, with more

Sarah Vaughan

traditional classics, mostly ballads, which she interpreted with some affectation, but also a sense of mischief.

Bebop singers

In singing, bebop (an onomatopaeic word derived from the rhythm of a style which appeared in the early forties and renewed the concept of 'classical' jazz) takes two different forms. In 'Scat', words are replaced by sounds, syllables or nonsense phrases (see Dizzy Gillespie's repertoire of songs like 'Oop-Pop-A-Da', 'Ooo-Shoo-Be-Doo-Be', 'Ool-Ya-Koo' . . .); vocalese is the name given to the adaptation of new texts to themes that were originally instrumental, or to carefully transcribed solos.

The invention of scat singing is generally attributed to Louis Armstrong, though this form of expression was in use as early as the 1920s and Cab Calloway became famous in the 1930s with songs like 'Hi-De-Hi-De-Ho' and 'Zah Zuh Zah' (which is the origin of the French word 'zazou'). But it was in fact the boppers who made the most intensive use of it, followed by vocalists like Ella Fitzgerald, Sarah Vaughan or Mel Tormé, who then included it in their repertoire.

'Scat' singers

Dizzy Gillespie (see p. 84) never gave a performance without including two or three scat numbers for the pleasure of a public that was greedy for these vocal acrobatics; his duets with the singers Kenny Hagood in 1948, then Joe Carroll from 1949 to 1953, were pretexts for entertaining rivalry and excesses bordering on verbal delirium.

Previously, another scat pioneer, the crazy singer **Leo Watson** (1898–1950), had teamed up with one of the champions of the absurd, the hilarious Slim Gaillard.

Both a scat expert and an adept of the vocalese style, singer and poet **Babs Gonzalez** (1919–1980), composer of 'Oop-Pop-A-Da', played in the orchestras of Lionel Hampton and Charlie Barnet before launching his own group, Babs' Three Bips And A Bop. He also adapted his own texts on instrumental solos with devilish gusto.

The Vocalese Style

Eddie Jefferson (1918–1979) was the first singer in the 1940s to adapt his own words from famous solos, following the inflections and modulations of the great instrumental versions.

King Pleasure (1922–1981) became famous through his version of 'I'm in the Mood for Love' in 1952, singing Jefferson's words to James Moody's tune. He perfected the art of writing his own words on improvisations by Lester Young, Stan Getz, and Charlie Parker. This kind of transcription inspired the vocal group **L.H.R.** (**Dave Lambert-Jon Hendricks-Annie Ross**). The trio became famous for their vocal interpretations of Count Basie's recordings, pulling off the incredible achievement of vocally reproducing their orchestral features, sometimes with the aid of over-dubbing techniques.

Under the impetus of singer and song-writer **Mimi Perrin** the group called **Les Double Six** was formed in France in 1959. Their poetic texts and perfection of their voices and phrasing were applied to classic Bebop and their success was considerable, but ephemeral, since after changing vocalists several times, the group disappeared in 1965.

Betty Carter (1930), one of the last Bebop singers, hit the limelight after a recording she sang with Ray Charles in 1962. A dynamic scat singer, she was also influenced by the sonority and phrasing of instruments, which she reproduces with perfect technical control.

Ray Charles

1930, Albany

A synthesis of all vocal types

The blind young man from Georgia became 'the Genius' for the black community and the white public.

Few artists have succeeded as Ray Charles has in stimulating enthusiasm in such a varied public. During a concert by this wizard of *Soul Music*, absolutely nobody, whether a rock fan, blues freak, 'fired' by Gospel Music, obsessed by boogie, a lover of 'country' or infatuated by romance, can resist this voice, which is both rough and gentle, raucous or luminous, often rasping, almost breaking, always heart-rending, vibrant and warm. It is hard not to be carried away by these breaking waves of rhythms which induce a trance-like state; hard not to melt when he becomes persuasive. His sensitivity is accompanied by a penchant for incantation, or oscillates with a gentle growl which is always charming and sometimes sentimental.

The reasons for his success can be found in audiences' perception of his sincerity, his voice, and his 'preacher's' tone, expressing joy as well as rage, as in 'I Got a Woman' (1954), 'Hallelujah I Love Her So' (1955) or 'What'd I Say' (1959). He himself plays piano or organ in the big bands which most frequently accompany him, together with his backing singers, The Raelets. He followed the path marked by the branding iron of the blues, an exemplary route dotted with pitfalls, notably drugs, which he managed to overcome.

He took part in 'jazz' recording sessions, including his record *Genius + Soul = Jazz*, and with Milt Jackson). In 1960, 'Georgia on My Mind' rose to first place in the hit-parades in the United States. For ten years now his American career has been devoted exclusively to interpreting *country and western*.

Nat King Cole

1917, Montgomery — Santa Monica, 1965

Ray Charles recognized the influence of this pianist and singer who rapidly became a star at the end of the 1940s. A pianist with an elegant touch and a supple, airy swing, he was the first to invent a modern concept of the trio, using piano, guitar and double bass, in which each musician had a prominent role, and which was to influence Ahmad Jamal and Oscar Peterson. Oscar Moore was the guitarist of this trio, so unlike all the others, from 1939 to 1949.

Nat King Cole gradually gave up the piano, and won the public's favour as a popular singer.

> **In Ray Charles's own words:**
> 'When I wrote *What'd I Say*, I only had one rhythmic plan which I liked; I composed it in one evening . . . I was brought up in the Baptist school, and this is why I like songs with a real rhythm' (*Jazz Magazine*, August 1976).

From crooners to virtuosos

Launched by the radio in the 1940s, a new kind of vocalist mingled charm, humour and swing.

Frank Sinatra (1915), together with Nat King Cole, is the ideal model for all crooners, those singers of charm on the borderline of jazz who became the rage in the 1940s. Sinatra was deeply marked by his early years in the big bands of Harry James and Tommy Dorsey, and always liked them, cutting sumptuous discs with Ellington, Buddy Rich, Woody Herman, Count Basie (*Live at the Sands*) and Quincy Jones. His infallible swing, even at a very slow tempo, was fantastic when he 'crossed swords' with favourite soloists like Stan Getz or Harry Edison.

Mel Tormé (1925) is ten years younger than Sinatra, and if he is less well-known (at least in Europe), this is largely because he was definitely more modest and discreet! He had also made his debut in the big bands, first with Chico Marx, then Artie Shaw, and his lightly veiled tone earned him the nickname of 'The Velvet Fog', which he hated. A poet and novelist, and an excellent composer of ballads, he preferred the intimacy of clubs and the spontaneity of jam-sessions, where he gave the whole measure of a vocal imagination which made him far more than a crooner.

Leon Thomas (1937) sang with Earl Coleman and Johnny Hartman, and is one of the rare baritones in jazz. His career defies the usual distinctions of style and generation. The singer in Count Basie's band at the beginning of the 1960s, he found himself shortly afterwards in the real avant-garde, alongside saxophonist Pharaoh Sanders. An author-composer, he continued to navigate between very different styles, utilizing his amazing scat singing and an impressively wide range of vocal effects. He changed his name to Leone in 1976.

Al Jarreau (1940) embodies the removal of barriers between vocal styles from the beginning of the 1970s. For this shepherd's son, with a degree in psychology, anything that 'moved' was worth singing. Blues, gospel, jazz, samba, Californian rock or pure Motown soul, he did not hesitate to brew all these categories together in the same record or concert, to make a sort of polyrhythmic performance with neither age nor frontier. He became, with George Benson, the most popular 'jazzy' singer of the 1980s.

Manhattan Transfer is a vocal quartet which was very influenced by the *doop-wop* of the 1950s, but which was mainly dedicated to vocalese (like L.H.R. and Les Double Six; see page 10). Formed in 1972 by a New York taxi-driver, Tim Hauser, the group has moved to California, and scored a world-wide success with its vocal version of 'Birdland' by Weather Report's Joe Zawinul (1980).

Bobby McFerrin (1950) is the great 'vocal phenomenon' of the 1990s. His parents were both opera singers, and he benefitted from a totally eclectic musical training, learning to play the piano as well as several wind instruments before devoting himself entirely to voice. It certainly deserved it, for with no other artifice than the astonishing dexterity of his vocal cords and great skill with the mike, he can hold the stage alone, improvising spontaneously on a repertoire stretching from Bach to James Brown, via Mozart, Bud Powell and Coltrane. Like the Mills Brothers, he imitates all kinds of instruments, but he is also able to create truly unheard-of sounds, although at the price of exhibitions which are sometimes futile. He became the mascot of jazzmen of all kinds, but refused nonetheless to be merely their favourite 'gimmick', and seems to be moving towards a more 'conceptual' form of music, in line with the great scat singers.

From spiritual to funk

The voice of the Lord and the way of pleasure

The role of the sacred, the rite and trance can never be over-stated in the whole history of Afro-American music. Almost all the great creators of jazz periodically drew their inspiration from the repertory, and especially from the way of singing and proclaiming their faith that was current in the black churches.

After the Civil War and the abolition of slavery, a fanatic, institutional racism developed in the debilitated States of the South, which soon imposed total segregation in the very heart of Christian communities. The 'African' Methodist, Episcopalian or Baptist churches had a huge success among former slaves and their families, and during the 1860s founded more than 20,000 places of worship. At the end of the century, they were joined by the Pentecostal Churches, notably the 'Sanctified Church of God in Christ', a true museum of black rites and songs. Coming from the North, hundreds of emissaries of the American Missionary Society opened numerous schools and institutes for literacy. In these two places — church and school — flourished the art of the *negro spiritual*, based on hymns and psalms sung most frequently a cappella, most often harmonized for four voices.

October 6 1871 saw the birth of the first great season of spirituals, of the eleven 'Jubilee Singers' from the school of Fisk (Tennessee), a true epic which took them right to the courts of the Czar, Frederic III and Queen Victoria, and which revealed to the whole world the wealth of Afro-American music, even if in a slightly sweetened rhythmic form. The European composers (Dvorak, Delius, Ravel) were enthusiastic, and a lot of works and collections of transcriptions were published. From the 1920s, recordings enabled singing preachers and pastors to shine outside their churches, and some of them, including the Reverends Nix, Gates, Taggart, Kelsey and Franklin, even became stars. Until our day, all this religious expression constituted a real parallel 'show-business', not only in the United States, but throughout the English-speaking world.

After the Crash of 1929, it was the *Gospel Song* (evangelical hymns) which acquired its classical form thanks to the great 'converted' blues pianist and composer, Georgia Tom Dorsey. The frontier between the profane and sacred version of Afro-American singing continued to be eroded. The *rhythm'n'blues* of the 1950s, the *Soul Music* of the 1960s and 1970s, and even *funk*, borrowed the essential elements of their dynamic potential for expression from Gospel music. In these fields, it goes without saying that 'great creators' abound, and we have only been able to introduce here those who have directly or indirectly contributed to the history of jazz. It remains true that without this irreplaceable background which they collectively represent, most of the heroes of this Odyssey would be missing the essential part of their soul.

13

Holy voices

Choral singing is the most widely recognized form of Afro-American music. The church benches have always been a primary jazz school, and very few musicians have escaped the fascination of this transition of the word to song, which is perhaps the most obvious resurgence of African sources on American soil.

Vocal Quartets

The Spirit of Memphis, founded in 1928, was rebaptized after the name of Lindbergh's aeroplane the *Spirit of Saint Louis*. Still active under the lead of the veteran Earl Malone, it included in its ranks such future stars of rhythm'n'blues as O.V. Wright and Joe Hinton.

The Golden Gate Quartet, founded in Virginia (1934), was the most popular of all, adapting the Mills Brothers' imitations of instruments to spirituals. Its repertoire also includes standard jazz pieces, and it continues its triumphant tours throughout the world, led by one of its founders, the bass Orlandus Wilson.

The Soul Stirrers of Texas, created in 1935, offered a more exalted expressionist singing, expressionist. The great pioneer of Soul Music, Sam Cooke, was a member between 1950 and 1965.

The Swan Silvertones of Alabama, founded in 1938 by the master of falsetto Claude Jeter, also included some remarkable 'shouters' like Soloman Womack and Bob Crenshaw. They recorded masterpieces like 'My Rock' and 'Jesus Remembers' for James Brown's King label.

The Sensational Nightingales started in 1949 under the leadership of the extraordinary baritone Julius Cheeks, a well-known militant anti-racist. Their aggressive style contrasts strangely with their name 'nightingales'.

The Harmonizing Four led by Thomas Johnson have recorded hundreds of spirituals since 1943, some of which are heart-rending.

The Five Blind Boys from Alabama are an extended quartet (quintet or sextet) focussing on ecstatic gospel singing.

Female Groups

The Ward Singers were the queens of gospel singing from the 1940s, thanks partly to the charisma of the turbulent Clara Ward (1929–1973), and even more so to that of Marion Williams, who remodelled the group without Clara in 1958, renaming it **Stars of Faith**.

The Staple Singers (Mavis, Cleotha, Yvonne and their father) began in 1950 in Chicago and managed to record real 'hits' of Gospel with no commercial concessions, such as 'Uncloudy Day', before making a spectacular adventure into soul at the end of the 1960s.

Several Great Soloists

Female singers: Vanessa Armstrong, Shirley Caesar, Bessie Griffin, Marie Knight, Sallie Martin, Willie Mae Ford Smith, Marion Williams. Without forgetting the Afro-American lyrical singers, who interpreted in their own way the spirituals and gospel songs, like **Marian Anderson**, **Barbara Hendricks**, **Jessye Norman**, **Leontyne Price**, and also **Dionne Warwick**, a product of the famous Drinkard Singers. Male singers: Alex Bradford, Solomon Burke, James Cleveland, Sam Cooke, Andrae Crouch, Al Green, Edwin Hawkins, Little Richard.

Mahalia Jackson

1911, New Orleans — Chicago, 1972

The Callas of Gospel

Refusing all the temptations of a profane career, her genius made her the only star of sacred music.

The song of the sirens has always solicited this incorruptible believer of the Baptist church. From her early childhood she absorbed the most genuine forms of Afro-American singing, in the Mount Moriah Church next to her humble family home. Her father, a barber, was preacher on Sundays, and there was no organ and no choir. Hymns burst forth to the sound of drums, and West African trance brought natural rebirth. Mahalia always admitted that she was fascinated by this 'Joyful noise unto the Lord' to which the Psalms refer, and which is in such contrast with the austerity of Protestant rites. In her adolescence, though, she secretly listened to the songs of Bessie Smith, who (together with Caruso!) was to remain her idol. When she was sixteen she started a small cosmetics shop in Chicago. The Windy City was then going through a fantastic

musical whirlwind which was lifting the taboo separating the 'music of God' from the 'music of the Devil'. Thomas E. Dorsey (born in 1899) was the pioneer of modern gospel and became its most inspired composer 'Precious Lord', while a few years earlier, under the name of Georgia Tom, he had been one of the most sarcastic bluesmen.

Mahalia cut her first disc in 1937. Dorsey became her mentor, and their duo found success with 'Move On Up a Little Higher' (1947), which sold more than two million copies, and then with 'Silent Night'. She triumphed at Carnegie Hall, had her own television show and toured in Europe. In 1958, she sang at the Newport Festival, and recorded with Duke Ellington a new version of his famous 'Black, Brown and Beige Suite'. She was very close to Martin Luther King, lending her voice to the civil rights movement, putting on shows all over the world despite her heart problems. But her universal fame was only a superficial facet of a life entirely dedicated to her Church. As soon as she arrived in Chicago she refused the golden opportunity she was offered by Earl Hines, who was the most famous band leader in the city of a thousand night clubs. Similarly, her fierce independence and the belief that her 'natural' talent was an unalterable gift of God, made her refuse any singing lessons and barely accept affectionate advice from her peers, Sallie Martin and Willie Mae Ford Smith. Strangely, her glory and her contract with the 'white' label CBS made her lose her own audience, the ghetto populations whose most sacred expression she had revealed to the whole world. Her autobiography, *Movin' On Up*, was published in 1966.

The 'miraculous' Newport concert

'She got on stage and said softly, as if she were talking to children: "I wonder if you are prepared to stay and listen to me under this rain, I'll just try to warm us up". Then, under a shower of applause she sang *Didn't It Rain!* No one had ever sung it like that, not even Mahalia. The storm grew calm. The rain stopped falling. And soon God's firmament was filled with stars' (Rudi Blesh, *O Susanna*).

Sister Rosetta Tharpe

1915, Arkansas — Philadelphia, 1973

From the Cotton Club to the Baptist Church

Refusing to sell her soul to jazz, she nonetheless gave it her youth before dedicating her incredible swing to spirituals.

If we have already seen that the border between the sacred and the profane is never quite water-tight, the case of Sister Rosetta Nubin is unique in the history of jazz. The marvellous ease with which she literally 'swings' between the two shows more than just versatility, but also a deliberate will to defy conventions and taboos. She became the leading gospel star in the 1940s, while at the same time being triumphant on the 'unworthy' stage of the Apollo in Harlem. She paid dearly for this impertinence, being rejected by the pious community of the Pentecostal Church to which she owed her rise to stardom, and joined the Baptists, who were more accommodating.

Trained from her earliest childhood by her mother Katie Bell Nubin, who directed

the choir in her small home town of Cotton Plant, Rosetta had her first success at the age of six in a big Chicago church. At nineteen, she married a pastor called Thorpe in Pittsburgh, and when she divorced after a short time she kept the name, changing just one letter. In 1938 she became the first gospel singer, which was a new genre at the time, to sing in a night club, and not just any old dive; first she performed with Cab Calloway, then with the dancer Bill Bojangles Robinson, in the Cotton Club shows which had just left Harlem for Broadway. Soon after, she made her first records for the Decca label, and on December 23 she took part in a historic concert in the Carnegie Hall, *From Spirituals to Swing*. Then, to the fury of the New York clergy, she did not hesitate to 'evangelize' jitterbug fanatics, singing with torrid big bands such as Andy Kirk's and Lucky Millinder's, or accompanied by pianists like Mary Lou Williams and Sammy Price. Wearing a boa of ostrich feathers she drove around in limousines, and was featured in *Life* magazine, which did not prevent her from recording the Good Word for the 'V Discs', aimed at the morale of the troops rather than at their morality. Her versions of 'Rock Me' and 'Trouble in Mind' were amongst the great 'black' hits of the war.

From 1947 Rosetta sang with the singer Marie Knight and concentrated exclusively on recitals of religious music, but she still managed to hit the headlines. For her third wedding in 1951, she had 25 000 paying guests! She was very popular in Europe during the 1960s and starred in Hugues Panassié's film *L'Aventure du Jazz*. As well as her ardent and irresistibly syncopated singing style, her talent as a guitarist made her one of the most communicative personalities of her generation.

Says Sister Rosetta Tharpe:

'My mother used to hold me on her knees while she played the harmonium in church. I would tap out with one finger *Nearer My God to Thee* and she would accompany me with the left hand ... It was one our friends who gave me the nickname 'little Sis' when I was a kid; but I'm not in holy orders, I sing gospel because I like it: I'm what they call a *holy roller* singer, I sing anywhere people will have me'. (*Jazz Magazine*).

Aretha Franklin

1942, Memphis

The soul that sublimates love

By refusing to choose between 'Love Supreme' and 'Love Forever', the most beautiful voice of our time turns every song into a hymn.

Eroticism and religion overlap throughout Afro-American culture, and the lives of all the great soul musicians walk this tightrope which tries to separate religious expression from the expression of the body. Marvin Gaye and Sam Cooke were the sons of pastors, and Al Green and Little Richard became preachers. As for Aretha, she is the niece of the great singer Clara Ward and the daughter of the most famous preacher of the Baptist Church. Mahalia Jackson and Marion Williams, to name just two, were among those who saw her in her cradle. The countless sermons by C.L. Franklin, her father, on the 'Chess' label are 'hits' in their own genre. In the New Bethel Church in Detroit, Aretha and her

Says John Hammond:
'The most 'natural' singer I've heard since Billie Holiday' (*Downbeat*).

Atlantic Soul
The famous producer Jerry Wexler made this prestigious jazz and blues label, founded in 1947 by the Turk Ahmet Ertegun, into the best soul music recording company, alongside Stax and Motown. Their catalogue includes: Otis Redding, Ray Charles, Wilson Pickett, Ben E. King and, of course, Aretha Franklin.

father keep the most ardent flame of the gospel alight between triumphant tours.

It was in Detroit too, the future capital of the *Motown sound* that she made her first records. They were strictly religious and were cut on the J.V.P. label. Sam Cooke, a friend of the Franklins, encouraged her to persevere, and the double bassist Major Holley introduced her to Columbia Records. She was just eighteen when she made her first non-religious recordings, which were real masterpieces. Nobody, except for Ray Charles, had so instinctively and intimately crossed the blues, gospel and jazz traditions, without sugaring them up to suit the new soul-pop context. An accomplished pianist, Aretha became known as the 'female Ray Charles' of the prestigious Atlantic label in 1965, and two years later was established as the most famous American singer. She recorded 'Respect' with Ray Charles and 'Lady Soul' with Otis Redding.

Aretha is also very influenced by her childhood, her mother's death, her father's exhausting 'Gospel Caravan', tours and a divorce which affected her very deeply. Although she 'flirted' sometimes disappointingly with rock musicians like Eric Clapton and Eurythmics, she always seems to fall in with the best orchestrators like Quincy Jones and Curtis Mayfield, and her religious dimension always comes through, as can be seen in her masterpiece 'Amazing Grace' (1972). A few months before, she sang the last adieu to Mahalia Jackson with 'Precious Lord', which the latter had howled over the body of Martin Luther King. She is true to the tradition, but always looking for new sounds, and knows how to take risks without sacrificing the essence of her art. She gambles her life without ever losing her soul.

Mahalia Jackson
singing in the new temple she had built (1961).

Stevie Wonder *at Bercy (1984).*

Soul music

The secularized form of gospel was taken immediately to its highest form of expression by Ray Charles, Aretha Franklin and James Brown and gained universal recognition in the 1960s. Its greatest artists practically all come from two well-defined areas.

The Great Lakes school

The Great Lakes region (Chicago, Cleveland, Detroit) gave birth to a school which stresses tenderness, elegance, a high register and a certain sophistication. The Motown company, founded in Detroit in 1960 by Berry Gordy, a Ford factory worker, attracted the singer-author-composer **Smokey Robinson** (1940), whose enlightened musical direction provided an essential part of popular music in the 1960s. The history of Motown continued in the following decade with **Stevie Wonder** and **Diana Ross** (1944). After leaving her brilliant vocal trio The Supremes, Ross became a major star, partly thanks to her films, which include *Lady Sings the Blues*, (1971) in which she played Billie Holiday. She also served as a godmother to the Jackson 5, whose youngest member, Michael, allowed Motown to repeat the miracle of the prodigal son already achieved by Stevie Wonder. The Detroit stables also included **The Temptations**, another vocal quintet, fairly ordinary but with great stage presence, and above all two of the greatest gospel soloists, **Al Green** (born in 1946), whose airy falsetto was just as romantic as the hymns which he eventually devoted himself to entirely, and **Marvin Gaye** (1938-1984), whose charisma and sensuality culminated with *What's Going On* (1970) and *Let's Get It On*. Gaye was tragically shot by his father, a minister, during an argument.

The Chicago gospel choirs gave birth to several major figures of this northern soul, who were inspired and gutsy at the same time. The great historical pioneer of this type of singing, **Sam Cooke**, (1931-1964), leader of the Soul Stirrers, was the first to softly open the secret door which led from the temple to the hit-parade. His tight-rope phrasing, his charisma and his infallible swing were to have an incredible impact, well after his mysterious murder. His former guitarist, **Bobby Womack** (1944) married his widow and perpetrated his style brilliantly, in the heart of a talented family. **Lou Rawls** (born in 1937), another disciple of Cooke, a former member of the famous Pilgrim Travellers, at first associated with the pianist Les McCann and illustrated a very refined form of soul jazz in his records for Capitol. Finally, **Curtis Mayfield** (1942) imposed his piquant falsetto on a style of orchestration which is both graceful and serene, first with the Impressions, and later as a soloist.

The Southern School

The other great nursery of soul, is obviously the South, the cradle of the blues and of jazz. **Percy Sledge** (1941), whose 'When a Man Loves a Woman' was the hit of the summer of 1966, came from Alabama, as did **Wilson Pickett**, whose tough male accents clearly expressed a certain kind of southern machismo. **Otis Redding** from Georgia (1941) was another to illustrate this, but in a spectacular, feline way. He was killed in an airplane crash in 1967, at the height of his fame. His best albums, like *Pain in my Heart* or *Sings Soul Ballads* are the jewels of Stax, the celebrated Memphis label, which also recorded the two most beautiful voices of the town, the practically unknown **O.V. Wright**, and **Isaac Hayes** (1943), a brilliant pianist whose *Hot Buttered Soul* and the original score for the film *Shaft* have made his messianic attraction and almost symphonic orchestration famous all over the world. His compatriot, the veteran **Rufus Thomas** (1917), cruder but no less charismatic, and his sister Carla, were an authentic link

19

between classical rhythm 'n' blues and Memphis soul, represented by the younger **Allen Toussaint** (1938), who became the musical soul of New Orleans as pianist, composer and producer.

Last but not least, the most famous of these 'Southern voices' (at least in Europe), summarizes and contains them all. Born in North Carolina in 1933 as Eunice Waymon, the sublime **Nina Simone** excelled in all registers and nuances of an infinitely varied spectrum, which radiated from gospel to modern jazz, passing through blues, soul and even extending to a dramatic repertoire of European origin. An accomplished pianist and organist, uniting the tradition of the spiritual with the solid base she gained in the Juilliard School, this lively, totally unpredictable rebel was one of the unique geniuses of Afro-American culture, able to transcend better than anyone else a universal repertoire stretching from Gershwin to Brel without ever betraying the original mystery which is best expressed by the word 'soul'.

Stevie Wonder (1950)

If prodigal children are too often only wise monkeys, the terms 'miracle' and 'little genius' do not seem excessive on sleeves of the earliest records of Steveland Morris. From the age of nine, he was treated as a sort of Amadeus, with Berry Gordy, the founder of Motown, in the role of Mozart's father. Gordy re-baptized him *Wonder*, and moved mountains to launch him. Stevie has never left this 'home' of records, where he felt at home among the godfathers of soul at the time, Smokey Robinson, Marvin Gaye and the Supremes. Blind from birth, he acquired perfect mastery of piano, organ, harmonica and percussion instruments, but his first 45 rpm records — 'Thank You Mother', 'I Call It Pretty Music' — first and foremost emphasized

the childlike grace of his voice. After a triumphant concert at the Apollo in Harlem, the 'toughest' hall in New York, he recorded better records live, one after another, marking the rhythm'n'blues epoch, notably *'Fingertips'*, and *'12 year old Genius'*. He also started to compose, but he spent the 1960s mainly as a brilliant harmonica virtuoso and interpreter of fashionable hits like 'Blowin' in the Wind' by Bob Dylan. Among those who influenced him was Ray Charles, of course, but also the Rolling Stones and Stan Getz.

In 1972 the second Stevie Wonder was born, as the best 'pop' composer of his generation. His albums — *Music of My Mind, Talking Book, InnerVisions* — grew more and more sophisticated. Worked out as real orchestral suites, they provided dozens of superb melodies to enrich the repertory of singers, but also of jazz musicians. At the same time, his impressive mastery of synthesizers began to have an effect, especially after the monumental triple album *Songs in the Key of Life*, in memory of Duke Ellington. Thereafter each composition appeared as a homage or a testimony clearly linked to the destiny of his people, or some sublime episode in his love life. Tirelessly militant against racism, Apartheid, and the misery of Africa, he managed to have Martin Luther King's birthday declared a public holiday in the United States. This account by the great blues singer **Sippie Wallace** is a good description of his personality: 'One day Stevie Wonder chanced to enter my local church. He started to sing 'Have a Talk with God' sitting at the piano, but he found it out of tune, so he moved over to the big organ. Well, that was child's play for him. Blind or not, he leant back and forth, and made it reverberate like synthesizers and the whole kaboodle! The three choirs sang 'Oh Happy Day', and he took the solo. Later, he offered us a new piano!'

James Brown

1933, Augusta

The inimitable godfather

The 'No 1 Soul Brother' is approaching sixty, but retains his energy from the 1960s. Funk owes him everything, and he knows it.

With over 90 albums and about 200 45 rpm records, not counting the even more numerous productions under the name of the artists for whom he acted as 'godfather' (he gives the term its full sense!), Mr. J.B. has never been out of work since February 4, 1956. That day, James recorded for the first time for the King company a 'non-religious gospel', which was already the original atom of an unequalled explosion in the history of dance music. He recorded 'Please, Please, Please' with the Famous Flames, formed two years earlier, and had an instant success. The young black public identified more and more with this indomitable rebel with steel nerves forged by a wretched childhood, whom educational specialists had tried in vain to 'straighten out' by means of a thousand tortures. His broken but nonetheless flexible voice, his falsetto like the cry of a wounded wild beast, made him a sort of Ray Charles, with a soul just as ravaged but harder. His interminable tours to the depths of the most forlorn suburbs of the United States, and all over the world, notably in Africa, assumed an importance which outstripped the musical phenomenon. His physical commitment was so complete that he was seen as a politician by a community at the peak of its struggle for civil rights. As well as pushing what he called *Sex Machine* to the full, and without renouncing the gospel repertoire which he enlivened by a high ratio of trances, he delivered the crowds in the ghettos a simple, rough and direct message which his 1968 hymn summarizes — 'Say it Loud, I'm Black and I'm Proud'.

Almost always animated by the JBs, a reduced but highly effective big band led by saxophonist Marceo Parker, the James Brown show is an immutable ritual which nevertheless constantly renews itself, where this 'cartharsis' functions marvellously in making it the most convincing profane version of Baptist services. Implacable but syncopated rhythm made this 'Brownian' movement the unsurpassable archetype of *funk*, a music much closer to the urban blues than rock, in which jazz frequently intervenes as a model for collective improvisation. Since the beginning of the 1980s, James Brown has adapted perfectly to the electro-funk of the new hip-hop generation, recording with rappers like Grandmaster Flash, Kurtis Blow and Full Force. In fact, the dashing godfather is furious at being systematically exploited by innumerable disciples since the advent of 'samplers and sequence machines'.

A few hints to dance like J.B.

'I always stuck to the latest steps in fashion: the slop, the funky chicken, the alligator, the camel walk that Louis Jordan had already made famous in the forties, but I added some pizzazz. Not to be confused with Michael Jackson's Moon-walk, which is in fact Charlie Chaplin's bicycle done backwards . . .' (*James Brown, The Godfather of Soul*, autobiography, Fontana-Collins 1988).

From funk to rap

In the 1970s and 1980s soul music exploded in three distinct directions. It retained its great creators like Stevie Wonder or Aretha Franklin, who gladly assimilated the technological innovations and inspired the new voices of Randy Crawford, Luther Vandross, Anita Baker, Whitney Houston and Chaka Khan. The mid-1970s vogue for disco, an off-shoot of the sophisticated sound of Philadelphia, made stars of Bostonian Donna Summer (born in 1950) and the Californian Barry White (born in 1944). In reaction to these commercial forms, Funk developed as a more radical and agressive type of soul which had a considerable influence on contemporary jazz.

The term *funk*, which evokes the smell of sweat, had already been in use since the 1950s to baptize the great return of jazz to its physical association with blues and gospel. Henceforth, it described a precise style of dance music, whose binary rhythm, solid but syncopated, depended mainly on the electric bass played in the *slap* style. James Brown's original influence was omnipresent, and it was his ex-bass player Bootsy Collins, together with singer George Clinton, who animated the Detroit community baptized 'P. Funk', a truly surrealist group which generated two of the best bands of this kind, **Funkadelic** and **Parliament**. But the recognized pioneer was the Texan Sylvester Stewart, whose group **Sly and the Family Stone**, exercised a seminal influence in the late 1960s, notably on the evolution of Miles Davis and the birth of *jazz-rock*.

Another legendary formation, **Earth, Wind & Fire**, was formed in 1970 by Maurice White, a famous jazz and blues drummer in Chicago. Clinton, Sly and White gave funk an ethnic and even esoteric dimension which made it something more than music, a real festive and tribal culture of the modern ghettos. Like all previous forms of rhythm'n'blues, funk has preserved its decentralized, regional and very diversified character. In Washington D.C. what is perhaps its closest relationship to jazz developed in *GoGo Music*, played by real big bands of whom the most famous are **Trouble Funk**, **Experience Unlimited**, and the **Soul Searchers**.

By the end of the 1970s, the phenomenon had expanded beyond the Afro-American public. The first world-wide successes of **Michael Jackson** — *Off the Wall*, then *Thriller* — popularized funk in a very sophisticated form in the nervous and highly-coloured orchestration of **Quincy Jones**, a true jazz-funk idol.

While funk groups such as **Cameo**, **The Commodores**, **Kool and the Gang** and **Slave** multiplied, jazzmen were increasingly interested in this flexible and muscular rhythm. Miles Davis clearly adopted this style in the 1980s, as did trombonist Joe Bowie's group Defunkt, Herbie Hancock, Ornette Coleman and his former sidemen, drummer Ronald Shannon Jackson and guitarist James Blood Ulmer, one of whose titles summarizes this trend very well: 'Jazz is the teacher/Funk is the preacher'.

Orchestral funk, having become a classic and considered as 'a left over' from the 1970s, was soon supplanted in the ghettos by *rap*, a cruder and more primitive form in which a stupefying ingenuity is shown in the craftsmanlike use of ultra-sophisticated but also ultra-basic electronics. Hence *scratch*, which consists in playing two records at the same time, mixing them and altering the speed of rotation (thus the pitch) with the finger tips. The term *rap* like the *jive* of the jazzmen, mean something like 'sweet-talk' or 'chatter', and illustrates the durability of a way of scanning and even rhyming street-slang, which is the very essence of the Afro-American culture.

Since the 1960s, the pianist **Gil Scott-Heron**, the dramatist **LeRoi Jones**, and the New York group **The Last Poets**, have given respectability to this form of rhythmic recitation, a kind of 'swing' equivalent of the German 'Sprechgesang'. As pop music, rap was revived in about 1980 in the New York ghetto of the Bronx, on the little Sugarhill Records label, and by picturesque personalities, both singers and *disc-jockeys*, like **Grandmaster Flash** or **Africa Bambata**, the founder of the 'Zulu nation'. The texts, often militant and encrusted with puns and hermetic allusions, are largely improvised and spouted at a dizzy pace. The music is a multi-faceted collage of many different riffs and vocal or instrumental sequences, played by a sampler. Associated with *break dancing*, a reappearance of the acrobatics of the *swing* era, rap has given rise to this 'hip hop' culture which Max Roach does not hesitate to name 'the bebop of the 1980s'. Among the best rappers of this decade are Eric B & Rakim, Jazzy Jeff & Fresh Prince, Stetasonic, Jungle Brothers, LL Cool J, Public Enemy, De La Soul, Tone Loc, Run DMC, Ice-T, Fab 5 Freddie, Kool Moe Dee, and Digital Underground.

Prince (1958 . . .)

In spite of the supremacy of the 'national' scene since the 1950s, the United States retained a certain form of provincialism in music, which the local radio and television stations contributed to maintaining. Thus among many others, a 'Midwest sound' still exists, a style both highly strung and refined, of which Prince has been the catalyst since his first album, *For You*, recorded when he was twenty years old in conditions which have remained legendary. Shut up alone in a studio for several months, he was responsible for all the choral parts (where the classical harmonization of the spiritual with four voices could be found) and orchestral parts (at least twenty different instruments). The result was spectacular as regards melodic imagination; as for the sins of youth (certain excesses of sickly sentimentality, a slightly monotonous rhythm), they became blurred after the following albums, especially *Dirty Mind*, and *1991*, where one discovers the fever of the best records of James Brown in a more sophisticated register.

Soul and funk were not the essentials of his musical culture. His father, John Nelson, was a famous local jazz pianist, and his mother sang as a fervent follower of Billie Holiday. Jazz, the blues and gospel, but also white rock, were very popular even in the black quarters of the Midwest, and constituted the explosive mixture which made Prince's music one of the most representative of his generation. Ostensibly a libertine, but at the same time secret and exhibitionist, and passionate about the cinema and the music-hall as much as with new sounds, he sought the recipe for a total spectacle, entirely subjected to his own imagination. His grandiose tours, his refined albums, his films and videos and especially his experimental maxi-singles, illustrate his nostalgia for the major glamorous reviews, for the Moulin Rouge as for the Cotton Club. Jazz plays a major role in this superproduction, with episodes where swing is omnipresent and where clever quotes proliferate, from Duke Ellington to Charlie Parker. Surrounded by a real court which is also a sort of musical army, Prince reigns as a monarch over the domain of Paisley Park, a magnificent studio-laboratory from which small masterpieces regularly emerge, some unfinished or rejected through pure perfectionism, like the experimental piece made with Miles Davis, which is already a myth, or the *Black Album* which was scrapped, perhaps the best 'jazz' of an already impressive discography.

Bud Powell

Thelonious Monk

Knights of the keyboard
The elite and versatile piano players

Back in New Orleans where they were called 'professors', the pianists were a sort of elite in the jazz world, which is explained by the 'orchestral' nature of the instrument and the 'musical preparation' necessary to master it, but perhaps also because it was essentially through the keyboard that jazz assimilated and interpreted the European musical heritage in its own way. Moreover, contrary to a far too widespread belief, from the very start most of the great jazz pianists have a serious classical basis, which they often acquired in a religious context. Nevertheless, without wishing to make those who play other instruments jealous, it will be observed that the history of jazz can be read through the chart of the stylistic development of the pianists, in their progressive but rapid apprenticeship in independence, in voicing, in polyrhythms, in all kinds of non-conformist ways of using the instrument, and especially in the modern harmonic language, all the eminently pianistic techniques which musicians and bands have been able to exploit.

On a professional level, even if the jazz pianist is not the star, he is a sort of aristocrat, a knight errant. He is practically alone, with the organist and the guitarist, and if necessary he can manage by himself. This independence is not always synonymous with freedom. Reduced to the thankless role of pianist in a bar, our knight errant cuts a truly pathetic figure! One evening or another, most great jazz pianists have experienced the fearful solitude of the musician playing in the midst of total indifference, even if their subtle art often deserves the reception which still seems to be the exclusive privilege of classical interpreters.

For some years, thanks to the invention of synthesizers, the keyboard has commanded a sound process which is far more complex than the thump of the hammer on the cords. This has led to considerably increased respect for the role of the pianist in jazz. In the centre of the band, it is in his field that technology has gathered the essential jazz materials of the year 2000. To the infinitely variable sound of traditional keyboards, he can add the sound of all the other instruments, as well as an infinite number of combinations of unheard of tones. However, those who give up the acoustic instrument are rare, and it is probable that in jazz as in all western music, 'daddy's piano' still has some good years ahead of it.

Scott Joplin

1868, Texas — New York, 1917

The first great Afro-American composer

A perfectionist in syncopated music, he was the great creator of 'jazz before jazz'.

Joplin's destiny could be compared to that of his contemporary Charles Ives, the only difference being that death prevented Joplin from enjoying his recognition as a pioneer of American music, which came several decades too late. The son of a railway labourer violinist and a maid who scraped away at the banjo, he had all it takes to be an obscure blues player, dedicated to interpreting folk-songs from Texas. But his access to the piano, which at the end of the last century had become very widespread even in farms, decided otherwise. Several free lessons from a German neighbour enabled him to

---

From ragtime to jazz

Generally conceived to be played at a medium tempo, ragtime, which appeared under this name around 1895, was accelerated and somewhat perverted by the craze for the mechanical piano. It also evolved towards an orchestral style dominated by the banjo, and was closer to *country music* than jazz. As well as Joplin, several other pianists should be mentioned: James Scott (1886–1938), Tom Turpin (1873–1922), Eubie Blake (1883–1983), Joseph Lamb (1887–1960) and May Aufderheide (1890–1972). The transition to pianistic jazz took place mainly in New Orleans in about 1910– 1920, with Jelly Roll Morton, then in Harlem during the 1920s with the advent of *stride*: James P. Johnson, Fats Waller, Willie Smith, Cliff Jackson and of course Duke Ellington, whose first known theme was 'Soda Fountain Rag'.

---

discover the 'classical favourites' of Romanticism, which were henceforth to haunt him, though without making him forget his rural background.

Although he was an itinerant pianist, Joplin never adopted the flashy and dissolute life style of his peers. His timidity, but also his ambition, led him to settle in Saint Louis around 1885, where he perfected his skill in a Methodist college. He took an active part in the musical life of Missouri, playing the cornet and directing a dance band. He had scarcely started to write ballads when he was carried away by ragtime fever, which at the turn of the century, literally swept all other kinds of light music out of its way. He associated himself with a certain Johnny Stark, a small farmer turned piano salesman, who was henceforth to be his publisher. The first score he published, 'Maple Leaf Rag', instantly became a best-seller, and sold more than a million copies in the very first year. An exacting composer, in twenty years he wrote only thirty-three ragtime pieces, each more complicated and ingenious than its predecessor. In 1907, he settled in New York and devoted himself entirely to composition. After a first opera, *A Guest of Honour* (1903), which has unfortunately disappeared, he undertook a second, less exclusively imbued with ragtime. *Treemonisha*, which is a kind of *Porgy and Bess* thirty years in advance, describes the spiritual and emotional lives of the blacks on the plantations, and was produced in Harlem in 1915 at the composer's expense. The public's reaction was so indifferent that Joplin died of disappointment in a mental asylum. In the 1970s the jazz composer Gunther Schuller, who had dedicated himself to rehabilitating Joplin's reputation, made this extraordinary work into a Broadway hit.

Jelly Roll Morton

1885 (?), Gulfport — Los Angeles, 1941

An unlicensed inventor, but a forerunner with a patent

A cross between a black slave and a French colonialist from Louisiana, he was the creator of the first musical 'hybrid'.

His father F.P. LaMenthe quickly left his family and was replaced by a certain Morton, a hotel porter. Young Ferdinand learned to play the harmonica very young, then the bombard and the guitar, which he played in a fiddle band from the age of seven. With some reticence, he admitted, he was converted to the piano, which was then considered an effeminate instrument. But it was also the key to the brothels or sporting houses of Storyville, where the pianist played a lot more than his own role. 'Jelly Roll' attracted attention there from 1902, and it was there he earned his famous nickname, the name of a kind of 'swiss-roll' with a very evocative look about it.

Morton did not stay in New Orleans until the clampdown hit this famous 'French quarter'. He became a nomadic musician, circulating between Los Angeles, Saint Louis, Houston, New York and Chicago, where he arrived in 1923. Here, with his band the Red Hot Peppers, he became the star pianist of the Victor firm, for whom he recorded about 175 sides of 78rpm records, of which approximately fifty were piano solos. These reveal, if not a virtuoso, at least an accomplished instrumentalist, largely emancipated from the 'pumping' of ragtime and stride, with a resolutely polyphonic style which made him, with Earl Hines, the best pianist around, at least according to the unanimous testimony of New Orleans musicians.

As for his orchestration, it reveals an innate sense of colour and a formal diversity which makes him comparable with the early Duke Ellington.

A pioneer in everthing, he was unfortunately the first jazz player to fall a victim to the Great Depression. In 1930, record production in the United States fell by 65%, as compared to two years before. Jelly Roll was forced to sell his Cadillacs

With **Rex Stewart** *(on the left)*

and the diamonds he had had fixed to his garters, and even in his molars. He undertook all kinds of picturesque activities; in turn he became pimp, professional gambler, boxing impresario, and even 'pharmacist', the hawker of a miracle medicine whose ingredients he later swore were totally innocuous — 100 per cent Coca-Cola!

In 1937, passing through Washington, he was 'rediscovered' by the great musicologist Alan Lomax, who set him up for five weeks at the piano in the Library of Congress. In these solemn surroundings, Jelly Roll related in detail the dream-history of his life, and these long hours of monologue punctuated by dazzling solos and Creole songs are the most genuine witness we possess concerning the genesis of Jazz, albeit an unreliable one.

Even if the whole of 'coloured' America actually 'invented' this uniquely collective music, Jelly Roll was the best incarnation of all its paradoxes: mixed blood, dandy and rascal, a loner and a tricker of men, a full-time composer whose work was only written in whirlwinds which bore him from one town to another, according to his picaresque adventures. At the end of his life, his visiting card read as follows: 'Ferdinand-Joseph LaMenthe, known as Jelly Roll Morton, Inventor of Jazz.'

Having thus described his identity, he hastened to add that he had also invented the metal brush! He needed no persuasion to tell his life story with the gravity and precision of a real tale-teller. He was taken for a mythomaniac but jazz historians have proved ever since that the reality of his life far exceeded the stories about it.

Whether his name was LaMenthe or according to some sources, LaMothe, it is certain that Ferdinand-Joseph was born in Gulfport (Louisiana), and 20 September 1885 seems the most likely date. His family belonged to that very special milieu of 'slightly coloured' Creoles, and was strongly marked by French culture, which suffered greatly from the racial laws promulgated at the beginning of the century in New Orleans, which put an end to the relative integration which made the 'Cité du Croissant' a haven of tolerance in a South which was still restive at the anti-slave laws imposed by the 'Yankees'. All his life, from town to town, Jelly Roll Morton fled the trap of negritude which was closing inexorably on these Creoles who had been reared in a European culture and were somewhat scornful of the proletarian *niggers* with whom they were being forced to integrate.

Unfortunately, he did not have the time to pick the fruits of the *Dixieland jazz* revival at the end of the 1930s. After one last burst of glory which gathered Sidney Bechet, Albert Nicholas, Zutty Singleton and several other great pioneers of Storyville around him, he was to die of exhaustion in Los Angeles on 10 July 1941.

Stride and boogie woogie

These popular styles of the 1920s and 1930s share an emphasis on the left hand, which must be able to supply the tempo to the wildest dancers. They remain a fundamental basis in the apprenticeship of jazz pianists.

Stride, which developed in Harlem on the crest of the 'Harlem Renaissance', reached an inimitable level of virtuosity with **Fats Waller** and **Art Tatum**. It is a modernized form of ragtime, based on the 'pump', an alternation of bass notes on the up-beat and octave chords on the down-beat. Its other great exponents were:

James P. (Price) Johnson (1894–1955), who seems to have been its pioneer with 'Carolina Shout' (1921). The favourite accompanist of the great female blues singers and composer of symphonic works, he recorded numerous 'pianola' cylinders. His very free and swinging style had a deep influence on the following generations, from Duke Ellington to Thelonious Monk.

Willie Smith (1897–1973), who diversified the playing of the left hand, and introduced European melodic references acquired in the trenches in 1914–1918, where his attitude earned him the nickname 'The Lion'.

Joe Turner (1907–1990), who settled in more peaceful circumstances in France, after alternating with Tatum, who had a deep influence on him, as the accompanist of the singer Adelaide Hall.

The *boogie-woogie* (onomatopoeic word probably originating with railway workers) was born in Chicago, as an urban variant on the twelve bar blues already played by pianists in the *barrelhouses* and *honky-tonks*. Based on a strolling bass rhythm, played in *ostinato* by the left hand, thus freeing the right of any rhythmic function, boogie-woogie was to have an enormous impact on the dance bands of the 1930s and 1940s, and on the great creators of rhythm'n'blues and rock'n'roll.

Jimmy Yancey (1898–1951) is more or less its archetype. He divided his life between baseball and the piano, which he also played 'hell for leather', in an old-fashioned style which was very moving. He was not recognized or recorded until after 1938.

Like him, his disciple **Pine Top Smith** (1904–1929) was originally a singer and tap-dancer in vaudeville. Just before his death, he recorded the superb 'Pine Top's Boogie Woogie', the first title which explicitly referred to this style.

Meade Lux Lewis (1905–1964), another admirer of Yancey, was the son of a railwayman, and recorded the railway-oriented 'Honky Tonk Train Blues' in 1927. Its huge success was not enough for him to avoid a tough working-man's life before he received well deserved recognition at the end of the 1930s.

Albert Ammons (1907–1949) and **Pete Johnson** (1904–1967) were the great classics of the elaborate boogie of the swing era, as it was then played in its birth-place, Kansas City. As a duo or a trio with Lewis, they were to be its top stars after their famous Carnegie Hall concert *From Spirituals to Swing* in 1938.

Sammy Price (1908) is a pure product of Texan blues for whom boogie is merely the touchstone of a multi-coloured palette. He accompanied Sidney Bechet and Red Allen.

Lloyd Glenn (1890–1985), also a Texan, but who had emigrated to California, was an authentic, thundering virtuoso, who made boogie roll through extremely varied and hilly landscapes.

Thomas 'Fats' Waller

1904, New York — Kansas City, 1943

An impulsive virtuoso

The first great organ expert and a master of stride piano, he was a sort of Rabelais lost in Harlem.

In the New York of the 1920s, a twenty year-old pianist could be heard at rent parties (where money was raised to pay the rent). The high-spirited adolescent also took an active part in *cutting contests*, a form of musical jousting between several musicians, among whom the public chooses the winner. Generous and dynamic, Thomas 'Fats' Waller's motto was 'to live the life I love'. He was without a doubt the first to adapt the organ to the language of jazz. As a pianist, his left hand became famous for its power, which provided a solid backing for the right hand to embroider delicate variations rich in ideas and imagination, strewn with astute paraphrases. To his technique as a 'band' pianist he added a 'sound' characterized by his complete exploitation of the keyboard, a sensitive and forceful touch noticeable in his solo works or within his sextet. As an unparalleled leader, he was able to support and encourage his partners by solid agreements punctuated with cheeky humour.

As the leader of his group (from 1934 to his death), his popularity was at its height. His public seemed to appreciate him more as the singer with untarnished verve and ferociously destructive humour of the kind he used to make fun of the hackneyed tunes of the time, than as a pianist. He was a prolific composer, and is the author of classics such as 'Honeysuckle Rose', 'Ain't Misbehaving', 'Black and Blue'. He made numerous short films, notably *Stormy Weather*, and died in a train, during one of his exhausting tours.

> **By John Hammond:**
> 'Waller's great musical talent never got the renown it deserved. It was easier to use him like a buffoon or a clown than like the great musician that he was.'

Earl Hines

1903, Duquesne — Oakland, 1983

The jovial father of a numerous 'crop' of pianists

His first records were solo or with Armstrong, and next to him he was the most influential jazz musician of his generation.

When one earns the nickname of 'Fatha' (Father), it is not without reason. The first great creator of jazz, a native of the north of the United States, Earl Kenneth Hines won a bet when he was twenty-five years old, the stakes of which were perhaps no less than the future of jazz as serious music. It was a question of knowing whether the piano, with all its percussive, melodic and harmonic resources, would become a great solo jazz instrument, equal to the clarinet and brass.

Hines, whose father played the cornet, learned this instrument at the same time as the piano. He instinctively worked out a blaring, thundering style at the keyboard, which enabled him to compete with the 'blowers'. His tapering fingers and his innate sense of contrast gave this trumpet-derived piano style a formidable effect.

'At a time which was longer ago than one thinks, (. . .) Hines declared himself to be more lastingly 'modern' than Al Haig, Cecil Taylor, and Chick Corea put together. Having brought his weird but rigorous instrument up from the stone age plough and the spasmodic loom, he had harrowed and carded in advance for them the whole stretch of ground, and showed them that their way to freedom lay over hills, dales and boundaries. (Jacques Réda, *L'Improviste*, Gallimard).

Plunged into the extraordinary musical effervescence of Chicago in 1924, where he formed his own group, Hines found himself miraculously in the next door flat to Louis Armstrong. It was as his pianist at the centre of the Hot Five and the Hot Seven, or in memorable duos, that he revealed his gifts as a soloist. Their collaboration served as the initial model for all small jazz groups until about 1940.

From 1929 to 1948, at the *Grand Terrace Ballroom* in Chicago (the equivalent of the *Cotton Club* in New York), Hines conducted a big band through which the major creators of modern jazz were to pass, notably Dizzy Gillespie, Charlie Parker and Sarah Vaughan.

Hines was also one of the first jazz pianists who played and recorded solo (from 1928). Sparkling with invention and swing, he made a decisive impact with his records and through radio broadcasts on the generation to come, including Art Tatum, Teddy Wilson, Count Basie, Nat Cole, and even Bud Powell, through the mediation of his pupil, Billy Kyle. But he himself always honestly recognized the influence of Fats Waller.

The 'Hines style' was quick to materialize. It is very complex, alternating stride and strolling bass, with intervals of tenths played by the left hand, while the right hand produced long monodic sequences suddenly interrupted by a trill, a silence, the jumping of an octave, and other surprise effects, switching suddenly to rhythmic double time for a few bars, with highly syncopated off-beat rhythmic intervals from the left hand. All this was already far from pure stride, which nevertheless remained the predominant style right to the end of the 1930s, to the immense displeasure of 'Fatha'.

Duke Ellington

1899, Washington — New York, 1974

The draughtsman beneath the painter

His sketches at the keyboard provided the basis for the richly coloured palette of the most beautiful jazz band.

The hero of *L'Ecume des Jours* by Boris Vian invented the most refined pleasure conceivable, playing 'piano-cocktails' which caused Duke Ellington's chords to turn into alcohol! It is true that the modernity of his harmonic concepts as well as his art of ellipsis and his resolutely percussive approach in the 1920s and 1930s opened up one of the royal ways for contemporary piano, which was to be illustrated by his disciples, from Thelonious Monk to Cecil Taylor. Like Picasso, to whom he may justifiably be compared, Duke Ellington represents a dizzy bridge stretched between a past, where the academic (composition), the primitive (blues, gospel, stride) and the most radical modernity are reconciled. The double impact of the piano conceals all the potentials to be developed evening after

From the pianist, Aaron Bridgers, who heard him in the 1920s: 'it was enough for him to play a single note or chord for anyone normal to feel a warmth, an intensity, an incomparable presence, nobody would have played the same notes that same way. His tone was also as unique as that of Tatum, Monk, Wilson, Hines or Evans, those rare pianists who have nothing in common save their originality and their distinction.'

evening by the voicings of the band. All his life he was to conduct from the keyboard, juggling with the keys, gesturing and snapping his fingers so that his music ceaselessly twirled from the piano to the music stands. While studying the decorative arts, Edward Kennedy Ellington took his first piano lessons from a Mrs Clinkscales, whose name seemed to predict the whole future style of her pupil! In his autobiography *Music is My Mistress*, the Duke — a nickname given him by his schoolmates, inspired by his elegance — remembered that 'She played the high notes while I played the 'dumpy-dump' which served as the basis for this entire aspect of the piano that I came to love later'. So it was ragtime pieces, and above all the stride of Harlem, which first seduced him. His first recording (on a cylinder) was a stride called 'Jig Walk' in 1923.

Busy all the while with his orchestral task, Ellington never recorded as a soloist before the 1940s, when he played duets with the bass player Jimmy Blanton (1941), then with his alter ego, arranger Billy Strayhorn (1950). He became interested in small groups, recording with a trio on *Piano Reflections* (1953), *Piano in the Foreground* (1961) and in particular *Money Jungle*, with Mingus and Max Roach (1962), a duet with Ray Brown on *This one's for Blanton* (1972), and the quartet on *Big Four* (1973). His *Suites* and his *Religious Concerts* often included solos and in 1966 he recorded his *Symphonie pour un monde meilleur* at a private concert in the Chateau de Goutelas-en-Forez. His tough, rolling style proved as immutable as it was fashion-resistant, thanks to his mastery of dissonance which brought him into line with his contemporaries Stravinsky, Bartók and Prokofiev.

Art Tatum

1909, Toledo — Los Angeles, 1956

1000 fingers for 88 keys

God for Fats Waller, a mad Chopin for Cocteau, this extraordinary virtuoso personified everything it was possible to do on a piano.

Pianists, and not only jazz pianists, have no words strong enough to express what they think of Art Tatum. Vladimir Horowitz stated his astonishment at his technique; Samson François declared that 'he really was a genius in his way of composing while improvising'; Count Basie called him the eighth wonder of the world, Oscar Peterson the best jazz instrumentalist of all time, while Herbie Hancock admitted that nobody could equal him.

Heir at the same time to the stride tradition and the innovations of Earl Hines, he succeeded in giving equal importance to both his hands, each able to play different rhythms with a refined sense of harmony, which allowed him to perform tempo changes and impressive 'prestissimos'. *A tempo* introductions were the preludes of themes (by composers from Gershwin to Kern, Dvorak or Massenet), swarming with arpeggios, quotations, and arabesques, a multitude of elements which sometimes seemed to drown the tune.

Born almost blind into a musical family, Art Tatum began classical studies very early, then played in clubs and on local radio. He arrived in New York in 1932, and recorded four solos the following year, including a memorable 'Tiger Rag', which it was thought was played by two pianists.

He became the first soloist *after hours* at the *Onyx Club*, in 52nd Street, before performing in numerous clubs throughout the United States, and formed a very highly thought of trio with the double bass player Slam Stewart and the guitarist Tiny Grimes. From 1953 to 1955 he recorded one hundred and twenty titles for piano solo, at four sessions supervised by Norman Granz, who organized other sessions with Ben Webster, Lionel Hampton, Benny Carter, Buddy Rich, and Jo Jones.

He gave one last solo concert in 1955, and continued to record until the summer of 1956, before dying of an uraemia crisis.

Billie Holiday *with* **Big Sid Catlett** *and* **Oscar Pettiford**.

Thelonious Monk

1917, Rocky Mount — Weehawken, 1982

An arranger of silence

A revolutionary composer and a pianist with a controversial disputed technique, he was one of the most unusual geniuses of the 20th century.

In 1941, in Minton's Playhouse, the little Harlem club open until dawn, an enigmatic character could be seen and heard during the turbulent jam-sessions, *a pianist*, with a piercing gaze, accompanying young musicians who worked out with him the new music which was to be called *Bebop*, and of which he became the 'High Priest' or 'Prophet'. That was Thelonious Monk. The first thing one noticed was his way of playing flat-handed, his fingers held horizontally, like an extension of the palm, but what was intriguing, or disconcerting, was his rhythmic treatment based on discontin-

---

In Thelonious Monk's own words:
'I think it is easier to play fast than to build something interesting on a slow tempo.'

Julio Cortazar:
'(. . .) Coming from the back of the stage and making a completely useless detour, a bear wearing a half-fez and half beret, advances to the piano putting one foot before the other with such effort that one can't help thinking of mine fields or the flower-beds of Sassanid despots where any trampled flower certainly meant a slow death for the gardener.' (extract from the *Tour du Piano* by Thelonious Monk, in *Around the Day in Eighty Worlds*, Gallimard).

---

uous playing, and a harmonic development based on dissonance. His sequences were sometimes disturbing to his partners; indeed, Miles Davis refused to be accompanied by him during a superb performance of 'Bag's Groove' in 1954.

Monk invented a style which was devoid of any virtuosity, relying on an impeccable rhythmic rigour, which gave priority to unusual structures made of dissonances and small, asymmetric intervals. He cut his first records in 1944 with Coleman Hawkins, and played in Dizzy Gillespie's big band in 1946, before signing for his first records as a leader with the Blue Note Company. After being sentenced for possessing drugs in 1951, he was banned from playing in the New York clubs for six years.

Monk recorded with Sonny Rollins in 1956, and played *At the Five Spot* with John Coltrane, then with Johnny Griffin and Roy Haynes in 1957. His association with the saxophonist Charlie Rouse lasted from 1958 until 1970. Charlie Rouse was an ideal partner who was perfectly in tune with the pianist's universe. They embarked on their first European tour, and performed all over the world. Their repertoire varied little, Monk ceaselessly polishing and repolishing the same compositions, some of which became classics, such as the omnipresent 'Round Midnight', one of the most played themes in modern jazz.

A composer with a hallucinatory imagination, of a breadth comparable to that of Duke Ellington, Monk was to become the object of numerous tributes, proof of the up-to-date and avant-garde quality of an original and inimitable achievement. After a European tour (1971) in the Giants of Jazz Group and a series of recordings either solo or in a trio, he shut himself up in silence from 1972 at the home of his friend, Baroness Nica de Koenigswarter, until his death.

Bud Powell

1924, New York — New York, 1966

The perfect stylist of bebop piano

He had an almost obsessional need to express entirely and faithfully the musical ideas which sprang from his mind.

It used to be said that Bud Powell was to Charlie Parker what Earl Hines had been to Louis Armstrong, a pianist who adapted to the resources of his instrument the innovations contributed by the greatest soloist of his generation. It would be more correct, however, to admit that there was a similarity of spirit and musical thought, which was reinforced by an obvious influence.

After studying classical works from Bach to Debussy, from the age of six, Powell heard the creators of bebop at *Minton's Playhouse* in 1941, in the company of his friend Monk. He developed the features of his style very early on, notably on the level of harmonic sequences (tone scales and chord changes), and was hailed as the most representative pianist of the bop movement from 1946 onwards. He worked with Dizzy Gillespie and Don Byas and took part in

Bill Evans:
'If I had to choose a single musician according to his artistic merit, and the originality of his creation, but also for the greatness of his work, it would be Bud Powell. Nobody could measure up to him' (Paris, 1979).

many recordings, especially for Savoy notably with Dexter Gordon, J.J. Johnson, Sonny Stitt and Charlie Parker ('Cheryl', 'Donna Lee', 'Chasin' the Bird') before recording his first sessions under his own name in 1947, in which we can admire the speed of his thinking combined with the fantastic speed of his execution, the impeccable rigour of his phrasing and tempo, a profusion of melodies and extreme tension finding a perfect balance between his concept and his technique. Between 1949 and 1951, he recorded a large number of pure masterpieces for Blue Note and Verve, in a trio or in a small group, including 'Un Poco Loco', 'Parisian Thoroughfare', 'Glass Enclosures', and 'Bouncing with Bud'.

But his career suffered highs and lows because of shaky health. After his first depressive crisis in 1945, with periods in psychiatric hospitals, frequent bouts of alcoholism and drug use, his hands could no longer follow the trend of his ideas. He made his first appearance in Europe in 1956, and settled in Paris in 1959. He played at the *Blue Note Club* in Paris, with Pierre Michelot and Kenny Clarke and regained a certain balance thanks to his friendship with Francis Paudras, who made him welcome and had him treated. He had tuberculosis (1963), but returned cured to the States the following year, playing for a while at *Birdland*, but was obliged to cease all his activities before he died in a Brooklyn hospital.

Bud Powell was to influence a number of pianists, including Bill Evans, Horace Silver, and his followers Barry Harris and René Urtreger.

The bop pianists

*In the footsteps of Duke Ellington and Art Tatum, Thelonious Monk
and Bud Powell had freed jazz from the pianistic conventions limiting
its horizon. The jazz pianist now had a tool at his disposal which
would permit him to improvise pieces which vied in complexity — and
especially in density — with the modern European repertoire.*

Hank Jones (1918), like Bud and Monk, had already assimilated the rich and varied style of Tatum before he adopted the Bebop language. Following his debut with his brothers, trumpeter Thad and drummer Elvin, he became a sideman with a very full timetable, playing with Coleman Hawkins and Benny Goodman, as well as Ella Fitzgerald and the other stars of Jazz At The Philharmonic [J.A.T.P.]. In the 1980s, his Great Jazz Trio further contributed to his reputation.

John Lewis (1920) was one of the pianists who was a beacon of the first Bebop era, succeeding Monk in Dizzy Gillespie's big band, and recording historic tracks with Charlie Parker and Miles Davis. But his very thorough classical training led him to blend this quality into a more eclectic language, ending in the creation of the famous Modern Jazz Quartet in 1951. His chiselled playing, crystalline yet bluesy, made him a 'silken bridge' between Basie and Monk.

Irving 'Duke' Jordan (1922) owes his nickname to his youthful passion for Ellington. He inherited Ellington's percussive quality and his great talent as a composer, which were transformed by the influence of Charlie Parker, whom he accompanied on the piano.

Tommy Flanagan (1930) was something of a tranquil father of bop. He was the pianist of Ella and Hawkins, and also of Coltrane, Miles Davis and many others. He also occasionally played in a duo with Hank Jones. A great interpreter of ballads, he dedicated himself thoroughly to Thelonious Monk's compositions.

Al Haig (1924–1982) worked out an airy style of great harmonic subtlety in the shadow of Parker and Dizzy Gillespie, whom he often accompanied. He played

and recorded a great deal in Europe, re-interpreting standard classics.

Phineas Newborn Jr (1931–1989) was a prolific virtuoso after the fashion of Oscar Peterson, but faithful to the blues idiom which imbued his first career in rhythm'n' blues in Memphis. He integrated all the harmonic subtlety of bop in a tumultuous style in which polyrhythmics played an important role.

Bobby Timmons (1935–1974) also refreshed Bebop from the springs of blues and gospel. From the Jazz Prophets of Kenny Dorham to the Jazz Messengers of Art Blakey, his playing was solidly anchored, but without sacrificing a taste of ornamentation and the unexpected, which is one of bop's charms.

Barry Harris (1929) has the bearing, the science and the experience of a master, maintaining in New York the flame of this music which he passionately rediscovered as the pianist of the *Bluebird Club* in Detroit. This is how he was able to accompany 'passers by' such as Parker, Miles or Lester, before becoming the pianist of Max Roach, and then Cannonball Adderley. His balanced worship of Monk and Powell is sufficient to guarantee the quality of his 'anthological' style.

René Urtreger (1934) is also a 'faithful among the faithful' of this double allegiance, but he succeeds marvellously in the challenge of translating this music, which is essentially New Yorkian, into a language which simultaneously evokes the jargon of the Parisian kid, and the ironic tenderness of the French lover. In this way he contributed a lot to the character of his music, inspired by numerous sessions in the company of greater jazz musicians on tour in Europe, from Chet Baker and Lester Young to Dizzy Gillespie and Miles Davis.

Lennie Tristano

1919, Chicago — New York, 1978

An ardent freshness

Founder of a style and leader of a 'school' of capital importance in the evolution of post-Bebop jazz.

While the Bebop revolution was at its peak in the clubs of 52nd Street in New York, in Chicago Tristano was working on a vocabulary which was different from that of the founding fathers of this movement. Blind at nine, he studied the piano and several wind instruments, at the same time as pursuing his studies at the Conservatory, which he left in 1943 with diplomas in piano and composition. Having shown a deep attachment to Bach, his interest then focused on the works of the Viennese school, and Bartók. He then turned to teaching, perfecting a method which was to make him the greatest teacher in the history of jazz. He developed a theoretical and analytical point of view on the evolution of jazz, and Charlie Parker's music which he admired. He also performed as a pianist and earned the critical acclaim of being 'father confessor to all the avant-garde

musicians in the city'. He settled in New York in 1946, and continued his teaching, which was rich in innovations as regards harmony, tempo and phrasing, thus offering Bebop an alternative, an extension rather than a departure, which opened the doors to the *Cool jazz* from the West Coast. When he was elected 'musician of the year 1947', he presented two studies where he wrote that bop was an essential moment in the evolution of jazz, but that young musicians, content with repeating the clichés of their masters, risk extinguishing what constituted the treasures of the music of Parker and Gillespie. Tristano played at Parker's side (1947), was elected 'pianist of the year 1948', and in 1949 recorded in the company of his pupils and followers, guitarist Bill Bauer and saxophonists Lee Konitz and Warne Marsh, a series of masterpieces, including 'Intuition', and 'Yesterdays', free improvisations both with and without a harmonic framework, which anticipated the free jazz of the 1960s. He opened a recording studio in 1955, where he used a re-recording process for improvisations, dubbing in several piano parts which each had its own metric development, with some passages being played in 9/8 and others in 13/8.

The features of his style (thematic renewal, or rather suppression of the theme concept, free rhythm, renunciation of expressionist symbols, work on sound) have earned his music accusations of intellectualism, coldness, abstraction, where there was rigour, strictness and inspiration, the qualities he needed to make himself a real jazz musician.

In Lennie Tristano's own words:
'I have a very clear feeling that the French think that white musicians cannot play jazz. When I found myself in Paris (1965) I spoke to many people of these problems, and they in some way confirmed this impression that I had: in France, it is thought that Whites do not do it as well as Blacks.' (*Jazz-Hot*, 4 July 1973).

Erroll Garner

1921, Pittsburgh — Los Angeles, 1977

A delay ahead of its time

The best way to play doing the splits with the hands.

Garner was popular with a public that could have been totally indifferent to jazz, because he played in a way which combined the most contradictory elements of the old and new styles, and succeeded in inventing an original language, which was immediately identifiable. All the same, he did not belong to any specific school and had no direct influences.

What is immediately striking is the light lingering, the subtle and infinitesimal delay of the right hand over the left, what is known as the 'Garner amble'. A strong generator of swing, his left hand was comparable to a rhythm section which marked the four beats in chords, while his right hand, with a varied touch, phrased very

swiftly, in simple notes or in chords which were superimposed on those played by the other hand. His sequence was punctuated with themes and paraphrases, and could reach a tragic dimension in the blues.

Self-taught, Garner claimed that he could not read music. He learned by watching the family teacher play. However, he mastered all the piano techniques, and became an improviser with a fertile imagination, showing humour and a sense of suspense in his sometimes lengthy introductions, or in the interludes or codas of which he was particularly fond.

He settled in New York in 1923, and played in the trio of the double-bass player Slam Stewart, replacing Art Tatum. His first recordings, 'Play Piano Play' and 'Laura', attracted the public's attention, but it was in 1950 that he reached the ranks of the stars with his composition 'Misty', written during a flight between San Francisco and Denver. The recording of a trio concert at Carmel, *Concert by the Sea*, earned him a gold disc in 1958. It illustrates all the aspects of a style that could grab the audience with a succession of emotion and euphoria. It was worth seeing him perched on his stool, raised on a telephone book, groaning with pleasure, with his permanent mischievous smile, flooded by the pink colour of the spotlights he asked for at the concerts he gave all over the world since 1957.

Errol Garner *in concert*

René Urtreger:
'I discovered Garner at the age of 12. It was a miracle for me! He made me want to play the jazz piano, which did not prevent me from discovering Bud Powell and Bill Evans. On the contrary, thanks to him I was able to discover the others; he enabled me to have access to the geniuses.'

The art of the trio

At the end of the 1930s, pianists claimed an independence which the supremacy of the big bands made it difficult for them to assume. Even the most illustrious — Art Tatum, Teddy Wilson — were reduced to 'one night stands' in bars and restaurants to be able to express their creativity freely. In this humiliating context, and to ward off the solitude and the exhausting work it required, pianists were to find the ideal formula, the piano/bass/drums or piano/bass/guitar trio, sometimes augmented by a percussion player who mainly played the congas.

The charismatic model of this type of music has been provided since 1939 by Nat King Cole (with the guitarist Oscar Moore and the bass player Wesley Prince), and imitated in 1943 by Art Tatum with Tiny Grimes and Slam Stewart. From that time, it is amusing to observe that each year a new pianist founded a prestigious trio, beginning with Oscar Peterson (1944); Erroll Garner (1945); Lennie Tristano and George Shearing (1946); Thelonious Monk (1947); Ray Charles (1948); Paul Bley (1949); Ahmad Jamal (1950); George Wallington (1951); Horace Silver (1952); Russ Freeman (1953); Hampton Hawes (1955); Bill Evans and Phineas Newborn (1956); Wynton Kelly (1957); Red Garland (1958); Bud Powell (1959); Martial Solal (1960). Dozens of others were to follow, notably Hank Jones, Monty Alexander, Chick Corea, Herbie Hancock, Keith Jarrett, Georges Arvanitas, Joachim Kühn, Marc Hemmeler, André Persiany, Michel Petrucciani, Tete Montoliu, Enrico Pieranunzi, Kenny Barron, Tommy Flanagan, and many more.

Ahmad Jamal (alias Fritz Jones) deserves to feature as the central personality of the chapter. He was really the one to bring the art of the trio to the highest level of collective expression in modern jazz. Born in 1930 in Pittsburgh (like his elder, Erroll Garner, whom he was to rival with the general public to a certain extent), he had a solid basis of classical study before he created The Three Strings (1950) with guitarist Ray Crawford and bass player Eddie Calhoun. Their 'Billie Boy' was to Jamal what 'Nature Boy' had been to King Cole, a success which went far beyond the jazz framework.

In 1956, he opted for double-bass (Israel Crosby) and drums (Vernell Fournier), and the albums of this new trio were even more successful. The most subtle and coherent combination of sounds, syncopation and sighs gave the music a dreamy, poetic dimension, with an almost extra-sensory communication between the members of the group, which fascinated all musicians at the end of the 1950s. Miles Davis adopted many of the themes recorded by the trio, and always honestly recognized his debt to the pianist.

Fritz Jones renamed himself Ahmad Jamal when he converted to Islam, and his interest in mysticism — notably Sufism — is evident in his music, even if this aspect escaped the public at the time. After a trip to North Africa (1959) and the failure of his Alhambra club in Chicago, his musicians left him for George Shearing in 1960. In spite of several very successful records with Impulse, 20th Century and Atlantic, he never recovered the magic of this legendary trio which enchanted the amorous evenings of the 1950s.

Oscar Peterson

1925, Montreal

A torrent springing from the blues

A super-talented and versatile pianist, he has been swinging energetically for fifty years.

This virtuoso has multiple roots. He admits to having been originally influenced by Teddy Wilson, whom he found full of 'fire and finesse', by Art Tatum, whose perfection he somehow prolongs, by Bud Powell, who was his contemporary, by Nat King Cole for the choice of his tempos, and . . . by Lester Young, with whom he shared a room during the *Jazz At The Philharmonic* tours (quoted in *Jazz-Hot*, April 1973).

He was admirably capable of making the most of these youthful fascinations, and combining them to reveal a warm, brilliant style which was to make of him one of the most appreciated masters of jazz by different publics, which he immediately seduced by his exceptional agility as a pianist, his lyricism with 'bluesy' tones, enhanced by the twin qualities of simplicity and complexity, both easy and effective. No spectator could resist the serenity of this 'Apollonian art', so highly praised by the critics.

A coloured Canadian, Oscar Peterson became popular in the clubs in Montreal and Toronto, where he played solo. He was noticed by the producer Norman Granz, became a permanent member of the JATP from 1950 to 1955, and toured the States and Europe. In the meantime, taking as examples the small groups of Tatum and King Cole, he had formed his own trio with double-bass player Ray Brown and, subsequently, with guitarists Barney Kessel and Herb Ellis, who was replaced in 1959 by Ed Thigpen on drums. Several changes in partners took place until 1967, with Peterson performing solo and in duet, trio or quartet, notably with the Danish double-bass player, Niels-Henning Ørsted Pedersen, and the guitarist Joe Pass. He became the 'house pianist' of Pablo Records, and performed with fabulous soloists such as Dizzy Gillespie, Milt Jackson, and Sarah Vaughan.

Jazz At The Philharmonic (JATP)

Meetings in jam-sessions of several groups of musicians, sometimes with different styles, on the initiative of **Norman Granz**, JATP began in July 1944, with concerts in the Los Angeles Philharmonic Auditorium.

Responding to the public's enchantment with this kind of contest, Granz multiplied the number of tours throughout the world, lasting until 1967. It was no longer possible to count the star musicians who, stimulated by the crowds, playing blues or standard melodies and encouraged by emulation, gave the best and sometimes the worst of themselves. Oscar Peterson was an attentive and reliable accompanist as well as a flamboyant soloist.

In Oscar Peterson's own words:

'When I play, I sing at the same time as the notes sing out on my piano . . . This is due to the fact that I used to play the trumpet before becoming a pianist . . . I often sing well ahead of what I am going to play, or I sing to accompany what I am playing on the piano.'

Bill Evans

1929, Plainfield — New York, 1980

The sublimation of melody

His quest for perfection and need to transmit his emotions led him to explore ceaselessly the same themes.

From 1960, Bill Evans had the same fate as Bud Powell: both turned out to be the most influential pianists of their generation, especially Bill, since he continues to be an example and a point of reference.

As the creator of an aesthetic quality rather than a style, he profoundly modified harmony, phrasing and the rhythmic concepts of the instrument. He renewed the pianist's art to such a degree that he totally did away with the notion of musical categories. He was a keenly sensitive musician, introspective, lyrically serious, overwhelmingly emotional, with a 'classical', sensitive touch, and he transformed the favourites he fondly played so often, by arranging the notes of a chord (voicing) or its sequences, with imperceptible arpeggios resulting in the 'swingiest of swings'. Contrary to pianists who use their left hand to support the rhythm or the harmony, he lightened its role, using it to punctuate the melodic design which he developed with the right hand, employing inversions of chords which lent a varied touch of harmonic colour. His repertoire consisted almost exclusively of standard classics, with a preference for waltzes, some of which were his own compositions. At the *Village Vanguard* in New York in June 1961, in the company of double-bass player Scott LaFaro and Paul Motian on drums, he recorded the masterpieces which illustrate his concepts of the piano/double-bass/drums trio, a three-part conversation in which each player has an equal role.

The trio, one of the most famous jazz trios, was reformed after the death of LaFaro, and achieved further success with bass players Chuck Israels, Eddie Gomez, Marc Johnson and drummers Jack DeJohnette, Marty Morell, Eliot Zigmund and Joe LaBarbera. Bill Evans was particularly fond of playing solo, and was to improvise on two or three pianos using the device of multi-recording, in several 'conversations with himself'.

Bill Evans

In Bill Evans's own words:

'I had to work terribly hard and spend a lot of time searching, diving and extracting, before I managed to achieve something' (*Jazz Magazine*)

'I often said that it's not enough to create a piece of music, one must live with it ... It's better to work on the same piece for twenty-four hours than on twenty-four pieces in one hour'. (*Jazz Magazine*)

The wizards of the keyboard

Unclassable but of great class, many pianists transcended the successive fashions and styles to exploit, often alone, the inexhaustible riches of this 'king of instruments'.

To a certain extent, and in spite of himself, **Herbie Nichols** (1919–1963) resembled a drawbridge between two epochs. Obliged to play Dixieland to survive, he was actually one of the most acid and advanced composers of the 1950s (under the influence of Monk, it must be said). The author of 'Lady Sings the Blues', he loved the rhythm of the waltz, stride and everything with an irregular and dizzy swing.

Jaki Byard (1922) was a band man, and a living encyclopedia of jazz. He played many instruments, but first became the pianist of Maynard Ferguson in the 1950s, then of Mingus. His style (which consisted in having none!) was typified all the same by a very percussive touch, as adapted to stride as it was to 'Monkian' flights, which made for some surprising escapades into atonal and even arhythmic music.

Dick Twardzik (1931–1955), prematurely reduced to silence by an overdose of heroin during a stay in Paris with Chet Baker, streamed through the early 1950s like a meteor in full flight. This disciple of Tatum and Bud Powell, whose great classical culture included the school of Vienna, was a genuine hipster; his chords are as pure and hard as a diamond, and each one of his compositions is a rare pearl of detached humour and swing.

Hampton Hawes (1928–1977), was the son of a pastor, a self-taught and eclectic virtuoso who, at the price of his own 'personal problems', crossed the teeming universe of rhythm'n'blues, bebop and West Coast jazz, of which he was the greatest pianist. Close to Bud Powell in his manner of guiding the whole theme in his right hand, and in the stupifying speed at which his harmonic ideas followed, he had nevertheless studied European music far less. His playing emphasizes the primacy of blues and the specific inheritance of jazz, marked in particular by his frequent use of *block chords*.

Paul Bley (1932), the child prodigy of Montreal, took on the trio of his idol Oscar Peterson when only 17, when he emigrated to the United States. He accompanied Parker, and became the pianist of Chet Baker, Ornette Coleman, and Mingus, and fully participated in the birth of Free Jazz. However, he is a real musician throughout his sustained nuances, whose solid classical training is constantly challenged during a passionate spell of improvising which obscurely echoes the introspection of his own personal life.

Ran Blake (1935) appears eccentric by virtue of eclecticism, blending all the musical imagination of a New England intellectual from gospel to Monk, in his ambitious epic compositions (examples of the so-called 'third stream'), not to mention Debussy, Stravinsky and Bartók.

From his Haitian origins, **Andrew Hill** (1937) has retained his taste for swaying melodies and piquante chords, integrated without excess in the masterly theme which he develops in the royal footsteps of his great masters (Tatum, Monk, Powell...), which made him one of the main leaders and composers of the Blue Note label and style in the 1960s.

Don Pullen (1944), at first a pupil of Muhal Richard Abrams and close to the Chicago avant-garde, then became the accompanist of Nina Simone before entering the quintet of Mingus, where he made friends with the sax player George Adams. Their quartet, formed in 1979, highlights in particular the extreme diversity of this energetic, forceful pianist, capable of integrating gripping 'clusters' in a very sophisticated harmonic development.

From the organ to the synthesizer

Pioneered by Fats Waller and Count Basie, the Hammond organ quickly became one of the most popular jazz instruments. The technical difficulties of this cumbersome instrument soon made it the prerogative of specialists. The jazz organist is a 'mover' by vocation, simply because it is true that swing is his primary raison d'être. Today synthesizers have done away with the irreplaceable pedals which were really a double-bass played on tiptoe, but the God Hammond still has a lot of devotees.

Milt Buckner (1915–1977) first made himself justifiably famous by developing (at the piano and at the organ), the famous block chords style (simultaneous movement of the two hands playing chords together) with Lionel Hampton. A keen soloist who jumped to fame and an excellent blues man, he played in a trio and a duet with the drummer Jo Jones, becoming a great star in Europe.

Wild Bill Davis (1918) played the piano at Louis Jordan's before devoting himself to the organ at the end of the 1940s. He became one of Duke Ellington's favourite partners, and pushed the instrument towards a fully orchestral style, which also showed in his remarkable arrangements for big band (particularly with Basie), which were carried on by his pupil, **Bill Doggett** (born in 1916).

Brother Jack McDuff (1926), self-taught and at first influenced by W.B. Davis, emerged as an accompanist of saxophonists like Benny Golson, Roland Kirk, Gene Ammons,and Sonny Stitt, but above all by developing the henceforth classical organ/guitar association with Kenny Burrell, Grant Green, then George Benson.

Jimmy Smith (1925) literally blew up the Hammond Organ with his devastating swing: although his style was enriched by the harmonic language of bebop and hard bop, it consisted especially in the torrential reappearance of rhythm'n'blues in its instrumental form. Funky and above all churchy, he improvised on the keyboard with the fluidity of a saxophonist, but his playing relied on impressive strolling basses, the tips of his toes skimming over the pedals. Often accompanied by major guitarists like Kenny Burrell, or Wes Montgomery, or the best big bands (Oliver Nelson, Thad Jones/Mel Lewis), around 1960 he was the most popular jazz musician of his generation.

Larry Young (1940–1979) illustrates the gentle transition (although in a 'highly charged' atmosphere) of the organ to the current electronic keyboards. He was formed in the double school of rhythm'n' blues and bebop, and became something of a rival to Jimmy Smith at Blue Note. He came from the same funky-blues mould, but evolved at the end of the 1960s towards a more eclectic and contemporary style. He took part in the historic birth of the jazz-rock movement at the heart of the Lifetime Trio with Tony Williams and John McLaughlin, then with Miles Davis. He was a virtuoso obsessed by the discovery of new and exotic sounds and modes. Together with Eddy Louiss he was the main organist of the post-bebop period.

Martial Solal

1927, Algiers

The jazz kaleidoscope

Like a set of mirrors and Chinese shadows dancing on the keyboard, his fast style is a cascade of allusions and powerful images.

A many faceted and unusual personality, Solal the pianist, composer, arranger and band leader escapes any simple classification. Two essential characteristics seem most suitable to define him as a musician: rigour and humour. His rigour is apparent in a perfectionist approach to piano technique, while his humour shows in his playing, or rather the playful style in which, thanks to his rigour, he performs all his works, with a 'tweak of the ear'. He renders standard classics unrecognizable, inserting them into his own universe, turning them upside down, inside out, or vice-versa, with slaloms, skids, gear-changes, short circuits, all punctuated by paraphrases, quotes, or quotes of quotes ('Oléo' for Solal becomes 'Ah! Léa'). All these acrobatics are the work of an architect who is passionate for freedom; they are not gratuitous, gimmicky effects intended merely to impress. This born improviser, whose imagination is boundless, whose harmonic range is inexhaustible and whose arsenal of rhythmic combinations is limitless, also possesses an acute sensitivity beneath his cool appearance, rather like one of his favourite partners, the saxophonist Lee Konitz.

As a pianist he plays solo, in duo (with the pianists Hampton Hawes and Joachim Kuhn, or with Michel Portal and Jean-Louis Chautemps) and has performed in trios with Guy Pedersen and Daniel Humair (1960–1964) and Gilbert Rovère and Charles Bellonzi (1965–1968). As a composer he wrote and performed his *Suite in D flat* for a jazz quartet in 1959, and in 1981 a *Concerto* for a jazz trio and orchestra. He has also written pieces for the harpsichord player Elisabeth Chojnacka, for the accordionist Marcel Azzola, for the barrel-organist Pierre Charial, for the 'Percussions de Strasbourg', and for the cinema (*A bout de souffle, Léon Morin pretre* . . .). As a self-styled orchestrator, in 1956, 1981 and 1984, he formed large ensembles on which to 'play the orchestra' like the piano, in other words with the same virtuosity and creativity, tonal freedom and rhythmic overlaps, and paid a tribute to his friend André Hodeir by recording the most significant works by this composer.

He has published a series of didactic pieces for jazz, comparable to Bela Bartók's *Mikrokosmos*, formed a Dodecaband, improvised on Marcel L'Herbier's theme *Feu Mathias Pascal* and he presided over the first Marcel Solal International Jazz Piano Competition in 1989, which was won by Aydin Esen.

In Martial Solal's own words:

'I have always considered that for an improviser, playing is not working. I have noticed it myself: if I do not work, even when I am performing in concerts or in clubs in the evening, I lose a little bit of my muscle. One must avoid relying indefinitely on the fingering or the scales one already knows, it does not lead to progress. For a young musician today it is essential to become a real instrument specialist. Twenty or thirty years ago in jazz, you could be mediocre in playing the piano and still create an illusion. Today, really knowing how to play is a minimum requirement . . .' (*Jazz-Hot*, November 1980).

Cecil Taylor

1933, New York

The master of the hammers

A rebellious disciple of Ellington and Monk who explored in total freedom the percussive potential of the keyboard.

It would be limiting to classify Cecil Taylor with the Free Jazz musicians, because his music extends beyond this movement of the 1960s and 1970s. He belongs to the Afro-American tradition (Ellington, Monk, Tristano) as much as to contemporary European music (Schoenberg, Bartók, Boulez) and traditional music (African and American Indian).

He learned the piano when he was very young, playing classical music, and his interest in percussion led him to try to imitate the drummer Chick Webb. He listened to the big dance bands, discovered Fats Waller, the boogie-woogie pianists and (the revelation!) Duke Ellington. He took courses in arrangement and harmony, studied the works of modern composers, and was impressed by pianists such as Bud Powell, Lennie Tristano, Mary Lou Williams and Dave Brubeck. He accompanied the trumpeter Hot Lips Page, and played in the Johnny Hodges Band. By 1953 he was directing his own first group, playing at the *Five Spot* in New York and at the Newport Festival. From 1960 he was considered one of the main exponents of the avant-garde, and started working with his most faithful collaborator, the saxophonist Jimmy Lyons, who remained in all his bands until he died. In 1969 he featured at the 'Nuits' of the Maeght Foundation in St-Paul-de-Vence, collaborated with dancers and choreographers, played with Max Roach in 1979, and with the Art Ensemble of Chicago in 1985 and 1990.

Cecil Taylor is primarily an organizer of sound who builds his music as he improvises, two objectives he pursues powerfully and energetically. Liberated from traditional structures, he rejects any uniformity of tempo, hammering frantically out of the whole range of the keyboard an avalanche of notes, or on the contrary, distilling silence with self control. Ridding himself of the traditional conflict between tension and relaxation, he raises the question of what really belongs to jazz. The intensity of his playing creates a trance-like feeling through accumulations, repetitions, explosions created by bunches or packs of notes (clusters) which he plays at a phenomenal speed. His concerts are often compared to physical performances in movement, suggesting a sort of dance on a diabolical keyboard.

In Cecil Taylor's own words:

'What I find fascinating in working with other musicians is that however precise my compositions may be, they are never finished. The minute a musician starts to play, new ideas emerge. Then we try to assimilate what's been brought in, we ask questions, and they do the same. That's one of the magic aspects of the process, the opposite of mathematics.' (*Jazz-Magazine*, October-November 1981).

McCoy Tyner

1938, Philadelphia

An exceptional continuity

He shows the same serenity, as an accompanist or solo, playing with Coltrane or as leader.

Vaguely related to Tatum through his taste for ebullient phrasing, Tyner has a few points in common with two other pianists. Like Bill Evans, he develops a modal concept of the piano through his delicate touch in playing ballads; like Cecil Taylor, he has powerful, clear fingering, making full use of his left hand whose role he is keen to promote, which gives him a wonderful sound as he uses the whole stretch of the keyboard, sometimes with cluster effects to punctuate his melodies.

In 1953 Tyner directed a group of young musicians and accompanied visiting soloists. He played for the first time with John Coltrane in 1956, and joined the Jazztet at the same time as its leaders, the trumpeter Art Farmer and the saxophonist Benny Golson. In 1960 Coltrane asked him to come back to his quartet, where he stayed until 1965. During that time he was the stable element in a turbulent universe, providing a climate of enchantment as background to the patches of sound, cries and whispers of the saxophone's fury. Alongside the permanent rhythmic challenge of the drummer Elvin Jones, he provided an alternative, calmer, more serene air of force and certainty, expressed in the confidence and skill of his accompaniment and solos, always seeking simplicity and broader melodies.

Like Coltrane he was to live a mystical experience. Converting to Islam, he took the name of Saud Sulaiman. Together they made more than twenty records for Impulse. Tyner left when Coltrane hired a second drummer, claiming that 'it was very difficult for me to hear between Elvin (Jones) and Rasheid (Ali)'.

After his departure he made a few records with Blue Note, in which he seems to be trying to throw off the Coltrane imprint and find a new direction. He then accompanied Ike and Tina Turner and made a new start in 1972 with his record *Sahara*, with the sax of Sonny Fortune and drummer Alphonse Mouzon. He became a top star, and got the prize for the best record in 1973 for *Enlightenment*, in which his music explodes with joy and sensuality. Later he used the percussionist Guilherme Franco, and included African and Oriental elements in his music.

At the beginning of the 1980s, he directed his work to reviving standard and classic bebop numbers in a more moderate style.

In McCoy Tyner's own words:

'I think it is good to use the past as a base; it's good for anyone to have foundations to use as a starting point, because the stronger and deeper the foundations are, the further one can progress. You don't have to become the best technician, but you need to explore your inner self' (*Jazz-Hot*, December 1974).

Herbie Hancock

1940, Chicago

Well-tempered funk

With his technique and universal culture, this unique rhythm man reigns dominant at the crossroads of all contemporary styles.

One might have expected the young Herbie to embark on a career as a classical musician, for as a child prodigy at the age of eleven, he played Mozart's *Piano Concerto in D major* with the Chicago Symphony Orchestra. Yet his interest lay in jazz. He transcribed Oscar Peterson's solos, and soon decided at the end of the 1950s that he would become a jazzman. He was to reach the summit of popularity using all the different styles he mastered, keeping an elegant, delicate touch due to his classical experience, enriching his art as much through his early influences as through that of Bill Evans, and above all preserving his sonority, an essential pianistic quality. All this brought him to the notice of such musicians as Coleman Hawkins, Lee Morgan, and Donald Byrd, whom he was to follow to New York. Thanks to him, Herbie made

In Herbie Hancock's own words:
'I am consciously seeking to reach the largest possible number of people, without sacrificing any of my personal integrity. What I have tried to do is to get a better understanding, to be more aware of how I can relate to a greater number of people rather than just addressing the privileged few who already appreciated my music' (*Jazz-Hot*, December 1974).

his first record on the Blue Note label, *Taking Off* (1962), from which his 'Watermelon Man', based on a gospel-inspired rhythm, became a huge success. In 1963 Miles Davis invited him to join him in starting his new quintet which was to become one of the most important small groups in modern jazz. During that period, whether as leader or as accompanist for Miles Davis, he skilfully produced some motivating sound-scapes for the wind instrumentalists. As a soloist he developed a style which is full of contrasts, basically simple, and in which his left hand provides a strong rhythmic support.

In 1968, after five years with Miles Davis — with whom he saw the developments which led to jazz-rock — Hancock formed his own quintet, revealing his talent as an arranger. In order to reach a wider audience, he turned to electric and electronic means at about the same time as his old partner Wayne Shorter founded Weather Report with Joe Zawinul. His music, which cleverly blends rhythm'n' blues and soul music, or else blues and swing, is full of furiously binary rhythms heavily scanned by the drums and supported by synthesizers. The records *Headhunters* (1973), *Man Child* (1975) and *Secrets* (1976) enjoyed big sales with a young audience attracted by the new sounds. He presented three different groups in a single day dedicated entirely to him at the 1976 Newport Festival.

From that date, Hancock alternated his genres and instruments, returning to acoustic instruments with the group VSOP, and in a duo with Chick Corea. He rose to the hit parade with a number called 'Rock It', and he received an Oscar for the sound track of Bertrand Tavernier's film *Round Midnight*.

Chick Corea

1941, Chelsea (USA)

A matter of 'feeling'

He bases his career on resisting neither his impulses, nor his desire to communicate by any possible means.

Like his friend Hancock, this Italo-American has a taste for diversity, and even the need to visibly assert his refusal to allow himself to be imprisoned in any given genre. He therefore passes without transition, and according to his whim, from accoustics to electronics, from Latin rhythms to bebop, from Stan Getz to Miles Davis. From Miles Davis to Anthony Braxton (free jazz), from Hollywood-style 'Hispanic' (La Fiesta) to classical (the recording of the *Concerto for two pianos and orchestra* by Mozart, 1982), from Monk's music to the Elektric Band (1986, the year when his own *Concerto for Piano and Orchestra* was performed), investing in action each

time, while dreaming of troubles to come.

Jazz first had an effect on him when he heard the records of Charlie Parker and Bud Powell on the family gramophone. He played in the dance band directed by his father and soon took advanced piano courses at the Juilliard School. Having played in various groups where the construction of his solos in concise sequences, and his facility for different rhythms, attracted attention, he replaced the vibraphonist Gary Burton in Stan Getz's quartet. He later played in a duet with Burton. He recorded his first records (including *Now He Sings, Now He Sobs*, with Miroslav Vitous and Roy Haynes), replaced Herbie Hancock in Miles Davis's group, playing the electric piano on the *In a Silent Way* and *Bitches Brew* albums. In 1972, he formed the jazz-rock supergroup group Return to Forever with the Brazilian couple Airto Moreira and Flora Purim, and bassist Stanley Clarke, and later performed in the company of guitarist Al DiMeola.

Chick Corea was an active Scientologist, who went off in the tortuous direction we know, sometimes letting himself be tempted too far by siren's songs based on pop tunes. His laudable desire to reach the widest possible public did not proceed without a few compromises, which he was quickly able to make people forget by his more 'serious' and less accessible works (*Piano Improvisations, Children's Songs*). A complete pianist, he knew in both cases how to express and transmit delicate emotions with confusing sincerity or tasteful cunning, through splendid compositions ('Return to Forever', 'Crystal Silence', 'Armando's Rhumba') romantic or realist, dancing or abstract.

Chick Corea himself:

'Improvisation is less a technique than a frame of mind. You need to trust your imagination. When you are working on technique, you absolutely have to realize that it's only technique. In other words, it's not the way you manipulate the instrument, the most correct way to express feelings . . . (*Jazz-Hot*, August 1981). 'I am not drawn by the solo for electric keyboards, I prefer the sound of a band and I have no control over the sound of others. We play together, everything relies on interaction.' (*Jazz Magazine*, June 1986)

Keith Jarrett

1945, Allentown

Pianist body and soul

His physical involvement is total in his struggle with the substance of sound.

When Jarrett played for the first time in France (Antibes Festival 1966, at the centre of the Charles Lloyd Quartet), the public and critics were spellbound by this little man who dived greedily into the belly of the piano, going wild on the keys, squeaking and grinding chords, sprinkling his song and dance solos with *free* passages overflowing with extreme lyricism. Already, the 'Jarrett style' had appeared, that of a modern romantic nourished with the Black Church, stride, American folklore, pop music, avant-garde, and later by Schumann, Ravel, John Cage and . . . Jarrett. Far from resembling a patchwork, his music fed itself as it unrolled in perpetual motion.

Keith Jarrett himself:

'I think that people have forgotten the importance of lyricism.

It is here that music began and here where it will end. Music *is* melody. Certain musicians have no sense of melody in themselves, and I think this is a major defect for one can learn everything except lyricism.' (*Jazz Magazine*, March 1970).

'I find that electric music is something extremely dangerous' (*Jazz-Hot*, February 1976).

Before he transferred to Lloyd, he was briefly one of Art Blakey's 'Jazz Messengers'. Later, he formed a trio with Charlie Haden and Paul Motian, before joining Miles Davis (1970–1971), who asked him to play the electric piano and organ. Jarrett recorded *Facing You*, a piano solo, for the Munich company, ECM, and triumphed with this formula during many concerts in Europe which have been recorded: Bremen, Lausanne (1973), Cologne (1975), Munich (1981) not to mention an album of ten records, *Sun Bear Concerts* (1976) from Japan.

Jarrett became the darling of a larger and larger public. He did not sacrifice himself to the electronic fashion, and mastered his progress, which consisted in adventuring into modal worlds whose climates varied, intervening with constant availability, fluidity, generosity, and a tendency to mannerism; labyrinthine meandering, long sequences ending in their midst with a sort of melodic and rhythmic enchantment, a gradually appeasing paroxysm, if not the intricate weaving of ecstatic hypnotic sensations, the whole forming 'something like Chopin and Art Tatum coming together down a river in a canoe', as the critic S.Davis described it.

He formed two quartets between 1972 and 1979 (an 'American' one with Dewey Redman, Haden, Motian, and the European-based 'Belonging', with the Norwegian Jan Garbarek), and recorded with symphonic orchestras, before returning in 1983 to the jazz classics which he transcends, in the company of Gary Peacock on bass and drummer Jack DeJohnette, informed by a new joy in playing.

**Keith Jarrett
Gary Peacock
Jack DeJohnette**
*in Vienne (Rhone)
(1986)*

An 'electrified'
Django *at home in
Samois sur Seine*

Acrobats on six strings

The jazz guitar

Guitarists occupy a somewhat select place in the jazz world, where they form a sort of fraternity, weaving a complex network of influences and technical emulation. The fact that their instrument is the most widespread in all kinds of popular music, urges them to eclecticism, while the guitar also has a para-doxical image. It is the main blues instrument and at the same time, its sound and harmonic potentials are practically unlimited, which leads to a constant dialectic throughout the history of jazz, between a certain archaism and a permanent revolution in 'guitarist' technology and language.

Jazz nevertheless took quite a time to adopt the guitar, first preferring the banjo of African origin for a more effective sound in the epoch when amplification did not exist. It made a discreet entrance into the jazz band, at first content with a rhythmic role very well illustrated by Johnny St Cyr in Louis Armstrong's band, and was then brought to an unequalled perfection by Freddie Green in Count Basie's big band. Among the pioneers who tried to assume a soloist's role, notably with Ellington and Jelly Roll Morton, one naturally finds blues players such as Teddy Bunn and Lonnie Johnson (see p. 63). But it was in these white bands in the 1920s that the guitar heaved itself up to the level of brass, with Snoozer Quinn in New Orleans, and especially Eddie Lang (1902–1933) in Chicago. This native Italian discarded the banjo for the guitar from 1923, and developed by teaching himself an original technique, using either fingers or pick, and phrasing in chords or in *single notes*. His too brief career nevertheless enabled him to make a lot of records with his childhood friend the violinist Joe Venuti, and with the great leaders of the era, from Armstrong to Paul Whiteman, not to mention Benny Goodman and King Oliver. At the beginning of the 1930s, in France, an elderly Argentinian boxer of Indian origin, Oscar Aleman, launched by dancer Josephine Baker, worked out a no less personal style, playing with the help of plectrums a joyful music full of contrast, rich in arpeggios and harmonics. Despite considerable success, he could not compete with the lightning rise of the first genius of the jazz guitar: Jean Baptiste Reinhardt, known as Django.

Django Reinhardt

1910, Liverchies (Belgium) — Fontainebleau (France), 1953

The blue 'Nuages'

A meeting of jazz and the gypsy heritage, Django's music has a completely unique nostalgic flavour.

In his semi-retirement, Django Reinhardt spent quiet days in Samois painting and fishing. At the beginning of January 1953 he met Norman Granz, who asked him to join Jazz At The Philharmonic for a tour, a unique privilege for a European jazzman. He went to the studio for the last time on 8 April, together with Martial Solal and Pierre Michelot; on 15 May he had a stroke and died that night. That was how this unusual, sweet and dreamy personality disappeared. He had become the greatest jazz guitarist, the first to emancipate the instrument and to give it an orchestral dimension.

Jean-Baptiste, known as Django, was a gypsy, born in the family caravan. He taught himself the guitar and, at thirteen, would play at village balls with accordion bands. He had to re-educate himself in guitar playing after a fire which destroyed his caravan in 1928. Having lost the use of two fingers on his left hand, he developed a personal technique to cater for his atrophied hand. First noticed in Toulon by the painter Emile Savitry, Django discovered jazz with his brother Joseph, and played in clubs on the Côte d'Azur. Back in Paris, he frequented the jazz world, playing with the violinist Michel Warlop. In 1934, with the violinist Stephane Grappelli, he founded the Quintette du Hot Club de France, and recorded its first tracks on the Ultraphone label. It had immediate success, due as much to its formula of using one violin, one solo guitar and two playing rhythm, and a double bass, unique in the history of jazz, as to the intimate, refined and warm swinging style of the music. Django became the first European musician to have an influence on American guitarists, and he played with the great soloists who passed through Paris, including Coleman Hawkins, Benny Carter and Barney Bigard. He produced a swing version of the *First Movement of the Concerto in D minor* by J.-S. Bach with the 'Black Angel of the Violin', Eddie South, and Grappelli. In 1940 his 'Nuages' put some colour back into the black night of the occupation, during which he was to become the most popular jazz star in France.

After the Liberation, he joined Grappelli, who had stayed in London, and reformed the quintet, with or without him, after playing in the United States with Duke Ellington's band. He took up the electric guitar, adapting to it marvellously, and played with some of the young boppers, but gigs were getting rarer. Finally he settled in Samois, where he is commemorated with an annual festival.

Jean Cocteau:
'Django's death is the death of a gentle beast in a cage. He lived as one dreams of living, in a caravan. And even when it was no longer a caravan, it was still a caravan. His soul was mobile and holy. And his rhythms were his own, like a tiger's stripes, shine and whiskers. They were under his skin . . .'

Charlie Christian

1916, Dallas — New York, 1942

A shooting star

In the course of his short life he freed the guitar by electrifying it, and contributed to the development of bebop.

Despite his very short career — only five years, for he died of tuberculosis at the age of 26 — Charlie Christian was to establish the electric guitar as a solo instrument. Before him it had only been used in the rhythm sections of big bands because of its weaker sound volume. He was to influence all the guitarists that came after him (except for Django) and took part, with Monk, Gillespie, Parker and a few others, in the sessions in the Harlem clubs in 1941 that gave birth to bebop.

The most significant features of his style are his new conceptions of accompaniment and improvisation, the balance of his harmonic innovations (passing chords, frequent use of the minor seventh) and of his melodic daring, and the use of legato phrasing in an almost 'saxophone style', perhaps derived from Lester Young. In his solos he would insist on one note, and

> **Oscar Pettiford:**
> 'I have never heard anybody play with so much love. It was simply that: a pure love of jazz and the joy of doing a thing called music.'

develop gorgeous swinging riffs, with a rigorous sense of timing, flexibly stressing the four beats, sometimes punctuated by impressive breaks. His sound, which was percussive, but full and rounded at the same time, was inimitable, and recognizable at the first notes. It remains one of the finest ever produced on this instrument.

Christian started his career as a musician on the double bass, having also learnt the trumpet, the saxophone and the piano. When he took up the guitar, he played all over the Middle West with different bands. In 1937 he met the guitarist Eddie Durham, who had been the first to use an amplified electric guitar in Jimmie Lunceford's band (1935–1937). Impressed by this young prodigy, the pianist Mary Lou Williams phoned the producer John Hammond, who recommended him to Benny Goodman and he was hired. Staying with the band from 1939 until his death, he took part in many concerts, including the second *From Spirituals to Bop* event, and big band recording sessions, as well as recording in sextets (*Waiting for Benny*, 13 March 1941) and quintets.

His participation in the clarinettist's groups made him famous, and he gained top ratings in polls. As soon as concerts were over, he would rush to *Monroe's Uptown House* or *Minton's Playhouse*, where he would find his bopper friends for endless jam-sessions. He went to hospital in July 1941; a rapid recovery was expected, but he died a few months later in the Seaview Municipal Sanatorium. With his death, jazz lost the musician who, with Django Reinhardt, was to remain a model for all future guitarists.

From bop to bossa

After Christian's death, the guitar was somewhat overshadowed, but it came back powerfully in the 1960s, with the rise of hard-bop, *followed by* bossa-nova.

Barney Kessel (1923) is the greatest 'Christian' follower, who preserved the dynamic style of his idol by giving priority to swing and a clear development without any 'guitaristic' effects. His recordings as a sideman are prestigious (Armstrong, Billie Holiday, Parker, Ben Webster), and he was one of the regular guitarists of the JATP, a role he shared with **Herb Ellis** (1921), an ex-swing band player who took over from Kessel in the Oscar Peterson trio, and then had a great career as a sideman, notably with Ella Fitzgerald.

Jimmy Raney (1927) was the first great stylist to emerge after Christian. His knowledge of harmony and counterpoint (see his famous duet with Stan Getz) earned him the reputation of being the best guitarist of the generation which saw the birth of both bop and cool.

Tal Farlow (1921) is a genuine virtuoso, whose impressive hands earned him the nickname of Octopus! As expansive as Raney is introverted, but also influenced by Christian, he belongs to the bop avant-garde with the trio he put together with Mingus and Red Norvo. He then became the great 'translator' of hard bop for the guitar, a style whose expressionism suited his personality perfectly.

The Belgian **René Thomas** (1927–1975) grew up in the shadow of Reinhardt and Raney, until he developed, alongside his countryman, the saxophonist Bobby Jaspar, a singular, lyrical and spontaneous style which made him one of the favourite musicians of the great American 'tenors', such as Getz and Rollins.

Kenny Burrell (1931) applies his brilliant technique, acquired by listening to Django and Christian, to the blues, which permeate every note he plays, and enable him to cross barriers between styles and generations. Equally at home with Benny Goodman, Jimmy Smith or Dizzy Gillespie, he deservedly became one of the two favourite guitarists of the famous Blue Note label.

The other was **Grant Green** (1931–1978) who was also deeply rooted in blues and rhythm'n'blues, which enabled him to make the *soul jazz* style popular for the guitar in the 1960s. It was very melodic, but also direct and good for dancing.

Giuseppe Passalaqua, or **Joe Pass** (1929), is in a class of his own. His speed and the undemonstrative vigour of his phrasing make him a guitar equivalent of Oscar Peterson, with whom he often plays. His eclectic range of music and his infallible swing make him a great interpreter, independent of fashions and generations.

Jim Hall (1930) is one of the most subtle harmonizers on the guitar, and his refined sound makes him the greatest acoustics specialist for the electric guitar, which in his hands can achieve the finest nuances of the classical guitar. This admirably modest and discreet 'quiet fellow' has in fact contributed enormously to several key recordings of modern jazz, notably alongside Jimmy Giuffre, Bill Evans and Sonny Rollins. He is also one of the pioneers of the bossa nova in the United States.

But it was **Laurindo Almeida** (1917), a Brazilian disciple of Django's who, playing with the saxophonist Bud Shank in California, inaugurated the American version of this refined cocktail of jazz and samba which was already flourishing in Rio, where **Charlie Byrd** (1925), a specialist on the nylon string guitar, discovered it in 1961. A year later in Washington, he and Stan Getz were to record *Jazz/Samba*, which was an incredible success.

Wes Montgomery

1923, Indianapolis — Indianapolis, 1968

The man with the golden thumb

With his brilliant technique and his incomparable blues style, he was undoubtedly the greatest guitarist of the 1960s.

From the moment he was 'discovered' by Cannonball Adderley in 1959 until his sudden death from a heart attack, Wes Montgomery was seen both as 'the new Charlie Christian' (which is right) and 'the Coltrane of the guitar' (which seems

---

Johnny Griffin:

'He was a great guy, he didn't drink, didn't 'smoke'; he was terribly particular about food, he'd only eat what his mother used to give him, no frogs' legs, no snails; he wouldn't even taste them when he came to France!'

George Benson (1943)

There are four distinct periods in the career of this direct descendant of Montgomery, who from the little eight year old singer that he was (Little George Benson), became an extraordinary left-handed guitarist, with a clear sound and swing phrasing, and was a star of the pop scene in the 1980s.

Rhythm'n'blues and rock in his youth; funky with the organist Jack McDuff; virtuoso with the great beboppers; and pop star since 1976 (*This Masquerade*), dubbing his own guitar to his singing voice. In his latest recordings he is now ostensibly flirting with a *jazzy* sound.

---

excessive). He was a serene innovator who, in the footsteps of Charlie Christian and Django Reinhardt, broadened the instrument's potential and opened up new avenues which successive generations of guitarists have followed.

As a self-taught guitarist (he learnt to play at nineteen by listening to Christian's recordings, and still could not read music when he joined Lionel Hampton's big band in 1948) he nonetheless became an accomplished and very versatile guitarist, who had the singular characteristic of not using a pick, but the thumb of his right hand. This gave his playing a soft, warm and colourful, velvety tone, somewhere between the electric and the acoustic guitar sound. Another singular characteristic was his disconcerting ability to play in chords just as well as he could in single notes or in octaves. In complex thematic developments he could give the intensity he wanted to each note, a special meaning to each phrase, without any virtuoso effects, playing hard bop and standard classics as easily as ballads, in which he was a master of subtle melodies. He was also an outstanding bluesman.

After leaving Hampton in 1950, Montgomery played with two of his brothers as The Mastersounds, and recorded, first as a trio, then with Tommy Flanagan and the Heath brothers, *The Incredible Jazz Guitar of Wes Montgomery*, which earned him the highest awards. Later he played with Milt Jackson (*Bags Meets Wes*), and Johnny Griffin (*Full House*, which was recorded in public in 1962). He also made some more commercial recordings accompanied by string sections or big bands.

John McLaughlin

1942, Yorkshire (England)

An eclectic virtuoso

On the fringes of jazz, this over-endowed guitarist manages to blend a Djangoesque style, flamenco and the sitar.

This self-taught musician came to London at nineteen. He was familiar with blues and rock, had discovered flamenco, Django Reinhardt and Tal Farlow, and was interested in India (its culture, philosophy, religions and music), practised yoga and listened to Ravi Shankar and vina players from South India on the radio. His life was then devoted to studying the spiritual elements of Indian music, while at the same time playing in rock and blues groups, and later with the Blue Flames and the Graham Bond Organization. He easily mastered a skilful synthesis of Afro-American and Indian music, acquiring an impressive rhythm technique and fabulous speed which earned him the reputation of being 'the guitarist who plays faster than his shadow'.

He got some avant-garde experience with his own group in 1968 (the record *Extrapolation*), before he was recommended to drummer Tony Williams, whom he joined in New York to play in his group,

Lifetime. Invited by Miles Davis to record *In a Silent Way*, he took part in the birth of jazz-rock with the trumpeter, with whom he made five records between 1969 and 1973, contributing his blend of English rock and Jimi Hendrix-influenced music to the group.

In 1970, McLaughlin became a disciple of the Indian guru Sri Chinmoy, who gave him the name of Mahavishnu (Creator). He started the Mahavishnu Orchestra with the drummer Billy Cobham (*The Inner Mounting Flame*, 1971), then with the violinist Jean Luc Ponty in 1974 (*Visions of the Emerald Beyond*).

Returning to the acoustic guitar, he formed the group Shakti in 1975 with the violinist L. Shankar and tabla virtuoso Zakir Hussain, in which he blended western and eastern music. From then on, McLaughlin oscillated between East and West, acoustic guitar (flamenco with Paco de Lucia, the classical pianist Katia Labèque) and electric groups (One Truth Band), working with Chick Corea and David Sanborn, the guitarists Larry Coryell, Al DiMeola and Christian Escoudé, before putting together, for one recording and a tour, a new Mahavishnu, with the collaboration of the saxophonist Bill Evans, and Jonas Hellborg on bass. In 1985 he performed *Mediterranean*, his concerto for guitar and orchestra, and participated in Bertrand Tavernier's film *Round Midnight*. Recently, he has performed with a trio featuring percussionist Trilok Gurtu.

Always looking for perfection, he continues to explore the potential of his instrument, both violently and serenely, guided by the musical styles he has mastered passionately, humbly, sincerely, totally.

In John McLaughlin's own words:
'I am not aiming at an Indo-jazz fusion, I want a new music with the flavour of all the cultures, and of course something more' (*Jazz Magazine*, June 1988).

Pat Metheny

1954, Lee's Summit

A moderate futurist

He rounds the corners of state-of-the-art technology with his subtle sense of melody and a beautiful sound.

Being appreciated equally by the fathers of bebop, the rock generation, the Free Jazz veterans and the convinced fusionists is no mean feat for a jazz musician. Pat Metheny (who looks like the eternal student) carries this off with ease thanks to his musical open-mindedness (he admits to liking the country singer Dolly Parton as much as Ornette Coleman, a founder of Free Jazz, and he composes for David Bowie), which permeates his work. He offered an alternative to McLaughlin's tense virtuoso style,

Lyle Mays:
'I think we belong to a generation which has no fear of technology. We have grown up with it, through electric guitars. It seems natural to me, by extension, to use the possibilities offered by rhythm computers . . .' (Guitares et Claviers, July 1987).

In Pat Metheny's own words:
'The Synclavier is an incredible tool; think of anything and you can do it. It is no longer enough to conceive of good melodies or to have good ideas, you have to find a new sound, a new tone with this technology' (Jazz Hot, April 1985).

with seductively simple melodies, a very lilting, sax-like development, and a profusion of new tones, cleverly blending acoustics and electronics (from the good old Gibson to the Synclavier, including the Ovation and the twelve string guitar).

At the age of 12 he manifested his interest in jazz by listening to Ornette Coleman, for whom he developed a religious passion, often playing his work, and actually playing with him in 1985, on the record *Song X*. At 20, he met the vibraphone player Gary Burton, and played with him until 1977, while teaching at the Berklee School of Music. He recorded his first record, *Bright Size of Life*, with Jaco Pastorius and formed the Pat Metheny Group with his friend Lyle Mays. His record *American Garage* was enormously successful. In 1980, with Michael Brecker, Charlie Haden and Jack DeJohnette, he made the record *80/81*, and also played with Sonny Rollins and with Brazilian musicians.

Since 1978, Pat Metheny has been interested in the most recent equipment, like the first guitar-synthesizer which he used in *Offramp* (1982), and the Synclavier. Like Stevie Wonder, Frank Zappa and many other young musicians, he approaches these new electronic machines by saying that he 'uses the Synclavier like a writer using a word processor', while adding that 'despite (his) taste for technology, nothing can beat the sound of an acoustic instrument.'

His group, with the addition of two vocalists and a Brazilian percussionist, went all over the world in 1987–1988. Pat has composed music for films such as John Schlesinger's *The Falcon and the Snowman*, in which David Bowie sings the theme song.

Masters of the eclectic guitar

By the 1960s the guitar had become the favourite instrument for exploring the common ground between jazz, rock, funk, and contemporary European music. Each year brought a new batch of electronic improvements: chorus pedals, wah-wah, distortion, delay, harmonizers, octave couplers and finally, the magic instrument, the guitar-synthesizer. Most improvisors on the guitar embarked on the path frayed by Jimi Hendrix, but they soon followed new tracks. There were soon as many styles, and above all 'sounds', as there were soloists.

Derek Bailey (1930) is British, self-taught and in the 1960s, was a pioneer and theorist of free improvisation. Like John Cage, he rejects conventional rules for the guitar and his concerts are a sort of minimalist happening.

Sonny Sharrock (1940) is another great master of the 'free' style, and sometimes plays with Bailey. He started playing with Olatunji, Pharoah Sanders and then Herbie Mann, developing an original technique based on the good old bluesman's *bottleneck*. He was linked to the activities of the group Material, and has since evolved towards a funkier style.

Ralph Towner (1940) is the great specialist of the twelve string guitar. He is also a good pianist in the Bill Evans line, and occasionally plays trumpet. After a sound on-the-job training in the New York clubs, he hit the limelight through a recording with Weather Report (*I Sing the Body Electric*, 1971), and went on to found Oregon. His 'gliding' style is loaded with harmonics, and is very free rhythmically.

James Blood Ulmer (1942), the son of a baptist minister, went naturally from gospel and rhythm'n'blues, after a short time with the Jazz Messengers, to playing with Ornette Coleman. Fascinated by the latter's music, he became his regular partner, moving very fast to a highly personal fusion of blues, funk and free jazz which was particularly effective in concerts.

Philip Catherine (1942) has developed a refined and lyrical style, using chord sequences reminiscent of Django (who was also Belgian!) and, amongst those who use the full range of modern technology, is probably the one whose links with bebop are the most evident.

Larry Coryell (1943), who used to play with Catherine, is a self-taught virtuoso who had a very personal itinerary from country-rock to jazz, playing in groups with Charles Lloyd, Chico Hamilton and

---

The case of Stanley Jordan

Only time will tell if this expressive and intense soloist — very reminiscent of Hendrix in blues mode — is simply being 'original', or whether he is a truly revolutionary guitarist heralding a new era for the instrument. In any case, the amazing technique he has developed has yet to find other adepts, despite the infinite possibilities it seems to have. Playing with both hands on the fret board, he hammers the strings with all ten fingers rather than plucking them. This pianistic approach, only occasionally used by Hendrix and a few rock guitarists like Van Halen, allows for all sorts of daring harmonic effects in the context of jazz without, however, depriving the electric guitar of any of its unique expressiveness.

Born in 1959, he abandoned classical piano for the guitar at the age of eleven when he discovered Hendrix, then he studied electro-acoustic music at Princeton. As a street musician in Chicago and then in New York, he was encouraged by his colleagues Mike Stern and Blood Ulmer. After an initial success at the New York and Montreux festivals in 1984, his first record marked the revival of the famous Blue Note label. Since then he has regularly been playing solo or in a trio with the pianist Bernard Wright and the amazing drummer, Kenwood Dennard, or, more recently, bass player Chornett Moffat.

Gary Burton. As an unconditional admirer of Hendrix, he keeps that heritage alive within a context of bebop-based improvisation.

Mick Goodrick (1945) is to some extent the 'guru' of the Berklee School. Metheny's partner with Gary Burton, he developed a way of playing without a pick, defined as 'pianistic', which combines much harmonic research with the use of electronic effects.

John Abercrombie (1944) was a real rock'n'roll fan until he learnt all the subtleties of contemporary jazz guitar and the Hendrix style. He is a favourite sideman with drummers (Billy Cobham, Chico Hamilton, Jack DeJohnnette, Peter Erskine), and possesses a notably fluid style which remains very clear rhythmically. He is a specialist on the mandolin-guitar playing a very wide range and resolutely defies classification.

Terje Rypdal (1947) is one of those musicians who have been perhaps hastily grouped under the name of 'ECM school'. This Norwegian wilfully plays an ethereal music, which is both 'electric' and very lyrical, with a 'windy' and sometimes heart-rending sound.

John Scofield (1951) studied with Goodrick at Berklee, and entered jazz by the front door at the Carnegie Hall where he played at 23 with Chet Baker and Gerry Mulligan. He went on to play with Billy Cobham, George Duke, the Brecker brothers, then Gary Burton, Richard Beirach and Dave Liebman, recorded with Mingus and, in 1979, formed a spectacular swing trio. Hired by Miles Davis between 1982 and 1985, he has since pursued various activities both as a leader and as a sideman. He is considered one of the most complete and inventive guitarists of his

generation, playing with long sinuous phrases full of distortions, but his music still remains very close to the blues.

Bill Frisell (1951) also graduated from Berklee, but appears as a kind of 'researcher' figure in his generation. His singular style, full of glissandos, contrasts and effects, evokes country *steel guitar* as well as the *bottleneck* of the blues.

Mike Stern (1953), a friend of Frisell's since they studied together at Berklee with Metheny, played in the group Blood, Sweat and Tears and in Billy Cobham's group before joining Miles Davis, and being his main sparring partner for three years (1981–1983, and again in 1985). He also accompanied Jaco Pastorius, then Dave Sanborn and Steps Ahead, and played in trios or quintets. His vigorous syncretist style enables him, in the same chorus, to change a few bars of blues into a typical bebop phrase, then a hard rock riff, without changing its meaning, quite the opposite. He is probably the most spectacular of these 'mutants', who from being rockers have become the heirs of jazz.

Hiram Bullock (1955) competes seriously with Stern (whom he plays with frequently in clubs) as regards scenic effects. He is a real 'stage burner'; strongly influenced in his youth by Jimi Hendrix, he became a favourite soloist in many bands, from Pastorius to Carla Bley, including Gil Evans and Dave Sanborn. He is very much in demand in the recording studios, starred for a while in a show on NBC-TV, and is well known in Japan, where he was born and where his own group, the 24th Street Band, with the spectacular drummer Steve Jordan, is well established.

B.B. King, *'Preacher' of the blues*

The roots of the blues

Born in the South

Like all music from an ethnic tradition, the blues has more of a geography than a history. Its story is a slow odyssey from the south to the east, then to the north-east, and finally to the west, following the successive changes which have affected the Afro-American population, the decline and fragmentation of the cotton plantations, institutionalized segregation reinforced by terror, urbanization and proletarization.

Born in the delta of the Mississippi at the end of the last century, the blues has practically erased or absorbed all other forms of non-religious Black music, and profoundly transformed White music. The blues rapidly gained the cities in the upper reaches of the river basin (Memphis, Saint Louis and finally Chicago), spreading also to Texas and the Appalachians. The spread was accelerated by the success of travelling *vaudeville shows* and then, in the 1920s by the spectacular distribution of the portable gramophone in the Black community. Until the 1929 crash, *race records*, made by white producers, represented a large share of the market and encouraged a high degree of emulation amongst musicians.

The paradox of the blues man, the troubadour of the modern era, is to be both a territorial musician and a spreader of his poetry. The road, the river and to an even greater degree, the train are in fact the major themes in the blues repertoire. The lives of most blues musicians are punctuated by ceaseless travel. The great styles or schools have to some extent usurped the names of the regions and towns through which the blues have passed. Amongst this crowd of nomadic artists so attached to their roots, thousands have shown original talent and instrumental innovation. But very few of them have had a real professional career, and it would be vain to attempt to select from their ranks a handful of 'great creators'. The musicologist Paul Oliver, in the prologue of his *History of the Blues*, stresses 'that it is the history of humble, obscure and unpretentious men and women, only a few of whose names have become familiar . . .'

We have therefore highlighted the ones who are particularly interesting with regard to the history of jazz. In any case, it is impossible to 'hear' the message of the great jazz creators without constantly referring to the fundamental background in which words and melody are confused, where the 'soul blues' become the notes. The blues is basically the collective and spontaneous work of the greatest jazz creator of all: the whole of the Afro-American people.

Delta blues

The cradle of the vocal blues and also of the bottleneck *guitar style (played* glissando *using the neck of a bottle), the Mississippi Delta includes the state of that name, Arkansas, Alabama, a part of Tennessee, and Louisiana. The mostly black population suffered years of poverty, isolation and segregation, which offers some explanation for this heart-rending, tormented and very 'African' style.*

Charley Patton (c.1887–1934) was the father of all blues guitarists, a virtuoso who accompanied his own voice with unusual independence, and whose style was like a wild cavalcade, as in his famous 'Pony Blues'.

Bo Carter (1893–1964) left his family's 'string band' to go all over the South in a Model-T Ford, before he went blind at about 40. He was the leader of the Mississippi Sheiks, then a crude but anti-alcoholic soloist, he was both a virtuoso guitarist (specializing in dobro) and a great joker.

Tommy Johnson (1896–1956) is the other great pioneer of the Delta, less frequently recorded but more influential as a composer ('Canned Heat', 'Cool Drink of Water'), and a singer specializing in falsetto.

Skip James (1902–1969) was the great blues player of the 1929 Depression, a sedentary musician from the Mississippi, misanthropic and deeply religious at the same time, with a strangely contrasting instrumental style at both the piano and the guitar.

Big Joe Williams (1903-1982) was an indefatigable vagabond. His abundant discography illustrates the typical career of a first generation blues player marvellously, enlivening picnics, railroad builder's camps, and dives. He was the author of the famous 'Baby Please Don't Cry', and he invented a curious nine-string guitar, enabling the bass strings to be doubled.

Son House (1902), the ancient *preacher*, is at the same time one of the great masters of the *bottleneck*, but also one of the most exemplary blues players, due to the refined inter-dependence of his voice and his guitar. His influence on his two illustrious pupils, Muddy Waters and Robert Johnson was considerable.

Robert Johnson (1912–1938) was perhaps the most legendary of all: although it was so brief (he was certainly murdered), his career not only influenced practically all the blues players of the post-war period, but also Bob Dylan, Jimi Hendrix and the Rolling Stones. His songs ('Crossroad Blues', 'Love in Vain') have almost all become classics. In spite of his almost constant use of a boogie bass, his complex guitar playing marked the ultimate perfection preceding the advent of the electric guitar.

Chester Burnett, known as **Howlin' Wolf** (1910–1976), found the equivalent of his powerful and aggressive voice in this new instrument, amplified to saturation point. He became the great star of the Chicago clubs until the end of his life, and he retained all the authenticity he had inherited from Charley Patton and Tommy Johnson.

Robert Nighthawk (1909) perfectly illustrates the transition between the Delta and Chicago styles. An agricultural day labourer in Arkansas, he played in the *Medicine Shows* then in the Memphis Jug Band, before becoming a star of the Bluebird label. His *bottleneck* playing had a big influence on Earl Hooker, Muddy Waters, and many more.

Elmore James (1910–1963), a pupil of Robert Johnson, owes his fame to returning to the themes of the latter in his original style, using the bottleneck on the electric guitar.

The South East blues

More relaxed but also more brilliant than the Delta blues, the style relied more on ragtime guitar. *The South East blues were born in the region of the Appalachians, in North Carolina, Virginia, Kentucky and in eastern Tennessee. Segregation was milder in this area, and the difference between blues and the white farmers' country style was less pronounced, and their common repertory of love ballads scored a triumph for* Nashville *sound. Blind musicians were numerous among the great blues players of this region . . .*

Arthur Phelps, known as **Blind Blake** (1890–1933), was the pioneer of ragtime guitar. His serene voice, his straight tone and his impressive dexterity have affected the whole history of East Coast blues.

Blind Willie McTell (1901–1959) was the pioneer of the twelve-string guitar imported from Mexico. He was a solitary traveller in spite of his blindness, a poet as much as a musician. He radiated around his home town of Atlanta, and ended his life as a preacher.

Blind Gary Davis (1896–1972) was a preacher nearly all his life, proclaiming the Gospels through the New York streets. A disciple of Blind Blake, he incarnated one of the first examples of the blending of blues and gospel songs. He became a famous figure in the struggle for civil rights, and was the hero of a French film made in 1968.

Blind Boy Fuller (1908–1941) was inspired by Blake and Davis. He simplified their way of playing by putting more emphasis on the bass strings. His humorous repertory left a deep mark on tobacco country.

Hudson Whittaker, nicknamed **Tampa Red** (born in 1900) first joined the pianist Georgia Tom (the future pioneer of gospel, Thomas Dorsey) before becoming one of the blues heroes of Chicago, next to Big Bill Broonzy and Big Maceo. He was a sober and elegant guitarist whose shrill voice was to have a strong influence on the first rhythm'n'blues singers.

Blind Sonny Terry (1911), as good at

harmonising as his father, made his debut with Gary Davis and Blind Boy Fuller, before becoming the most celebrated blues player of his generation, together with his partner the guitarist **Brownie McGhee**. The husky voice of Sonny and the more velvety voice of Brownie earned this widely recorded duet unparalleled success.

Lonnie Johnson: a suspension bridge between blues and jazz

A major blues figure in New Orleans, Alonzo Johnson (1889–1970) was one of the most eclectic geniuses of Afro-American music, and the first to be heard in Europe, in 1917. A violinist, a singer, but above all a guitarist, in 1925 he became a key musician of the famous firm Okey, and recorded with Armstrong, Johnny Dodds, Ellington and Eddie Lang. In this privileged circle, it was he who introduced the guitar into jazz as a solo instrument in its modern form. The inventor of the style of playing with a pick, note by note, he did not neglect the urban blues scene, which had a long-lasting effect on his vocal style as well as on his instrumental phrasing, rich in *blue notes*. His influence was felt by musicians as different as Charlie Christian and T-Bone Walker, the other great pioneers of the electric guitar. He was very popular before the war, but suddenly and inexplicably declined in popularity soon afterwards. Nevertheless, his reputation was rehabilitated in the 1960s by the American Folk Blues Festival.

The Texas blues

From the devastation of the cotton fields by weevils to the oil boom, this region in the throes of radical economic changes witnessed the development of a sub-proletariat deeply marked by a new form of slavery, and with it, a highly unusual style of blues, which had hints of the Mexican and even flamenco in its polyrhythmic basses and rich ornamentation for the guitarists, and imagination overflowing in a tragi-comic vein for the singers.

Henry Thomas, better known as **Ragtime Texas** (1874–?), was a legendary pioneer, the only blues player of his generation who recorded. Those 23 sides (1927–1929), including two gospel songs, are precious traces of the original blues of the *hoboes*. These were itinerant musicians who wandered along the railroad tracks, and whose style still closely resembled the *square dances* which relied on anonymous repertories, both eclectic and exuberant.

Blind Lemon Jefferson (1897–1929) does not look like a ball of fire in the single, famous photo which shows his round, impenetrable face. In spite of being blind from birth, he was a jack of all trades, both a musician and a wrestler at the fair! He became the most prolific, most famous blues player of the 1920s, and recorded more than 85 titles for Paramount, each of which is a masterpiece. Louis Armstrong himself admitted how much he owed him as a singer. With his bitter and expressive voice, he evokes a misery which he knew from the inside, his own compositions remaining very close to the work and gospel songs of his youth. He was an unorthodox guitarist, who often resorted to picking at his guitar with a knife, to improve the sound of the instrument.

Huddie Ledbetter, known as **Leadbelly** (1889–1949), borrowed this technique from him during those years in which they enlivened the hot neighbourhoods of Dallas, before he found himself 'in the shade' for many years. He was discovered in a *chain gang* in the 1930s by Alan Lomax, the musicologist who had him freed and

took him to New York, where he became the favourite singer of the Greenwich Village intellectuals. His stentorian voice and his energetic 'twelve string playing' was perfectly suited to his repertory of folk songs that often dated back to well before the blues.

Texas Alexander (1880–1955) was another who immortalized these work or prison songs, some of which would have been lost if it were not for his records. Exclusively a singer, he was accompanied by the best guitarists of the era who were very much influenced by his imperious vocal style and oratory.

It was with him in particular that **Lightnin' Hopkins** (1912–1982) made his debut in the streets of Houston, where he was to play the role of catalyst from the 1940s. Influenced as a guitarist by Jefferson and as a singer by Alexander, he soon developed one of the most profound and original blues voices, to which he gave a personal, autobiographic and amusing tone which was truly exceptional. The intelligence with which he used the microphone and amplification also caught on.

Mance Lipscomb (1895–1972) practically never left the Brazos region, where he was a tenant farmer during the week, and did not make his debut as a professional musician until he was 65. He made his first record with the famous Arhoolie label. Influenced by Jefferson, and deeply marked by the context of cotton plantation balls, he numbers among the ranks of those 'archaic' *songsters*, who often have a repertory a lot older than the blues.

Memphis and Saint Louis blues

On the docks of Memphis, cotton was unloaded by thousands of Black emigrants who went the same way as the Mississippi river to escape the misery of the plantations. The capital of Tennessee naturally became that of the blues well before the 1920s when a style typical of that seething city emerged.

It was here that the clever cornet player and minstrel **W.C. Handy** (1873–1958) published numerous traditional songs in 1908 in his name, which earned him the title he appears to have somewhat usurped of 'inventor of the blues'. The most famous of them, 'Saint Louis Blues', takes its name from the next stopping place, upstream on the Mississippi at the confluence of the Missouri, a city which was to rival Memphis before Chicago's supremacy was affirmed.

Frank Stokes (1887–1955) has every right to dispute the paternity of the Memphis blues with his lesser known compatriot Jim Jackson. The thirty discs made by Stokes are as many humorous and picturesque masterpieces, and reflect the social life of the port. His quavering tenor voice blended magnificently with the bouncy performance of the guitarist Dan Sane.

Furry Lewis (1893–1981), the occasional partner of W.C. Handy was the most original of the Memphis blues players, due to his loud performance on the guitar, often coloured by the *bottleneck*. Familiar with the *riverboats* and the *Medicine shows* (shows to attract the public to the platforms of quacks), late in life he was to be treated like a sort of historic monument in Memphis.

Lizzie Douglas, nicknamed **Memphis Minnie** (1897–1973) is both the most famous of the singers who stayed faithful to country blues, and an accomplished guitarist. She was a pupil of Frank Stokes and Lonnie Johnson. She represents the historic transition between Memphis and Chicago, where she made her career from the 1930s on. Some of her approximately two hundred recorded blues put her on the same level as Bessie Smith or Ma Rainey.

The **Memphis Jug Band**, to which Memphis Minnie at first belonged, was the best band of this type around 1930. The *jug* (a pitcher used as a wind instrument) was accompanied by the kazoo, the mouthorgan, the banjo, the mandolin and the guitar; their repertory also included Dixieland jazz and country tunes.

Sleepy John Estes (1899–1977) occupies a place on the very edge of Memphis blues. His utterly original style, which has been widely immitated, became the 'Brownsville blues' after the name of the suburb where he lived. An overwhelming singer (he sobbed with undeniable sincerity!), he interwove his voice with the plaintive mouth-organ played by his inseparable collaborator (and brother-in-law), **Hammie Nixon**, with whom for more than thirty years he formed one of the most beautiful duets in the history of the blues.

Roosevelt Sykes (1906–1983) settled in Saint Louis at the end of the 1920s, where he refined his thundering pianistic style marked by his use of noisy *barrelhouses* which animated the fairgrounds of the valley. When it was transplanted to Chicago, this style, which relied on spectacular strolling basses, attracted many emulators, including the pianist Peter Chatman, known as **Memphis Slim** (1915–1988). Sykes was also a singer full of humour, and a remarkable composer.

Leroy Carr (1905–1935) had very little time to excite the Saint Louis scene, where he arrived two years before his death, with his alter-ego the guitarist **Scrapper Blackwell**. The unprecedented cohesion of their duet, and Carr's unusually refined pianistic style and the caustic, blasé tone in which he deals with the crudest subjects with a vein of black humour, make him one of the great forerunners of modern urban blues.

The Chicago blues

Since the start of the century, the terminus of the Illinois Central, the railway running from New Orleans, the capital of the Midwest, was the great pole of attraction for Blacks emigrating from the South. In the 1920s, segregation and prohibition were less strict here than elsewhere. Lester Melrose founded the Bluebird label in the 1930s, and his studio immediately became the crucible for Chicago blues, dominated by the rhythm section — especially the piano — and a style of improvisation close to the local jazz.

William Lee Conley, known as **Big Bill Broonzy** (1893–1958) occupies a considerable place in blues history, practically all of whose styles he covered, from the simplest to the most urban. A swift, bounding guitarist playing in the difficult key of C in the ragtime style, he accompanied virtually all the great blues players of his generation, and he himself recorded hundreds of titles, many of which were his own compositions. At first he was typical of Chicago modernism, but from the 1950s to the 1960s, he was to revert to the *blues revival* of his origins. His autobiography, *Big Bill Blues* is an essential account of this period.

Robert Brown, called **Washboard Sam** (1910–1966), is a clear illustration of the ambiguity of the Bluebird blues, through the contrast between his primitive instrument (a washboard, beaten and scratched with the help of a thimble) and the generally very orchestrated context in which he performed.

James Kokomo Arnold (1901–1968) is one of the most individual and mysterious stylists of the Chicago blues. He was a *bottleneck* virtuoso, a loud jive singer, and as efficient as the still (for making hooch) which he had installed in his bath tub. This bootlegger remained an amateur musician, even in the years from 1934–1938, when he was a local celebrity, recording more than a hundred titles before sinking into oblivion.

Jazz Gillum (1904–1966) was the most popular harmonica player of his time, if not the subtlest, and a talented composer, very marked by his rough childhood in Mississippi.

Of a very different stature, **John Lee 'Sonny Boy' Williamson** (1914–1948) was a highly expressive singer, and above all the first great virtuoso of the harmonica which he made into a major instrument, first at Broonzy's side, then with a complete rhythm section. Literally screaming into his instrument with formidable intensity, all the while accompanying himself (probably the first) on the guitar, with the acute rhythmic sense he had gained from his experience at the drums, he was to be the great harbinger of the post-war blues, and a generous, Rabelaisian personality.

Major Merriweather, known as **Big**

John Lee Hooker

A native of Clarksdale (Mississippi), John Lee Hooker (1917) started in the gospel choirs in Cincinnatti, before he settled in Detroit in 1943. Five years later, still semi-professional, he won national success with what was to remain his fetish-title: 'Boogie Chillun'. From that time, his fame was to be increasingly affirmed, notably in Europe where he became in the 1960s the most popular of the blues players, and even a symbolic figure on the English rock scene. Staunchly running against the tide of his generation's predominant trend, he refused all prefabricated orchestration and played most frequently alone, accompanying himself on the electric guitar while marking the time with a well-nailed boot. Giving priority to riffs and intensity of expression, he decorated his solos very little. His music, therefore, is a very genuine recreation, in a contemporary context, of that which cradled his childhood in the Delta. One could say of him that 'he had done the rounds of the blues'.

Maceo (1905–1953), also marked this capital transition at the beginning of the 1940s. His sulphurous voice and his voluble performance on the piano, imbued with boogie-woogie, exercised a decisive influence on all the blues pianists of the following generation.

Aleck 'Rice' Miller (1901–1965) certainly deserves the nickname of 'Sonny Boy Williamson', which he borrowed from his great predecessor. This fugitive from Memphis was already fifty when he became one of the international glories radiating from Chicago. In fact, this 'usurper' was equal to his namesake, especially in his astounding mastery of the harmonica, even if his reputation as a man was at opposite poles from the former. Moody and caustic, gifted with an exceptional sense of the theatre, he impressed all those who approached him, and influenced almost all the great showmen of the blues revival, whether black or white.

Willie Dixon (1915) dominated the post-war Chicago blues, less by his vocal talent than by his favourite instrument the double-bass, and especially his dynamism as a producer, a conductor, and *talent scout*. A prolific composer, he presided at the end of the 1950s, over almost all the notable recording sessions of the Chicago blues players, but also the pioneers of rock'n'roll (Chuck Berry, Bo Diddley). He is a poet as much as a musician, and his own records (notably with Memphis Slim) are a curious contrast with his usual modernism because of their stolidly traditonal atmosphere.

McKinley Morganfield, known as **Muddy Waters** (1915–1983), became the most popular of the young blues players from Chicago as soon as he arrived in 1943. This child of the Mississippi, a pupil of Robert Johnson, was 'launched' by Broonzy, who immediately recognized the potential of this acid guitarist, who used the *bottleneck* on the electric guitar better than anyone, and doubled as a singer with an overwhelming charm. His passionate and gravelly voice was also as little urban as

possible in an ultra-electrified context which, from the end of the 1940s, foreshadowed the best aspect of rock'n'roll. In spite of his youth, he already played a paternal role as regards the whole of the new Chicago generation, which passed through his groups like a sort of living conservatory of the great Delta tradition. His career then became that of an uncontested master. He was famous worldwide, and to list his pupils would be like publishing a 'Who's Who' of modern blues, and also soul and rock, since it would range from Ray Charles to Jimi Hendrix, including the Beatles and the Rolling Stones, whose name is taken from one of his many compositions, which are usually marked by the traditional blues of the south. Everybody claimed him as their own.

Less well known in Europe, but much better known in the United States, **Jimmy Reed** (1925–1976) equally represents the effect of the Chicago style with a 'southern accent'. He also came from the Mississippi, and his sober and relaxed guitar style had almost as much influence on American pop music.

Little Walter Jacobs (1931–1968), having been a street musician in the famous Maxwell Street market, revealed himself alongside Muddy Waters as the great 'electrifier' of the harmonica, adapting all the technical possibilities of amplification to an admirably ornate theme, which made him a blues improviser comparable to the most subtle of jazz players. A sombre and aggressive character, he died prematurely in a fight, leaving some of the most beautiful solos recorded for the Chess and Checker labels.

Otis Rush (1934) is a remarkable singer with a quivering falsetto, and an ultra-sensitive guitarist, influenced by Kenny Burrell and T-Bone Walker. He represents, with **Buddy Guy** (1936) and **Magic Sam** (1937–1969), the expressionism of the 'West Side Sound' which completely renewed the Chicago Blues in the 1950s and 1960s.

Bessie Smith

1894, Chattanooga — Clarksdale, 1937

The empress of the blues

Her flexible phrasing and powerful and expressive voice became a model for all the early jazz singers

Edward Albee's play *The Death of Bessie Smith* has not quelled the polemic: according to certain witnesses, a 'white' hospital is supposed to have refused to give her treatment after her car accident. We shall never really know whether it was segregation that cost her life. In any case she died as she had lived, on the road. For this little orphan started her nomadic singing career in the travelling *Minstrel Shows* at eighteen, in the same troupe as her senior and first model, Gertrude 'Ma' Rainey.

By 1921, her personality was established in her own band, which she took to the Northern cities. Two years later, a contract with Columbia and the recording of 'Down Hearted Blues' was to to put her in the lead over contemporary blues recording artists like Mamie Smith, Ida Cox, Alberta Hunter, Victoria Spivey, and Ethel Waters and she soon became the first superstar of black showbusiness.

Until 1930, Bessie Smith was to record about a hundred masterpieces, accompanied by the greatest jazz-men, including Armstrong, Coleman Hawkins, James P.

Johnson, Fletcher Henderson and her own manager, Clarence Williams. Her realistic but non-political songs give raw descriptions of poverty, love pains, and natural catastrophes in a style which is more heart breaking than plaintive, often marked with angry feminism. Under the big top or in the most luxurious theatres, her flashy beauty and elegance, her plain speaking and her fighting instinct, which did not spare the whites, made her singing tour a local event. In spite of her very free life-style, she went to church every Sunday wherever she was, and the innumerable *preachers* she listened to avidly had a great influence on her profane interpretations.

Alas, after the Great Crash her style fell out of fashion, and she experienced a certain decline, emphasized by her divorce and chronic alcoholism, which she mocked in the film *Saint Louis Blues*, which Warner dedicated to her in 1929.

By means of her great rhythmic freedom and her most subtle diction, in the space of a few too brief years, Bessie Smith was able to skim over a considerable distance, from the somewhat square accentuation of rural blues to that persuasive or thoughtful balance that Billie Holiday and Ella Fitzgerald were later to discover. Better, she discovered all the tacit codes which make the jazz singer a fully-fledged member of the band.

T-Bone Walker

1910, Linden — Los Angeles, 1975

The patriarch of the electric guitar

Like Coleman Hawkins for the saxophone or Lionel Hampton for the vibraphone, he was at the same time both pioneer and archetype.

When in 1933 Aaron Thibeaux Walker made friends with the young Charlie Christian and formed an ephemeral but nourishing duet with him, they did not suspect that they would separately become the archetypes of the two rural approaches to electric guitar, the 'sitting' jazz guitar and the 'standing' guitar of modern blues, then of rock'n'roll.

Walker, who was six years older than Christian, had already acquired a solid experience with the singer Ida Cox, then with Cab Calloway's big band. He settled in Los Angeles after having been the accompanist of Ma Rainey, and adopted the 'clip- on-microphone' at about the same time as the pioneers Floyd Smith and Eddie

> **B.B. King:**
> 'He has a strange way of holding his guitar, he lies it at a distance instead of letting it simply rest flat against his stomach . . . and one could say that it was enough for him to scrape along the strings with his pick, I do not even know how he manages to hit the right one . . . and yet, what a touch! I've done all I could to find that sound, I've come close but I've never really reached it. T-Bone is the first electric guitarist I ever heard . . . and it is the most beautiful sound I shall ever hear in the whole of my life!'

Durham. His 'T-Bone Blues' recorded in 1939 with Les Hite's big band, enabled him to make his name as a blues player, and to claim the paternity of the 'plugged-in' guitar. It was the first record where the guitar sounds really 'electric'. Moreover, T-Bone already had the attitude on stage which was to be typical of all the *guitar heroes*, whose ancestor he claimed to be, a contrasting and acrobatic performance, all in *single notes*, at first tortuous and soon torrential. His success enabled him to form a band that included a brass section where saxophonists Eddie and Maxwell Davis were to play, and which for a long time was to be an obligatory passage for young Californian jazz players.

In the 1940s, T-Bone was the black musician who sold most records in the United States, and he was unanimously acclaimed by all the trends of criticism. Regularly invited to play in the great jazz festivals and the JATP tours, he was never to deny that he belonged to the world of blues. Nostalgic for his native Texas — like a lot of blues and jazz players he had some Indian blood, Cherokee as it happens — his models were Blind Lemon Jefferson, Lonnie Johnson, and especially the Leroy Carr/Scrapper Blackwell duet. As for his pupils, those closest to him were Lowell Fulson, Clarence 'Gatemouth' Brown, Pee Wee Crayton, and Johnny Guitar Watson, but he influenced pratically all the subsequent singer-guitarists; in fact, he inaugurated a whole stage and musical system which dominated show-business in the 1950s. From Jeff Beck to John Winter, but also Chuck Berry and Jimi Hendrix, there is not a single one who would not cite him as the absolute term of reference for perfect cohesion between voice and electric sound.

B.B. King

1925, Indiana

A blues player of the Gospel School

The most celebrated and imitated singer-guitarist made his perennial and brassy show into a true celebration of the blues.

In the same tradition as James Brown, Riley King has natural charisma, a gift of the gab, and showmanship which gives his concerts a quality of communication with an audience which goes way beyond blues fans. And yet his repertoire is almost exclusively made up of blues, which distinguishes him from the great soul singers whose aura he shares. In spite of his origins, his style draws less from the blues players of the Delta than from the three heroes who charmed his adolescence: Lonnie Johnson, T-Bone Walker, but also Charlie Christian. For, more than any other, he is a guitarist born lovingly rocking his instrument, which he baptized 'Lucille', and treats like a girl-friend, and which he plays with remarkably controlled vibrato and *glissando* effects which recall the *bottleneck* styles of the past.

An orphan at the age of nine, he already had to work on the plantations, and his only school was the church, where he soon got his own vocal quartet together. At twenty, he sang in the streets of Memphis, where he learned to play the guitar with Bukka White and Robert Lockwood, and where he became popular as a disk-jockey in a local radio station, where he was given the name of 'B.B.' (Blues Boy).

From the 1950s, he travelled all over the United States with a group inspired by T-Bone Walker's (with a rich panoply of brass), and his success continued to grow, lined with hits like 'Three O'Clock Blues' and 'Sweet Black Angel'. His career ran parallel to that of James Brown, whom he has been wrongly accused of copying. Their common way of singing, a blend of chanting and restraint, quite simply had the same origin in preaching, faintly tempered by the influence of the crooners then in fashion.

In the 1970s, both were treated as itinerant ambassadors of modernity and the Afro-American tradition. They were welcomed triumphantly in Africa of course, but also in Europe and Japan. They travelled like princes, installing a turbulent court in the hotels wherever they stayed. But if at that time, James Brown appeared like a minstrel of the struggling negro race, B.B. King tended rather to exalt integration and the social struggle.

His pupils, as many singers as guitarists, could be counted in hundreds, but nonetheless, Albert and Freddie King (no relation), Bobby Bland, Little Milton, Luther Allison, Mickey Baker, Eric Clapton, Johnny Winter, and above all Jimi Hendrix when he played the blues, must all be mentioned.

James Powell:
'I have seen B.B. King play a good many times, and he must have done what he did a thousand times, yet each time it's a true revelation. I've seen women faint when he ended a solo, when he retained a note or when he threw himself into a drawn out and plaintive falsetto' (*Down Beat*).

In B.B. King's own words:
'There are some people for whom the blues is almost sacred. But there are others who can't bear it. And when I can't manage to make them understand, I get really upset'.

Ebony concerto

The sound of the woodwind

Somewhat neglected today because of its extreme technical difficulty, the soprano clarinet (in B flat) played an essential role in the first decades of jazz. In New Orleans, the first soloists used the Albert model with keys, which was easier to control than the classic Boehm system. The 'ebony dancer' in the hands of the improvisers who were often geniuses (Lorenzo Tio, Jimmie Noone, Johnny Dodds and of course, Sidney Bechet), was the queen of Dixieland jazz, twining her tendrils around the cornet and ensuring an expressive and penetrating response. In Chicago, white musicians like Frank Teschemacher, Jimmy Dorsey and Pee Wee Russell courted her cleverly, while in New York, she contributed definitively to the elaboration of Duke Ellington's *jungle* style, thanks to Barney Bigard, the renegade from New Orleans. She was to be submerged by the flood of saxophones, but kept her noble title thanks to Artie Shaw, Woody Herman, and in particular, the virtuoso Benny Goodman. In the heart of the *Dixieland revival* (Bob Wilder, Claude Luter, Maxime Saury), she flirted with bebop (Buddy DeFranco, Tony Scott). Contemporary jazz allotted her a marginal but original role (Roland Kirk, John Carter, Perry Robinson), but frequently preferred her big sister, the bass clarinet (Anthony Braxton, Michel Portal, Hamiet Bluiett, Howard Johnson).

The only 'wood' among the wind instruments used in jazz (where the oboe and the bassoon are still very rare), the clarinet became first and foremost the occasional 'mistress' of numerous saxophonists, some of whom mastered her absolutely (Lester Young, Phil Woods, Art Pepper, Eddie Daniels, Tony Coe, Louis Sclavis, André Jaume), including at least one, Eric Dolphy, who made the bass clarinet his favourite instrument for his most radical experiments.

The Creole style

This brilliant playing, full of contrast and rich in vibratos and trills, deserves this name all the more since it may have originated in the French Antilles, but it was in New Orleans that it became part of history . . .

Alphonse Picou (1878–1961), the first soloist who escaped anonymity, played from before 1900 with the best groups in Storyville, including Buddy Bolden's. Presumed author of the famous solo in 'High Society', played ever since by all the Dixieland clarinettists, he composed many themes, some of which were adopted by King Oliver.

Lorenzo Tio (1884–1933), the son of a real dynasty of clarinettists, became the teacher of almost all the first 'historic' generation around 1910. The four whose names follow developed his elegant, articulate style, but adding the dimension of their improvisations.

Johnny Dodds (1892–1940) took the same road as Louis Armstrong, playing with Kid Ory, Fate Marable and King Oliver, before becoming his alter ego in the heart of the Hot Five and the Hot Seven. But well before his association with the trumpeter, he had proved himself an ardent improviser with an aggressive vibrato. Known for his temperance and discretion, and nicknamed 'Toilet', he was nonetheless, of all the great New Orleans soloists, the one who best translated the rough language of the blues into an urban framework. In the 1920s, he became an ancestor of the session musician, recording a lot as a sideman, but also with his own groups, including a trio which gave the star part to the clarinet, with Lil Armstrong at the piano. Having switched to the real estate business, he died too soon to profit from the *Dixieland revival* other than through his influence on the likes of Mezz Mezzrow, Buster Bailey, or Claude Luter, or Kenny Davem and Cy Laurie in a later generation.

Jimmie Noone (1895–1944) represents the other side of the Creole style. He was more a product of classical European influence, blessed with a superb technique. He was a pupil and friend of Bechet, and really took off in Chicago, first with Freddy Keppard, then above all by becoming the star of the *Apex Club* with Earl Hines (1926). In the 1940s, the *Dixieland revival* offered him a second career with Kid Ory, with whom he provided the musical animation on Orson Welles's radio broadcasts. His 'woody' sound and very logical phrasing were to have a decisive influence on Benny Goodman's generation.

Albert Nicholas (1900–1973), was the most travelled, of all Noone's pupils, from China to Switzerland — where he died — by way of Egypt and France. His fluency and his immediacy made him a precious element of the best swing bands (Armstrong, Chick Webb, John Kirby).

Omer Simeon (1902–1959), another follower of Tio, Dodds and Noone, emigrated very young to Chicago, and also illustrates the transition from Dixieland to Swing, recording with Oliver and Jelly Roll Morton, then Earl Hines, Fletcher Henderson, Coleman Hawkins and Jimmie Lunceford, with a happy sense of contrasts and collective improvisation.

Barney Bigard (1906–1980) united all the qualities of those who preceded him in a magnificently coherent style which caused him to become one of the 'pillars of Ellington' from 1927 to 1942, then to play with Armstrong's All Stars from 1947. Moreover, he recorded those two historic periods in his memoires, *With Louis and the Duke*. His incomparable swing, the diversity of sounds he obtained in the different registers, the modernity of his contributions to the masterpieces of counterpoint composed for him by the Duke — 'Mood Indigo', 'Solitude', 'Clarinet Lament' — make him one of the most fascinating sidemen in all jazz.

The bird-catchers

There would have been no link between these clarinettists and 'those with the job of catching or caring for birds' if critics had not accused them of producing 'warbles, chirrups, and twitters' (!)

Under the double influence of the great black clarinettists of New Orleans, Johnny Dodds and Jimmie Noone, whom he went to hear in the South Side districts of Chicago, **Frank Teschemacher** (1906–1932) (who was of German descent) became the most famous clarinettist of the Chicago style. Although his playing was technically limited, his graceful and fluctuating tone created a style in which chaos reigned with lyricism, within phrases sometimes chopped up, sometimes cut off, with a sense of rhythm similar to that of the trumpeters of the epoch. He influenced Benny Goodman at the start of his career.

For the general public, the name of **Artie Shaw** (1910–1989) was linked to 'Begin the Beguine', which was a triumph in the year 1939. Directing the most modern band of the Swing Era, he was able to distinguish himself from other bands by his *cooler* atmosphere, relying on string sections after 1935, and getting together a little group in 1940, the Gramercy Five. Close to Goodman in tone, he was (like Goodman), one of the first to present 'integrated' (black and white) groups to the public, including such soloists as Roy Eldridge, Hot Lips Page and the singer Billie Holiday in their ranks.

Pee Wee Russell (1926–1969), one of the most original jazz figures, proved a musician with an insatiable curiosity, since his career took him from the Chicago style (he played beside Bix Beiderbecke) to avant-garde jazz, recording compositions by Ornette Coleman and performing in Thelonious Monk's quartet. Until 1951 he was one of the most asked-for jazz musicians, and attracted attention by his preference for the low register of the instrument, by the vehemence of his improvisations with contrasting figures, and

especially, by his *dirty* tone and his sustained *growl* effects. In 1953, after a serious illness, he took part in numerous international tours, and towards the end of his life discovered he had some talent for painting.

Buddy DeFranco (1923) was the first (with the Swede Stan Hasselgard) to transpose the bebop vocabulary to the clarinet, thanks to his infallible technique, his exceptional mobility and fluidity, and his ease in the service of his smooth and mellow tone in all registers. He made himself heard in the big swing bands before confronting big soloists (Dizzy Gillespie, Oscar Peterson, Art Tatum), and directed the Glenn Miller Orchestra (1966–1974) before finally performing freelance.

When Barney Bigard left Duke Ellington (June 1942), **Jimmy Hamilton** (1917) had the difficult task of succeeding him. Influenced by Goodman, he possessed qualities of restraint, melodic clarity, and an undeniable concern with modernity, enhanced by a virtuosity which he rarely abused.

Famous for his composition 'Four Brothers' popularized by Woody Herman's band, in which he played with saxophonists Stan Getz, Zoot Simms, Herbie Stewart and Serge Chaloff, **Jimmy Giuffre** (1921) is at the same time a saxophonist, flautist and arranger. He is without a doubt the most 'West Coast' of all musicians, a forerunner, in his multiple experiences, of all the trends of present day jazz. The inventor of minimal orchestral formulas, adept at undulating melodic lines, he distinguished himself by his work on tone, breathing, and the substance of sound. At the same time, he is both on the fringe and a harbinger of all the adventures of post-bebop jazz.

The first jazz group which openly defied segregation: the Benny Goodman Quartet *(in 1937) with from left to right* **Lionel Hampton**, **Goodman**, **Teddy Wilson**, *and* **Gene Krupa**.

Benny Goodman

1909, Chicago — New York, 1986

A link between styles and races

An accomplished instrumentalist, this cheery charmer tamed all the styles, from blues to baroque, big band to quartet.

Beyond his qualities as a clarinettist, as the conductor of an orchestra, and his commercial success — his coronation as the 'King of Swing' at the *Carnegie Hall* in New York in 1938 — it would be fitting first of all to salute him as the man who brought about the abolition of racial discrimination in the heart of bands by integrating coloured musicians in his own (Teddy Wilson, Lionel Hampton, Charlie Christian, Cootie Williams). It would nevertheless be unjust to reduce his contribution to jazz to this alone (which moreover he was able to exploit), for Goodman was able to create a very seductive personal style, nourished by the Chicago school and the contributions of

---

In Benny Goodman's own words:

'During recording sessions, there was no question of beating about the bush or wasting time. If for one reason or another, things weren't going well, we stopped everything and went home . . .'

'In a trio or quartet, you need instrumentalists who are all first class and who know what each one's contribution will be, and what, according to one another's suggestions, could be made of the music while it is being played. I also like bands where one works on a clearly established formula, for example, a good arrangement by someone like Fletcher Henderson, what a joy!'

Sidney Bechet and Barney Bigard. His music is one of fullness: full of charm, full of simple joy and happiness of being alive, magnified by effective and clever orchestration by the best arrangers of the time (Fletcher Henderson, Benny Carter, Mary Lou Williams). A clarinet virtuoso, he based his style on the modulation of short, sometimes precious phrasing, with arabesques and curlicues expressing his bent for ornamentation. A strict perfectionist with himself as with others, Goodman — well managed by the producer John Hammond, who became his brother-in-law — knew how to please a white public greedy for fashionable tunes, as well as the crowds of dancers invading the ballrooms. He diversified his appearances with small groups (from trio to sextet) in the original orchestral style, in which the soloists had the lion's share, and Gene Krupa intervened with crazy exhibitions (drum solos).

The way which led this child of an immigrant Jewish tailor — all of whose sons became professional musicians — from the band of the synagogue where he started to play at eleven, to the symphony orchestras which accompanied him in Mozart, Bartók or Hindemith, was a royal one. When he was seventeen, he entered the group of Ben Pollack, a great talent scout. He was very much in demand on Broadway for radio, recordings and musical comedies, and accompanied two of the greatest blues and jazz singers, Bessie Smith at the end of her career and Billie Holiday at the beginning of hers. In helping to steer jazz out of its ghetto, he became the most famous clarinettist in the world. A film, *The Benny Goodman Story* (1955) was dedicated to him. After the International Exhibition in Brussels in 1958, he played in the Soviet Union in 1962, with the first American jazz group allowed to play in that country.

The premature death of **Theodore 'Fats' Navarro** *has unfortunately made people forget that, like* **Dizzy Gillespie** *and* **Miles Davis**, *he was a great pioneer of the modern trumpet.*

The jazz pavilion

The sounding brass

Legend has it that the two first great jazz soloists were Bunk Johnson (1879–1949), who only recorded at the end of his life, and Charles 'Buddy' Bolden (1877–1931), who never made a disc, but (accounts tell us) was famous in New Orleans from 1895. His nickname, The King, which was to be inherited by his heir, Joe Oliver, described the role of his instrument rather well. The cornet with valves was in fact the king of parades and picnics, because of its very direct attack, due to its conical bore. Nonetheless, in 1926, after hesitating for a long time, Armstrong gave back the cornet to the shop selling jazz accessories and opted for the trumpet, whose register and tonality (B flat) are the same, but whose brilliant tone compensates the slightest facility. A thousand leagues from New Orleans, and already far from the blaring style of a Freddie Keppard or the sober and velvety style of 'Papa' Celestin, the jazz trumpet hoisted the flags of the Prohibition-era Chicago and the New York of the 'Harlem Renaissance' to new heights. The royal route goes from Oliver and Armstrong to Tommy Ladnier, Jabbo Smith, Joe Smith and above all Henry 'Red' Allen. On the white side (musical segregation was total at the time), Bix Biederbecke and his pupil Bunny Berigan took a shady path in a harmonious countryside, landscaped by listening to Debussy.

The impetus of the great bands led trumpeters to specialise. Each had to play a well defined role according to his register, his ability in the use of mutes, or his ease in the high pitches. Duke Ellington's band was also to be a real workshop for the polishing and chiselling of brass, revealing stylists as different as Bubber Miley, Cootie Williams, Rex Stewart, Cat Anderson or Clark Terry. From Roy Eldridge to Fats Navarro and Dizzy Gillespie, it was the synchronized speed of brain and fingers which opened the era of the virtuoso. From Clifford Brown to Wynton Marsalis, not to mention Lee Morgan and Freddie Hubbard, the valves opened up capricious paths, visited by all the other instruments. At the same time, the almost vocal emotion which really belongs to the trumpet was magnified by the most economical soloists like Miles Davis and Chet Baker, and the richness of its tone attracted new explorers to the jungle of sounds, such as Lester Bowie or Don Cherry. However, along the path of its research, the trumpet never ceases to bring us back to the origins of jazz, perhaps because of its incomparable ability to modulate the *blue notes* and to compete with, without however imitating the matrix of all music, the human voice.

King Oliver

1885, New Orleans — Savannah, 1938

The spiritual father of 'hot' jazz

Prematurely overtaken by his disciple Armstrong, he was the real inventor of structured improvisation.

With the three choruses by Joe Oliver — nicknamed The King because he was the greatest New Orleans cornetist of his generation — in 'Dippermouth Blues', recorded in Chicago with his Creole Jazz Band on 6 April 1923, jazz was to be freed of the strictly polyphonic concept of the New Orleans style (which he had himself created) by structuring collective improvisation. It is therefore no exaggeration to consider him one of the fathers of jazz, since he was the first to conceive of a truly orchestral form for a very wide range of different elements (fanfares, marches, polkas, traditional melodies, blues), which left a little space for improvisation, and then to emancipate this formula into what became the Chicago Style, retaining the constant essential element of jazz — Swing, in its earliest form.

Jacques Réda:
'Like a flickering point of light in the wind and dust, revealing distant outlines standing obstinately bidding farewell, that is how — after half a century of fuss and noise — the grooves still yield the tender and poignant call of the Creole Jazz Band' (*Jazz Magazine*, April 1980).

His cornet playing was sober and unadorned, but robust and powerful, relying heavily on the tempo, innovative through its use of 'blue notes' and the newly invented mute. King Oliver was also a composer whose themes like 'West End Blues', 'Canal Street Blues', 'Doctor Jazz', were to become massive landmarks in the history of jazz.

Between 1908 and 1917 he played in New Orleans parades and brass bands, and became a friend of Kid Ory. In 1922, his 'Hot' Creole Jazz Band (in which Louis Armstrong played as second trumpet) attracted (and influenced) young white musicians from Chicago, including Bix Beiderbecke. It was in Richmond, Indiana that he recorded, between March and December 1923, about twenty historic masterpieces, featuring the first recorded improvisations by the young Armstrong, playing with the Dodds brothers and Lil Hardin on the piano. In 1924, after the departure of Armstrong, whom he considered his spiritual heir, the King turned his back on the style that had made his name, and changed formula, putting together a ten-man band, the Savannah Syncopators, playing compositions in the style of Fletcher Henderson, and trying his luck in New York. He got there too late. His own disciples, especially Louis Armstrong, were already getting all the success. He made a few records, but was soon forgotten. In an attempt to survive, he made a few disappointing tours, and gave up his musical career in 1937, by which time his health was failing. Having settled in Savannah, he died there completely destitute.

Grandeur and decadence both featured in the life of this first great 'King' in the history of jazz.

Louis Armstrong

1901, New Orleans — New York, 1971

A genius through and through

By raising improvisation to the highest form of musical art, he turned jazz into the music of the century.

Armstrong's achievement was not only to codify improvisation in the form it was to retain through all the styles and generations of jazz. The unanimous acclaim he received in the 1920s actually became the cement that enabled the skyscraper of jazz to be built on those foundations. As luck would have it, he was sixteen when the adventure of recorded music began. His first recordings in 1925–1928 with the Hot Five and Hot Seven remain the basis of any record collection. Thereafter, jazz became music for the soloist, relegating to the past the blurry interpretations which, even with King Oliver and Jelly Roll Morton, still had charm, but also the limitations of New Orleans polyphony.

'Satchmo' (satchel-mouth) established what might be called the golden rule of jazz — 'blowing is not playing!' His genius consists in giving each note an attack, a duration, a height, an intensity, a tone and a colour, making it a snap of emotion, while showing perfect mastery of the logic of his 'phrases'.

The emotional force of his playing is due largely to his virtuosity, which is unsurpassed. But it also comes from his ability to 'live' a music which has never had to face the eternal problem of adapting individuality to culture.

Miles Davis:
'As soon as you blow into an instrument, you know that you'll never get anything out of it that Louis hasn't already done.'

Louis Armstrong's life is the ideal personal assertion of the Afro-American identity, espousing all the changes it has been through, coming up from the South to the northern cities, the difficult struggle for recognition, adaptation to modernism and 'business', involvement in the growing 'black' movement. His biography could have been one of those 'black novels' in the form of a saga through which America seeks to discover its roots that have never been quite buried.

Often described as the eternal child, Louis never had a childhood. His early years in the poorest parts of Storyville are those of a 'street urchin' left to his own resources from the age of five, put up rather than brought up alternately by his grand-mother (born to slavery), and by his mother, Mayann, (a part-time prostitute), to whom he nevertheless remained deeply attached all his life. Jewish neighbours, the Karmofskys, befriended him, and employed him with their own children as a 'rag and bone' man. But above all they lent him a little cornet with valves, which was his first instrument. They also gave him a taste for singing, so Louis entered a vocal quartet which performed in the *tent shows* of the neighbourhood, and attracted Sidney Bechet's attention. On New Year's Day 1913, he was arrested for firing a shot into the air. So he acquired an elementary musical training in the reformatory, and learned the orthodox way to play the cornet. When he was released the following year, he made his debut in the Storyville clubs, and profited from Oliver's advice. In 1918 he entered Kid Ory's group and played on the *river boats* and in a cinema with Fate Marable, before joining Oliver in Chicago (1922), then, two years later, Fletcher Henderson in New York. He also accompanied blues singers, including Ma Rainey and Bessie Smith, and recorded with Clarence Williams. On returning to

Chicago, he played in the band of his second wife, the pianist Lilian Hardin (who came after the prostitute Daisy Parker), and formed his Hot Five with her, Johnny Dodds on clarinet, Kid Ory on trombone, and Johnny StCyr on guitar, followed by the Hot Seven, which added John Thomas on trombone, Peter Briggs on tuba, and Baby Dodds on drums. Finally, he discovered his ideal partner in Earl Hines.

But his decisive meeting was with the impresario Joe Glaser, a 'toughie' with whom he made an everlasting friendship, although they seemed total opposites in character as well as 'race'. With no written contract, Glaser took charge of the career of Louis, who was shortly to become the most famous musician in the world. At first he was invited to play by the best known club bands, then he led his own big band in the 1930s, toured Europe triumphantly (in 1932 and 1934), and made dozens of film

---

The four faces of Armstrong's genius

The musicologist Gunther Schuller: — the supreme choice of his notes and the resulting form of his melodic line; — the unique quality of his basic tone; — his incomparable sense of swing: in other words the dexterity with which his notes are integrated in the continuum of the tempo, and the remarkably varied nature of the attack and delivery in his phrasing; — finally and above all, the subtle repertoire of vibratos and inflections with which he colours and embellishes each of his notes.

---

clips and sequences. This first period ended in apotheosis on the stage of the Metropolitan Opera House in 1944. In 1947, Armstrong created his All Stars, a sextet which brilliantly blended the spontaneity of New Orleans jazz and the typical *riffs* of the big bands. In spite of the lip problems which had plagued him since the 1930s, he refused to be relegated to being only the most famous voice of pop singing, even if this role dominated his recordings from 1950. Very few musicians have experienced such daily involvement in their art. A Rabelaisian character, Louis Armstrong compensated for his greed by a canny diet of herbs, in which marijuana always had the place of honour. But this inveterate smoker imposed his own motto on his musicians — 'Never before the job!' What is more, his almost austere professionalism contrasted strangely with his irresistible love of life, which he communicated to the whole world. His humour, which was sometimes misinterpreted as heedlessness (his temper, however, was proverbial!) affected jazz as much as his music, since he invented or imposed most of the *jive vocabulary*, the jazz player's slang.

The constant accusations of 'Uncle Tomism' applied to an artist who had been persecuted by the F.B.I. for his frequent and severe public declarations against segregation, also seem unfair. But the fact is that, by means of his triumphant tours, 'Pops', together with Lucille (a Cotton Club dancer who in 1942 became his fourth and last wife), was the most convincing ambassador of the United States, at a time when American prestige was very low.

From the cornet to the trumpet

From the 1920s, the development of broadcasting and recording had an impetus on all instrumental techniques. As soon as a new first-rate soloist appeared, he was heard everywhere, and his innovations were dissected, imitated and, above all integrated and synthesized by his brother musicians. The cornet, and even more so the trumpet, evolved spectacularly during the between-the-wars period.

Muggsy Spanier (1906–1967) was an avowed disciple of Oliver and Armstrong. A star of the Chicago radio bands, a great specialist in the use of mutes, he was to be one of the initiators of the *New Orleans revival.*

Bunny Berigan (1908–1942), with Muggsy and Bix (like the latter, he often confused the mouthpiece with the bottle), was the great white trumpeter of his generation and by far the most popular in New York. He was a soloist in the most celebrated big bands of Whiteman, Dorsey, and Goodman, where he shone through his perfect mastery of the low register and his interpretation of ballads.

For a long time, **Henry 'Red' Allen** (1908–1967) followed Armstrong's itinerary step by step, from his native New Orleans to Chicago and New York, from King Oliver to Fletcher Henderson, to finally enter Satchmo's band (1937). However, his immense virtuosity, the diversity of his style, his rhythmic and harmonic modernism made him a fully-fledged master in his own right.

Jabbo Smith (1908) is also one of the great virtuosos of this generation. A high flying improviser, he was underestimated for a long time because of his too frequent imitations of Armstrong, and a badly directed career, which nonetheless enabled him to record with the greatest jazz players of his time.

Tommy Ladnier (1900–1939), the regular partner of his friend Bechet, was a great blues player in particular, whose style, unadorned almost to the point of asceticism, ripened in the shadow of singers like Lovie Austen, Ida Cox and Ma Rainey.

Joe Smith (1902–1937) also provided the backing for *blues girls* (Mamie Smith, Ethel Waters), before becoming one of the favourite soloists of the first big bands, forming an admirable duo with Ladnier in Fletcher Henderson's. His delicate and sensual style makes him closer to Bix and Satchmo.

James 'Bubber' Miley (1903–1932) first accompanied the blues singer Bessie Smith, before becoming an attraction in the New York clubs. A happy parenthesis in a brief and chaotic career, his collaboration with Duke Ellington (1923–1929), with whom he co-signed his first masterpieces, was a great moment in the history of jazz. An unequalled master of the *plunger mute*, he invented the wah-wah style, raucous and plaintive, which was to be an essential element of orchestral sound.

Charles 'Cootie' Williams (1910–1985) succeeded Miley with the Duke, and played with him until 1940, and again from 1962. Between times, he directed a remarkable big band where Bud Powell made his debut. His bluesy performance with unexpected accentuations, with or without a mute, make him one of the most moving soloists of his generation. A singer and a composer, he was the co-author with Monk of the famous 'Round About Midnight'.

Rex Stewart (1907–1967) soon escaped the double influence of Armstrong and Bix, to become, in turn, one of the great Ellingtonian soloists. An inspired melody man, who stayed faithful to the cornet, he developed a style that was both expressionistic and elegant, using various mutes and reducing pressure on the valves.

Bill Coleman (1904–1981) came to France in the 1930s. He settled there definitively at the end of the 1940s, after a brilliant New York career, with Fats Waller in particular. His elegant playing, both supple and imperious, is very marked by his love for gospel and the blues.

Bix Beiderbecke

1903, Davenport — Newport, 1931

The archetypal romantic jazzman

Fragile and refined in the chaos of Prohibition era Chicago, he provided a fleeting alternative to Armstrong's genius.

He became a legend both as the first great white musician of jazz and as the first doomed artist of jazz. His life — in many points identical to F. Scott Fitzgerald's creators of the jazz age — was fast and furious, devoured by music and destroyed by alcohol. It inspired the novelist Dorothy Baker in her novel *The Young Man with the Trumpet*. Tormented and dissatisfied ('I think it's because he was a perfectionist that he drank so much' says the trumpeter Jimmy MacPartland who is one of his disciples) he brought a romantic flavour to jazz, with an indefinable melancholic air, a touch of impressionism, and a refinement which made him the first cool soloist in the history of jazz, a forerunner of Miles Davis. A very personal use of the vibrato, a tone

Says Irving Riskin:
'There were probably dozens of cornet players who were technically better than Bix, but there's never been one to compare with him for musical instinct.'

rich in harmonics, and a soft and warm sonority were the characteristics of this passionate musician's work.

He was self-taught, and invented his own fingering technique for the cornet. He could play any piece by ear on the piano, and in the only solo he ever recorded on that instrument, 'In a Mist', he revealed his knowledge of European composers like Ravel, Debussy and Stravinsky.

Beiderbecke discovered jazz at fifteen by hearing the bands playing on the river boats. He played there himself in 1923, before going to Chicago to join the Wolverines, the first white band to play with some swing, of which he later became the star.

In 1925 he played in Charlie Straight's band, learning the arrangements by heart because he could not read music. In that same year he met the saxophonist Frankie Trumbauer again, and the two of them joined the Jean Goldkette group.

The following year they recorded under the name of Bix Beiderbecke's Gang, before joining Paul Whiteman, who was wrongly known as 'The King of Jazz'(!) and 'Apostle of Symphonic Jazz'(!). In the despair of not achieving his great ambitions, Bix drank more and more and had to undergo a spell of treatment which left him a broken man; Whiteman did not renew his contract. He continued to play sporadically, but his frail constitution could not withstand the pneumonia which killed him at dawn on 7 August 1931. He was only 28.

Roy Eldridge

1911, Pittsburg — New York, 1989

A petulant and remorseless blower

A typical swing trumpeter, Roy expresses the transition from Armstrong's classicism to Dizzy Gillespie's bebop.

It would be wrong to see Roy Eldridge only as a sort of link between two very different styles, because he had the intrinsic qualities of a musician, with a crazy kind of energy which left its own mark, as witnessed by the influence he had on his companions Charlie Shavers, Harry Edison and Joe Newman. As one of the last generation of the Swing era, he was also, like Charlie Christian, a harbinger of bebop, shattering the universe of classical rules and broadening the concepts of his early masters, Rex Stewart, Red Nichols and Louis Armstrong. He hammered out a language of his own which was particularly physical in its character, a kind of generous effervescence.

In Eldridge's own words:
'I arrived at a hall where we were supposed to be giving a ball and the guy at the door won't let me in saying: 'it's a white ball in here', when my name Roy 'Little Jazz' Eldridge is on the billboard at the door. I got someone to identify me and he lets me in. I had tears in my eyes when I started in on the first number and by the end tears were rolling down my cheeks. I went to the changing room and stayed there crying for half an hour, wondering what I was doing in this place anyway.'

Says Dizzy Gillespie:
'During my years of training the only style I liked was swing, that was all I played. Roy Eldridge was my idol.'

With his taste for brio and speed, he never resisted the temptation of engaging in dangerous fireworks of carefully worked out dialogue, jousting greedily with tremendous swing and insolence, juggling with the notes, sometimes cracking them like a whip — he managed to conceal occasional imprecisions in skilful and witty pirouettes — and defying all the rules of conventional technique.

He started as a drummer, and showed special interest in the saxophone, going as far as to reproduce on the trumpet Coleman Hawkins's solo in 'Stampede', as recorded by Fletcher Henderson. He played in different bands, including Elmer Snowden's alongside Otto Hardwicke, who gave him the nickname 'Little Jazz'. He formed his own bands several times (1933–1937). While playing in the white bands of Gene Krupa (1941), with whom he recorded one of their greatest hits, 'Rockin' Chair', and Artie Shaw (1944–1945), he was exhibited as a kind of special attraction, and sadly experienced racial discrimination. He received some consolation, however, through his victory in the 'Down Beat' referendum over his white rivals. He made a series of recordings including one with his own Little Jazz and his Trumpet Ensemble, where he shows dazzling punch in his extremely physical style. He stayed in Paris after a tour with Benny Goodman, then joined Norman Granz's JATP, and crossed swords with the boppers, whom he had already met in the historic sessions at Minton's. Between 1963 and 1965 he accompanied Ella Fitzgerald, before going freelance until he suffered a heart attack in 1980 which forced him into semi-retirement.

He was also a composer and singer and he never failed, at least in his French concerts, to include 'Une petite laitue', a burlesque vocal which became one of his standard pieces.

Dizzy Gillespie

1917, Cheraw

A delicately mastered delirium

Pyrotechnician of bands and vocals as well as the trumpet, he spiced up jazz with all his verve and devilry.

One might think that two persons inhabit the same man. The trumpeter, the great technician and virtuoso, whose wonderful tone reaches even the highest of high notes, the true revolutionary who became, with Charlie Parker, one of the creators of the bebop style, a serious and demanding innovator. And then there is Dizzy, the crazy showman, the hilarious singer, the remarkable eccentric entertainer. But there is no division. Gillespie *is* all that at the same time, and has been ever since the beginning of his long career.

As an instrumentalist he has, in the words of André Hodier, 'elevated the art of the trumpet solo to a level that was unknown until his appearance on the jazz scene'. He led the first bebop big band in

1946, and introduced Afro-Cuban rhythms into jazz by bringing in percussionists like the Cuban Chano Pozo on the congas. As a composer, he brought some singular compositions to jazz, which are now considered classics ('Night in Tunisia', 'Groovin' High', 'Dizzy Atmosphere', 'Anthropology'). As an arranger, together with Tadd Dameron and Gil Fuller he gave new punch and complexity to harmony and rhythm. As a singer and an entertainer, he took scat singing to the absurdly comic limit of verbal delirium in his duos with the singers Kenny Hagood and Joe Carroll. He was also one of the first to refuse to play the role of 'Uncle Tom' generally attributed to coloured musicians, while at the same time the spectacular side of his performances and his behaviour contributed greatly to the new music his 1948 concert in France had brought to Europe. That famous concert in the Salle Pleyel on 28 February was like a shock wave that will be remembered as one of the most important events of the immediate post-war period.

John Birks Gillespie had acquired early experience in big bands, and it was with Earl Hines in 1942 that he met Charlie Parker, with whom he was subsequently to perform in the clubs of 52nd Street, and record some masterpieces. Dizzy's own band broke up in 1950, and he played with small groups or with the JATP until he was asked by the Department of State to go on tour in the Middle East and Latin America in 1956 as an ambassador of jazz. He was a presidential 'candidate' in the 1963 and 1972 campaigns in the United States, and he is still blowing his turned-up trumpet all over the world with the same punch and enthusiasm.

In Dizzy Gillespie's own words:

'Strange as it may seem, I have never considered myself as a true interpreter of the blues. Charlie Parker was a master of the blues. I know that the blues represent our musical culture, the culture of my race, but I'm not a real blues-man. And I can't stand white musicians who say 'I'm a bluesman', because if I, who grew up and lived in the middle of it, can't say I am one, then . . .'

(extracts from *To Be or Not to Bop*).

Miles Davis

1926, Alton

The legend of the half-century

For the last forty years he has incarnated all the metamorphoses instrumental blues have been through in the tumult of the urban jungle.

Having become a kind of 'sacred monster' over the years, Miles Davis has shown himself to be the most adaptable of all the great creators of Afro-American music. His extraordinary ability in capturing, accompanying and even anticipating aesthetic developments, and his disdain for all forms of nostalgia, are in surprising contrast to his deep attachment to the roots of this music. 'I play like a preacher', he likes to say. He is a loner with a sort of sixth sense for collective needs. Over three or four generations, he managed to impose both his ideas as a soloist and his orchestral concepts. As a trumpeter he deliberately stood aside from the battle of titans his peers were involved in — Dizzy Gillespie, Fats Navarro, Clifford Brown — developing a restrained, pointilliste, confidential style, full of fragile serenity. His unbrassy tone, without vibrato, full of lunar beauty, is the most copied but the least imitable sound. As a leader, his charisma has no equal in the history of jazz, apart from

Key figure of a night time mythology, no longer confined to jazz, referred to by the press with such clichés as: 'the sphinx', 'the phoenix', 'the prince of darkness' — overcoming all his real or imaginary diseases, Miles pursues his obsession for eternal youth, driving his band ahead like a Ferrari, and always wearing dark glasses . . .

Duke Ellington or his friend Gil Evans. To have played in his group, if only for a few sessions, has been for hundreds of musicians like joining a sort of Pantheon.

Miles Dewey Davis III, like Ellington, is a pure product of the black bourgeoisie in search of recognition. The son of a famous dentist, he grew up in a residential part of East Saint Louis with a strong white majority, and he discovered racism in the schoolroom. His mother and sister were classical musicians, but jazz was highly thought of in the family, and it soon became, together with horse-riding, his main interest. At thirteen, 'little Miles' became the pupil of the trumpeter Elwood Buchanan, who had been one of Andy Kirk's Clouds of Joy. A neighbour of his, Clark Terry, then introduced him to jam-sessions and to boxing, a skill which he was going to need frequently later on in his career!

While he was at the Juilliard School, he became a regular in New York's 52nd Street clubs, where he found and followed his new 'guru', Charlie Parker, whom he had met together with Dizzy Gillespie when they had been in Saint Louis with Billy Eckstine's big band. Miles even lived with Bird for a while, and made his recording debut with him, on three tracks which have remained masterpieces of modern jazz, 'Now's the Time', 'Billie's Bounce' and 'Ko Ko'. Using poor equipment (a Heim mouthpiece and a Harmon mute), Miles struggled to heave himself by his finger-tips to the level of Charlie Parker, with whom he continued to play until 1948. A year before, he had seen his favourite trumpeter, Freddy Webster, die at thirty. That was when he put together an original nine-man instrumental ensemble (horn, tuba, trumpet, trombone, guitar, bass, piano, bugle, drums) and recorded twelve tunes for Capitol, later issued under the title *The Birth of the Cool*, which represent a real turning point in the early history of modern jazz. The names associated with these momentous orchestrations are Gerry Mulligan, John Carisi, John Lewis and Gil Evans, who stayed closest musically to Miles Davis until his death. Between 1950 and 1960, he composed in several albums (which include *Miles Ahead*, *Sketches of Spain* and *Porgy and Bess*) the perfect framework for clipped trumpet solos.

In 1949, at Charles Delaunay's invitation, he went to Paris, where he immediately became a star of Saint-Germain-des-Pres: cosseted by Juliette Greco, guided through the cellars by Boris Vian and in the open air by Jean-Paul Sartre, he discovered the pleasures of the star-system. He returned in 1956–1957 to play with the best Parisian jazzmen of that time (Barney Wilen, René Urtreger, Pierre Michelot and Kenny Clarke), and to record with them the music for Louis Malle's film *Ascenseur pour l'échafaud*.

In New York he alternated between quintets and sextets, playing with all the great boppers, before forming his first regular group with John Coltrane, Red Garland (replaced by Bill Evans and then Wynton Kelly), Paul Chambers and Philly Joe Jones (then Jimmy Cobb), and occasionally Cannonball Adderley. This was the state of grace, the 'golden age' of the classic Miles which produced *Kind of Blue* in 1959. Then came the 'modern' period with the 'virtuoso quintet' (George Coleman, then Wayne Shorter, Herbie Hancock, Ron Carter, Tony Williams) from 1963 to 1970, introducing the modal concept, with dazzling tempo variations and dissonances. The scene was already a 'mine field' when the 'electric fairy' appeared, considered by many to have damned the soul of the sorcerer Miles Davis.

He threw himself bodily into her arms. John McLaughlin's Hendrixian guitar, the aggressive bass of Dave Holland and later Michael Henderson, and the strident keyboards of Chick Corea, Joe Zawinul and Keith Jarrett, created around him an angular and throbbing environment echoing the crisis-ridden megalopolis that he hates, but that he cannot do without. The implacable drums of Billy Cobham, Jack DeJohnette or Al Foster, and African, Indian, or Brazilian drums completed this savage profusion of sounds and rhythms, a tribal music, joyfully despairing in the urban jungle, regally dominated by the 'wah-wah' trumpet, sometimes even approaching Stockhausen! After retiring for health reasons from 1975 to 1980, Miles made a spectacular return to the stage with a repertoire almost entirely composed of hit songs, surrounded by the latest in synthesizers and the best young soloists in the business, Mike Stern and John Scofield on guitars, Bill Evans, Branford Marsalis, Bob Berg, and Kenny Garrett on saxes, Marcus Miller and Darryl Jones on bass; and the ever 'exotic' percussionists, Sammy Figuerola, Mino Cinelu, Marilyn Mazur.

In Miles Davis's own words:

'I can never go backwards, nor listen to my old records. I would feel as though I had lost a child' (Interview with Gerald Arnaud and Jerome Reese, April 1989).

Gil Evans

'Miles is a great jazz creator because he has absolute confidence in his own taste, and he goes his own way. So many musicians are constantly spying on what the next guy is doing and wondering if they are hitting the right note ...' (quoted by Nat Hentoff).

From bebop to hard bop

The huge prestige which surrounds Dizzy Gillespie and Miles Davis is thoroughly justified due to their conceptual creativity and their historic role in the history of jazz. If judged purely from the point of view of instrumental skill (which cannot obviously be separated from their musical genius), the gap narrows which divides these two giants from a dozen of those who formed the most wonderful generation of trumpeters since the 1920s.

Howard McGhee (1918–1987) was influenced all his life by his 'childhood games', playing the clarinet and passionately listening to records by Armstrong and Eldridge. He was a soloist and arranger for big bands (Kirk, Hampton, Barnet), and was on 52nd Street at the right moment, which enabled him to learn the rules of bebop, and then, when living in California, to have Charlie Parker to stay and record his infamous 'Lover Man' with him. His career was hampered by the same 'personal problems', and he made periodic appearances with big bands (Ellington, Machito). In the 1940s, though, his complex phrasing and his ease in the high register had a deep influence.

Theodore 'Fats' Navarro (1923–1950) started by understudying McGhee in Andy Kirk's big band, and soon revealed himself to be as skilful as Dizzy Gillespie, who left him his place with Billy Eckstine. After playing with Illinois Jacquet, Hampton and Hawkins, he joined the pianist and arranger Tadd Dameron. They became one of the most creative teams on the New York scene, and Charlie Parker finally hired Fats just a few weeks before he died of tuberculosis. Of African, Chinese and Caribbean background, this child of warm Florida, nicknamed 'fat girl' because of his effeminate voice and manner, thus had only five years in which to insert himself into the Pantheon of jazz, in which he would probably have become as important a figure as Miles or Dizzy. His knowledge of harmony, his precise and biting tone, and the melodic beauty and perfection of his sometimes breathtaking phrasing, all reveal a slightly melancholic introverted personality which remained as a romantic model for many trumpeters who still mourn him.

Clifford Brown (1930–1956) was his main disciple, even if his round and brassy tone is almost the reverse of Fats's, whom he replaced briefly with Dameron. After a European tour with Hampton, he was recruited by Art Blakey on Charlie Parker's recommendation. A year later (1954), Max Roach lured him away to form a quintet, where the young trumpeter literally exploded, juggling with Sonny Rollins in an absolute state of grace. Sadly, a car crash killed this fugitive genius who had managed to stay clear of drugs. The solos he recorded constitute a complete work in the true sense of the word, a brilliant and accomplished synthesis of all the bop innovations by as pure and competent a performer as Armstrong or Beiderbecke. His influence was as great as that of Miles, Dizzy or Fats on all the great trumpeters of subsequent generations.

Art Farmer (1928), who knew him with Hampton, dedicated one of his best works to him, 'I Remember Clifford', written with Benny Golson. He is one of the few survivors of this generation, from which he stands out because of his velvety tone which he got from Bix and Harry James, but especially from Lester Young, whose 'on the job' training taught him 'how to tell a story'. 'You have to know how to let a note stay alive' he once said. And that is what he has always done, particularly in his many records and tours with the Jazztet he co-directed with Golson. This very subtle and sober aesthetic approach likens him to Miles Davis, and even more to Chet Baker, whom he frequently replaced in 1958 with Gerry Mulligan. Based in Vienna since 1968, he has given up the trumpet for the flugelhorn, and plays mainly in Europe.

Kenny Dorham (1924–1972), who

recorded 'The Bebop Boys' with Navarro, is another typical figure of this generation. A Texan, who often wore cowboy clothes, he was steeped in the southern blues tradition, which he transformed with a keen sense of modern harmony. Living in New York, he played with Dizzy's and Billy Eckstine's bands. In 1948 he replaced Miles in the Parker quintet. After a spell with the Jazz Messengers in 1955, he started the Jazz Prophets along the same lines, before replacing Clifford Brown in Max Roach's band. In his very active last years, which often took him to Paris, he recorded with Rollins, Coltrane, and Cecil Taylor, showing his preference for ballads and the bossa-nova, of which he is the best interpreter on the trumpet.

Lee Morgan (1938–1972), murdered by an irate 'ex', left an impressive collection of recordings. He was mostly a studio musician who recorded one of the few rave hits of jazz, 'The Sidewinder' (1965). He deservedly became the emblematic figure of the Blue Note label, being as deeply influenced by the blues as by bebop. His playing was full of subtly nuanced inflections and variations, and had the sincerity which is the stamp of true jazz. His Philadelphia childhood gave him the opportunity to 'jam' with Clifford Brown, Fats Navarro and his fellow citizen John Coltrane. By the age of eighteen he was recording with Horace Silver, then he played with Dizzy's big band and the Jazz Messengers. He was very much a prodigy, and took a while to purify his rather ebullient style, but he often showed himself worthy of the unfailing comparison with Clifford Brown. He had an explosive technique, and knew how to use references and quotes without falling into cliché. The son of a gospel pianist, together with Jimmy Smith and Horace Silver he animated a powerful movement for the revival of spiritual roots in the hard bop years of the 1960s.

Booker Little (1938–1961) had only

three years in which to explore the hard bop register, during which time he became Max Roach's ideal partner, then worked with Coltrane, and with Eric Dolphy. His playing was full of dissonances and all sorts of surprises, which made him the ideal link between hard bop and free jazz, which was just beginning at his death.

Freddie Hubbard (born in 1938) was in exactly the same state of mind as Little around 1960, and he was the one who got the opportunity to record, with Dolphy and Ornette Coleman, the famous record that was to become the signature tune of free jazz, *Out to Lunch*. Since then, this technically fantastic trumpeter (perhaps the most spectacular in the whole history of jazz) has continuously hesitated between the avant-garde and creative classicism, which has made him into a sort of contemporary Louis Armstrong, whom he actually resembles physically. His versatility and his multifaceted talents have enabled him to 'mutate' each time he has changed producer or record label. He took over from Lee Morgan at Blue Note, flirted with 'disco' at CTI, and tried to occupy Miles Davis's territory at CBS. Such a patchy catalogue casts a shadow over this relatively young talent, who explodes in the all-star concerts where he is generally the driving force. Like his classical counterpart Maurice André, he is a sort of school model for contemporary trumpeters.

Whether their bop was be-, hard- or post-, we must also mention **Red Rodney**, who played with Charlie Parker in 1949–50; **Blue Mitchell** and **Carmell Jones**, who partnered Horace Silver; The Jazz Messengers; **Bill Hardman** and **Valeri Ponomarev**, **Woody Shaw** and **Terence Blanchard**; **Hannibal Marvin Peterson**, star soloist with Gil Evans; **Randy Brecker**, Michael's brother, and the delicate **Tom Harrell**, who was Bill Evans's, and especially Phil Woods's, sideman.

Chet Baker

1929, Yale, Oklahoma — Amsterdam, Netherlands, 1988

Cry and whisper

Translating into concentrated emotion a tragic destiny, he sang and played with moving reserve about his own drama.

He was a stylist of the very top class who refused to use any of the flashy gimmicks of his contemporaries. Chet Baker is without any doubt the most lyrical trumpeter in the whole history of jazz. He was one of the most moving musicians due to his delicate legatos of an extremely refined quality, in the direct tradition of Bix Beiderbecke. His life and his career were full of stormy and shady periods; drug use and time in prison left their mark on the man, who looked like James Dean, and who, by the end of his turbulent life, had acquired a ghostly silhouette, a battered face and an infinitely sad look in his eyes.

Chet Baker in his own words:
'I think the musicians of today are a hundred years ahead of the people who listen to their music. I hope the gap is not getting any wider. It's a question of ear, and the ability to understand what music is. It seems to me that people don't want to take the time to learn, they want to have their heads bashed by rock drummers and are not so interested in thinking about music. That's probably why jazz will soon be a lost art' (*Jazz Magazine*, December 1986).

He achieved glory with Gerry Mulligan's pianoless quartet with his solo in 'My Funny Valentine' which was recorded on 2 September 1952. That was when the Baker 'sound' was noticed, well described by Gilles Gautherin in *Jazz-Hot* in May 1976: 'either an almost ethereal linear development, interrupted, now and then, by a few more assertive bars, or, on the contrary, a kind of murmur, a breath which gets strangled at the same time as it is blown.' With his own quartet, he was able to develop the other side of his talent, as a singer. His sweet, ethereal, transparent voice transformed the ballads, almost whispered with great control, into heart rending confessions. In 1955, he was to record in Paris a series of absolute masterpieces with the pianist Dick Twardzik and a number of French musicians, among them Jean-Louis Chautemps, René Urtreger, and Jean-Louis Viale.

There followed a long period of travels between California and Europe. He stayed in Europe from 1959 to 1964, and on returning to the United States, he was mugged in 1968, and left with a broken jaw and many teeth missing. He fell into oblivion, and was even reported dead, but with the support of Dizzy Gillespie, he picked up the trumpet again and made a come-back.

Until his tragic death, he played with many different musicians, usually in small groups (trios or quartets with Philip Catherine, Doug Raney, Michel Graillier, Niels Henning, Ørsted Pedersen), with a gravity and a serenity that never quite concealed his despair, but had great emotional impact.

Don Cherry

1936, Oklahoma City

The traveller of the avant-garde

Pioneer of 'world music', fascinated by the infinity of planetary sound, he hunted everywhere for purity amidst the tumult.

At the end of the 1950s, the meeting of this young coloured trumpeter of mixed Black and Indian blood (his mother was of Choctaw Indian descent) and the saxophonist Ornette Coleman was decisive for what was soon to become known as Free Jazz, of which the records *Something Else* and *Tomorrow is the Question* were the harbingers. A number of other fruitful associations were to follow, with John Coltrane for the recording of *The Avant-Garde* (1960), the same year in which Coleman's double quartet album *Free Jazz* was recorded; with Sonny Rollins on *Our Man in Jazz* (1962); with Archie Shepp in the New York Contemporary Five (1963); Albert Ayler (1964); Gato Barbieri, and the warm Parisian nights at the Chat-qui-Pêche (1965); Giorgio Gaslini, for the serial writing and free improvisation

In Don Cherry's own words:
'I feel caught in a sort of acoustic expedition with no limits or boundaries. (. . .) I am completely in favour of dancing, a kind of jazz ballet where the creative act is between dancers and musicians. Even bebop was a kind of dance music, and when Monk played, he would get up and dance himself. I feel that a great deal of the present frustrations are due to the fact that people don't dance and laugh enough any more. Jazz has become too intellectual.' (interview with Gerald Arnaud and Xina Vasconcelos, 1982).

(also 1965); the Jazz Composers Orchestra and Carla Bley (1968–1971).

His open nature and his spirit of adventure sent him travelling from 1970 in search of universal music ('I am a musician of the world'), to integrate elements from other cultures into his own music. This is how he studied and practised the music of countries such as India (with the Pandit Pran Nath), South Africa, Bali, Turkey, or Morocco. Hunting for as many rendez-vous as possible, greedy for all experiences, Don Cherry faced Jimi Hendrix and Frank Zappa with the same availability as the contemporary music of Krzysztof Penderecki or Lou Reed, the tabla player Ustad Latif Ahmed Khan or the saxophonist from Cameroon, Manu Dibango. He was to play in the Liberation Music Orchestra of Charlie Haden, and in the new-wave-jazz-funk-group Rip, Rig and Panic, together with his daughter Neneh. He willingly deserted his pocket trumpet and cornet for piano, flutes and percussion instruments before returning to the companion of his early years, Ornette Coleman, with whom he re-formed the quartet which played their first New York engagement at the Five Spot, and played with his electric Prime Time Band in 1987.

His phrasing on the pocket trumpet (he never played on a full-sized trumpet) proceeded either in small angry segments often propelled into a very high pitch at the time of his libertarian period, or by refinement of the melody, returning increasingly to the simplicity of the song, or rather the chant. ('I never really considered myself a trumpeter, rather thought of singing with the trumpet'.) The ecumenism which he claimed showed in the most convincing way in the Codona Trio (1980–1984), with the Brazilian percussionist Nana Vasconcelos and Colli Walcott at the sitar and the tabla.

Wynton Marsalis

1961, New Orleans

A purist with a great heart

The young herald of an 'artistic music' devoid of all venality, he brilliantly perpetuated the splendour of 'jazz before rock'.

The young prodigy of the 1980s could have let himself be seduced by the siren songs of jazz rock, like most of the musicians of his generation. He was the son of Ellis, a widely respected teacher and pianist, who called him Wynton out of respect for Wynton Kelly. He was one year younger than his brother Branford, a saxophonist and another virtuoso. Wynton Marsalis also chose another way, or rather a double direction: he was to be a jazz player — as he would claim insistantly — as well as a classical concert performer. When he was fourteen, he played the *'Concerto for trumpet'* by Haydn with the New Orleans Symphony Orchestra, but also let himself be heard in bands which played jazz and funk, when he was not listening to records by Miles Davis, Louis Armstrong, Fats Navarro, Clifford Brown and Freddie Hubbard (those who influenced him the

most), or studying classical music in the New Orleans Center for Creative Arts, and then in 1979 at the Juilliard School.

Engaged in Art Blakey's Jazz Messengers, where he joined his brother, and also working in the Brooklyn Philharmonic, the following year Wynton Marsalis was integrated in the quartet composed of Miles Davis's former companions, Herbie Hancock, Ron Carter, and Tony Williams. His style was strengthened by his contact with these giants, who encouraged the young man, who looked very proper, to record his first astounding record as a mature musician. In conjunction with the extension and the development of bebop, notably through the changing of chords and the modal concept of improvisation, his playing, which he mastered to perfection (one can seek his defects in vain) was combined with a deep sense of swing (a very particular kind of binary phrasing on a tertiary rhythm). With a broad clear sound, with a hint of copper tones and effects inherited from his experience of classical music, Marsalis (who recorded Haydn, Hummel and Leopold Mozart concertos in London in 1982) imposed his strong personality, with a faintly haughty assurance, in his subsequent records.

This new star has a warmth of expression typical of New Orleans musicians in these kinds of meditative drifts on a slow tempo, where strange atmospheres emerge when his fury leaves him. Like Miles Davis in the 1960s, he let his fellows, all great soloists, express themselves at length. They included the pianist Marcus Roberts, and the drummer Jeff 'Tain' Watts. He continued to play with symphony orchestras alternating with his quartet, which was sometimes augmented by a saxophonist, as was the case in the Great Jazz Parade in Nice in 1988, where he really triumphed.

In Wynton Marsalis's own words:

'People confuse speed and technique, it isn't that; feeling is one aspect of technique, the key of all music. Before understanding what it is to prolong something, you really must understand what the thing is, if you don't study it, if you don't understand it, you mess up the part of the programme which to me is the most important. The tree comes from its roots . . .' (*Jazz-Hot*)

Coleman Hawkins *(here with* **Miles Davis** *in 1945) is not only 'the inventor' of the tenor sax, but also a genius of harmonic progression which 'bridged the gap' between classical jazz and modern jazz.*

The advent of reeds

The new sound of the sax

It was only after the First World War that the invention of Adolphe Sax spread in the United States and it was jazz which was to ennoble it in the 1920s. Indeed, its incomparable qualities were revealed in improvisation: manageability and expressivity, which permitted each artist to develop a sound and phrasing which were highly individual. In New Orleans however, it was still confined to the role of accompanist, or an extra instrument for clarinet players. It was two of them who were the first to use it as a solo instrument, Barney Bigard (the tenor) and Sidney Bechet the soprano.

The first important stylist was the white Chicagoan Frankie Trumbauer, who made the saxophone in C (little used after him) an elegant and subtle instrument in counterpoint with Bix Beiderbecke's cornet. But it was Coleman Hawkins who 'invented', or at least explored the potentials of, the tenor in B flat, which he and Lester Young made into a major tool in the elaboration of modern jazz. On a parallel, Benny Carter, Jimmy Dorsey, Willie Smith and Johnny Hodges discovered the expressivity of the alto, used until then within a limited perspective in the new European classical repertory. Charlie Parker, in the 1940s, was to make it the ideal medium for polytonal improvisation.

The collective role of saxophones was also affirmed from the 1930s in the heart of the big bands, in compact sections (usually two altos, two tenors, and a baritone), frequently harmonized like real choirs, providing increasingly complex riffs and prolonged tutti. Ellington's sections and the 'Four Brothers' of Woody Herman's big band are the best examples.

Sidney Bechet

1897, New Orleans — Paris, 1959

An inspired popularizer of original jazz

Impervious to the march of time, his genius confirmed the myth of natural and impulsive improvisation.

On 14 May 1959, the death of a jazz musician took on the dimensions of a national event. The French (and international) press put it all over the front page — 'Sidney Bechet has died!' 'This death' wrote the critic Leonard Feather, 'bitterly highlights some of the paradoxes of jazz history. For many years Sidney only had insignificant gigs, unworthy of his talent; it was only late in his life that he received in France the acclaim he had not been given in his own country.'

The course of events which was to take the young clarinettist, a celebrity with Louis Armstrong, from the New Orleans style to composing 'Les Oignons' (1949), and becoming the master of the soprano saxo-phone which he first used in the early 1920s, was full of movement. A professional in 1915, he accompanied King Oliver in 1917, and came to Europe for the first time with the Southern Syncopated Orchestra (1919), where he was to be praised by the conductor Ernest Ansermet. On his return to the United States, he recorded with Louis Armstrong, and after returning to Europe, worked in the Revue Negre with Josephine Baker (1925), and stayed in Paris playing at Les Ambassadeurs with the musicians of Noble Sissle, whom he met in New York after eleven months of prison and expulsion following a brawl in Pigalle. There, he was to form the New Orleans Feetwarmers with the trumpeter Tommy Ladnier, but, in the onslaught of the economic crisis, he was obliged to open a clothes boutique. Hugues Panassié (who was to have him record with Tommy Ladnier and Mezz Mezzrow) and the New Orleans Revival enabled him to reach new heights.

Sidney Bechet was invited by Charles Delaunay to the Jazz Festival in the Salle Pleyel in Paris in 1949, where he was triumphant. He settled in France the following year; from being a distant figure whose discs were known to a few, he became the symbol of this revival which was all the rage. His great lyrical inspiration, the flame which seemed to consume the sax player, his special way of mingling tradition with tunes accessible to the widest public, made him a great popular star, who was thus able to contribute to the popularization of jazz. With Claude Luter and André Reweliotty, he recorded groove after groove (Disque d'Or in 1955), then he played at the Paris Vieux Colombier, and at the one in Juan-les-Pins, where he married amidst a New Orleans carnival atmosphere. He composed 'Petite Fleur' and 'Dans les rues d'Antibes', which were a huge success, as well as the music for the ballet *La Nuit est Une Sorcière*.

Charles Delaunay:
'You leave only friends behind you. And I am not thinking only of musicians ... but of taxi drivers, waiters in bars and even passers by, who when they bumped into you in the street, ... like an old friend, instinctively held their hand out to you, which you shook without hesitation, showing the good humour and simplicity that you always had' (*Jazz-Hot*, June 1959).

Maxime Saury
'Going somewhere with Sidney was never a problem because his extraordinary personality, his knowledge of tempos, his utter strictness in putting in his phrases and his punch, galvanized us all, and the rhythmic sequence could not drift for an instant with such a metronome.'

Coleman Hawkins

1904, Saint Joseph — New York, 1969

An incomparable sculptor of arpeggios

Through his supreme mastery of harmony and sound, he developed the 'vertical' dimension of improvisation.

It was in the extraordinarily fertile environment for soloists of Fletcher Henderson's band that Coleman Hawkins elevated the tenor sax (which he had started to learn at the age of nine) to the nobility of a solo instrument, an honour which until then had only been reserved for the trumpet. This was why, although he was not the only musician to use the instrument, he received the prestigious and unrivalled title of 'father' or 'inventor' of the saxophone. He contributed greatly to the spread and development of this invention of Adolphe Sax's in jazz, and to the many new vocations for the tenor sax.

Getting away from the harsh staccato

Rex Stewart

'Coleman Hawkins was so impressed by Tatum's playing that he immediately started to work out a new style based on what Tatum had played. It was from that time that he completely abandoned his systematically staccato style' (James Lincoln Collier, *The Adventure of Jazz*).

Coleman Hawkins on 'Body and Soul':

'I will never know why this recording became such a 'classic'. I just played it the way I play anything else.'

style, Bean (one of his nicknames) was very melodic in extremely fluid solos, with a pronounced vibrato and mellowness of tone, becoming insistent in rapid tempos and waxing lyrical in ballads. In his composition 'Queer Notions' (1934), which makes use of augmented chords, Hawkins shows a perfect knowledge of harmony, which he would often study on the piano.

'The most famous sax player in the world' went to Europe in 1935, played in Paris, and recorded there in 1937 alongside Benny Carter and French players Alix Combelle and André Ekyan. Returning to the States in 1939, he found himself in contact with other important young musicians, including Lester Young, who had very different styles. After a recording session with Lionel Hampton, in October he recorded 'Body and Soul', his absolute masterpiece in which he lyrically, sensually and intensely adorns this (beautiful) melody with sparkling changes in a whirling tumble of chords on a soft cushion of air, providing the classic example of an elaborately structured chorus phrase. He was to repeat this achievement in 1943 with 'The Man I Love' and in 1947 with 'Picasso', an unaccompanied improvisation on the basic harmonies of 'Body and Soul'.

But Hawkins was already listening attentively to the young boppers, taking Thelonious Monk into his band, who was later to return the compliment in 1957, becoming a fellow-traveller of the young rebels, while helping them to become better known. He played with the JATP from 1946 to 1951, co-directed a quintet with Roy Eldridge, and played at many festivals until the great tired 'Hawk' died still blowing with his last breath.

Altology 1 . . .

In the 1930s, the alto saxophone in E flat, the only one of the whole family to have a repertory in modern composition, also found its place in jazz orchestras, large and small.

Frankie Trumbauer (1901–1956) is really a misfit on this page, because his playing the alto was only incidental. He preferred the very rare tenor in C, devised for the transcription of piano and violin repertoires. But this ideal partner of Bix Beiderbecke's (the famous Bix & Tram tandem), who reached stardom with Paul Whiteman's band, had a great influence primarily on the alto players, and also on tenor player Lester Young. His precision, his clarity and his fluidity made him the 'lightest' of all the sax blowers of his generation.

Benny Carter (1907), still active and in fashion at over 80, largely exceeds the limits of this page, because of his qualities as a trumpeter, a clarinettist, and above all, for his great talent as an orchestrator. He is to the alto what Hawkins is to the tenor, a yardstick against which all the great specialists of this elegant and ambiguous instrument, whose register and tone might be defined as 'bisexual', have been measured. Carter was the first to create the ornate, sinuous style later adorned with Charlie Parker's arabesques, Cannonball Adderley's sequences, and even Eric Dolphy's tootling. This erudite gentleman with the charming smile, like Hawkins, also went through all the revolutions of jazz, armed with his sense of melody and rhythm which neither bebop nor its extensions ever outmoded.

Willie Smith (1910–1967), who must not be confused with the pianist of the same name, also known as 'the Lion', was more of a cheetah of the alto sax, pouncing and stalking through the jungle of the big bands (Lunceford, Ellington, Goodman, etc.) with a virtuoso style that was a trend setter,

especially for his famous disciple Earl Bostic. From the 1930s, he was strongly influenced by Johnny Hodges.

Johnny Hodges (1906–1970) dominated the alto scene before Charlie Parker, but he first started on the soprano sax, under the patronage of Sidney Bechet. At 22, he joined Duke Ellington's band and remained a constant member except for five sabbatical years (1951–1955), during which he led his own big band. He was a tender interpreter of Ellington's lyricism, with a voluptuous and fantastically subtle phrasing based on his great theatrical sense of 'diction', treating melody like a text of which every syllable is worthy of a whole range of expression. All the great classic sax players (those referred to as the 'beardies') considered him both as the most orthodox (technically) and as the most inimitable (aesthetically) of jazz alto sax players. Nicknamed 'Rabbit', but also 'Jeep', he scanned rather than taking pieces at a vivacious tempo, and knew how to meander lazily through the complexities of a ballad. This charming serpent from the Ellingtonian jungle made many of its 'songs' his own, from 'I Got It Bad' to 'On the Sunny Side of the Street', as well as 'Warm Valley', 'Passion Flower' and 'In a Sentimental Mood', which Coltrane, having played in his band, later recorded with the Duke in his honour.

'My passion for him', said Julio Cortazar, 'made me buy an alto sax in the hope that one day I could make the Hodges sound. I soon understood that it was like wanting to paint *La Ronde de Nuit* or the ceilings of the Sistine Chapel!' (interview with Jacques Chesnel, 1977).

Princes of the sax

As though the 1929 Crash was a depression that jazz alone would alleviate, the 1930s opened up a golden age for brass instruments, and the whole range of Sax's horns were mobilized to oppose a generous and positive theme to the threatening vociferations of another Adolf. In the big bands, the lead tenor became a sort of vanguard in charge of preparing the ground. Tactics were diversified, and here only the most famous players will be mentioned, with the risk of arousing the wrath of critics for not including soloists as expert as Bud Freeman, Prince Robinson, or Gene Sedric.

Chu (or Chew) Berry (1910–1941) only just had time to impose himself as the undisputed rival of Hawkins to whom he owed everything, even his choice of instrument, inspired by listening to 'Hawk's' records with Fletcher Henderson's band, which he himself joined in 1935. But it was in the four years preceeding a fatal car accident that he surpassed himself, becoming the instrumental trade-mark of Cab Calloway. His swift but relaxed performance, fiery and explosive, perfectly reflects his habit of compulsive eating which earned him the nickname Chew, and which also enabled him to shovel in a lot of 'cakes'.

Herschel Evans (1909–1939) was no luckier, dying from a heart attack when he was only 30 years old. The archetype of the 'Texan tenor' and an extrovert, he was the perfect counterpart to the slender Lester Young in Count Basie's big band (from 1936). Their contrasting styles is one of those miracles of balance which punctuate jazz history.

Buddy Tate (1914), a pupil of Evans and a Texan like him, was quite naturally his successor with Basie for ten years of intense, communicative swing, and in turn, he was to assume Lester Young's 'vice-presidency'. He is a warm and honest soloist, who went on to embody the classicism of those swinging tenors who were pure products of the big bands of the 1930s.

Ben Webster (1909–1973), like Charlie Parker, came from Kansas City, the capital of the night-birds, with its interminable jam sessions. He was also, after the example of Hawkins and Young, although basically less inventive, one of the giants of the tenor sax. After imposing himself as a tough soloist in the heart of the best big bands of the 1930s (Fletcher Henderson, Benny Carter, Andy Kirk, etc.), he was able to remain an artist available to serve and magnify the music of others, while affirming himself as an unrivalled master. Compared by Rex Stewart to 'Dr. Jekyll and Mr. Hyde', he excelled as much in the forceful driving style, as he magnificently illustrated with Ellington in the 1940s, as in the art of the ballad, which he brought to its peak in the following period. His expressionistic vibrato, humid and breathy, damp and torrid, won him the most varied pupils, from Paul Gonsalves to Archie Shepp. Woody Allen paid him the tribute of basing an entire film on the story of one of his historic duets with Art Tatum, 'September Song'.

Eddie Davis (1922–1986) certainly deserves his strange nickname, 'Lockjaw', because of his truly 'tetanizing' playing, charged with electric currents of infinitely varying intensity and 'voltage'. One of Basie's leading soloists from the 1950s, performing unbridled duets with Johnny Griffin, he represented the ideal synthesis between the styles of Hawkins and Webster, with an admirable propensity to blow the spirit of the blues like a draught of pure air amidst the most sophisticated orchestration, passing through the swing tradition and the transition from bebop as swiftly as an arrow.

Honkers and shouters

These turbulent performers are intoxicated with improvisation, featuring screaming and howling, or frantic tempos or routines, producing a 'white heat' impact on the audience through their sheer extravagant madness, driving to the limit in paroxysms of extreme tension (and attention), but equally often balanced by their sensuality and emotion in ballads.

Arnett Cobb (1918–1989), born in Houston, was a typical 'Texan Tenor', nicknamed the 'savage of the saxophone'. After replacing Jacquet in Lionel Hampton's band (1942–1947), he recorded a series of discs that the rhythm'n'blues sax players of the 1950s and 1960s were to take as a model, copying his guttural explosions, grunts and groans. After a car accident in 1956, he had to use crutches, but he continued to play with his customary fury and generosity.

Illinois Jacquet (1922) popularized the use of the shrill treble, turning it almost into a screech. Ardently 'white hot', this heir of the Count Basie sax tradition had no equal until the 1960s, in enthralling the audiences of the JATP with spectacular effects. A soloist in big bands, he also led trios in the company of the organists Milt Buckner and Wild Bill Davis. With Cobb and Buddy Tate, he started the Texas Tenors group before going on to form the Jazz Legends Band. He is one of the few jazz musicians to play the bassoon.

Flip Phillips (1915) and **Charlie Ventura** (1916–92), both of Italian origin, are famous for their torrid flights. The former plays with crude, sometimes outrageous frenzy, while the latter showed his attachment to bebop by starting the group Bop for the People.

The Canadian **Georgie Auld**, a brilliant, more controlled soloist, easily made the transition from classical to modern jazz.

Together with Dexter Gordon and Sonny Stitt, **Gene Ammons** (1925–1975) propagated the very popular 'chase' form in the 1950s. More of a soul and funky musician, with a broad sound 'as big as a mountain', he builds his music up in large dramatic fragments, mostly in ballad form, at which he excelled.

A solo can sometimes bring fame to a musician; it was Jacquet's case with the sixty-four bars of his 'Flyin' Home', as it was for **Paul Gonsalves** (1920–1974), the soloist in Duke Ellington's band, with his twenty-seven choruses in 'Diminuendo and Crescendo in Blue' at the 1946 Newport Festival. Under Ben Webster's influence, his phrasing was fluid, effervescent and fiercely swinging, yet capable of expressing the most lyrical melodies. He stayed with Ellington for nearly twenty years, and died ten days before his great friend and leader.

The more typical 'howlers' are **Red Prysock**, **Sil Austin** and **Willis Jackson** together with **King Curtis** (1935–1971), who was one of the most typical rhythm'n' blues musicians, and the sax player and singer **Eddie 'Cleanhead' Vinson** (1917–1988), who howled after the manner of the blues shouters, similar to Charlie Parker's alto sax.

Lester Young

1909, Woodville — New York, 1959

The bard of a thousand and one notes

Named 'the President' by his friend Billie Holiday, he became the sensitive story-teller of his own scorched life.

More than anybody else, Lester Young brought to jazz 'total relaxation in the act of spontaneous creation; this relaxation was sometimes more of an appearance than real; some think that, at times, in the last years of his life, it had actually changed to resignation'. Those words were used by the critic Nat Hentoff to define the essential characteristics of the inventor of cool jazz, an expression he is reputed to have coined himself, with a style diametrically opposed to that of the prevalent 1930s saxophone style, of which Coleman Hawkins was the archetypal exponent.

A loner who acted strangely, who held

In Lester Young's own words:

'I played the drums from when I was ten to when I was thirteen, and I stopped because I was sick of putting everything away. I used to look at girls after the show, but the time it took me to tidy up all my stuff, they had gone . . .'

Billie Holiday:

'When Lester plays, he almost seems to be singing; one can almost hear the words. People think he is 'self-satisfied' and pleased with himself, but in two seconds you can hurt him deeply; I know. I realized it once, when I had done it. We were hungry together and I will love him for ever, him and his music'.

(extract from *Lady Sings the Blues*).

---

his instrument at forty-five degrees, liked to wear a flat, broad brimmed 'pork-pie' hat, and whose utterances were as scarce as they were original, was in fact the first to foreshadow modern jazz, since Charlie Parker and a few other boppers were influenced by his playing in the 1935–1940 period, and then a whole generation of musicians reacting to bebop saw him as the forerunner of the Cool and West Coast jazz movements.

By alternating different phrases brimful with notes and unadorned passages, shattering rhythmic concepts and accepted notions of swing, by gliding through up and down beats and freeing melody from the tyranny of chords, he developed new relationships with the themes whose 'story' he liked to 'tell'. He tried to keep emotion at bay, delicately revealing his inner lyricism, his intimate concept of music, as if he were a stranger to his own creation. Diametrically opposed to the fashionable 'big sound', he offered colourless tone and an almost inaudible vibrato, which gave the impression that he was playing with the tip of his tongue.

Between 1936 and 1940, recordings with Count Basie's Band ('Tickle Toe', 'Every Tub', 'One O'Clock Jump') made his reputation. Mobilized in 1944, he never recovered from his stay in the army. During some Alladin sessions (1945–1948) he recorded some of his most beautiful interpretations and then enlarged his public during his tours with JATP (1946–1950). He then played freelance, often visiting Europe from 1952. He died a few days after his last engagement at the Blue Note in Paris, having made records of an infinite and unbearable sadness. Bertrand Tavernier's film *Around Midnight* (1986), which recaptures the end of the life of a musician, was inspired by his life, and that of Bud Powell.

Charlie Parker

1920, Kansas City — New York, 1955

The greatest inventor of instant music

*A genius at paraphrasing, he
opened jazz up to polytonality and
freed improvisation by turning
basic themes and rhythms into mere
pretexts.*

One night in 1939, during a jam session in a
Harlem pizzeria, Charlie Parker suddenly
became aware of the musical revolution he
was about to accomplish. 'I realized that by
using the high notes of the chords as a
melodic line, and by the right harmonic
progression, I could play what I heard
inside me. That's when I was born.'

Harmony had for a long time been an
obsession of this self-taught musician, who
one year earlier, had not hesitated to get
hired as a dish washer in the café where his
idol, Art Tatum, was playing. His only
musical education was in fact to have
listened analytically to the two musicians
he had recognized before anyone else as the
two great innovators of the late 1930s,
Tatum and, above all, Lester Young.

From adolescence, Charles Christopher
Parker methodically equipped himself with
an extraordinary technique which was to
enable him to give sublime expression to his
genius. A master of all tones and fingerings,
even the most acrobatic, he could express in
'real time' the most complex themes at a
dizzying tempo.

When, at eleven, his mother gave him his
first saxophone, Kansas City, the capital of
drunken cattle breeders, had become a
kind of sleepless Babylon run by the
gangster Tom Pendergast who, like his
colleagues Al Capone and Lucky Luciano,
had a providential passion for jazz! The
Parkers were living in the ghetto, two
blocks from the Reno Club where under-

age Charlie had to stay on the doorstep. He
would stay there for hours, listening to his
elders, particularly to Lester Young, who
unknowingly taught him all about
rhythmic freedom, and whose recordings
with Count Basie were to become his staple.
Listening, copying and extrapolating
endlessly, he became proficient enough to
join Buster Smith's group. This alto player
helped him to improve his tone and tidy up
his phrasing. Charlie was only seventeen,
but he was certainly not a kid any more. He
had been married for two years, and had
already got to know the 'artificial paradise'
that was going to cost him his life.

Shortly after his arrival in New York, he
joined the band of another musician from
Kansas City, the pianist Jay McShann,
with whom he recorded his first solos.

The two years that followed (1942–1944)
were a turning point in the history of

The trumpeter Cootie Williams:
'Armstrong changed the world of 'brass', but
after Bird it was the musicians who had to
change the way they played, from drummers
to saxes, including pianists, bassists, trumpets
and trombones.'

**Some of Parker's disciples on the alto
sax:**
Sonny Stitt, Frank Morgan, Cannonball
Adderley, Charles McPherson, James Moody,
Lou Donaldson, Art Pepper, Sonny Criss,
Charlie Mariano, Bud Shank, Ornette
Coleman, Eric Dolphy. . .

Dizzy Gillespie:
'He was too fragile to last. It's terrible to be
black in this society. If you let all these
pressures reach you, they drag you down and
they do you in.'

improvised music, but they were accompanied by a musician's union strike and recording ban, which makes it difficult to follow Parker's development during this period. The actual birth of modern jazz came about through his playing in the big bands of Earl Hines and Billy Eckstine, and especially during the sessions at Minton's with Monk, Kenny Clarke, and Gillespie. In 1945, he put together a quintet with the trumpeter, which became the crucible of bebop.

Increasingly perturbed by heroin abuse, and as yet little known by the public, he nonetheless became the hero of young avant-garde musicians, who flocked to hear him or talk to him on New York's 52nd Street. These included the trumpeter Miles Davis (19 years old) and the drummer Max Roach (20 years old), who participated in making his first major records. Parker then travelled to California (1946) and, after a cure in the Camarillo hospital, to Europe (1949–1950).

Bird's works:

The 'official' part includes: with Savoy (1945–1949), the great classics in original version ('Koko', 'Donna Lee', 'Parker's Mood'); with Dial (1946–1947), the California sessions ('Ornithology', 'Lover Man', 'Bebop') and the New York sessions with Miles Davis ('Scrapple from the Apple', 'Dexterity'); with Clef/Verve (1948–1955) quartets with strings or in big bands, on a repertoire often made up of pop hits of the time (mambo and boleros in particular). But it is probably in the live 'pirate' recordings, mostly made by amateurs, that one finds the quintessence of Parker genius, unhampered by the constraints of the studio, and galvanized by an audience of mesmerized musicians.

The impresario Norman Granz took charge of his career, and he became a living legend, the consecration of which was the opening of a New York club in 1948 which bore his name, Birdland. But the narcotics police took away his professional licence, and the last years of his life, punctuated by a few good moments like the Toronto concert (1953), were rather tragic. He died at the age of 35, of a haemorrhage in the house of the Baroness Nica de Koenigswarter. During the weeks that followed his death, the walls of New York were covered with the defiant and enigmatic graffiti: 'Bird Lives'.

Even if the anecdotal origin of his nickname was his liking for chicken ('Yardbird'), none could better sum up Parker's own style, a capricious fluttering flight around a melodic line which is sometimes barely perceptible, but ever moving towards a distant goal, chasing to the horizon all the predictable boundaries of improvisation. Whoever his partners were, and whatever theme was chosen, Parker's solo would always be an adventure on the brink of amazingly unheard of sounds, a succession of freely taken risks, heroically surmounted obstacles. The prodigious diversity of stresses, syncopations, silences, appoggiatura, used not as mere adornments but as true parentheses, full of meaning, everything in his playing is the fruit of a dazzling, almost inhuman intuition. No wonder that he became the main target of such fundamentalists as Panassié, who saw his records as the 'satanic verses' of bebop!

And yet Parker always remained a genius of the blues, and his own compositions consistently respected the traditional form, when they were not actual remakes of standard pieces of the 1920s and 1930s ('Koko' comes from 'Cherokee', 'Donna Lee' from 'Indiana', 'Ornithology' from 'How High the Moon').

Sidney Bechet *and*
Claude Luter *at the*
Vieux-Colombier in the
'grande époque' of Saint
Germain des Prés
(1950).

'Bird and Diz'
Charlie Parker *and*
Dizzy Gillespie

Both of them were disciples of Charlie Parker: the two giants of modern tenor sax — **Sonny Rollins** *(above) and* **Stan Getz** *(right), or the fire and the fresh water.*

Sonny Rollins

1930, New York

A fiery but fragile colossus

With torrential solos of blinding sound, between doubt and jubilation, he expresses his unquenchable thirst for musical absolutes.

He is as much of a giant physically as he is musically. And yet he is passing through modern jazz, from bebop to today, carrying deep within him a permanent doubt on his own creative capacities, which explains the inner searchings which led him into periods of retreat, in 1959–1962 when he played alone, for himself, on the Brooklyn and Williamsburg bridges; from September 1969 to July 1971). He emerged like a phoenix from these ashes, both different and the same person. Impervious to fashions, he pursued perfection with rigour and austerity in a ceaseless exploration of jazz.

In Sonny Rollins's own words:

'... I really want to reach the stage where I don't have to think of what I am playing. So I try to stay prepared, keeping in shape by practising the chords I might need, then I wait until it comes to me, that is essential, to let the music flow over me rather than constantly trying to create it. I simply want to reach a level where I will never cease to make progress. I know I will not be satisfied with myself every evening. It is probably impossible, but I am trying to improve my standard. I should be better than I am. So that, even the bad evenings, I may never be bad enough to despair' (*Jazz Magazine*, March 1987).

After playing bop with the greatest, he became the unrivalled master of the hardest of hard bop, joining Clifford Brown and Max Roach, competing with Coltrane in a memorable 'Tenor Madness', recording the imposing *Saxophone Colossus*, all in 1956. Subsequently he preferred to play in smaller groups (trios without a piano, duets, solo), and became interested in jazz in 3/4 time (the 'hot waltz'). When he emerged from his first silence, he was clearly appeased in *The Bridge*, before his meeting with the slashers Ornette Coleman and Don Cherry (*Our Man in Jazz*), and his return to standard themes.

When he emerged from his second retreat, he had an unconvincing flirt with jazz-rock. But at the beginning of the 1980s, serene at last, he became the most adventurous, impetuous and superbly lyrical improviser, removed from his anxieties, applying all his natural versatility to the development of his discourse, endlessly blending tradition and contradictions, reconciliations and detours.

Despite these episodes, there are constant references to the great master Hawkins, with the 'fat' tone coming from the middle of the instrument, and to Parker in the freedom of his improvisation. Rollins also frequently refers to the folklore of his origins in the Caribbean calypsos like 'Saint Thomas', or 'Don't Stop the Carnival', with a jumble of themes, a stretching of introductions and codas, the inclusion of unexpected quotes (hymns, nursery rhymes), sardonic humour, changes, sequences and deviations of rhythms and moods, breathing techniques like circular breathing, and tones.

At sixty, Sonny Rollins tirelessly pursues his unique and exemplary career as an adventurous improviser constantly expressing both his need and joy in playing with confounding lyricism and wit in each of his performances.

Stan Getz

1927, Philadelphia — Los Angeles, 1991

A glider on the 'cool' wave

An incomparable master of the pastel blues, he gave the tenor sax the ideal voice and diction to express tenderness and nostalgia.

For forty years, since his historic improvisation in 1948 on 'Early Autumn' (composed by Ralph Burns, in the cool style), Stan Getz remained the most important white modern jazz saxophonist. A virtuoso capable of playing anything, he distinguished himself by his immediately identifiable tone, of great purity, smooth and velvety, airy, not very resonant, in full harmony with his own musical universe, and by his supple and elegant playing, refined but with a virile touch, nonchalant or fiery, tender and sometimes crude, suggesting more than he affirmed.

Nicknamed 'The Sound', this improviser with the fertile imagination and playful character always preferred to play melody with the relaxed phrasing he acquired from

In Stan Getz's own words:
'I do not discover young musicians, it is they who come to see me. They want to express themselves through their music, and they know they have a chance with me. I never try to boss them about, but on the contrary, try to let them develop their talents. I do all I can to help them, because I think love is an essential element for whoever wants to create music. The two capital things, in fact, are love and an open spirit, an openness towards other musicians and towards oneself and the world which surrounds us. One cannot behave like a horse with blinkers. One must open oneself to life, to music . . .' (*Jazz-Hot*, September 1978).

Lester Young, but without forgetting the concepts dear to the boppers he met in 1949, after he had left Woody Herman's second group, where he was part of the saxophone section known as the Four Brothers, with Zoot Simms, Herbie Stewart, and Serge Chaloff. He contributed to the evolution of hard bop, his playing becoming more sculptured, his tone gaining in fullness as well as in firmness, John Coltrane recognized that he was his first influence. In 1952, he signed with Norman Granz and joined the JATP, before settling in Europe at the end of 1958, after a series of personal problems. On his return to the United States, he recorded 'Focus', a sort of concerto for saxophone and string band composed by Eddie Sauter. At the beginning of the 1960s, the bossa nova, which he discovered through the guitarist Charlie Byrd, was to make him a universal star. He recorded compositions such as 'Desafinado' and 'The Girl from Ipanema' which were huge commercial hits, with the guitarist and singer Joao Gilberto, the pianist Antonio Carlos Jobim and the singer Astrud Gilberto.

In 1965, we discover a more energetic Getz, surrounded by young musicians (Gary Burton, Chick Corea, Steve Swallow), and in 1970 with the Europeans René Thomas, Eddy Louiss and Bernard Lubat. He did not pursue an experimental adventure with electronic and rock rhythms, which did not seem to agree with his distinguished romanticism, and henceforth performed in a quartet, with pianists such as his old accomplices Lou Levy and Jimmy Rowles, or younger ones like Joanne Brackeen, Jim McNeely and Kenny Barron. Health problems in 1988 forced him to interrupt an international tour, but he reappeared a few months later stimulated by a new entourage, poetry continuing to pour from his saxophone.

Bop-sax

Jazz saxophonists hurled themselves into the breach opened by Charlie Parker and the tenor sax became the privileged instrument of the bebop 'combos'. Most tried to find an identifiable, personal sound in innumerable aspects of Parker's dialogue.

The Tenor Sax

Carlos 'Don' Byas (1912–1972), son of a Cherokee Indian, achieved a magnificent synthesis between Hawkins and Young (whose place he inherited in Count Basie's band), and like them, quite naturally accepted the transition to bebop. In 1944, he even took part with Stan Getz in the historic recording sessions which were the first to clearly define this style. A great Parisian figure in the period which immediately followed the Liberation, he perpetuated a flamboyant and voluptuous lyricism in modern jazz, which is reminiscent of Swing. This romantic craftsman of exquisite ballads was also the first to record 'Laura', from the Otto Preminger film, but also showed himself to be a thoroughbred at a gallop.

Dexter Gordon (1923–1990) is physically and musically another giant of the tenor saxophone. He is as much a pupil of Hawkins as of Young. Starting with Lionel Hampton, he moved on to Armstrong before becoming a kind of Californian ambassador of New York bebop. His drug problems complicated his career and made him an archetype of the marginal jazz player, while as an accomplished actor he acted in plays (*The Connection*), then in films (*Round Midnight*). In the 1960s he became one of the stars of Blue Note records, and developed a direct, clear and electric melodic style, while his keen tone, stinging with harmonics, was painstakingly studied by Coltrane and Rollins. He improvised expertly on themes which were often close to rhythm'n'blues, and exploited them with a sure sense of crescendo which made him a true 'preacher' of imperious and persuasive tones.

Wardell Gray (1921–1955), who was often the alter ego of Gordon (*The Chase*

1947–1952) superbly illustrates his merging of the styles of Young and Parker, with whom he recorded. Evolving from an elegant, velvety style towards a more spectacular manner, he contributed greatly to the 'modernization' of Count Basie's music around 1950. Murdered for obscure reasons, he left few records in his own name, but a great number of recorded sessions as sideman in the most varied contexts.

Johnny Griffin (1928) completes this 'triumvirate' of tenor sax players with grinding, sharp and scratchy names, who sharpened their beaks listening to Bird. Nicknamed the 'little giant', he was the youngest, the most virtuoso and most voluble of the three. Bounding from one octave to another, harvesting his bunches of triplets at an infernal tempo, he made thorough use of an expressionist palette with a generosity which was sometimes verbose, but with an incomparable effect. He was the equal of a Coltrane and a Rollins to a certain point, before they rose to a mystic plane where this great lyrical interpreter dared not adventure, rooted as his inspiration was in the simple faith of gospel.

James Moody (1925) could have taken as his motto 'any more bop and you die!'. He matured in the sumptuous seraglio that was Dizzy Gillespie's big band (whose favourite partner he was always to remain), he produced, on both tenor and sax (and on the flute, of which he was one of the greatest stylists), the 'general audience' version of Parkerian music. One could even say that he 'was fluent in' bebop, rather than played it, with a fluid and natural elocution, an intense swing and a lot of humour.

The Texan **Harold Land** (1928) can be associated with bop, although he is insensitive to fleeting fads and so capable (culpable?) of going off in different directions, which took him from Eric Dolphy to accompanying Tony Bennett, but also playing in the Clifford Brown-Max Roach Quintet, and the one he himself was to form with the vibraphone player Bobby Hutcherson.

Alto-Sax

Julian 'Cannonball' Adderley (1928–1975) was the most famous of the 'post-Parker' alto saxophonists. Starting with an almost perfect imitation of Bird's style, and as his most inventive heir, he was soon able to make an impression as leader of one of the best known 1960s jazz groups. After forming a quintet with his brother Nat (trumpet), inspired by Parker's with Dizzy, he joined Coltrane in the Miles Davis group (1958–1959), becoming one of Davis's few close friends. His quintet then carved itself a place as one of the most famous jazz groups of the 1960s and 1970s, with an impressive selection of talented young pianists, from Bill Evans to George Duke, by way of Wynton Kelly and Joe Zawinul. Evolving towards an increasingly 'bluesy and funky' jazz, he was to be one of the first to electrify his saxophone. In spite of his nickname, 'Cannonball', which comes from a story of greed like Parker's, it was not so much his speed as his 'solidity' which was the mark of his game, ever apt to make real hits out of themes anchored indisputably in the great Afro-American tradition, such as 'Sermonette', 'This Here', 'Work Song'.

Sonny Stitt (1924–1982) could almost have been Parker's perfect double, a thankless role he was often expected to play at the JATP 'fairs'. But the fact that he was one of the rare saxophonists who was able to master the alto sax as well as the tenor, and his very personal sense of the blues, always earned him the respect of his peers including both Bird and Gillespie. Even if he is not one of the greatest improvisers of modern jazz, he sometimes reached their level during his impressive recording career, which enabled him to play with practically all of them notably on the Verve label.

Lou Donaldson (1926), son of a preacher, represents a seductive extrapolation of Parkerian blues. He was an ardent disciple of Bird in the 1950s, and later, after a spell with Horace Silver, became one of the musicians most frequently recorded by Blue Note. For a while he also played with the Jazz Messengers. An expressive and swinging alto, he regularly came to play in Europe, accompanied by his faithful pianist, Herman Foster.

Phil Woods (1931) is without any doubt the most virtuoso and the most faithful disciple of Parker, whose widow Chan he married, and whose 'Koko' was decisive in his career as a musician from the age of thirteen. His career as a sideman is impressive: amongst others, he played with Lennie Tristano, Dizzy Gillespie, Buddy Rich, Quincy Jones, Benny Goodman and Thelonious Monk. The founder of the European Rhythm Machine with George Gruntz, Henri Texier and Daniel Humair, he made a name for himself in the 1970s as the best alto sax player, and also one of the most brilliant clarinettists, of his generation. Then his quartet, often augmented by the trumpeter Tom Harrell, became one of the major groups of 'neo-bop', which he played, usually without amplification, in the largest halls, thanks to the exceptional power of his tone. Lyrical and sinewy, his playing ideally prolongs Parker's, but also Cannonball Adderley's, with whom he shared a fiery passion for vigorously expressed blue notes.

The cool sax

The adepts of 'soft sax', all of them more or less disciples of Lester Young, cultivated swing in voluptuous arabesques.

The tenor saxophonist **Warne Marsh** (1927–1987), the most orthodox pupil and disciple (with Lee Konitz) of Lennie Tristano, was a retiring, even shy musician, with an overwhelming tone devoid of any vibrato, and very mobile, fluid phrasing with complex rhythmic motives, all of which heralded the Free Jazz revolution. He played with Lee Konitz for a long time (the similarity of their tone has been pointed out), with the pianist Lou Levy, and was part of the Supersax group formed on the initiative of the double bass player Buddy Clark. Its originality consisted in transcribing Charlie Parker solos. Marsh passed away in the most beautiful way possible for an artist; he died on stage, at the begining of an improvisation on 'Out of Nowhere'.

Zoot Sims (1925–1985), the swingiest of the Four Brothers in Woody Herman's band, and an improviser with a passion for playing under the double influence of Lester Young and Ben Webster, formed a notable quintet (1957–1969) with another tenor saxophonist, **Al Cohn** (1925–1988), who was also in the 'President's' tradition, (lyricism, harmonic invention, distance, a cool sound), and who made friends with Zoot while playing with Herman (1947–1949). As a composer and an arranger, he worked for cinema and television, and appeared regularly until the mid-1970s, always with Zoot, for the famous duets which did so much for their reputation.

The immense shadow of Lester Young looms over **Bill Perkins** (1924) too, and **Richie Kamuca** (1930–1977), two tenor sax players who also met in Woody Herman's band, in 1954. They then played in the Lighthouse Club in Hermosa Beach, in Stan Kenton's band, and in 1956 made a record showing the similarity between them (their supple phrasing), and their differences (tone, closer to Getz in Perkins's playing). As well as this collaboration, Bill Perkins mingled very young with the big bands, and worked after 1956 as sound engineer and art director. He played in Toshiko Akiyoshi's big band and with **Lew Tabackin** (1974–1977), then could be heard again with Shorty Rogers in 1982 and 1985. He was the inventer of the saxophone synthesizer interface-MIDI. Richie Kamuca, of Indian origins, trained in the bebop school in his youth (friend of Clifford Brown, and substitute for Charlie Parker). He worked with the drummers Stan Levey and Shelly Manne, and in Gerry Mulligan's Concert Jazz Band.

Since his debut in 1953, **Barney Wilen** (1937) was to remain faithful to the spirit of Lester Young, in spite of several 'free jazz rock' and African adventures. From *Ascenseur pour l'échafaud* with Miles Davis (1957) to *French Ballads* in 1987, he kept his relaxed lyricism intact, but it was sometimes spiked with brief and sudden tensions.

Saxophonist of the Dave Brubeck Quartet (1951–1967), and composer of 'Take Five', **Paul Desmond** (1924–1977), a typically West Coast musician who was extremely educated and witty (see his collection of souvenirs *How many are there in a quartet?*), possessed an admirably pure tone. His phrasing, he said, was 'the slowest in the world'! His way of playing was a source of perpetual discovery, with a delicate and permanent swing. He played ballads marvellously, and in 1963 recorded with two of his favourite accomplices, guitarist Jim Hall and drummer Connie Kay.

The 'tenors' of the baritone

No longer playing the oaf of the band, this semi-heavy member of the sax team gained its freedom as a soloist due to its extensive register.

Some musicians had already proved excellent on this instrument (Joe Garland, the author of 'In the Mood', Adrian Rollini) when **Harry Carney** (1910–1974) was engaged to play in Duke Ellington's band, aged sixteen. Until then, baritone players always 'doubled', either on the tenor saxophone, the alto or the clarinet. A fan of Coleman Hawkins, he was to enter jazz history as the first baritone soloist. He was not only the indispensable fifth man of the formidable tone colour which provided so much Ellingtonian reed section, but also an improviser with serene phrasing and a powerful tone, robust and deep. He remained with the band until the death of his leader, surviving him only by a few months.

Cecil Payne (1922) and **Serge Chaloff** (1923–1957) were the first baritone sax players to play bebop. Payne, with an incisive style, played in the big band of Dizzy Gillespie (1947–1948), replacing **Leo Parker**, an audacious harmonizer in the bands of Lionel Hampton (1963–1964) and Woody Herman (1966–1967), and in the New York Jazz Repertory Orchestra (1974). In the playing of Chaloff, the baritone sax player in the first Four Brothers section, it is possible to distinguish the combined influences of Carney and Charlie Parker, in his very intense treatment in an airy, broad tone, which a kind of strangled sobbing made intensely

moving. Before he moved to Herman's band (1946–1949), he played in various bands, including Tommy Dorsey's. Afterwards, he played with Count Basie's Octet, although his health problems and use of drugs forced him to reduce his musical activities.

Bob Gordon (1928–1955), represents the West Coast style of baritone sax, with his sober, virile performance, and his clear, unwavering tone. He played with Chet Baker, Clifford Brown, Shelly Manne, Stan Kenton, in the quintet of Lennie Niehaus, and in a duet with the tenor saxophonist Jack Montrose.

Nicknamed 'The Knife' by Stan Kenton's musicians (referring to the clean-cut quality of his solos and his trenchant, coarse, and husky tone), and described by Philippe Carles as 'the most baritone of baritones', **Pepper Adams** (1930–1986) was a musician whose harmonic qualities of rare finesse are evident in very different contexts; the boppers of the Thad Jones-Mel Lewis Orchestra, as well as the dashing Californians, and Benny Goodman, Lionel Hampton and Charles Mingus. He played in Europe with various rhythm sections, including the impeccable trio of Georges Arvanitas in France.

The Englishman **John Surman** (1944) made his debut with the best British musicians, then with Barre Philips and Michel Portal, and was a member of the sax trio S.O.S. He was the leading baritone sax player of the Free Jazz era of the 1960s and 1970s, and a multi-instrumentalist specializing in playing in high registers on baritone and soprano saxophones, clarinets, flutes, and synthesizers. Since working with the choreographer Carolyn Carlson, he has turned towards repetitive music with electric and acoustic effects, drawing on jazz, contemporary jazz and folk melodies.

Gerry Mulligan

Because of his predominant position in the 'West Coast' movement as a composer and arranger, the description of this most famous baritone saxophonist can be found on page 111.

Altology 2

Few modern saxophonists have escaped the irresistible attraction of the Parker style. By fighting against servile and vain imitation, the new altos have had to learn to fly with their own wings in Bird's groove.

While young musicians at the end of the 1940s followed the example of Charlie Parker, **Lee Konitz** (1927), under the influence of his teacher and companion, Lennie Tristano, anticipated the avant-garde forms of the 1960s. His transparent tone, his mellow, sinuous phrases in pursuit of the melody, which often resolve to a whispered shrill, are all elements of a luminous universe, highlighted in the duet form he loved so much (with Warne Marsh, Red Mitchell, Martial Solal, Michel Petrucciani), through a dreamlike, ironic re-reading of standard classics.

The Californian **Art Pepper** (1925–1982), first affiliated with the West Coast sound, became an original stylist with a way of playing imprinted with a breathtaking lyricism, which revealed the inner wounds of this live wire. His singing, tender or violent phrasing, translates intensely lived emotions. After his multiple eclipses, he returned to the limelight five years before his death, redoubling his recording sessions.

Gigi Gryce (1927–1983), whose playing resembles the Parkerian language with the influence of the Cool style, is equally a talented composer and arranger, who benefited from the teaching of Nadia Boulanger and Arthur Honegger in 1952 in Paris, where he recorded for the first time under his own name, with Clifford Brown and the pianist Henri Renaud. He then founded the Jazz Lab Quintet.

Because Charlie Parker sometimes asked him to stand in, **Jackie McLean** (1932) was rather too hastily relegated to the ranks of his imitators. Marked by bebop, he was also a bluesman, who found on the West Coast the nostalgia which, together with the strange and gentle violence of Ornette Coleman, was to give him his sulphurous tone, capable of transforming the most hackneyed classical piece, reinforced by a biting, metallic edge. McLean increased his exchanges with the boppers until, feeling himself close in temperament to the Free Jazz musicians, he took on his relationship with Ornette Coleman (the records *Let Freedom Ring* and *One Step Beyond* in 1963). In 1967 he managed to give up drugs, turned towards Islam, and studied during a long retreat the history of jazz from its origins. In 1975, he haunted the Five Spot in New York for two weeks with his son René, also a saxophonist, and then made a detour via Jazz-rock, funk and disco, before returning in the 1980s to bebop.

Arthur Blythe (1940), close to McLean in his tone and melodic invention, united in an ample and lyrical style the different sources of Afro-American music. Rooted in the blues, gospel and bebop, 'Black Arthur' found himself constantly at the side of the greatest names in contemporary jazz, affirming himself as the most original voice of the alto saxophone of these last years.

West Coast

From 1952 until 1958, the focal centre of jazz moved from the East Coast to the edge of the Pacific. The main Californian musicians mostly came from Stan Kenton's band. These exceptionally competent musicians, most of whom were white, gathered round trumpeter and arranger Shorty Rogers, who, supported by saxophonist Jimmy Giuffre and drummer Shelly Manne, became the leading figure in the movement.

The jazz they played had no well defined rules. What united them was the importance they gave to the arrangement. Like Minton's Playhouse at the beginning of the 1940s in New York, the Lighthouse Club in Hermosa Beach, under the direction of double bass player Howard Rumsey, was the meeting place for these young people who were to open up the frontiers to many different influences, and widen the range of tone by introducing instruments seldom used till then like flute, horn, or oboe.

A pillar of the Lighthouse Club from 1953, **Bob Cooper** (1925) was one of the principal promoters of the West Coast movement. A tenor sax player with a superb tone (he was soloist in Stan Kenton's band from 1945 to 1951), a composer, arranger and band leader, he was also the first jazz player to give an important role to the oboe and the French horn, providing new colour and sophistication, as can be seen from the baroque style of his arrangements. He joined Shorty Rogers in the West Coast Giants group for a European tour in 1985.

The companion of all the well known Californians, **Bud Shank** (1926), an alto and baritone saxophonist and a flautist (one of the best), was another who played in Stan Kenton's band and in the Lighthouse All Stars group, and had quite a success with his flute-oboe duets with Bob Cooper. Associating with the guitarist Laurindo Almeida, he recorded 'Braziliance' in 1953, a famous forerunner of the bossa nova. He played the flute with an admirable mastery, delicate and nuanced,

and not lacking in grace, and played alto sax with a modesty which counteracted his controlled exuberance.

Born in Los Angeles, **Buddy Collette** (1921), a virtuoso on all saxophones, flutes and clarinets, is supposed to have been the first black musician to be accepted in a Hollywood television studio. He made a considerable number of records, in which one is aware of his fluid phrasing, nonchalant and dreamy, and his limpid tone.

Although he did not want to be thought of as a West Coast player, New Yorker **Gerry Mulligan** (1927) had a definite influence on West Coast jazz. Close to the Cool in his melodic inspiration, he is in the ranks of the Californians by virtue of his rhythmic sequences and his deference to the classics. An arranger of great talent (he collaborated on Miles Davis's *Birth of the Cool* and worked for Stan Kenton's band), he was to become, from 1952, one of the most popular musicians, after forming a quartet with Chet Baker without piano, in which he put into practice a contrapuntal form of improvisation. He made the baritone saxophone a fully-fledged solo instrument. His rich tone, like the sound of a cello, combined voluptuously with supple or incisive phrasing, voluble without being chatty. Passionate about composing, he led several big bands; avid to meet people, he recorded with Thelonious Monk, Charles Mingus, Johnny Hodges, and the bandoneon player, Astor Piazzola. He was to play with the alto saxophonist Paul Desmond in Dave Brubeck's group from 1968–1972.

John Coltrane

1926, Hamlet — Huntington, 1967

A spiritual master

With an immense respect for the instrument, the public, and the sacred role of the artist, he extended the horizons of jazz to an entranced celebration of the universe.

The premature death of John Coltrane was such a tragedy that contemporary jazz is currently qualified as 'post-Coltrane', and his influence reached the dimension of a real cult. The last seven years of his life swept away the rules for improvisation as radically as the first years of Armstrong, or the middle period of Parker's career. Unlike Parker, it was only when he was 33 that all the singularity of his genius was revealed, with *Giant Steps*, then *My Favourite Things*. It seems that it was aesthetically necessary to by-pass bebop, to first reach past a 'new' technological 'boundary', while Charlie Parker's virtuosity seemed a sort of 'sound barrier' that was impossible to cross.

Keith Jarrett after Coltrane's death:
'Suddenly we all felt an enormous void. But that's not what he would have wanted: he would have preferred us to feel we had more space to do what we had to do.'

Archie Shepp:
'He proved it was possible to play an uninterrupted, constantly constructive, original and imaginative solo for thirty or forty minutes. And he showed us that we should have enough mental and physical stamina to put up with such long flights.'

The long maturation of 'Trane' represents the ideal course for a musician of his generation. He successively practised fanfares, rhythm'n'blues, bebop in a big band (the *Apollo*, then Dizzy Gillespie's band), and then played with two of the greatest saxophone virtuosos, Johnny Hodges and Earl Bostic. It was then that Miles Davis brought him out of anonymity to the front of the stage. A deep friendship developed between them, and a musical complicity comparable to that which united Parker and Gillespie. Their quintet (which was to include Cannonball Adderley) developed very fast. At first quite shy, Coltrane gradually asserted himself, acquiring in those last months of 1959 an energy and a level of creativity which plunged Miles into a certain disarray. In the meantime, the saxophonist rubbed shoulders with Monk, whose influence was to prove decisive on his harmonic and rhythmic concepts, recorded his first album *Blue Train*, and got 'unhooked' from heroin and alcohol.

It was then — after *Kind of Blue*, in fact — that Coltrane literally took off. Indifferent to the opinion of Miles, who reproached him for his lack of precision, he developed his solos at greater and greater length, enriching his playing of cleverly controlled harmonics, of dissonant emissions, and of his 'sheets of sound', which his interest in the harp inspired. Not only did his range on the tenor exceed three octaves, but his tone is grandiose, even in the extreme registers. He adopted the soprano in 1960, and soon became the major expert on this formidable instrument. His melodic imagination was increased tenfold by his knowledge of modes absolutely unknown in the western tradition. While it is true that it was under Miles Davis's influence that he was able to make full use of it, his musical education was also of great help — he had studied polytonality and modal improvisation — as was his growing interest in Indian ragas,

African pentatonic scales and the poly-phonic music of the Pygmys.

Founded in 1960, his quartet with McCoy Tyner (piano), Jimmy Garrison (bass) and Elvin Jones (drums) immed-iately became an absolute laboratory of collective improvisation, unequalled in its lyricism and subtlety. Trane serenely assimilated the influence of Ornette Coleman, John Gilmore (Sun Ra's tenor sax) and above all Eric Dolphy, who joined the group for a few historic sessions. From then on nothing could stop the crazy drift which had started, and was to lead, five years later, to the disintegration of the quartet, the piano becoming too much of an anchor to western rules of harmony. As if he knew his days were numbered — as indeed they were, alas! — Coltrane started a frantic race, in which the only objective seemed to be to leave as much evidence of his research as possible. Surrounded by devoted young musicians — Pharaoh Sanders, Archie Shepp, Rashied Ali, his second wife Alice — he practically played day and night, and took advantage of a providential contract with Impulse to make many recordings.

The titles he gave to his records — *Im-pressions, Transition, Ascension, Crescent, Meditations, Om, Sun Ship* — clearly indicate his will to move beyond the playful tradi-tion of jazz to a mystical dimension, which was indeed the challenge of that period, when the hippie movement flourished, and in a very similar context Jimi Hendrix was beginning to evolve. These two giants the blues had produced were to die suddenly within three years of each other, as Charlie Parker and a few others had done before them, as if to pose the painful question, is there a threshold in the mind beyond which music can become deadly?

Both as a man and as a musician, he radiated 'love supreme'

In John Coltrane's own words:
'Monk taught me how to play two or three notes simultaneously on the tenor sax. With fake fingering and adjusting the lips, one can make perfect chords! Harmony then became my obsession. I sometimes had the feeling I was playing through ground glass!'

Archie Shepp

1937, Fort Lauderdale

In memory of the black people

His style, full of inspiration and contrasts, is like a summary of the previous episodes of the whole of Afro-American music.

Through all the aesthetic changes that he accepted wholeheartedly, he remained faithful to the blues and gospel traditions, and when he had made nearly sixty recordings, he dedicated two of his most beautiful to them, with pianist Horace Parlan. After graduating in literature and drama, he settled in New York in 1959, where he embarked on a career as a playwright and musician, playing at first with Afro-Cuban bands. Cecil Taylor then hired him, and convinced him to dedicate himself entirely to his music. He also encouraged him to go beyond his early influences — Lester Young, Sonny Stitt, Charlie Parker — and to improvise outside harmonic progressions.

In fact, Shepp was already under the influence of Coltrane, who became his friend and produced his first album — *Four for Trane* — in 1964. In that period, he left Taylor to form pianoless groups with trumpeters like Bill Dixon, and later Don Cherry, or the alto saxophonist John Tchicai, who 'doubled up' with him in the New York Contemporary Five. The formula — three horns, bass and drums — became the standard in Free Jazz. From 1965 (the year in which he recorded *Ascension* with Coltrane), he was a pioneer in developing a frantic solo style in an orchestral context inspired by Mingus, but with deliberate reference to the music of West Africa, with records like *Mama Too Tight* and *The Magic of Ju-Ju*. Daring by nature, but a traditionalist due to his great culture, he embraced all the trends of Afro-American music, from gospel to bop, passing through the blues and Ellington, whom he venerated above all. His sound is like a potted history of the tenor sax, from Ben Webster to Coltrane and Rollins.

Like the poet LeRoi Jones, the author of *Blues People*, he was in search of the origin and deep character of the 'Great Black Music', which for him replaced the term 'jazz'. Shepp sporadically returned to rhythm'n'blues — *Attica Blues*, *Cry of My People* — to increase his popular audience for a political and cultural message that was beyond the scope of music. Around the mid-1970s, he made a spectacular return to the history of jazz, which he taught at university. With his rich sensual tone on the tenor, reminiscent of Ben Webster or Don Byas, a plaintive whine on the soprano, sober, slightly archaic piano style, a broken 'hoarse' voice, which chants more than sings the blues, he gleefully reviewed a repertoire ranging from Ellington to Parker, heavily stressing its relevance today.

LeRoi Jones:
'Shepp sprung immediately to the front line of 'post-Coltrane tenors', but he is only playing his own role, like all those of his generation who learnt from Ornette Coleman and Cecil Taylor to give vent to the deepest roots of their emotions and who managed to express a song of their very own' (sleeve of the record *Four for Trane*, Impulse A71)

Ornette Coleman

1930, Fort Worth

An impatient questioner of tomorrow's music

From Free Jazz to free funk, the most 'alternative' of alto sax players turned improvisation into a primitive art, without hesitating to subvert his own melodic genius.

The titles of Ornette Coleman's 1958 and 1959 recordings are revealing: in *Something Else!*, *Tomorrow is the Question*, *The Shape of Jazz To Come*, *Change of the Century*, his music was already tracing the outline of future jazz. He provoked an almost general outcry; a few musicians, including John Lewis, the pianist of the Modern Jazz Quartet, encouraged his efforts to put new life into 'modern jazz, once so daring and evolutionary, but which in many ways had become established and conventional' said Coleman). With his white plastic saxophone, he shared his spontaneous creativity with Don Cherry, the bassist Charlie Haden, and drummer Billy Higgins, who provided classic tempo. Going even further out, his manifesto-record *Free Jazz* (1960) was an absolute bombshell of liberated music. The musicologist Gunther Schuller once said that 'His musical inspiration operates in a world that is not confined by conventional bars, usual chord changes or the beaten track.' After two years of inac-

Ornette Coleman

tivity, he came back with a trio, with Davis Izenzon and Charles Moffett, playing trumpet and violin in an unorthodox style that had many people gritting their teeth.

Controversial as an improviser, Ornette Coleman was accepted more readily as a composer. In 1972 he created a piece for his quartet and a symphony orchestra, *Skies of America*, constructed according to his theory of 'harmolody', which considers all melodies, harmonies and rhythms as equal. He went on to make use of electric instruments (two guitars and two basses) in Prime Time, where he mixes Free Jazz, rock and funk.

In Ornette Coleman's own words:

'Harmelody allows everybody to be an individual, who does not have to imitate anybody else ...'

Steve Lacy

1934, New York

A high-pitched low note

From the soprano saxophone, of which he was the greatest expert since Bechet, he made an instrument of shrieks and contrasts.

Steve Lacy entered the jazz world as an adolescent, through photography, taking pictures of musicians who ended by dragging him after them. From this original approach, he has retained a visual dimension which appears as much in the scrupulous design of the sleeves of his albums as in his constant interest for painting, and notably for the magic world of Paul Klee. Like the latter, he transcends fashions and styles by his direct access to the essential, which some take for naivety. From his first discs, his legendary *Jaguar Sessions* in 1954 with the trumpeter Dick Sutton, his music traces the shortest way between Dixieland and music improvised on a razor's edge. It was after listening to Ellington's 'The Mooche', recorded by Sidney Bechet in 1941, that Steven Lackritz (his real name) chose to learn the clarinet, and in Bechet's footsteps he definitively opted for the soprano saxophone. At the beginning of the 1950s, he became a sideman of the best soloists of the *revival* and Swing, from Red Allen to Pee Wee Russell, by way of Rex Stewart, Willie 'the Lion' Smith, Hot Lips Page and Zutty Singleton. He then deepened his musical knowledge at the Manhattan School, and without transition, became the privileged partner of Cecil Taylor, with whom he recorded, precisely, *In Transition* (1955). Taylor became a true 'guide', making him listen to Webern (whose works Steve transposed), Stravinsky, and especially Thelonious Monk, with whom Lacy was to record in 1960. His first record in his own name, *Soprano Today* (with Wynton Kelly), was the first of a long list dedicated to Monk's work, which perhaps he plays better than anyone. He became one of Gil Evans' favourite soloists, and went on to get to know all the great contemporary improvisers, from Miles Davis to Eric Dolphy.

Steve Lacy participated in experiment with Free Jazz with Ornette Coleman, Jimmy Giuffre and Don Cherry. With Cherry he discovered Europe, where he ended up settling at the end of the 1960s first in Italy and finally in Paris. There, he became the centre of an intense activity of musical exchanges between the United States, Europe and Japan, where he stayed regularly. He finally formed a stable group with Steve Potts (saxophone), Irène Aebi (violin, cello), Bobby Few (piano), Jean Jacques Avenel (bass) and Oliver Johnson (drums). His compositions are as many abstract postcards which testify to his tireless curiosity to discover, and he does not cease to expand the limits of his dizzy instrumental exploration.

From the Italian critic Gianni Gualberto

'Steve Lacy's music seems to scatter itself all over the place, because it is made of a continuous juxtaposition of short sequences delivered with the logic of a chess player placing his pieces'.

In Steve Lacy's own words:

'The blues is the carcass, the flesh and the blood of my music. It is implacable and irrepressible, it is both universal and ancient. Why do we make music? One of the basic reasons is to soothe sadness. Perhaps music began with the blues . . .'

The expressionists

Around 1960 the saxophone became the ideal 'megaphone' for the revolutionary aspirations of Afro-Americans. A whole generation (too diversified to be called a 'school'), which had grown up in the golden age of bebop and rhythm'n'blues, followed in the footsteps of Ornette Coleman, John Coltrane and Eric Dolphy, rejecting orthodox instrumental practice, giving priority to volume, length, emotional content and freedom of expression which sometimes bordered on the vertiginous. And yet its roots were firmly planted in jazz.

The Texan **Booker Ervin** (1930–1970) may be considered the forerunner of these saxophonists, with his big rough sound, played in all registers, but with a preference for high notes, and a rapid, exasperated phrasing. He recorded with Mingus in *Ah Hum*, and in *African Cookbook* alongside Randy Weston.

John Gilmore (1931) started off with Earl Hines and Sarah Vaughan, and then became the regular tenor sax player of the Sun Ra Arkestra, but also played for a short time with the Jazz Messengers. He was admired by Coltrane, and is considered a pioneer of Free Jazz, while he is in fact an imaginative exponent of the 'contrasted fluidity' style used by Wardell Gray and Rollins.

Clifford Jordan (1931) is almost a 'twin' of Gilmore's, with whom he studied the tenor sax and made some records between two long periods of playing with Max Roach. He was a prominent figure in the hard bop movement; a lover of blues and African music, he later developed a more aggressive style, playing with Mingus and Dolphy, under whose influence he took up the flute.

Dewey Redman (1931) grew up in Fort Worth in Texas with Ornette Coleman, whom he ended up joining in the 1960s, after many wanderings, and later founded a Coleman-like quartet, Old and New Dreams. But he is not only a historic figure of Free Jazz, as his rather oriental recordings with Keith Jarrett confirm. His

unusual phrasing and very 'oral' tone make him one of the most disconcerting contemporary musicians, on the alto as well as the tenor sax, and even on the African flute known as the musette.

Rahsaan Roland Kirk (1936–1977), who went blind at the age of two, was a polyinstrumentalist: he could play three saxophones at once, sang into his flute, and used a whole range of equipment, from the hooter to the flexaphone. His was a feverish type of music rooted in gospel and blues.

Pharaoh Sanders (1940) is also a rhythm'n'blues progeny, influenced by Coltrane, with whom he played in the last two years of his life, becoming a sort of posthumous missionary, firstly with his widow Alice Coltrane, then under his own banner, full of mystical and exotic references. Based on a sound basic classical technique, his tenor playing represents a fascinating exploration of the extreme limits of the instrument, using harmonics, leaping from one register to another, with dissonant squeaks, brays and roars, he races to the borders of audible sound.

George Adams (1940) embodies a harmonious balance of exploration and tradition, between the fever of the avant-garde and the sweat of city blues with which he started, and which he sings superbly. With Roy Haynes, Mingus, Gil Evans and finally with the pianist Don Pullen, playing both the tenor sax and the flute, he is a real 'showman' with an often hilarious patter.

Wayne Shorter

1933, Newark

A marvellous 'dream blower'

In his admirably chiselled compositions and solos, he explores the timeless land of dreams.

Having replaced the saxophonist Hank Mobley for a tour with Art Blakey's Jazz Messengers, Wayne Shorter stayed with the group from 1959 to 1964, becoming its musical director, revealing his talents as an original composer and soloist who could free himself of the distant Coltranian influences he had revealed in his early work with Horace Silver. And yet it was with some Coltrane musicians (McCoy Tyner, Elvin Jones) that he made his remarkable first recordings for Blue Note. In the summer of 1964 Miles Davis asked him to join his quintet; as he had done with Blakey, he had a considerable influence on

the repertoire, writing most of the new compositions. With themes tending to be minimalist in character, of undulating elegance, performed in unison often with a slightly off-beat timing, Shorter shows his liking for tonal and rhythmic ambiguities, which he handles with the greatest assurance, even in the most frenetic passages of his improvisations, and especially in concert. In 1968 he began to play the soprano sax, mainly because its rather nasal tone provided greater contrast with the new electronic instruments Davis was using more and more. He participated just as much as the trumpeter in the group's evolution towards jazz-rock.

With the keyboard specialist Joe Zawinul, who had also just left the Miles Davis group, Shorter founded and co-directed Weather Report, in an attempt to escape the stylistic constraints and to seek new horizons. His new themes were either ethereal, as in 'Mysterious Traveller', or dance-like and even funky, as in 'Heavy Weather', while in his solos sharp figures or long notes either blend or contrast with the sound layers from the synthesizers.

Around the mid-1970s, Shorter's role as composer for the group became less important, and the members changed constantly. He seemed to enjoy these new encounters more than other musicians of his generation, and made recordings with artists as different as the Brazilian Milton Nascimento or the Italian Pino Daniele. At the request of Herbie Hancock, he then played in the V.S.O.P. quartet, and finally left Weather Report in 1985. Since then he has played mostly in an electro-acoustic environment with young musicians (Geri Allen, Terri Lyne Carrington), with new lyrical compositions that possess the same dreamy poetic quality.

In Wayne Shorter's own words:

'I often ask myself: is what I'm doing worth anything? For me, creating something of value in life is like feeling immortal, you get the feeling of being eternal, and you can live without fear. Music is an illusion, but if you can transform that illusion, turn it into an eternal child, it's fantastic. In other words, I do not make what I am, I am what I make ...'

'I had a telephone conversation with Miles a little while ago: 'We don't really have to play together in the future', he said. 'But what good moments we had, during those six or seven years. You and I, we really brought the house down.' (*Jazz-Hot*, October 1986).

The sax athletes

After Coltrane's death, and partly due to the development of jazz schools, there was a new wave of virtuosos for whom the saxophone was a philosophy and even a kind of religion. Many of them led double lives as studio session players during the day, jazzmen during the night.

Joe Henderson (1937) developed Coltrane's modal style, with great intelligence and infallible swing. Copiously recorded on the Blue Note label, either under his own name or as a sideman (with Horace Silver, Kenny Dorham, Herbie Hancock, Freddie Hubbard, etc.), he contributed greatly to the survival of the powerful but subtle hard bop tenor.

Grover Washington Jr (1943) has been a real 'sax symbol' since the 1970s, whose cuddly sound accompanies plenty of mischief on the back seats of Cadillacs. He was a child prodigy, played a long time with the drummer Billy Cobham, and started piling up Golden Discs ('Winelight', 'Mister Magic') while at the same time reviving some of the great standard ballads ('I Love You Porgy', 'Summertime').

Ernie Watts (1945), like Washington, is a master of the whole range of Selmer saxophones. He is invited to countless pop and soul sessions (from Zappa to Whitney Houston), and is something of a new Earl Bostic, but takes the time to play more improvised music with his own group The Yellowjackets.

David Sanborn (1945) is one of the few current instrumentalists whose sound is immediately identifiable to a vast audience. He too features in hundreds of pop sessions (from Stevie Wonder to Steely Dan), but his own albums enjoy a fair amount of success, thanks to simple, seductive, bluesy themes, and above all due to his very 'vocal' tone both on alto and on soprano sax.

Michael Brecker (1949), a Philadelphian like Coltrane, is probably, with Rollins, the greatest living sax virtuoso. His tenor playing is prodigiously fluid and alert, and integrates the most diverse styles, thanks to an eclectic musical culture which he acquired methodically both from listening to records, and playing rhythm'n'blues and New York jazz, but mostly as a studio musician. For a long time he played with his trumpeter brother Randy in the Horace Silver band, then in the Brecker Brothers Band, then he participated in the Steps Ahead group, experimenting with the EWI (Electronic Wind Instrument), a kind of electronic saxophone. His career as a soloist became more important than his work as a sideman, and has revealed his great maturity as an improvisor, exemplifying the 'all round' tendencies of his generation.

Chico Freeman (1949), son of the legendary Chicago tenor player Von Freeman, embodies that city's 'avant-garde' tradition, and the new generation of the prestigious A.A.C.M. (Association for the Advancement of Creative Music). As a soloist with a strong presence on stage, he is an excellent ballad specialist, who by working on his tone was able to overcome an obvious fascination for Coltrane.

Bob Berg (1951), discovered by Horace Silver, then by Miles Davis, has persevered in the bebop tradition with great dynamism and a remarkable ability to communicate with the rhythm section.

Dave Liebman (1946) is perhaps the most spellbinding and the most complex of the contemporary 'blowers'. He entered the post-Coltrane jazz scene on a red carpet (Miles Davis then Elvin Jones), he is a 'purist' of improvisation, from which he manages to exclude any trace of clichés, and plays with admirably natural swing. Co-founder with his friend Richard Beirach of the Quest quartet, he has shown through recordings and tours that he is one of the best soprano sax players in the history of jazz.

119

The great maestros of three generations of jazz violinists together at the Paris Jazz Festival in 1969, from left to right: **Joe Venuti, Jean-Luc Ponty** *and* **Stephane Grappelli.**

Swing on strings

The adaptation of the violin

The violin entered jazz via different routes. At the beginning of the century, the black *string* band was an essential component of vaudeville and of street music; in the rural areas the fiddler had a choice position in white country music (and later in bluegrass), and also in the blues, before he was ousted by the harmonica player; in urban areas, closer to European traditions and technique, the violinist was the favourite soloist in *ragtime* & *novelty* bands, and in the klezmer music of Ashkenaze origin, which was very popular in New York and the North-East. In the 1920s, the vogue for 'symphonic jazz' earned Paul Whiteman (himself a violinist) the erroneous title of the 'King of Jazz'. In 1929, he hired the man who had become the first great jazz violin soloist, Giuseppe (Joe) Venuti (1894–1978). An Italian immigrant, like his alter ego, the guitarist Salvatore Massaro, alias Eddie Lang (1902–1933), he had developed — from a solid classical background — an ingenious and sophisticated improvisation technique which enabled him to rival the brass instruments with his powerful attack and robust phrasing. A very colourful character who loved tricks and practical jokes and was very fond of the bottle, he made a large number of records, the early ones having considerably influenced the young Grappelli.

From then on, while Eddie South and Stuff Smith developed a more highly syncopated style, and both became great figures on the Afro-American scene, it was in fact a European school that provided jazz with the greatest number of violinists, especially in France, but also in Scandinavia, Poland, and anywhere there were gypsies. From a backing instrument for a number of 'blowers' (the wonderful Ray Nance with Duke Ellington, and also Ornette Coleman), the violin became a formidable source of new and amazing sounds, a far cry from the sticky strings that were used in an attempt to 'whiten' the dirty blue notes.

Stephane Grappelli

1908, Paris

A Montmartre urchin in the court of the Kings

For the whole world he represents the 'French touch in jazz', and a fresh European romanticism livened up by swing.

From his first professional performance in 1918 to the concerts he gave to celebrate his eightieth birthday, Stephane Grappelli has been all over the world with his magic violin, arousing a lasting enthusiasm with the most varied audiences. With his insatiable thirst for life and creation, his lyrical and romantic style, his unfailing sense of swing and improvisation, he has been the most popular jazz violinist for forty years. He was the first, together with Django Reinhardt, to contribute to the rise of French and European jazz, with his Quintette du Hot-Club de France. By adapting the violin to jazz, rather than jazz to the violin, he managed to preserve the classic specificity of the instrument, embroidering (as he says) flowery motifs on

the themes, rather like the shirts he wears, avoiding complacency and routine, and giving a festive air to everything he plays.

In his youth he played in the streets and courtyards of Paris, learning his skills in cinema bands, sometimes replacing the pianist. He made his début in 1927 with Grégor and his Grégoriens. At his second meeting with Django Reinhardt, whom he had already met playing with Louis Vola's band at the Claridge Hotel, they started the famous 'Quintette' in 1934. Staying in London during the war, Stephane played with the pianist George Shearing, and occasionally with Fats Waller and Duke Ellington. On 31 January 1946 he and Django celebrated their reunion in a London studio by recording a swing version of the 'Marseillaise' which they called 'Echoes of France'. The quintet was put together again, but in 1947 Grappelli embarked on a solo career. As a leader of small groups he performed in concerts and festivals, including Newport (1969), Montreux (1973), and several times in Antibes, and was triumphantly applauded at New York's Carnegie Hall in 1974. He was loyal to his accompanists like the guitarist Marc Fosset ('the ideal partner') and the double bass players Jack Sewing and Patrice Caratini, but he occasionally played with the pianists Oscar Peterson and Martial Solal (with whom he made a recording for the first time in 1980) and the guitarists Philip Catherine and Larry Coryell. Fond of crossing 'bows' with fellow violinists, Stephane recorded with Eddie South — a swing version of the first movement of J.S. Bach's *Concerto in D minor* — Joe Venuti, Stuff Smith, Jean-Luc Ponty, Didier Lockwood and Yehudi Menuhin, who was fascinated by this amazing improviser.

With his less well known talents as a pianist, he prefers to interpret the works of Ravel and Debussy.

In Stephane Grappelli's own words:
'I feel freer with Marc Fosset today than I did with the Hot-Club. I am free, I can do what I want . . . I don't know whether it is my age, but I'm in a hurry to play . . . and I'm going to go on like this until my strength fails' (*Jazz-Hot*, March 1985).

'Free jazz is an old friend; we used to do it with Django forty-five years ago; the number of times we went off in total improvisation, with nothing arranged in advance. We would just look at each other, and we would be off, then we would arrive back together' (*Jazz Magazine*, November 1980)

The bows of jazz

On both sides of the Atlantic violinists have taken up the challenge of the brasses
and made their E strings roar and swing.

Nicknamed the 'black angel of the violin', **Eddie South** (1904–1962) was a child prodigy and could have become a classical concert musician, but he chose jazz instead. He was an impressive soloist (due to his technical background, his pure tone, his ease and the lovely way he could make his instrument sing with a delicate sense of swing), and had a fascination for gypsy music, which he studied. He recorded with Grappelli, Michel Warlop and Django Reinhardt.

Stuff Smith (1909–1965) was quite different. Self-taught, with little respect for the instrument which he 'tortured', with a fierce swing and a rough tone, he gave vent to violently expressionistic concepts, the 'mobster of the violin', its 'evil genius'. He was the first to electrify the instrument.

Michel Warlop (1911–1947) developed a passion for jazz around 1930, and met Grappelli when he was with the Grégoriens. He modelled himself on some of the great soloists, and was an imaginative and expansive musician. A pioneer of French jazz, he accompanied Maurice Chevalier, recorded with Django, and put together a string septet based on the classical formula.

Ray Nance (1913–1971), trumpeter, singer, dancer, soloist in Duke Ellington's band (his friends called him 'Floor Show'), was also a brilliant violinist, with a fantastically swinging style imbued with a true gypsy lyricism.

Another showman, the Dane **Svend Asmussen** (1916), 'The Fiddling Viking', a master of many instruments, played (with) the violin with superb technique and humour, flirting gleefully between jazz and pop.

A graduate of the Paris Conservatoire (First Prize for the Violin), **Jean-Luc Ponty** (1942) developed an early interest in jazz, and soon became a new star, in the midst of the Free Jazz and rock wave,

bringing an awaited renewal after Grappelli. With his electric violin he moved away from the traditional French jazz violin, and confirmed his position as a leader in the jazz rock movement, after playing with Frank Zappa and John McLaughlin's Mahavishnu Orchestra (where he replaced Jerry Goodman, an eclectic musician, who was the first to make the violin into a star instrument in rock music). Now living in California, Ponty, a tone specialist, cleverly combines extra-musical effects in the poetical and symphonic dimension, using synthesizers with dazzling virtuosity.

The paths followed by the Poles **Zbigniew Seifert** (1946–1979) and **Michal Urbaniak** (1943) were totally different. The former initially played the alto sax, but took up the violin exclusively from 1970. Influenced by Coltrane, he said: 'I try to play as he would have done if his instrument had been the violin.' Considered an authority on the modern approach to the violin, he died of cancer after a career in which he played with Joachim Kuhn, Philip Catherine, John Scofield, Eddie Gomez, and Jack DeJohnette. Urbaniak, also abandoning the saxophone, and as soon as he settled in the United States, turned to a sort of electr(on)ic jazz-fusion, imbued with the folk traditions of his homeland, until the 1980s, when he reverted to more classical (and acoustic) concepts of the jazz violin. He participated in the recording of Miles Davis's *Tutu*.

Don 'Sugarcane' Harris (1938), whose distinctly rhythm'n'blues and free rock style is strongly influenced by Stuff Smith, performed in the Johnny Otis show, alongside Frank Zappa and the British guitarist John Mayall.

Leroy Jenkins (1932) and **Billy Bang** (1947) took a different approach. Both were involved in the free movement to varying degrees, and ostensibly distanced themselves from western tradition. They strove to achieve the ingenuous style of the early blues violinists, while searching at the same time for new approaches to the instrument going beyond traditional rules and harmony. The former joined the A.A.C.M., founded the Revolutionary Ensemble, and played with Albert Ayler, Archie Shepp and Muhal Richard Abrams, before putting together a group inspired by Ornette Coleman's harmolody. The latter formed the New York String Trio in 1978, performed solo and with big bands, and played with Don Cherry.

Didier Lockwood (1956), of Franco-Scots origin, has kept the great French violin tradition alive since Grappelli and Ponty. In 1979 he symbolically received the violin Warlop had given to Grappelli, which the latter chose to pass on to Ponty. Claiming to have been 'moved and influenced' by Seifert, Lockwood asserted himself as the most impressive violinist of the 1980s, composing original and catchy themes, but sometimes abusing his own exceptional skill by the use of electronic effects.

After a classical training, Lockwood started a jazz rock group in 1973 with his brother Francis, an excellent pianist, who played with groups like Christian Vander's Magma, Zao and Surya, and then with the cream of European jazz musicians. In concert and at festivals, he achieved great success with the public. In 1984 he played with the guitarists Philip Catherine and Christian Escoudé, and in 1986 with the violinists Michal Urbaniak and John Blake.

The double bassist **Didier Levallet** founded the Swing String System (two violins, two cellos and a rhythm section), in which Lockwood played, and which introduced Dominque Pifarely and Pierre Blanchard.

Another facet is **John Blake** (1948) who, after studying in India and with Zino Francescatti, showed himself to be very eclectic within the soul/funk tradition. He played with Archie Shepp, Grover Washington Jr, in McCoy Tyner's group (1979–1983), and with Bobby McFerrin and Wynton Marsalis.

Didier Lockwood *at the New Morning, Paris (1987).*

Europe under hot tension

From the New World to the Old

The transfer of jazz to the Old Continent appears with hindsight as the major cultural event of this century. It was in fact the first time that America offered Europe an art form which owed little to its own influence, even if it was that 'little' that was to make it immediately familiar — the influence of quadrilles, mazurkas and other ancestral dances that were becoming obsolete over here, but which had provided the basic repertoire for the cake-walk and ragtime.

These two forms of 'prehistoric' jazz were the ones that caught on immediately. As early as 1898, the New York show by Willie Marion Cook and Paul Lawrence, *Clorindy, the Origin of the Cake-Walk*, brought thrills to London. Four years later, the *Joyeux Nègres* was a smash hit at the Nouveau Cirque in Paris. Debussy and his friend Satie were enthusiastic for what they saw as the music of the century that had just begun, while Picasso and Braque were fascinated by African sculpture. It was with a delicious thrill of primitivism, somewhat tainted with paternalism, that intellectuals began to cultivate a taste for the 'negro arts', of which jazz appeared as the most exciting. For the general public, things were quite different, and the *fox-trot* simply became the most titillating ingredient in the music-hall, which was then having its golden age. In the orchestra pits of the dream palaces of those crazy years, many musicians became jazzmen due to the demands of their work rather than through a liking for improvisation. But it was not until the 1930s that an avant-garde of enlightened amateurs began to distinguish 'true jazz' from its more or less sterile imitations. From that time, particularly in France, *hot jazz*, as opposed to the socially fashionable *straight jazz*, became a subject of erudite studies and endless speculations as to its authenticity. It was only then that European jazz really took off, and started to acquire a certain independence from its American model.

From music-halls to jazz-clubs

It was obviously through the ports of Western Europe that the invasion began. As early as 1914, the drummer (and minstrel) Louis Mitchell, playing in London, then in Brussels and Paris, was the vanguard of the American troops that came to the rescue of the Allies in 1917, supporting their morale with the all-stars of the very un-military band the *Hellfighters* (of the 369th Infantry Regiment). The band was led by a pianist with the appropriate name of Jim Europe. For his part, the ragtime pianist Joe Jordan landed in London in 1915. He was followed, in 1919, by the Original Dixieland Jazz Band and the Marion Cook Syncopated Orchestra, featuring the trumpeter Arthur Briggs and Sidney Bechet, who were both eventually to settle in Europe.

In Brussels, in 1924, the lawyer Robert Goffin published his poem *Jazz Band* and organized *Jazz Dance Parties* where Belgian musicians tried to reproduce the sound of the records they could find! Belgium, which had first applauded John Philip Sousa's cake-walk in 1881, and also exported the saxophone and quite a few saxophonists, remained a bastion of European jazz, organizing a jazz tournament in 1932, two years before the creation of the Hot-Club de France.

However, Paris in the 1920s also became an intellectual, social and professional centre of attraction for jazz bands which proliferated in different places: private houses, intellectual cabarets, like the famous *Boeuf-sur-le-toit*; classical concert halls, where Jean Wiener invited Billy Arnold, and of course, all the big music-halls. Coming from Saint Louis (Missouri), Josephine Baker landed in Cherbourg in 1925. The incredible fascination she exerted over a whole generation had repercussions on the music which accompanied the swing and brilliance of her dancing, as witnessed by a few minutes of the film *La Revue Nègre*. From the theatre of the Champs Elysées to the Casino de Paris and the Folies Bergère she became the queen of Paris by night, and her irresistible success

carried in its wake the jazz battalions: Pau Whiteman (1926) and his English discipl Jack Hylton (1928), who was to invit Coleman Hawkins to Europe in 1934; Te Lewis and Sidney Bechet (1928); San Wooding, Noble Sissle and Tomm Ladnier, Muggsy Spanier and Jimm Dorsey (1930); Fats Waller (1932 Armstrong (London, 1932; Paris/Pleye 1934); Ellington (Pleyel, 1933); Bi Coleman (1935)...

From 1929 Europe's night spots wer haunted by an amazing figure wrapped i an extravagant cape: Gregor Kelekian, dancer and boxer who had survived th Armenian genocide, whose unconvention band, the 'Grégoriens' brought togethe the cream of young French jazz mus cians... apart from the violinists Grappel and Warlop, there was the trumpete Philippe Brun (1908), a wonderful soloi who magnificently blended the styles Armstrong and Beiderbecke; there we also two remarkable sax/clarinettists: Al Combelle (1912–1978), who perfect assimilated the styles of Benny Carter ar Coleman Hawkins (with whom recorded) and later Lester Young; ar André Ekyan (1907–1972), anoth Armenian whose fluid and elegant sty became a trade mark of European jazz the 30s.

These three relaxed improvisers, wh were nonetheless still very much under t influence of their American idols, all fou themselves, like Grappelli and Warlop, orbit around the genius Django Reinhar but they also played in the many big ban which began to proliferate in the 193 Guy Paquinet, Ray Ventura and his 'C légiens', then Aimé Barelli, Jacques Héli Jerry Mengo... But their main activit were already very much in the jazz fie with the Hot-Club de France, founded 1932 by two Parisian students (Elw Dirats and Jacques Ozenfant), which a racted all those who were to help prom the passion for jazz in Europe: Hug Panassié, Jacques Bureau, Pierre Nour Charles Delaunay and Maurice Cullaz.

From the jazz-club to the festival

The 1930s saw the birth of the phenomenon of *hot-clubs*, which were at the same time more or less musicians' co-operative associations, semi-public discotheques, places for the rehearsal and performance of the few jazz cabaret shows that existed at the time and they even gave birth to some independent recording companies like Swing, founded in 1937 by Charles Delaunay. More important, however, was their role as centres for the study and propagation of 'true jazz' as a noble music, which is evident from the tone of some of the specialized magazines whose role was crucial in this respect: *Music* in Belgium (1929), *Jazz-Tango Dancing* (1930), and later *Jazz-Hot* (1935) in France, *Jazz International* (1934) in Switzerland, and *Music Echo* (1929) in Berlin.

For before the arrival of Hitler, Germany had also become a haven for jazz, where it was integrated with great originality into the repertoires of the Berlin cabaret and dance bands. Strangely, the Nazis were ambiguous in their attitude to 'negro music': banned from the air except in propaganda broadcasts abroad, jazz continued — in a rather sweetened form — wherever the Hitlerian troops went, to titillate the elite of the occupying forces. In France it was even better tolerated in the occupied zone than in the regions controlled by Vichy. . . as long as American titles were avoided: thus *Lady Be Good* became 'Les Bigoudis', *Take the A Train*, 'L'Attaque au Train' and, appropriately for the situation at the time, *Saint Louis Blues* was renamed 'La Tristesse de Saint Louis'. Django Reinhardt, who had several close shaves, became a teenage idol just as nearly a million other gypsies were taken off by train to the death camps. The real horror was that some camps even had their own jazz bands like the Ghetto Swingers (*sic*) which was formed for a visit from the Red Cross at Terezin, only to be gassed later at Auschwitz.

In any case, the Liberation was celebrated to the sound of swing from the grooves of the *Victory discs* that were churned out between 1942 and 1948 (nearly a thousand titles) to support the morale of the allied troops and the starving populations. The big shock came a bit later, when commercial records were unpacked from the Marshall plan supplies, and European Jazz fans discovered to their amazement that, because of the war, they had missed a revolution. . . indeed the bebop did not take long to appear in flesh and blood: Dizzy Gillespie's big band toured Sweden, Belgium and France (1948), then at the first Paris festival (Pleyel, 1949), where 'fans' from all over Europe flocked to hear Parker and Miles Davis, the vocations of a whole new generation of European jazzmen were born or confirmed.

But this was also a great time for *revival*: some of the great pioneers who had unjustly been forgotten were recorded just in time (Jimmy Noone, Tommy Ladnier, Jelly Roll Morton), while others, like Bunk Johnson, Kid Ory, Albert Nicholas and especially Sidney Bechet were 'revived', and embarked on a sort of second career based essentially in Europe, where they found not only ardent support, like the critic Panassié, but also fervent disciples, particularly among clarinetists and soprano sax players: in Britain, Chris Barber and Humphrey Lyttelton; in France, Claude Luter, André Reweliotty, Michel Attenoux and Maxim Saury. . .

This gave rise to what is known jokingly as the 'jazz war' between those Boris Vian refers to as the 'mouldy figs' (trad fans) and the 'sour grapes' (bop freaks), who for most musicians all boil down to the same thing. The only advantage of this polemic was to increase the animation which had already made Paris's left bank the unrivalled jazz capital of Europe, even if European Jazz as such was still in the making. . .

The Euro-jazz decades

It was an alien, musical force, exotic and fashionable, a wartime breath from the New World. But when Afro-American jazz captivated the Old World, the unexpected took root. Jazz found, slowly, a European voice.

The Twenties

There's no doubt that before 1920, some kind of jazz influence began to invade European cities, particularly Paris. Jazz, of course, is essentially an urban art form: in the United States it demonstrated this by finding a focus in New Orleans and Chicago, New York and Kansas City. So one of the first invaders, drummer Louis A. Mitchell, a Philadelphian, first took his Southern Symphonists Quintet to London in 1914. Later visits, in different formats, brought him to Glasgow in 1917 and eventually to Paris where his band played a five-year residency at the Casino de Paris. Syncopated music became part of the 'African style' which influenced painters as well as musicians.

This music has since been described as 'a rough blend of brass band music and ragtime'. But its deviation from the European tradition appealed to a public seeking release from the terrors of World War I yet ironically, it was this war which aided the import of jazz to the Old World through the 369th Infantry Regiment Band ('The Hellfighters') led by the black pianist and violinist James Reese Europe.

Born in Alabama in 1881, Europe became by 1917 the leader of New York's most famous black dance orchestra. He joined the regiment as a lieutenant charged with forming 'the best damn brass band in the US Army', in his colonel's words.

What Europe brought together was more of a travelling minstrel show than a military band. There were jazz players such as cornettist Jacon Frank de Braithe mixed in with dance musicians and bandsmen — with the famous Harlem dance star Bill 'Bojangles' Robinson as drum major. The 'Hellfighters' could produce from within its ranks smaller dance orchestras or theatre bands: apart from military music (freely interpreted!)

the repertoire included everything from cakewalks to novelty items. Its effect upon drab, wartime France during its 2000-mile tour was sensational.

At least two other American regiments formed similar outfits in an attempt to emulate Europe's success. But James Reese Europe is credited with having planted a 'jazz germ' in France which was to grow over the next decade. The leader himself was not there to see it: he died in Boston in 1919, stabbed by one of his drummers.

It was in that year that the all-white Original Dixieland Jazz Band travelled from New York to Britain, opened at the London Hippodrome — and were promptly fired and sent instead on a tour of variety theatres. Their brash energy was too much for politer audiences, but a nine-month stay at Hammersmith Palais established the health of the brawling jazz infant.

In Britain and on the Continent meanwhile, primitive forms of syncopated music were beginning to invade the dance and theatre orchestras. The connection between early jazz and popular theatre was cemented by the 1925 visit to Paris of the American show *Revue Negre*; it was not a success, although the black dancer Josephine Baker stayed on to become a star of the Folies Bergère.

Among the show's musicians was the New Orleans-born soprano saxophonist Sidney Bechet. In an earlier European tour with Will Marion Cook's Southern Syncopated Orchestra, he had been described by Swiss conductor Ernest Ansermet as 'an artist of genius'; but his abiding influence on the European jazz scene was yet to come.

In 1922 the first European jazz club opened in Paris, *Le Boeuf sur le Toit*. Here 'serious' composers like Maurice Ravel and Darius Milhaud were stirred and even shaken by the anarchic sounds of

128

American-inspired local musicians. But European jazz, as such, had not yet found its own voice.

The Thirties

American jazz musicians and orchestras travelled to the Old World in increasing numbers during this decade. Early performers included the Noble Sissle Orchestra with trumpeter Tommy Ladnier, as well as Sam Wooding, Muggsy Spanier, Jimmy Dorsey and Fats Waller. But this was leading up to the 1932 London visit of Louis Armstrong, followed by a European tour, and the two-week booking of the Duke Ellington Orchestra at the London Palladium the following year.

Armstrong had travelled alone (apart from his retinue) and thus had to appear with pick-up bands working from written arrangements. His first group of black musicians from Paris was generally mediocre; but a later British scratch group, including the tenor saxophonist Buddy Featherstonhaugh, filled the bill well.

Thus, in Britain and France, a core of young musicians had emerged whose music was based on the American model. But in 1932, the establishment in Paris of the Hot Club de France — the first jazz club in Europe — turned out to have great significance. Originally a place where students would meet and dance to records, it became a centre of debate on the nature of what was *le vrai jazz*. By 1934 it was able to present the first live concert by the Quintette du Hot Club de France, with the self-taught gypsy guitarist Django Reinhardt and the classically-trained violinist Stephane Grappelli fronting two rhythm guitarists and a bassist. This unique combination delivered the first truly independent European jazz style, one which still has its followers.

An important influence in Britain meanwhile was trumpeter Nat Gonella, who worked and recorded (in the Armstrong style) under such commercial bandleaders as Billy Cotton, Roy Fox, Ray Noble and Lew Stone. His own band, the Georgians, performed in a derivative American style during the late 1930s. Glasgow-born trombonist George Chisholm and fellow-Scot Tommy McQuater, a trumpet player, were among other native-born musicians to develop an impact, while other European countries began to produce their own practitioners — violinist Svend Asmussen in Denmark, Folke Andersson in Sweden, and Theo Mastman's Ramblers in Holland.

But equally important was the rise in Europe of jazz criticism. Ironically, Europeans seemed quicker than Americans to perceive that this music with its new vocabulary of sounds and its development of solo and collective improvisation, was in fact an original art form. During the 1920s, Belgian critic Robert Goffin published an early survey entitled *Aux Frontières du Jazz*; and he was followed in the 1930s by Frenchman Hugues Panassié with *Hot Jazz* and André Hodier with *Jazz: Its Evolution and Essence*. Another Frenchman, Charles Delaunay, became a jazz guru while British musician and arranger Spike Hughes wrote articles which helped to shape understanding of the music.

The Forties

At the outbreak of World War II, the Quintette du Hot Club happened to be in London. Reinhardt and three others returned immediately to Paris but Grappelli, who had no family there, stayed on to become one focus of jazz activity throughout the dark years. He worked with such British musicians as guitarist Denny Wright and pianist George Shearing. Curiously enough, Reinhardt continued to play in occupied Paris, although jazz had long been banned in Germany for anti-American and racist reasons.

Big band swing was then a dominant style. In a curious echo of the 'Hellfighters' of the First World War, the RAF formed a jazz orchestra called the Squadronaires to tour the airfields and raise morale; George Chisholm and Tommy McQuater were among the leading jazzmen recruited for it.

Towards the end of the war, the bebop style was emerging in New York City: but elsewhere a new phenomenon was rising, the revival of the New Orleans style from the pre-1920s and the white dixieland style. Collectively, this became known as the 'trad boom', although there were fiercely-argued boundaries between the 'purists' and others. While there were excellent Continental exponents of this reactionary movement, such as French trumpeter Boris Vian as well as the Dutch Swing College Band, the Roman New Orleans Band and (on a distant limb) Graeme Bell's Australian Jazz Band, the focus lay firmly in Britain.

The fathers of trad were pianist George Webb and trumpeter Ken Colyer, the latter dedicated to the unschooled charm of early jazz. They laid the foundations of a trend which was to occupy centre-stage in Euro-jazz for more than a decade.

The Fifties

It's been estimated that up to 3000 young British musicians, mostly in amateur bands, joined in the revivalist boom of the 1950s. Thus it was a popular movement, producing much music of indifferent quality. But among the leaders in the field who went on to professional careers — often developing their styles beyond the trad formula — were trumpeter Humphrey Lyttelton, trombonist Chris Barber, clarinettist Sandy Brown and cornettist Alex Welsh. In France, clarinettist Claude Luter's contribution was boosted by the return to that country of Sidney Bechet, to settle there permanently.

But contemporary American influence was still at work in Europe and the exciting new direction of bebop spawned many top-class players and bands. In Britain this produced saxophonists Tubby Hayes, Ronnie Scott (who opened a world-famous jazz club in London), Johnny Dankworth, trumpeter and arranger Jimmy Deuchar; in Sweden it produced saxophonists Arne Domnerus and Lars Gullin; and in France the Algerian-born pianist Martial Solal.

One important event on the British jazz scene was the ending in 1954 of a strange union-inspired arrangement which for more than 20 years had made it extremely difficult for American musicians to appear in Britain. At last, British jazz audiences could actually see the rising stars they had only heard on records, and for an entire generation of listeners this was a breakthrough of major proportions.

The Sixties

A decade now opened when Euro-jazz blossomed as never before. Young emergent talents were no longer content to follow an American lead, but explored new paths of their own: and in turn, some Americans came to be influenced by them.

Free jazz — shrugging off the constraints of time and strict harmonic rules — may not have been a European invention. But in Europe it found strong devotees and such outstanding British practitioners as the saxophonists Lol Coxhill, Tony Coe, John Surman and Evan Parker.

Pianist-bandleader Stan Tracey began to record splendid suites which, while inspired by Ellington and Monk, displayed a new European interpretation. The same was true of leader-composer Mike Westbrook, who drew players from the entire European jazz community to perform thoroughly original works, full of power and whimsicality.

Over the previous decade jazz ideas had taken root in South Africa. By the 1960s some outstanding musicians had emerged white and black and thus a source of embarrassment for the government of that time; but their American-influenced music with a distinctively ethnic flavour was happily absorbed into the Euro-jazz mix. Among these emigrés was the white pianist-composer Chris McGregor, saxophonist Dudu Pukwana, bassist Johnny Dyani and the outstanding pianist-composer Abdullah Ibrahim (formerly Dollar Brand).

The Seventies

Several musicians who had already developed individual strands of European style now began to receive due recognition and a wider audience. They were helped in this by the rise of European jazz record labels: and one which gave pioneering commitment to the new music was the German label ECM, founded in 1969 by former bassist Manfred Eicher. Among those he recorded (sometimes in sympathetic American company) were the Norwegian saxophonist Jan Garbarek, the German bassist Eberhard Weber, the Norwegian guitarist Terje Rypdal, the Norwegian bassist Arild Andersen, and the Italian trumpeter Enrico Rava.

Nearly all of these were also composers. Under their influence, Euro-jazz began to absorb folk music influences from Eastern as well as European sources, while South American performers such as Egberto Gismonti and percussionist Nana Vasconcelos introduced new instruments and rhythmic approaches. Rhythms and tonal flavours from rock music, including electronic instruments and devices like tape-loops, were freely adopted.

During the 1970s and into the 1980s, freewheeling experimental music continued to thrive under Europeans who by now had an international reputation — the German trombonist Albert Mangelsdorff (who introduced multiphonics on his instrument), the French virtuoso of the electronic violin Jean-Luc Ponty, the London-based Canadian trumpeter Kenny Wheeler, and the British guitarist John McLaughlin among them.

The Eighties onwards

The diversity of Euro-jazz is deepened by the rise of a new generation with at least three young British saxophonists — Tommy Smith, Courtney Pine and Andy Sheppard — developing independent strands from a Coltrane-inspired starting point. The Dutch *avant-garde* composer and saxophonist Willem Breuker took his iconoclastic Kollektief, with its wittily irreverent and theatrical performances, to tour North America.

In Russia, free expression in jazz had developed in comparative isolation: and now it emerged principally through the powerfully inventive trio led by pianist Vyacheslav Ganelin, with Vladimir Chekasin (saxophone). Ganelin has since emigrated to Israel.

Through the great international web of jazz festivals which developed since the 1960s, the influence of European jazz continues to spread and develop, contributing originality to a world music whose bloodstream is fed by change and adaptability.

Some other European musicians:

Piano: Gordon Beck, Keith Tippett, Charles Loos, Michel Herr, Misha Mengelberg, Jasper van'T'Hof, Bobo Stenson, Joachim Kühn, Wolfgang Dauner, Georges Grüntz, Giorgio Gaslini, Franco D'Andrea, Enrico Piernunzi, Tete Montoliu, Adam Makovicz, Michel Graillier, Michel Petrucciani, Antoine Hervé
Organ: Eddy Louiss
Guitar: Pierre Dorge, Hans Reichel, Bireli Lagrene, Raymond Boni, Christian Escoude, Gerard Marais, Claude Barthelemy, Marc Fosset
Trumpet: Palle Mikkelborg, Franco Ambrosetti, Valeri Ponomarev, Roger Guerin, Jean-Loup Longnon, Eric Le Lann, Paolo Fresu, Tomasz Stanko, Dusko Goykovich

Saxophone: Peter King, Steve Houben, Peter Brötzmann, Maurice Magnoni, Massimo Urbani, Maurizio Gianmarco, Jean-Louis Chautemps, François Jeanneau, André Jaume
Flute: Jiri Stivin
Drums: Han Bennink, Edvuard Wesala, Pierre Favre, Aldo Romano, Bernard Lubat, Andre Ceccarelli
Vibes: Gunther Hampel, Karl Berger
Bass: George Mraz, Aladar Pege, Jean-Paul Celea, Michel Benita, Patrice Caratini
Trombone: Glenn Ferris, Denis Leloup, Yves Robert
Big Band: Vienna Art Orchestra, Lumière (Laurent Cugny), Bekkumernis, Claude Bolling

Tommy Smith

1967, Luton, England

A chief of the young ones

Nurtured in Britain, honed in America, a child of the international jazz generation.

The only hint of 'Englishness' in Tommy Smith is the place-name on his birth certificate. He was still an infant when his family returned north to their roots in Scotland. He was brought up and educated in Edinburgh, but took his youthful musical talent to be honed in the United States. He speaks like an American: but in the voice of his saxophone, the Old World and the New mingle intriguingly. Of the new generation of British jazz players, he is probably the most cosmopolitan as well as being one of the most distinctive in the breadth of his ideas and the lavish tonality he can command.

By the time Tommy Smith won a scholarship to Berklee College in Boston in 1984, he was already a teenage phenomenon in Scotland. He had taken up the tenor saxophone at the age of 12, was soon sitting in with local mainstream bands, but at 15 he appeared on television with Oscar Peterson's bassist, Neils-Henning Ørsted Pedersen. His natural aptitude and excellent ear had been encouraged through a short-lived but highly fruitful jazz 'school' run in Edinburgh by the now-defunct Platform organization: soon some of Scotland's established musicians were calling him up to play, and in 1983 he was recorded with a trio and a quartet by two local record labels. The name of one, *Giant Strides* (GFM), established him as a musical disciple of John Coltrane.

Tommy's offer of a part-scholarship at Berklee came after he sent an audition tape to the college. Vibraphone player and bandleader Gary Burton has told what happened next: 'I first heard about Tommy when his playing caused a sensation among the Berklee students (I'm one of the administrators at the college). I finally heard him play at a special student concert in a group with Chick Corea, who was visiting the college. As we listened to Tommy rehearsing his featured number, Chick turned to me and said: "Burton, you should have that guy in your band. He's perfect for you".'

Thus by the age of 18, Tommy Smith had risen from being a promising young local player to find a foothold on the international jazz stage. His first work with Burton was on a two-week jazz cruise. But at the same time he had already formed his own group and had brought this band, Forward Motion, back to Britain for a short tour — and to a rapturous reception in Edinburgh.

Not only had Tommy's playing developed immeasurably in America, but he had come back sounding somehow more 'European'. The feeling for textures and moods that can be found in the music of, say, Jan Garbarek was now distinctively present in Tommy's work.

By the late 1980s Tommy had established himself back in a Scottish base as one of the young players with a big name on the world scene. He led a succession of groups, often including the even younger London pianist Jason Rebello. He was the subject of TV documentaries, a figure of Eighties 'hip'. A major step came in 1989 when he became the first Briton to be signed as a leader by the Blue Note label, which brought together a stellar American group including John Scofield and Jack De Johnette for the first album, *Step by Step*, playing Smith's own compositions. His second album, the 1990 *Peeping Tom*, with musicians of his own generation, found him in more congenial company; as if the international young community of jazz was saying that *its* day had arrived.

Tommy Smith, *Glasgow Jazz Festival, 1989*

Eberhard Weber

1940, Stuttgart

Five strings and a new sound

He moved the string-bass from the back to the front to give it an inventive role, rarely surpassed.

In an interview published in *Wire* magazine in February 1991, the great German bass player tells how the creation of Euro-jazz seemed from the inside. As a leader in the genre, he takes one of his important musical partners, the pianist Rainer Bruninghaus:

'What I like about his playing is that it is absolutely European. There is no fear of any jazz, so to speak. He *can* play that way, of course, but he's certainly a European musician and he plays in that style, not in the American style of accompanying one hand with the other.

'It's our tradition. It's the only thing we have against the Americans, for example. It wasn't allowed for many years — it always had to be jazz, bebop, everyone trying to copy the Americans. Suddenly, after all these years, the world opened its ears and said, ah, there's another way of playing. I think we need to take care to keep it and not lose it.'

These are important words because they articulate the struggle within a struggle which was the European musician's lot from the 1960s onwards. Weber was a soldier, latterly a general, in a battle which has been resoundingly won, with the myriad strands of European music both influencing the wider world and standing as a separate school.

But Weber, the son of a music teacher, had to find his own way through what was unmapped territory in the 1960s. He started to learn the cello at age six, switching to bass in his teens; and while working as a freelance theatre and TV director in his twenties, his music (with pianist Wolfgang Dauner and later with guitarist Volker Kriegel) moved into areas of free-jazz and jazz-rock.

But he was not happy with the compromise of using the traditional bass instrument with an electric pick-up: nor, it seems, was he particularly attracted to the electric bass guitar. He has told of how, in a second-hand instrument shop, he came upon a dilapidated Italian instrument basically an upright bass without the body designed purely for amplified playing. This became his five-string 'electrobass', the key to his monumental contribution toward the bass role in Euro-jazz.

Under his fingers the bass became a front-line instrument, moving easily between the rhythmic-harmonic role and the carrier of melody and extended improvisation. The mighty, sonorous timbres of the instrument — helped by limited use of electronic devices — has enabled him to give solo performances of great range and power. Equally important are his own virtuoso capabilities of articulation and ideas.

His first recording as a leader, *The Colour of Chloe* (ECM) was received with great critical acclaim, and was a statement of the direction he would continue to pursue. Eschewing the blues roots of American jazz, his way forward blended a sort of flowing romanticism with the creation of evocative tonal soundscapes. His compositions found great expression through his own group, Colours, first formed in 1975, as well as his collaboration in varying formats with the like-thinking saxophonist Jan Garbarek. Weber moves easily into Garbarek's world of misty plaintive and moody sounds, spiced by bass ostinatos and gentle eastern rhythms. In jazz since the 1930s, the bass has provided the key that locks the edifice together: so Weber is a master-key in the European dimension.

Eberhard Weber, *at the Queen's Hall, Edinburgh, 1990*

John Surman

1944, Tavistock

The West-country explorer

His first musical experiences came in the church, as with many of his American peers. A different church: a different result.

One of the most telling sound-images of John Surman can be found on his 1984 ECM album *Withholding Pattern*. It's a piece called 'Doxology', which reflects his musical beginnings as a choirboy at St John's Church, Plymouth, during the 1950s. It is performed on baritone and soprano saxophones, bass clarinet, recorder, piano and synthesizer — all instruments played by Surman and overdubbed, thus emphasizing his strongly individual contribution to European music. And it is produced on a German record label: reflecting the fact that it was on the Continent that Surman received his earliest serious acclaim as a major artist.

Several British musicians have, like Surman, found recognition on the Continental scene, particularly in Germany, while struggling to reach a decent audience in their own country. These prophets with minimal honour have included the clarinettist and saxophonist Tony Coe, and the pianist, composer and bandleader Mike Westbrook. What they had was a hungry urge to move the music onwards into new, original and sometimes complex directions.

So it was inevitable that Surman — and Coe, Westbrook and to a lesser extent Stan Tracey — were once thrown together into an *avant garde* ghetto from which they were allowed to emerge only in the late 1970s.

Like a significant number of modern Euro-jazz figures, Surman emerged from a classical background, the son of musical parents, and studied at the London College of Music. At the same time he became a sideman of the French-born bluesman Alexis Korner, whose influence on the British blues and early rock scene was immense.

At the Montreux Festival of 1968, playing with the Westbrook Orchestra, Surman was voted 'Best Soloist'. During that decade he had also been involved with other musicians whose work spanned the European-American orbit — pianist Chris McGregor, bassist Dave Holland and guitarist John McLaughlin.

During the 1970s, Surman formed two epoch-making small combos. The first, which he called simply The Trio, involved the emigré American bassist Barre Phillips and Stu Martin on drums. On tour, this band collaborated with the German trombonist Albert Mangelsdorff and the Norwegian 'vocalizer' Karin Krog, one of the performers whose jazz-singing took the art beyond the conventional limits of the songstress into areas of pure improvisation. Surman continued his innovative developments with Krog. But in 1973, his next important move was to found the saxophone trio SOS with fellow Britons Alan Skidmore and Mike Osborne.

During the 1980s, Surman continued to enjoy only sparse recognition in Britain although his music was appreciated by a growing band of devotees. But the Glasgow International Jazz Festival appointed him 'Composer in Residence' in 1989, commissioning him to write, perform and lead an instrumental and choral piece in Glasgow Cathedral which he titled 'Ovation'.

Karin Krog, as well as British pianists John Taylor and Gordon Beck, were involved here with the Glasgow Phoenix Choir. It was an event in which Surman touched his roots and his countrymen listened. A rare and rewarding event indeed.

John Surman, *at the Queen's Hall, Edinburgh, 1991*

Humphrey Lyttelton

1921, Eton

How British 'trad' was civilised

Under a questing musician and bandleader, the traditional jazz revival lost its leaden boots and found a spokesman.

The tall, mildly aristocratic figure of Humphrey Lyttelton has been familiar in British jazz for decades. Indeed, in 1988 he was able to celebrate 40 continuous years as a bandleader. He has been able to shrug off the popular image of being an 'old Etonian' and 'ex-Guards officer' jazzman because of two things: the consistent excellence of his playing and — within the broad church of the mainstream style — a readiness to try new ideas and slay, or at least deeply wound, a few sacred cows.

It was in the unlikely environment of the 'top people's school', where his father was a housemaster, that Lyttelton first heard jazz and started to teach himself the cornet. This involvement continued during service with the Grenadier Guards: by 1947, he was able to turn professional, taking the trumpet chair in George Webb's Dixielanders, first formed in 1943 and the spearhead of the coming 'trad boom'. This band's music was marked more by enthusiasm than subtlety with most of those who had been in its ranks unable to read a score. Not many months after joining, Lyttelton left, along with such promising players as the clarinettist-cartoonist Wally Fawkes ('Trog') and trombonist Harry Brown, to form his own band.

In the early days of the British revivalist movement, a curious schism appeared. Writer Jim Godbolt recounts in *Jazz in Britain: 1950-70* (Quartet) how the more 'studious' purist audiences, who felt the music should be listened to solemnly from a sitting position, found themselves confronted with younger devotees who wanted to dance wildly. Lyttelton was firmly on the side of the jivers.

His original playing style on trumpet was in the Armstrong mould. But Lyttelton was one of the first British 'trad' bandleaders to move away from the New Orleans-Chicago idiom of collective improvisation; he replaced the banjo in the rhythm section with a guitar; he introduced an alto-saxophone into his line-up: and both moves were seen as heresy to the more narrow-minded of British jazz followers.

But as a journalist and broadcaster as well as a bandleader, Lyttelton was well-placed to handle this sort of controversy. His own playing began to owe less to Armstrong than to such later stylists as Roy Eldridge and Buck Clayton, while his band's repertoire, through many changes of personnel, moved to embrace pieces from Ellington, Count Basie, and original tunes from English and West Indian folk roots which had no place in the purist book. To general surprise, his quartet version of *Bad Penny Blues* reached the Top Twenty in 1956.

Two years later, Lyttelton set new mould-breaking standards in the British jazz mainstream by employing a three-strong saxophone section — Tony Coe, Jimmy Skidmore and Joe Temperley. The saxophone has played a significant role at various points in 'Humph's' career: for in 1949, during the union-inspired ban on visiting American performers, the great New Orleans pioneer of the soprano saxophone, Sidney Bechet, appeared 'illegally' on stage with the band.

Throughout the 1970s and 1980s, Lyttelton continued to pursue an open policy of mainstream jazz, encouraging new talent generally in sympathy with his own ideals. These have been founded upon the American pre-modernist jazz vocabulary — but spoken with an Anglo-European inflection.

Humphrey Lyttelton, *in the Spiegeltent, Edinburgh Jazz Festival, 1985*

Stan Tracey

1926, London

Arranging the Euro-dream

A bit of Ellington, a bit of Monk. But a man who gave a distinctively European voice to the drama of the jazz ensemble.

The difficulties and the triumphs of Euro-jazz are found encapsulated in the career of pianist, bandleader and composer Stan Tracey. They are summarized in a liner note for a 1985 recording by Tracey's sextet Hexad, written by *Guardian* reviewer John Fordham: 'Stan Tracey, who has been at the forefront of the business for the past three decades and a professional musician for rather longer, was one of those who had the hardest job of all. He belonged to the first generation of British performers who were trying, in those restless, optimistic years after the war, to learn from the inspirations of Charlie Parker, Dizzy Gillespie and Thelonious Monk despite being 3000 miles away from the source, and then develop a style of their own in a culture that had never been hospitable to jazz.'

It's an interesting fact that Tracey, like several other original contributors to the European jazz scene (Garbarek, Brown, Lyttelton), was largely self-taught. This was, in many cases, due to the non-availability of formal jazz teaching when they were young. But with Tracey, as with Brown, the result was an instrumental technique so utterly unconventional that it became a factor in shaping his approach to improvisation: not an inadequate technique at all, but one which seemed to push his ideas into new directions — percussive and explosive bursts and excitingly dissonant interjections.

Stan Tracey started to work professionally at the age of 16: but his first jazz playing — on the accordion, oddly enough — was with a group led in the 1950s by the excellent British modern-style pianist, Eddie Thompson (d.1986). During that decade he also worked with the London-based bands of Ronnie Scott, Kenny Baker and Tony Crombie as well as the Ted Heath Orchestra, a versatile big band whose ranks sheltered several talented jazz musicians from economic hardship.

But one of the most important formative periods for Tracey came between 1960 and 1967 when he was 'house pianist' at Ronnie Scott's Club in Soho. This brought him into playing partnership with many of the top American touring jazz stars, from swing style players like Ben Webster to post-bop modernists like Sonny Rollins.

It was during this decade that Stan Tracey began to emerge as a composer of major significance. His first large work, the *Under Milk Wood* suite, was recorded in 1965 with a quartet including the Scottish-born saxophonist Bobby Wellins. He has gone on to write and arrange highly individual music for bigger ensembles — notably *The Bracknell Connection* and the *Salisbury Suite* for his octet and *Genesis* (1987) for his 15-piece orchestra. Such big undertakings, costly to produce and tour, couldn't be attempted without sponsorship or other funding: so while comparatively rare, they represent the height of Tracey's achievement.

Some of the distinctively European flavour in Tracey's work has been fostered through his duet work, on the fringes of the avant garde, with musicians like the pianist Keith Tippett and saxophonists Tony Coe and John Surman. He has marked his obeisance to Duke Ellington, arranging some of his compositions for the 1968 album *We Love You Madly*. But the under-stated, majestic sweep of his own themes, coupled with his idiosyncratic keyboard style, mark him out as a jazz figure of great individuality.

Stan Tracey, *at the Queen's Hall, Edinburgh, 1988*

Jan Garbarek

1947, Mysen, Norway

Jazz echoes from the North

The inspiration was black and blue: yet his jazz evoked a spirit from the Scandinavian roots of his childhood.

In the 1940s and 1950s, many young musicians were drawn to the saxophone by the sound of the altoist Johnny Hodges; by the 1960s, the bait was John Coltrane.

It may be seen as ironical that Coltrane, a musical hero of black America, should be the inspiration of a saxophonist who placed a firm European stamp on jazz. Yet in its way this was a development waiting to happen. Garbarek was able to distil from the essence of Coltrane a spirit which blended magnificently with his own Scandinavian outlook: a blend of intro-spective moods and haunting melodies drawn from his northern roots.

Critics of this strand of Euro-jazz have called it 'cold' and 'antiseptic'. But surely they ignore its pure foundations in the richness of Scandinavian folk music. Jan Garbarek has explained how he spent time searching the musical archives of Oslo to find the vital spark which sustains his own compositions: a stark simplicity generating huge emotional power.

Garbarek taught himself to play saxo-phone, principally tenor and soprano, and in 1962 — only one year after taking up the instrument — he won a competition for amateur players. He was starting at univer-sity, but dropped out as music inevitably took over his life. The first important groups he worked with, experimental in their approach, included other young emerging Scandinavians such as the guitarist Terje Rypdal and the bassist Arild Andersen.

At this point a second American musician became highly influential in shaping Garbarek's work. This was the composer-bandleader George Russell, who lived in Sweden for five years during the late 1960s and was given many composing and recording commissions by Swedish Radio. He also taught his theory *The Lydian Concept of Tonal Organisation*, on which the trumpeter Miles Davis's modal compo-sitions had been based. Russell's years in Sweden were to have an enormous impact on European jazz, and Jan Garbarek played and recorded with his sextet and orchestra.

The saxophonist made his first recording for ECM in 1970: he has since made more than 30 and his playing style, which record producer Manfred Eicher described as 'ascetic', is one of the most readily identifiable on the ECM palette. He is a creator of moods and textures rather than an improviser who strings together phrases; his musical ideas have been described as 'distilled thought'.

A government grant allowed Garbarek to make his first visit to the United States in 1970. Since then he has worked with several Americans, notably the guitarists David Torn and Bill Frisell, pianists Chick Corea and Keith Jarrett, and the pocket-trumpet player Don Cherry. As a leading 'post-Coltrane' saxophonist he has been highly influential in Britain and some of the subtleties and tonal variety of his playing can be detected, for example, in the work of Tommy Smith. During the 1980s, his collaborations with the bassist Eberhard Weber and the Brazilian percussionis Nana Vasconcelos have been amongst hi most highly-acclaimed performances.

Jan Garbarek, *at the Queen's Hall, Edinburgh, 1988*

Sandy Brown

1929, Izatnagar, India — London, 1975

The wayward man of 'trad'

His inspiration came from New Orleans. But he left behind him music of startling originality, from his own muse.

Jazz is an infectious, communicable music. In the early 1940s, the jazz condition was spread in Scotland mostly through records and a powerful strain of the virus took root in Edinburgh — then a distinctively douce and middle-class city having very little in common with the clamorous American working-class communities which had nurtured the music.

Was it even odder that jazz should find an active following among pupils of the Royal High School? This ancient foundation was then under the control of the Town Council, charging parents small fees for their children's education unlike the bulk of state schools. Therefore it had a slight tang of 'elitism' and of middle-class mores.

Here, in a small way, was an echo of the Austin High School Gang of 1920s Chicago. And the prime mover was an Anglo-Indian pupil, Alexander 'Sandy' Brown, who was later to become one of the most original clarinettists, bandleaders and writers to emerge from the British 'trad boom' of the 1950s and 1960s.

Sandy Brown took up the clarinet in 1941, largely influenced by the late-Twenties recordings of Louis Armstrong's Hot Five and particularly by the weaving New Orleans style embroideries of clarinettist Johnny Dodds. He was determined not to take formal music lessons: and to this, undoubtedly, can be attributed the unconventional, liquid intonation and powerful individuality of his improvised lines. He wrote hilariously

in *The McJazz Manuscripts* (Faber, 1979) of how in his early years 'there were hundreds of self-taught musicians about: skill was short or not even available at all. Coupled with this, the copies (of jazz) were being attempted by middle-class European whites whose grasp of anything to do with African music was impossibly tenuous.'

Among the Edinburgh musicians who played in Brown's early bands were pianist and drummer Stan Greig and trumpeter Al Fairweather with whom he formed a long-running partnership, which took them to London in 1954 leading the Fairweather-Brown All-Stars.

But the Brown and Fairweather combine soon established for itself a special niche for thoughtful and inventive music outside the 'purist' and 'dixieland' camps. As writers and performers, both were open to the influences of West Indian calypso music and African folk styles. At a time when about 60 professional 'trad' bands were on the road, jostling for work, the music played and recorded by Brown until his death in 1975 has remained uniquely adventurous, a spirit of discovery at large in the frequently mundane standards of trad revival.

Brown was one of the most outstanding blues-players to emerge from British jazz. In' the year before his death, he was recorded in New York with such veteran swing-era musicians as altoist Earle Warren, trumpeter Bill Dillard and trombonist Eddie Durham. This came about by accident: producer and writer Albert McCarthy, who had gone across from London to record some distinguished players who had faded from wider recognition, discovered Brown was staying at his hotel. The resulting tracks showed that — if Brown had been spared — he would have had a novel contribution to make to a music which was reaching growing world-wide audiences.

The drum kit kids

Laying down the tempo

As the only instrument actually to have been invented by jazz — the two were synonymous in Europe until the 1920s — the drums or drum kit was probably a rationalization of the 'one man band' of circus or street music. It is generally made up of a snare drum, a pair of tom-toms, a big bass drum and double cymbals (*high-hat* or *charleston*) with pedals, and other vaious cymbals and percussion accessories.

Initially used merely as a 'human metronome', marking two and then four beats, the drummer became a full soloist and percussionist in the 1920s, with the revelation of the first great stylists, Baby Dodds, Sonny Greer, Zutty Singleton, Dave Tough, Walter Johnson, Gene Krupa. In the 1930s, the latter together with Chick Webb, became the first of the great *drummer-leaders*. Big Sid Catlett with Armstrong, and Cozy Cole with both Cab Calloway and Lionel Hampton, invented the *one man show* in big band drumming. They started a tradition later to be developed by Buddy Rich, Sam Woodyard and Mel Lewis, while Jo Jones with Count Basie established the rules that were to make the drums into the 'gadfly' of the entire jazz band.

But it was bebop and Kenny Clarke that finally freed the drums of their subordinate role and put them on a level with the brass, and even (with Max Roach) with the piano. Art Blakey and Roy Haynes further deepened the role of the drums, while Philly Joe Jones and Billy Higgins literally made the cymbals take off. With Elvin Jones, Ed Blackwell or Jack DeJohnette, drumming was no longer a matter of scanning or stressing, it became the multiplication and abstraction of tempo. From then on jazz had left the 'black and white' of rhythm to express the full spectrum of swing.

From the primitives . . .

Often 'understated' in the 1920s and 1930s recordings, their impulsive strokes galvanized soloists and welded orchestras by battering the four beats in sprays of percussion.

The most representative drummer of the New Orleans style, **Baby Dodds** (1898–1959) was also the first important percussionist in the history of jazz. It was thanks to the micro-groove recording *Talking and Drums Solos* (1946) that the power and density of his playing, barely audible in recordings with King Oliver's Creole Jazz Band or Louis Armstrong's Hot Seven, was first appreciated. Military drum rolls, frequent use of wood blocks and cow bells, a pulsating cymbal and traces of his African roots were the characteristics of the first drummer to take *breaks*, thus opening the way for drum solos.

Zutty Singleton (1898–1975) had a major influence in developing the role of the drums, which until then had been treated merely as backing. He was the first to perform a full solo. His playing was diversified and very flexible, with subtle strokes, but also very regular on the bass-drum pedal. He was as rigorous with his timing and the precision of his punctuation when accompanying such different musicians as Louis Armstrong or Roy Eldridge, Sidney Bechet or Charlie Parker, as when turning a solo into a piece of true improvisation. He appeared in films alongside Fats Waller (in *Stormy Weather*) and Louis Armstrong (in *New Orleans*).

In the same line as Dodds and Singleton, **Kaiser Marshall** (1899–1948) came to light in Fletcher Henderson's band (1924). He was one of the first drummers to make regular use of the double pedal action or *charleston* cymbals, and managed to 'tell a story' on the *ride* cymbal, thanks to its wide range of sounds. He was often called upon to play in prestigious bands (Ellington, Calloway), and was regarded as a pioneer by his fellow musicians.

Ben Pollack (1903–1971), from Chicago, was one of the first drummers to lay stress on the down beats, developing this style with the band he formed in California (1926), in which he was joined by Benny Goodman, Glenn Miller, and later Harry James, the swing band leaders. As an innovator, he managed to adapt the Chicago style to the big band, adding to it, for the first time, a string section.

A companion of Duke Ellington's from the very beginning, **Sonny Greer** (1903–1982) stayed with the band until 1951. With his drums and cymbals, and an impressive array of percussion instruments (chimes, bells, tom-toms, gongs), he deployed a whole range of colourful sounds, like a misty haze around the Duke's works. Little heard as a soloist, his support was both firm and flexible, skilfully blending random elements with certainty, fire with elegance, rigour with the spectacular in the band's *jungle* period at the *Cotton Club*, 1927 to 1931.

His thirty years' service with the famous band put this master of sound and forerunner of modern percussionists in the shade, and made him one of the least known and most underestimated drummers in the history of jazz.

. . . to the virtuosos

Promoted to stardom with the big bands, their rolls, 'bombs' and shivers sent the great soloists of the swing era to the halls of fame.

A piece of bravura by the Benny Goodman band, 'Sing, Sing, Sing' gave **Gene Krupa** (1909–1973) the opportunity for a long solo, thrilling the crowds with his virtuosity and his qualities as a showman; at the height of the swing era, the drummer and the drums became, thanks to him, the focus and the star of the band. 'I am happy' he said, 'to have succeeded in making the drummer a top level instrumentalist and to have introduced more people to jazz'. Krupa was not only an exuberant soloist, shown to his advantage by orchestral arrangements, but also a solid accompanist and a perspicacious band leader in the choice of his partners (Roy Eldridge, Anita O'Day, Red Rodney, Gerry Mulligan).

Unrivalled as the King of the Savoy, one of the great dance halls of Harlem, **Chick Webb** (1909–1939), together with Krupa, was one of the first drummers in charge of a band. From 1931 to the death of its leader, his band was immensely popular with dancers. Physically handicapped, perched on the top of the cushions piled on his chair, Webb mesmerized everyone by his infallible tempo, his sense of swing, his drumming strength, the nuances of his tone and especially his way of carrying the band on the tip of his drumsticks. For the most part victorious in these jousts prized by the public, his formation included excellent musicians and arrangers, to whom we owe the famous 'Stomping at the Savoy' and a mischievous 'A-Tisket, A-Tasket', sung by a youthful Ella Fitzgerald.

Capable of playing in the company of musicians as different as Jelly Roll Morton, Dizzy Gillespie, and Charlie Parker, before founding a school for drummers with Krupa in 1954, **Cozy Cole** (1909–1981) was the archetype of the middle-jazz

drummer. The priority he gave to rigour and effect, his impeccable tempo inspired by a shuffle beat, which made it possible to 'create a propitious infrastructure for the support of the soloist', and the sobriety of his always pertinent interventions, which were always pertinent, made Cole the swinging master of the big drum and dry, fast drum roll.

The first to consider the drums as a melodic as much as a rhythmic instrument. **Big Sid Catlett** (1910–1951), who had colossal fists in which drumsticks looked like tooth-picks (according to the description of the drummer, Moustache), was not only one of the most complete drummers of the 1930s and 1940s, but also the inspirer of the rhythmic revolution to come. He, too was at ease in all the instrumental styles from New Orleans to bebop, and personified the transition between classical and modern by his combinations of tone and rhythm.

Another great middle jazz figure **Jo Jones** (1911–1985) was a drummer, but first and foremost a musician. The first advocate of the *four beat* from which stemmed not only his feline agility, his fluid style and his relaxed approach, but also his unequalled regularity as an accompanist, and the dynamism and dynamite of his effect on the band. Marvellous at manipulating drumsticks and brushes, sometimes caressing or slapping the skins with his bare hands, 'Papa Jo' was a brilliant soloist, and the source of exceptional sounds. In Basie's band, (from 1935 to 1948), he formed, together with the Count, Freddie Green and Walter Page, 'the best rhythm section in the world'. Of the 1500 records he made, only five were recorded under his name as leader.

Kenny Clarke

1914, Pittsburgh — Paris, 1985

The liberator of the drums

Rediscovering the polyrhythmic genius of Africa, and mastering the four elements of the drums, he made them an out-and-out solo instrument.

With him, drums made a radical entrance into the modern era at the beginning of the 1940s. A partisan of the first jazz revolution, inventor of bebop drums, the father of all the modern percussionists, 'Klook' (his nickname) overthrew the concepts of jazz which until then had relied on the big drum, with punctuation from the cymbals. He inverted their roles. His tempo was marked on the big *ride* cymbal, proliferating into a chabada and a constant 'ding ding' with a most flexible pulse, while punctuations and accents were assured by the side and bass drums, the latter releasing what he called 'bombs' which were most stimulating to he soloist. Thus the drum became an instrument which belonged to the concert and was no longer merely for dancing, freeing the double bass at the same time, which also became a solo instrument.

Kenny's innovations first attracted attention in the band of Teddy Hill (1939–1940), who entrusted him with the task of forming the combo to animate the famous jam sessions of *Minton's Playhouse*, a true laboratory of bebop. There he met the greatest innovators of the moment, married the singer Carmen McRae, played the trombone in the army, and then accompanied Billie Holiday and Sarah Vaughan, before joining Dizzy Gillespie's big band (1946). Freelance from 1949 to 1951, he often performed with Pierre Michelot, before he joined the Modern Jazz Quartet, which he left in 1954 'because', he said, 'I cannot limit myself to playing chamber music'.

Kenny Clarke settled in Paris in 1956, where he belonged to Jacques Hélian's band. He recorded the music for the film *Ascenseur pour l'echafaud* with Miles Davis, played at the *Club-Saint-Germain*, and became the permanent drummer at the *Blue Note* club in Paris from 1959 to 1966. He co-directed the Clarke-Boland Big Band for ten years from 1961, which was composed of international stars and European musicians, he played and recorded with both musicians passing through, and those who lived in Paris (Bud Powell, Johnny Griffin, Lee Konitz, René Thomas), and opened a school for drummers in 1967 with Dante Agostini. He became passionately interested in teaching. After twenty years of absence, he returned to the United States in 1977, and was moved to see the respect and interest he aroused in young musicians.

In Kenny Clarke's own words:
'When I played in Teddy Hill's band, I alternated with Chick Webb at the *Savoy Ballroom*. — When our set had finished, I used to sit down behind him to watch him and listen. In 1939, we played at the World Fair in New York. Chick came backstage and said to me' 'Well kiddo, you've come a long way, you play better and better every day. Fantastic!' This compliment was one of the elements which really proved to me that I was making progress. In all my life, it was one of those which gave me the deepest pleasure. (*Jazz Magazine*, March 1985).

Art Blakey

1919, Pittsburgh — New York, 1990

A major drum, an essential message

Pioneer of bebop, peerless discoverer of new talent self-taught and athletic, and the most 'Afro' of the drummers.

For more than thirty years, Art Blakey was at the forefront of the modern jazz scene, since his name was first associated with the Jazz Messengers, whose leader he became in 1955. This was one of the rare groups which was popular with the general public in the States and in France from the moment of its arrival in 1958.

The leading figure, with Horace Silver, of the hard bop style, and the *funky* movement of the 1950s, Blakey, who admired Chick Webb and declared he owed all to Kenny Clarke, was an extremely powerful drummer, madly impetuous, whose impressive rrrrrolling (*press roll*) indicated to musicians a change of tempo or

In Art Blakey's own words:

'We like to use a tempo that gets the audience tapping its feet, having fun. If they've forgotten how, we let the people feel they should learn something and they did not come for that. Music is there to chase away the dust of daily life . . . For me the stage is a Holy Land. You go there to play. If a musician gets up from his deathbed, it's to play.'

'We were the first to record live in public with *A Night at Birdland*. When I first suggested it to Blue Note they thought I was crazy; I just wanted that 'feeling' (*Jazz Magazine*, March 1988).

soloist, whose brusque and surprising silences or thunderous interventions were stimulating, enlivening and renewing for the soloist, and the whole band.

A master of polyrhythmic colour and form which came straight from Africa, he was the first drummer to go to Africa in search of his distant roots, and to study African rhythms and percussion techniques. He became a Muslim, and took the name of Abdullah Ibn Buhaina. His great skill showed in his use of *double time*, where the drummer plays at double the time played by the soloist. Originally a pianist, Blakey started drumming because he was forced to, as he explained: 'I became a drummer the day a gangster held a gun to my head and said "You wanna work here, kid, get with the drums and shut up."'

In 1939 he joined Fletcher Henderson's band, worked with Billy Eckstine's big band from 1944 to 1947, and got to know the young bebop musicians. In 1957 he recorded several masterpieces with Thelonious Monk, playing in trios or small ensembles (they were such a good match that they continued to meet regularly over the years for recording sessions until the pianist's last ones in 1971), and then organized a rehearsal band called The Seventeen Messengers with Miles Davis and Fats Navarro. After playing in Buddy DeFranco's quintet, he formed his first quintet for a legendary concert at *Birdland* in 1954 with Clifford Brown, Lou Donaldson, Horace Silver and Curley Russell. This became the Jazz Messengers, an ensemble with a variable composition which was a tremendously fertile breeding ground for young talent, and introduced many of today's great musicians.

At the beginning of the 1950s, Blakey made some duo recordings with the Cuban bongo player Sabu, and organized sessions for drummers and percussionists under the name *Orgy in Rhythm*.

The Jazz Messengers

'If we see some people not marking time with their feet or head when we play, then we know we are not doing it right. Because each time our message gets through, heads and feet start to move . . .' (Art Blakey in 1958).

The jazz of Art's Messengers was a superbly generous hard bop, completely unintellectual, which plunged frantically back to the roots of jazz, blues and gospel, imbued with black church singing, which appealed to both body and soul, and also carried some racial connotations. 'Our music is a statement against all the humiliations and injustices we have known for generations' said Blakey. The following are only the musicians whose creativity appears to us to have had a decisive influence on this ensemble which, thanks to the driving force of Art Blakey, was still sending messages right until his death in 1990.

Horace Silver (1928) made a recording in 1952 in a trio with Gene Ramey and Art Blakey. This meeting was decisive, and by 1954 Silver became the first pianist and musical director of the Jazz Messengers. With a style reminiscent of Bud Powell and Thelonious Monk (whom he resembles harmonically and in his manner of striking the keyboard), he became the main exponent of funky jazz, reviving certain aspects of boogie-woogie, aiming with the insistant repetition of short riffs at a sort of trance, a tension in which he reaches a paroxysm with complete physical involvement.

He wrote numerous compositions with a strong blues and gospel flavour, including 'The Preacher', 'Doodlin', 'Opus de Funk', and 'Senor Blues'.

Hank Mobley (1930–1986), who joined Silver and Blakey in 1954, was the first saxophonist in the Jazz Messengers, before joining Miles Davis. With his relaxed, intimate style and his mellow tone, Mobley was the 'coolest' of the hard boppers.

Benny Golson (1929), a prolific composer, wrote the themes that made the Messengers famous in the 1950s and 1960s, the 'Blues March', 'Moanin', and 'Whisper Not'. He was the musical director of the group in 1958. This tenor sax with baroque phrasing and a big, fruity sound, knew how to temper his fiery style in melodic ballads with a melancholy flavour, like his tribute to Clifford Brown, 'I Remember Clifford'.

The trumpeter **Terence Blanchard** (1962) took over from Wynston Marsalis in 1982, and was musical director until his departure in 1986. Together with the saxophonists **Donald Harrison** and **Jean Toussaint**, and the pianist **Mulgrew Miller**, he perpetuated the spirit of the group and contributed to its development with some daring pieces under the benign, watchful eye (and ear) of Papa Blakey.

A single touch of the cymbals is enough to recognize the unique sound of **Max Roach**.

Max Roach

1925, New York

The melodic rhythm man

This master of multiple sounds remained loyal to marching rhythms, proclaiming his rebellion blow by blow.

While developing a classical drumming style and assimilating Kenny Clarke's innovations, Max Roach was the first to use the drums as a 'melodic' instrument by composing musical solos, real rhythmic phrases with enormous tonal variety. Like an architect of sound and rhythm, he was the first to swing on the drums in 3/4 time and other unusual tempos for jazz (5/4 with 3/4), or to superimpose complex figures with tremendous rigour, infinite precision and a brilliant use of silences.

An established drummer by 1942, he would occasionally stand in with Ellington or Basie, and in 1945 he took part in the historic sessions with the Charlie Parker quintet. He was in Toronto on 15 May 1953 for the concert where Parker, Gillespie and Bud Powell played together for the last time, with Charles Mingus. There followed a long period of collaboration with Clifford Brown, with whom he co-led one of the most famous hard bop groups (1954–1956), and Sonny Rollins, including making a record which consisted of nothing but waltzes, *The Freedom Suite*. From 1960, he introduced an element of politics in his art, as witnessed by *We Insist — Freedom Now Suite*, a work which to some extent belongs to the Free Jazz movement, and is a homage to black students, Africa, and the singing cries of his wife, the singer Abbey Lincoln.

In September 1962 he recorded *Money Jungle* with Ellington and Mingus, a magnificent meeting of three great pioneers, and returning to his quintet formula, produced *Drums Unlimited* in 1966.

Between 1970 and 1976 Max Roach refused to record in the States as a protest against the economic exploitation of musicians, particularly as a result of re-issues, and spent much of his time teaching. In 1970 he formed M'Boom Re: Percussion, a ten-piece percussion orchestra (with bells, marimbas and timbales), while also playing with his own quartet (Cecil Bridgewater, trumpet; Odean Pope, tenor saxophone; Calvin Hill, bass), with the occasional addition of a string quartet. Since 1976 he has had a series of collaborations with musicians mostly involved with the free movement like Archie Shepp, Anthony Braxton and Cecil Taylor. Together with Eddy Louiss, Bernard Lubat, Manu Dibango and Salif Keita, he played for the liberation of Nelson Mandela.

> **In Max Roach's own words:**
> 'When I had to go by subway from Brooklyn to the Manhattan School of Music, I used to get lots of ideas hearing the wheels clattering along. It's incredible the rhythms a subway can create when you're interested in percussion . . .'
>
> 'The first drummers, 'Poppa' Jo Jones, Buddy Rich, etc., were tap dancers. And good ones; Philly Joe especially. So am I, actually . . . it was kind of inevitable. It was good for the feet . . .'
>
> 'The American drummer is a one man percussion orchestra' (extracts from *Jazz Magazine*, April, May, June 1988).

The hard and the soft

Liberated from the ghetto of tempo, with a demanding and powerful voice of their own, the great modern drummers are the masters of contrast and suspense.

Shelly Manne (1920–1984), a New Yorker, became the most famous West Coast drummer in the 1950s. He was appreciated for the fine subtlety of his playing, was a virtuoso on the brushes, and rejected the spectacular side of the instrument, preferring 'to play softly, giving meaning to what one plays, developing rhythm while thinking of the melody', instead of the other way round.

Chico Hamilton (1921) evolved an intimate and refined style with the groups he formed, with the original inclusion of the cello, after playing in Gerry Mulligan's famous quartet. With a continuous sizzle of cymbals, he creates a rich, subtle and flexible musical environment.

'Philly' Joe Jones (1923–1985) owes his reputation to the duo he and the bassist Paul Chambers formed in the Miles Davis quintet between 1955 and 1958. Filling the gap between Blakey and Roach, between bebop and modern jazz, he was a model of precision and balance. He was a master of the rim-shot, a specialist of the constant chabada, and the first to make an irregular use of the charleston pedal.

Roy Haynes (1926) is a rigorous rhythm specialist with a snappy punctuation on the snare drum and a thudding tone associated with the sound of quivering cymbals. In his career, which lasted forty years, he accompanied most of the top jazz musicians, from Lester Young to Chick Corea.

Ed Blackwell (1929), influenced by the percussion players of his native New Orleans, distinguishes himself by the way he plays the snare drum, his great sense of melody, and his interest in traditional African rhythms. He replaced Billy Higgins in Ornette Coleman's quartet in 1960 and was often to be found with the saxophonist Don Cherry (the duos *Mu* and *El Corazon*) Dewey Redman and Charlie Haden, in th group Old and New Dreams.

Paul Motian (1931), a sophisticate percussionist, expert with the brushes an indispensable partner to both great (Evans Bley, Jarrett) and young pianists alik (Geri Allen, Eric Watson) has since 197 led groups with no piano out of the heart c which has come the warm lyricism of Jo Lovano (tenor saxophone).

Billy Higgins (1936) is an accompanis drummer par excellence who, since th 1960s has perpetuated the tradition c rhythmic continuity with a wholl individual cymbal sound, has played wit the greatest jazz musicians, from middle jazz to free, and from Dexter Gordon to Pa Metheny.

The faithful companion of Charle Mingus since 1956, **Dannie Richmon** (1935–1988) was the indispensable elemen which held together the groups of th double bass player until his death. Fror time to time, he accompanied the singer Joe Cocker and Elton John, and played i the George Adams–Don Pullen quartet a well as in the Mingus Dynasty group.

When he was twenty, **Daniel Humai** (1938) left his native Switzerland an settled in Paris, accompanying the grea American soloists passing through, befor performing with René Urtreger, Pierr Michelot and Martial Solal (1960–1965 He is a virtuoso who developed an origina style, and carved himself a place among th greatest drummers in the world. He playe with Jean-Luc Ponty and Eddy Louiss (th HLP Trio), Phil Woods (the Europea Rhythm Machine), with Michel Porta and in trios with François Jeanneau an Henri Texier, Joachim Kühn and Jear François Jenny-Clark.

Elvin Jones

1927, Pontiac

A powerful dancer

A soloist 100 per cent of the time, he abolished the bondage of the accompanist to turn drumming into a wild and complicated ballet.

The younger brother of pianist Hank and trumpeter Thad, Elvin Ray caused a worldwide upheaval in the concepts of drummers, pursuing the emancipation of the drummer's role which had been initiated by Kenny Clarke, and developed by Philly Joe Jones and Max Roach, all three pushing bebop drums into a corner.

Self-taught, Elvin played with his brothers from the age of twelve. He attracted attention at the Newport Festival in 1955 playing with Charles Mingus. He played with Bud Powell, accompanied numerous musicians (Pepper Adams, Donald Byrd), recorded with J.J. Johnson, Sonny Rollins (*A Night at the Village Vanguard*), Miles Davis and Gil Evans, before John Coltrane called on him in 1960. Apart from a brief interruption in

1963, he remained for nearly six years with the famous quartet, only leaving it when Coltrane wanted to add a second drummer, Rashied Ali.

Stand-in drummer for Duke Ellington's band on a European tour, Jones only stayed four days. He then got various groups together, including Joe Farrell, Steve Grossman, Dave Liebman, Azar Lawrence, Pat LaBarbera, and started a series of tours all over the world. In 1975 he recorded in a trio with McCoy Tyner and Ron Carter, and formed the Elvin Jones Jazz Group at the beginning of the 1980s.

Gifted with exceptional power, Elvin broke with the tradition of continuous tempo. He abandoned drumming as a rhythmic unit, and invested all the elements of percussion (which no longer had clearly defined functions) in vehement and prolific polyrhythms. He created unusual, complex structures, which interlaced, tumbled over each other with rapid changes in speed, upheavals, and palpitations, which sent the simple rhythmic beat flying in all directions. He backed the soloist, and in particular at the time of his Coltrane craze (1963–1965), produced a river, a tornado of sound absolutely unprecedented in jazz. This did not prevent him from showing a swirling sweetness with the brushes in the record *Ballads*. His contribution determined the evolution of Coltrane's music, pushing the saxophonist to the limits of the possible, and he had a huge influence on the next generation.

Apart from his tours, he sometimes played in schools and prisons, and appeared in several films, including a short film dedicated to him, *Different Drummer*.

In Elvin Jones' own words:
'I've never felt that I have nothing left to learn. Moreover, there's always something that resists you, and you wonder how to get on top of it. That's exactly what makes drumming so passionately exciting. In fact,. every performance should be taken as a new challenge'.
(*Melody Maker*, December 1972)

Tony Williams

1945, Chicago

Life's tempo

Surmounting the binary divisions of time, he reinvented the art of galvanising a soloist by driving him on from all sides.

'He is seventeen years old' André Francis emphasized when introducing Tony Williams, the new drummer of the Miles Davis quartet on July 26, 1963 in Antibes.

Everything happened very fast for the little boy who, at the age of eight, played the drums in his father's band, and who was to have jam-sessions with Art Blakey and Max Roach after studying at the Berklee School of Music in Boston with Alan Dawson. He was 'discovered' by Jackie McLean, with whom he recorded *One Step Beyond* (April 30, 1963), and joined Miles a month later. He became famous as the symbol of modern drumming for the 1970s generation.

Respecting the traditional role of the instrument, and attached to the beauty and

purity of its sound, Tony excelled in particular in his use of 4/4 on the charleston cymbals, which he often kept open, and his refined use of the tom-toms, giving each percussion element its own tonal treatment, its own vocabulary. Proceeding in sound waves, by patches of sound, he nevertheless set a subtly suggested fixed tempo (Eric Dolphy, whose drummer he was for the record *Out to Lunch*, said that 'he does not create a tempo, but a pulse'). In these purely binary contexts he demonstrated his great metronomic regularity; in 1968, he reinvented the binary drums on Miles Davis's *Filles de Kilimanjaro*, and was to contribute to the birth and the evolution of the music which later became known as jazz-rock.

In 1965, Tony Williams recorded the records *Spring* and *Lifetime*, of which the saxophonist Sam Rivers, who participated in the recording declared, 'Whatever the fascination of his technique, one is always conscious of the sensitivity and feeling it expresses.' In 1969, having left Davis, he formed the group Lifetime with guitarist John McLaughlin and organist Larry Young (the records *Emergency* and *Turn It Over*). His Lifetime ensemble experienced a turnover of members, after a pause between 1972 and 1975, and eventually succumbed to a lack of commercial success. He reappeared with Gil Evans, McCoy Tyner, Sonny Rollins, before he became an integral part of the V.S.O.P. Quintet of Herbie Hancock in 1976. He took courses in composition at Berkeley University, joined the pianist Hank Jones and Ron Carter for the Great Jazz Trio, and invited jazz players of all styles, from rock to free, from Stanley Clarke to Cecil Taylor, to play in his *The Joy of Flying*. Since 1980, he has divided his time between modern jazz and jazz fusion.

> **In Tony Williams's own words:**
> 'I like the drums to sound like drums. In recordings, the sounds of the producer and the engineer can be heard, almost never the drummer. In the sound-booth, they need to hear certain things. And it ends by having nothing in common with what the drummer wants to hear ... One is always hidden away at the back of the stage, behind the drums ... it is hard for the public — and for the other musicians — to consider the drummer as a leader. In addition, for a long time we were considered as the least intelligent of the lot, those who were paid the least ...'

A historic trio of Jazz Messengers: **Art Blakey**, **Horace Silver**, *and* **Kenny Dorham** *(1955)*

The hard-hitters

Overtaking the false binary/ternary dilemma, a new breed of powerful drummers has taken over, who reconcile their energy with polyrhythms and melodic percussion.

Having played with the Brecker Brothers (in the Dreams group) and with Miles Davis, **Billy Cobham** (1944) helped to create John McLaughlin's Mahavishnu Orchestra in 1971, which revealed this pioneer as a virtuoso of binary drumming. A double bass drum, numerous tom-toms, an impressive array of cymbals including the one known as the 'Chinese block', and electronic effects, were all part of the attraction of this bruiser with exceptional speed and spectacular pyrotechnic solos.

Al Foster (1944) who was self-taught, played in various contexts from his debut (1960) until 1972, when he became drummer for Miles Davis, who appreciated his vigorous but sensitive accompaniment, his intuition and his subtlety. During the trumpeter's retirement from 1975–1980, he accompanied bebop pianists, and played with Sonny Rollins and McCoy Tyner, before returning to tour with Miles until 1985, adapting perfectly to the new orientation chosen by his friend.

The former partner of Albert Ayler, Ornette Coleman and Cecil Taylor, **Ronald Shannon Jackson** (1940), whose music is somewhere on the edge of rock, funk and Free Jazz since the creation of his group The Decoding Society, is a poly-rhythmic player at the height of power and precision, who was also to be found playing with the guitarist James Blood Ulmer in the Music Revelation Ensemble.

Jack DeJohnette (1942) studied clas-sical piano before hearing Max Roach led him to choose drums. He started in the blues groups in Chicago where he was born, frequenting the A.A.C.M. musicians. Until 1969, he worked with Jackie McLean, Charles Lloyd (when he met Keith Jarrett), Bill Evans and Stan Getz, and then joined the Miles Davis group,

which he left in 1972. His contribution was to be as decisive in the evolution of the group as it was in the evolution of his own style. He is one of the rare drummers capable of uniting ternary and binary rhythms (always relaxed on either side of the beat), combining the melodic elegance of a Roy Haynes with the polyrhythmic richness of an Elvin Jones. He formed several groups: Directions (1975), which was on the fringe of the fusion movement, New Directions, Special Edition and Gateway, playing more varied forms of music. Since 1986, he has been playing in the Keith Jarrett trio alongside the bassist Gary Peacock.

A typical studio drummer who works in different contexts (accompanying Stevie Wonder, Paul McCartney or Barbra Streisand), **Steve Gadd** (1945) has become a technical reference for the younger generation of drummers. His style is characterized by the dry strokes of his almost metronomic tempo. He first gained acclaim in the group Stuff, was one of the founders of Steps Ahead, and now tours since 1988, with his own Gadd Gang.

In the bands of Stan Kenton, Maynard Ferguson and Jaco Pastorius (Word of Mouth), or in the jazz-rock groups Weather Report (1978–1982) and Steps Ahead (1982–1986), **Peter Erskine** (1954) demonstrates the qualities of an all-round musician, a modern drummer. Open to technical innovations (musical soft-ware) he incorporates sophisticated electronic material into the traditional percussion elements which he uses with relevance. Also a composer, he has written stage music for Shakespeare's *Richard II*. In 1988, he played with John Scofield and Bill Frisell in bass player Marc Johnson's group Bass Desires.

Masters of the vibes

The rise of the vibraphone

No modern instrument has remained so close to its distant or immediate ancestors, from prehistoric lithophones to marimbas from Central America, passing by gamelan orchestras from Bali, and of course African balafons. Xylophones and metallophones have been a favourite accessory of jazz drummers since the 1920s. They naturally evolved towards the contemporary vibraphone, that magnificent airy-sounding invention which is in fact very 'solid', also called the *vibra-harp* in the U.S., or simply *vibes*. It consists of a double chromatic keyboard with metal bars. Beneath these bars are resonators, in which discs are set spinning by an electric motor. Duration of notes is also controlled by a damper pedal, which sustains notes and gives them a vibrato effect, and which forces the soloist to remain in an uncomfortable position, absolutely in keeping with the extreme ambiguity of the instrument.

It is not surprising that it should be a pianist-drummer (a rare combination) who gave it its title of nobility. In 1930, Lionel Hampton recorded the first historic vibes solo with Armstrong, which became the archetype of its kind. His lyrical and powerfully dynamic style even provided, beyond the originality of what was still a gadget, a sort of yard-stick for the swing to which the critic Hugues Panassié quite rightly often referred.

It was however, from a totally different example, the xylophonist Red Norvo, that the tonal concept and the structure of the 'vibraphonic language' evolved in the 1940s. After him, most of the masters of the instrument — whose names, astonishingly, almost all rhyme with 'on' — developed a multi-functional approach which made it a real rival of the piano as the harmonic nucleus of the band, through a more and more complete use of its exceptional potential by playing with four, and sometimes six mallets, controlled percussion, high frequency friction and vibration, which gives meaning to the etymology of the instrument by coming closer and closer to the vibrations of the voice.

Lionel Hampton

1909, Louisville

An wonderful player of blue notes

Even at eighty, he made everything he touched vibrate, and everything he played swing in an irresistible ringing.

On October 16, 1930, the young vibraphonist of the Les Hite Orchestra recorded his first solo on the vibraphone with Louis Armstrong. Lionel Hampton became part of the jazz legend by making the vibraphone a solo instrument. Shortly afterwards, he formed his first group, and in 1936, Benny Goodman engaged the already 'hot' musician, who played in his band and in a quartet with Teddy Wilson, Gene Krupa and the clarinet player. They had immediate success. The concert at Carnegie Hall in 1938 was triumphant. The R.C.A. Victor company opened its studios to him, and from 8 February 1937 to 8 April 1941, sixty-odd titles were recorded with the greatest soloists from the

---

In Lionel Hampton's own words:

There was a vibraphone in the studio and Louis Armstrong asked if anyone knew how to play it. I was young, and I said "I do". At the time, the vibraphone was quite new, I had never seen one. Armstrong asked me to play to him, and I played one of his own solos, note by note! I transposed to this instrument what I had learned from the keyboard, the xylophone and the drums. Armstrong was pleased, and so we recorded a piece that Eubie Blake had just composed for him, "Memories of You" ' (Interview with Gérald Arnaud and Maurice Cullaz, January 1985; about the session on October 16, 1930).

---

bands of Basie, Ellington, Goodman, Lunceford, Hines (Charlie Christian, Cootie Williams, Dizzy Gillespie (pre-bebop, Harry James, Benny Carter Johnny Hodges, Coleman Hawkins, Ben Webster.)

At the drums or the piano (he played in the upper reaches of the keyboard, basing his index fingers on the keys like the mallet on his vibraphone, which he used all the time), Lionel, a formidable swing player and inventive improviser, showed his mind blowing virtuosity and speed. These historic sessions contain pure masterpieces the quintessence of pre-war middle-jazz.

In 1940, Hampton left Goodman to form a big band, but it was only in 1942 that he was able to record. On May 26 'Flying Home' was to be recorded, with the famous solo of Illinois Jacquet which became an anthology piece. Concerts and recording followed one another with frequent changes in performers, apart from his faithful companion, the guitarist Bill Mackel. One can observe the presence of Arnett Cobb, Dexter Gordon, Johnny Griffin, Clifford Brown, Quincy Jones and Hampton's great discovery, the singer Dinah Washington. Anchored in rhythm 'n'blues, the band, whose riffs heightened the tension of his public to a paroxysm 'was hell paved with swinging intention led by a bounding devil who gets his message over to you bashing his mallets' a Michel Laverdure wrote about the concert at Olympia in 1956.

In charge of various groups, for nearly fifty years this occasionally capricious showman with staggering energy continue to flash his shower of sparks and his flamboyant lyricism all over the world with the support of his wife Gladys, who manages his career like a true company director.

'Hamp' (seen here in Nîmes, in 1976) is still the best showman of all jazz players, the one who knows best how to reach his audience.

Milt Jackson

1923, Detroit

Tremolo ma non troppo

With the tone of a wakening dream, he made the springs of gospel and blues flow into precious cascades of arpeggios.

Little disposed by his character to volcanic eruptions of the Hampton type, Milton 'Milt' Jackson, also known as 'Bags', forged his own style listening to the boppers while staying close to the spirit of blues and gospel which had nourished his youth. He often declared that he wanted 'to make his soul speak through his music'; his attachment and his taste for the funky caused him to be nicknamed 'Brother Soul' by Quincy Jones. Influenced by Monk, Gillespie and Parker, he was the first vibraphonist to play bebop, initially with a metallic tone which gradually became velvety as he developed a slower vibrato. His playing at once imposed an atmosphere typical of him, with long airy sequences of extreme musicality, melodic fluidity, and refined harmonies. He is a captivating

> **In Milt Jackson's own words:**
> 'Most guys like Hampton already played the drums and a bit of piano before switching to the vibraphone: that makes things a lot easier. Indeed, it's an instrument closer to the piano than the drums, except that in both cases you manipulate either drum sticks or mallets, but first and foremost it's a melodic instrument.'

> **John Lewis:**
> 'I don't like categories. For me there's only good music and bad music. You listen to good jazz like you listen to Mozart, Bartók or Beethoven'.

musician, remarkably easy and relaxed, and is known for his feeling for ballads.

He played in 1945 in the Gillespie-Parker Sextet, recording his first record with Dinah Washington, before playing in small groups and Gillespie's big band (1946–1947), where he met John Lewis, Kenny Clarke and Ray Brown. He returned to them after playing the piano in various other groups, and was also a partner in demand for Ray Charles, John Coltrane, Miles Davis and Oscar Peterson, and recorded with Monk (the famous 'Misterioso' in 1948). He formed the Milt Jackson Quartet, which in 1952 became the Modern Jazz Quartet, with Percy Heath replacing Ray Brown. Milt Jackson's career is closely bound up with that of the MJQ.

The Modern Jazz Quartet

The Modern Jazz Quartet was noticed right from the start thanks to two compositions by pianist and musical director John Lewis, which were to become its mascots, 'La Ronde' and 'Vendome'. Kenny Clarke, after a misunderstanding with Lewis, left the Quartet in 1955, and was replaced by Connie Kay, a drummer of great musical intelligence, a model of sobriety (the supreme art of silences) behind a battery enriched with small percussion instruments (triangle, finger cymbals). The four men in dinner jackets continued one of the most passionate adventures of modern jazz until 1974, with 'new concepts of playing which give greater freedom to improvisation while producing an even stronger form', said Lewis, a great composer (the sublime 'Django') and arranger, and a stylist stimulated by the art of counterpoint, a minimalist and delicate pianist. The MJQ, revived in 1982, is a long-lived jazz champion.

New vibrations

From the 1940s, jazz made the keyboard as 'rich' as the piano out of the full range of the percussion instruments.

Cal Tjader (1925–1982), with a sober, melodic approach, played at the beginning of his career with the pianists Vince Guaraldi, Dave Brubeck and George Shearing. Attracted by Latin American music, he went on to play with the salsa groups of Tito Puente, Machito and Eddie Palmieri.

Lem Winchester (1928–1961) first played saxophone and piano Lionel Hampton's way, before he changed to the vibraphone in 1947. With a clear and sparkling tone and an imperceptible vibrato, he distinguished himself by his imagination and in the art of shades and degrees of tone. He entered the police force in 1950, but continued to play semi-professionally until he died during a demonstration of Russian roulette.

In an attempt to escape Milt Jackson's influence (like the musicians already mentioned), **Walt Dickerson** (1931) owes his originality to the influence of John Coltrane, working at building up his solos from layers of sound. His particular tone is due to the use of rubber mallets instead of the usual felt. He recorded regularly in duos or trios from 1975 (after a ten year eclipse), notably with Andrew Cyrille, Richard Davis and Sun Ra, or solo with two vibraphones.

A fan of Hampton (percussion) and when he started, a disciple of Jackson (melody), **Bobby Hutcherson** (1941) represents the synthesis of bebop phrasing and modal improvisation while simultaneously experimenting with more libertarian musicians (Dolphy, Shepp) at the beginning of the 1960s, and at the same time developing his percussion playing on the marimbas. He formed a quintet with the saxophonist Harold Land (1969–1971), played with McCoy Tyner, and more

recently has experimented with Latin rhythms and jazz rock. In 1985, he proved himself as much an actor as a musician in Bertrand Tavernier's film *Round Midnight*.

Gary Burton (1943) is a dazzling virtuoso (the simultaneous use of four mallets enables him to play simple lines accompanying himself, or to play in four-note chords). He is also a tender, lyrical musician, with a pointillist romanticism, as his records show, especially those with Chick Corea (*Crystal Silence*, 1972). He was Stan Getz's sideman (1964–1966), collaborated with Carla Bley in an 'opera without words' (*A Genuine Tong Funeral*) and played with various groups which included Steve Swallow, Larry Coryell, Eberhard Weber, Mick Goodrick and Ralph Towner.

David Friedman (1943) started his career in a classical ensemble. In the 1970s, he founded an original duo, the Mallet Duo, with the vibraphone player David Samuels (they subsequently co-directed the Double Image quartet). He gave priority to tone and rhythm in his modal compositions. One can hear him in the New York Philharmonic Orchestra and in the Daniel Humair quartet with Jane Ira Bloom and Mike Richmond.

Working with Larry Coryell in the group Satyrs, **Mike Mainieri** (1938) became taken with electronics. In 1971 he experimented with a new amplification system, and worked on the production of the *Synthivibe* (a synthesizer electronically producing the sound of the vibraphone), which enabled him to renew the instrument's language. After several years in the group Image, he joined Michael Brecker, Eddie Gomez and Steve Gadd to form Steps Ahead, one of the most famous jazz-rock groups of the 1980s.

Charles Mingus

The pillars of the band

Plucking out the beat

When jazz was young, the 'bass line' was alternatively played by the strings and by the wind instruments (tuba, saxhorn, sousaphone, etc.). Numerous double-bass players, descendants from the 'old style' (Red Callender, John Kirby) are also virtuosos of the tuba, which was not ousted until the 1930s in most bands.

The double-bass with four strings, tuned in a fourth (E-A-D-G), or more rarely in a fifth, thus became the working peg of the jazz band, where it first supplied the basic pitch for tuning, but above all set the tempo. That is why the bow was soon abandoned for pizzicato, which was far more precise and detached. It fleetingly recovered its role with a few great soloists like Slam Stewart and Paul Chambers. Gut strings were replaced by metal strings, and the first concern of bass players is to make themselves heard, in particular by using the slap, which consists in clicking the string against the neck. It was not until the end of the 1930s that the first great improviser appeared. Jimmy Blanton (who died when he was 24) was the talented bass player in Duke Ellington's band. The two great bebop bass players, Ray Brown and Oscar Pettiford, were to develop his style. The latter (after John Kirby and a little earlier than Charles Mingus) was a true liberator who played a role equivalent to that of Kenny Clarke for the drums. Henceforth, the double-bass was not necessarily to set the tempo, but balanced its emphasis in such a way as to suggest it, and gave priority to its own autonomy in a constant dialogue with the successive soloists.

Born at the beginning of the 1950s, the Fender electric bass guitar almost immediately replaced the double bass in rhythm'n'blues, and played an essential role in the coming of rock, soul music, and even more in funk, in which it is the predominant instrument. But it was only in the 1970s that its pressure was really felt in the world of instrumental jazz, with the revelation of authentic improvisers, most frequently trained on the double-bass, like Steve Swallow, Stanley Clarke, or Miroslav Vitous. A new generation of 'totally electric' double-bass players emerged, dominated by Jaco Pastorius, the inspired pioneer of the fretless bass.

The first soloists

Like the drums, the double-bass became emancipated and wandered out of the rhythm section to become the four-stroke engine of jazz.

Initially a player of bass drum and tuba, **Walter Page** (1900–1959) became a double-bass player of extreme mobility, with a powerful sound, playing 4/4 with a great variety of nuances, a model of precision and swing who, for Philippe Carles and Jean-Louis Ginibre, 'constituted, before the War, a sort of ideal rhythmician for big band swing' (*Jazz Magazine*). He stayed with Bennie Moten from 1918 to 1923, and led the Blue Devils group which included William (the future Count) Basie and Jimmy Rushing. In the company of Freddy Green and Jo Jones, he was part of the most fabulous classical section in Basie's band (from 1936–1942 and from 1946–1949).

John Kirby (1908–1952) alternated between tuba and double-bass until 1933, when he finally opted for the double-bass. He contributed to the instrument's emancipation, with an approach considered audacious in the 1930s, harmoniously combining musicality and an effective beat. After various spells in the bands of Fletcher Henderson, Chick Webb and Lucky Millinder, he formed his own group (from 1937 to 1942), which was a considerable success, mainly because of its 'swing' adaptations of favourites from the classical repertoire. This sextet was notable for the care given to composing and arrangements (those by the trumpeter Charlie Shavers), for the quality of the soloists, and above all for its group spirit.

Israel Crosby (1919–1962) opted for the double-bass in 1935 after playing different wind instruments. He played with the pianist Jess Stacy and recorded one of the first double-bass solos in the whole history of jazz with Gene Krupa's band, 'Blues for Israel'. Because of his steady tempo, he was a sought-after accompanist, and an imaginative soloist. ('He played bass parts so beautifully that it was impossible to write any as good', said the pianist George Shearing, with whom he performed several months before his death.) Crosby was part of Ahmad Jamal's legendary trio (1951–1954), guaranteeing the pianist a rhythmic foundation which was essential to his performance.

Discovered by Duke Ellington in the ballroom of a Saint Louis hotel, **Jimmy Blanton** (1918–1942) caused the double-bass to enter the modern era by renewing the rhythmic concepts of the instrument, and granting it a role in melodic improvisation. He inspired the great modern double-bass players, Ray Brown, Scott LaFaro, Oscar Pettiford and Charles Mingus. During the period of the great Ellingtonian masterpieces, 1939–1941, and in a duo with the pianist, he showed not only his qualities as a solid accompanist, but also his exceptional gifts a an improviser in pizzicato or with the bow. He succumbed to tuberculosis and ended his days in a Los Angeles sanatorium.

The first virtuosos

It was really jazz which finally gave a concert role to this instrument which had been relegated to the back of the classical orchestra.

Red Callender (1918), the disciple of Blanton, the master of Mingus, was a rhythm expert who easily adapted to all contexts, from the traditional to bebop, from Louis Armstrong to Charlie Parker, and was an inspired soloist from whom the double-bass held no secrets. He could be found with the pianists Nat King Cole, Erroll Garner or Art Tatum and the greatest wind players (Lester Young, Dexter Gordon and Ben Webster). He took part in the concerts of Stan Kenton's Neophonic Orchestra playing the tuba, on which he was expert.

Another heir of Blanton, **Oscar Pettiford** (1922–1960), of American Indian origin, had an unparalleled technique and was a refined musician, better than anyone at making the instrument sing. A full, mellow tone, wavering tempo, and precision of articulation, were the best qualities of this fine melodist who, with Dizzy Gillespie, formed one of the first bebop combos in 1944. He went on to play in Duke Ellington's band from 1945 to 1948. For several months, he dedicated himself to the cello. After recording with Thelonious Monk and Sonny Rollins, he came to Europe where he decided to settle in 1958. He worked in France and Germany with Stan Getz and Bud Powell, until he died of a viral infection in Copenhagen where he had decided to live.

A rare rhythmic and melodic effect made **Ray Brown** (1926) one of the very top double-bass players of the modern rhythm section (he accompanied practically all the great musicians) and thus a first-rate soloist. He explored and exploited with dexterity and intensity all the registers of the instrument from the lowest notes to the highest, adding to this an infallible tempo, and a rare dynamism and swing. Pledged to Blanton when he started his career, Ray Brown was drawn to bebop as soon as he arrived in New York in 1946, and found himself engaged by Dizzy Gillespie; he was to stay two years with the trumpeter, in his small groups and in the big band. He then joined the JATP (1948) and accompanied Ella Fitzgerald. A member of the Oscar Peterson Trio, he stayed with the pianist for fifteen years; for many, Ray's presence accounted for much of their success. He settled in Los Angeles in 1966, worked for television and cinema, and recorded freelance. In 1972, Duke Ellington and he made a disc as a tribute to Jimmy Blanton, *This One's for Blanton*. A founder member of the L.A. Four, he toured with the group all over the world, and has performed most frequently with the pianist Monty Alexander in the last ten years.

Curtis Counce (1926–1963), a double-bass player with a robust and supple tempo, found himself playing with the best West Coast jazz musicians (Shelly Manne, Shorty Rogers), before playing in Stan Kenton's band. In 1956, he formed a remarkable quintet, which was dissolved upon the death of his pianist, Carl Perkins, in 1958.

Charles Mingus

1922, Nogales — Cuernavaca, 1979

A rebel rooted in blues territory

A devastating soloist, he used composition and the cohesion of the band to give jazz a controlled spontaneity which remains the code of contemporary improvisation.

Mingus's considerable contribution as a composer and bandleader has somewhat eclipsed his role as a formidable double-bass player from the very first years of the bebop revolution.

He contributed many technical innovations to the instrument: tremolos, flamenco features, a way of pinching the string while massaging it.

His enormous, aggressive sound, his 'slapping' style, ultra syncopated and almost angry, are like a symbolic echo of his radical rebellion against racism. His very choice of instrument was the result of this 'inhuman condition' which still belongs to the Black Americans of his generation, and which his autobiography denounces under the title of *Beneath the Underdog*. Indeed, although he already had a solid training in

---

Duke Ellington about the Money Jungle session:

'Max Roach's rhythmic subtleties could not have been more appropriate or sounded more genuine; and Mingus, with his eyes closed, just let himself be carried away with each gust of harmony, inventing new counterpoint as if he had played this theme — 'Little African Flower' — all his life. It was one of those mystical moments in which our three muses became one. We just recorded one take, I was in heaven' (Duke Ellington, *Music is My Mistress*).

---

the 'cello, his friend the trombone player Britt Woodman, made him understand that his colour was not frightfully appreciated in classical bands, and somewhat against his will, he opted for the double bass which he studied with Red Callender.

His childhood in the teeming ghetto of Watts in Los Angeles included the three musical strokes of fortune which were to determine his destiny. At college, he discovered romantic chamber music, and especially Bela Bartók; at church (Holiness Church), his mother-in-law initiated him to the most authentic and cathartic forms of gospel; and he was only ten years old when he heard Ellington on the radio for the first time.

Shortly after his debut with Buddy Collette and Lee Young (Lester's brother), Mingus became the bass player of Armstrong (1941–1943), who had to fire him because of his anti-segrationist remarks, while on tour in the South. He played with Kid Ory, then with the big band of Hampton (1946–1948), for whom he wrote his first arrangements ('Mingus Fingers').

Meanwhile, he passionately followed the evolution of Ellington and of his succession of double-bass players, Blanton and Pettiford. He occasionally played with Art Tatum, Fats Navarro (who led him to discover Afro-Cuban music), Charlie Parker (who dissuaded him from quitting music for a job as a postman), and his friend Max Roach, with whom he founded the record label Debut.

After a year he left the popular trio of Red Norvo and Tal Farlow, indignant at being replaced by a white player for a television broadcast. Then came his historic consecration in the legendary concert in Massey Hall, Toronto with Parker and Gillespie (1953), and the foundation of a co-operative of musicians, the Jazz Composers' Workshop, followed by th formation of his own quintet, the Jazz Workshop (1955).

Mingus showed himself, as a leader, to be the most creative disciple of Ellington, with whom he spent a few months in 1953, and later recorded the formidable *Money Jungle* in 1962, with Max Roach. Ellington radically changed Mingus's orchestral concepts; in the footsteps of this venerated master, he conceived open works, where each part magnifies the soloist's personality, but, at the same time, he arranged long transitions where spontaneous polyphony had free rein, a bit like with Jelly Roll Morton, but with a decisive atonal trend.

His preference for unexpected variations in tempo, alternating even and uneven measures, arhythmic and almost cacophonic passages cut short by a sudden impeccable return to the theme and the tempo, combined overall to be disconcerting, and yet magnificiently concerted.

Bizarre?

One evening, in a club where he was experimenting with one of his new compositions, and where the public was particularly noisy and inattentive, Mingus suddenly stopped the band and shouted at the crowd: 'If you find what we are playing odd, you only have to look at yourselves! (reported by Nat Hentoff in *Jazz Is*).

From the end of the 1950s, the name of Mingus incarnated in modern jazz a current increasingly distinctive from the *mainstream* represented by the Jazz Messengers or Miles Davis, and which developed into Free Jazz, while mobilizing some of the 'third stream' (see p. 208).

The Mingus universe perfectly integrated the strongest personalities: Dannie Richmond (his stalwart drummer since 1957), Roland Kirk, Jackie McLean, John Handy, Jimmy Knepper, Eric Dolphy, George Adams. His instrumentation was very diversified, from solo piano (at which Mingus was a master) to the big band, including up to three drummers, six saxophones, woodwind, etc. not to mention the whole range of smaller 'combos'. From *Pithecanthropus Erectus* (1956) to *Good Bye Pork Pie Hat* (1974) including the 'Fables of Faubus' (1960), 'dedicated' to a racist Arkansas senator and censored for ages by C.B.S., his records recreate the turbulent atmosphere of his concerts/happenings, and exalt the continuum of Afro-American culture, from the blues to Free Jazz.

After years of ostracism, the creator of the Newport Jazz Festival (1960) ended by being awarded an official tribute, one year before his death, by Jimmy Carter. His ashes were scattered in the Ganges, but his works will be perpetuated by the Mingus Dynasty group, in which most of the survivors of his fabulous venture are reunited.

Lyric basses

Bass players took giant steps through bebop harmonics to make their basses 'sing' without neglecting their responsibilities as rhythm specialists.

The idol of a whole generation, **Paul Chambers** (1935–1969) was not only the most sought-after accompanist, known to the best band leaders for his reliable tempo and perfect musicality, but also distinguished himself with his very lyrical bowed solos in a deep register, similar in tone to that of a tenor sax, which earned him comparison with Sonny Rollins. From 1955 to 1962, his vivacious bass phrasing and huge span on the strings drove the Miles Davis group and other combos he played with, firmly ahead. John Coltrane, with whom he recorded *Giant Steps*, dedicated a piece to him, 'Mr P.C.'. From 1963 he played in a trio with partners who had been with him in the Davis group, Wynton Kelly and Jimmy Cobb, and continued to play freelance until he died of tuberculosis.

Red Mitchell (1927) soon attracted the attention of musicians and jazz lovers with his way of playing long phrases in the manner of wind instruments, and his very personal sense of 'breaths'. A bassist with fine tempo, he knows how to avoid the clichés of the *walking bass*; full of inspiration, he is unrivalled in the treatment of lyrical themes. Another particular feature of his is that his instrument is tuned like a cello. He has had a major impact on the development of bass playing, and to describe his whole career 'would be impossible here.

Scott LaFaro (1936–1961), a 'natural virtuoso' as he was described by André Francis, emancipated the role of the double bass (as Kenny Clarke had done for the drums) by giving it total autonomy, breaking once and for all with the notion of regular tempo and turning accompaniment into a conversation with the soloist. His extraordinary mastery of technique enabled him to play melodic lines with extremely daring harmonies at an amazing speed, comparable to that of a guitarist. After playing with Chet Baker and Stan Getz, he was hired by Bill Evans in 1959, and their collaboration lasted until Evans died (in a car accident). It was with this fabulous trio (Evans, LaFaro, and Paul Motian on drums) that Scott achieved world fame; their historic sessions on 25 June, 1961 at the *Village Vanguard* were fortunately recorded. He also took part in the *Free Jazz* recording by Ornette Coleman, in whose quartet he replaced Charlie Haden. LaFaro's influence was fundamental, and there are few bassists who fail to recognize this.

Pierre Michelot (1928), the 'double bass man', Kenny Clarke's partner in a rhythmic duo of exceptional quality, has long been considered 'the best post-bop bassist Europe has produced'. The impressive list of records he has made is enough to prove the admiration in which he is held by other musicians throughout the world.

The 'basic basses'

Since the 1960s, the double bass has been exploring the full compass and malleability of its fretless strings, constantly diversifying its tradition.

In modern jazz, the double bass player has to provide a kind of vertical axis, firmly planted but in perpetual motion, around which the other musicians evolve, rather as if they were linked to this 'mast' by a sort of safety harness. Some have excelled in this sometimes unrewarding but essential role, refining both their own talents as soloists and even as leaders.

As a creator of 'sound climates', whether playing solo, pizzicato or with a bow, **Jimmy Garrison** (1934–1976) stayed attached to the basic harmonic and rhythmic role of the instrument through his solid, virile tempo, notably in the heart of John Coltrane's quartet from 1961 (when he replaced Reggie Workman) until 1966. Previously, he had made a remarkable twosome with Philly Joe Jones, playing with Lennie Tristano and Ornette Coleman. He then co-directed a group with the pianist Hampton Hawes, completed a tour with Archie Shepp, and joined the trio of his comrade Elvin Jones.

There is no doubt that **Ron Carter** (1937), a steady, rhythmic player with feline suppleness, is the most frequently recorded double-bass player, which shows how well he is thought of. He began in 1959 in the quintet of the great 'talent scout' Chico Hamilton, played and recorded with Eric Dolphy, on the cello ('Fire Waltz') and then formed one of the most legendary rhythm sections in jazz history, that of Miles Davis's quintet with Herbie Hancock and Tony Williams (1963–1968). He played with them again in VSOP, and later accompanied Wynton Marsalis. In 1975, he created a quartet with the pianist Kenny Barron, the drummer Ben Riley and another bass player, the excellent Buster Williams, himself playing the piccolo bass (the record *Pick'em*).

A great virtuoso master, **Eddie Gomez** (1944) added his lyrical sensitivity and his flat or round tone to the poetic aesthetics of Bill Evans for eleven years (1966–1977), extending the melodic and rhythmic concept inherited from Scott LaFaro. He then played with the pianists Chick Corea, Joanne Brackeen, McCoy Tyner, and in Jack DeJohnette's group New Directions, before participating in the creation of Steps and the Manhattan Jazz Quintet (with Lew Soloff, George Young, Dave Matthews and Steve Gadd). He joined up again with the latter when he formed his Gadd Gang.

One cannot enumerate all the American musicians who accompanied **Henri Texier** (1945), before and after he formed a quintet in 1965, and integrated Phil Woods' European Rhythm Machine, with Gordon Beck and Daniel Humair. With Aldo Romano, he then created Total Issue (ethno-rock jazzy), performed solo (various different instruments including the oud), participated in the different Units of Michel Portal, and since 1980 has multiplied his associations and experiences, as a leader, notably with the Bagad de Quimiperlé in 1987.

Marc Johnson (1953), then a member of Woody Herman's band, replaced Eddie Gomez in Bill Evans' trio in 1977. After the death of the pianist, he played with the LaBarbera brothers (Joe and Pat, respectively drummer and saxophonist), played in a duo with John Lewis and became the regular double bass player of the Mel Lewis big band, before forming his group Bass Desires with the guitarists John Scofield and Bill Frisell, with Peter Erskine on drums.

The bass unbound

Certain double-bass players feel more like improvisers detached to a certain extent from any constraining rhythmic function. Their melodic agility and the suppleness of their reflexes make them known as the indispensable 'freelancers' of collective improvisation.

Gary Peacock (1935), from being a drummer, pianist and flugelhorn player, became double-bass player in the band of his regiment in Germany (1954). He then embarked upon a career which took him from Paul Bley (1962) to Keith Jarrett (as from 1983) and Miles Davis, not to mention Albert Ayler (1964–1965) and Miles Davis, which showed the willingness of this disciple of Scott LaFaro to invest in all the adventures of jazz, from its avant-garde to a new interpretation of its standard pieces.

Charlie Haden (1937), self-taught, a bass player with a strong tone, giving more importance to the melodic aspect than to rhythm, accompanied Ornette Coleman (1959–1962) and directed his first Liberation Music Orchestra in 1969. He worked with Jarrett and Paul Motian (1967–1975), played in the group Old and New Dreams (with Don Cherry, Dewey Redman and Ed Blackwell) and formed, in 1986, Quartet West with tenor saxophonist Ernie Watts.

Steve Swallow (1940) occupies a unique place in jazz, since he is one of the rare, if not the very first players to have swapped his bass for an electric one (1970, in Gary Burton's quartet). He became a permanent element in the various groups formed by Carla Bley, set Robert Creeley's poems to music, and played with the Orchestre National de Jazz (1986) and in Henri Texier's Transatlantik Quartet.

Jean-François Jenny-Clark (1944), able to play legato with his left hand with a constant equality of sound, divided his time between jazz (from 1960, with Jackie McLean) and contemporary music. He performed in the group Pork Pie (Aldo Romano, Philip Catherine, Charlie Mariano), in a trio with Joachim Kuhn and Daniel Humair, and collaborated with Luciano Berio, John Cage, Mauricio Kagel, Pierre Boulez, Karlheinz Stockhausen, and Diego Masson in the group Musique Vivante.

The Dane **Niels Henning Ørsted Pederson** (NHØP) (1946), flawless accompanist and virtuoso soloist, first played in his country with a number of jazz players who were passing through (from Bud Powell to Albert Ayler), formed with Kenny Drew the rhythm section of the *Café Montmartre* in Copenhagen, then joined the Oscar Peterson Trio and recorded with the great soloists of Norman Granz's Pablo label.

Dave Holland (1946), a brilliant technician, played in London with the elite of British musicians, before Miles Davis engaged him in 1968. He stayed for two years with the trumpeter, and after leaving formed the group Circle (with Barry Altschul, Anthony Braxton and Chick Corea). He recorded a solo disc dedicated to the 'cello, and in 1983 formed a quintet with the Canadian trumpeter, Kenny Wheeler.

The Czechoslovak **Miroslav Vitous** (1947), who replaced Ron Carter for a week in Miles Davis's quintet in 1969, was a founder member of Weather Report, showing a 'gliding' sensitivity. He then played sporadically in various contexts (duo with Stanley Clarke), taught in Boston, and in 1981 rejoined his companions of the 1960s, Chick Corea and Roy Haynes, for the record *Trio Music*.

Electric bass

The usual reticence of jazz towards new instruments was finally swept away by the expressive qualities of Fender's second invention.

By a strange chance, most of the electric bass guitar's great virtuosos were born the year it was invented. In 1951, Fender launched this younger sister of his *solid body* guitar into the world. The *Fender Precision bass* with four strings — tuned in fourths (E-A-D-G) was followed by numerous imitations and derivatives, and led to a re-evaluation of the bass's role in pop music overall. First and foremost ensuring a rhythmic role of primary importance in rhythm'n'blues, soul and funk (James Jamerson, the bass players of Sly Stone, notably Larry Graham, Chuck Rainey, Bootsy Collins), used towards the end of the 1950s by Monk Montgomery (Wes's brother), it hit jazz with full force around 1970, and was often used as a more or less indispensable accessory by the double-bass players, notably Dave Holland, Miroslav Vitous, Steve Swallow, Ron Carter and Bob Cranshaw. But it also had its experts.

Stanley Clarke (1951) passed from violin to cello, then to double-bass, when as an adolescent he realized that it was perfectly suited to his imposing stature. But at the same time, he began to play the Fender in Philadelphian soul and rock groups. Becoming equally virtuoso with both instruments, he began an original double 'acoustic' career in the early 1970s, with the Jazz Messengers, Pharaoh Sanders, Stan Getz, Gil Evans, then Joe Henderson, where he met Chick Corea, with whom he formed the electric group Return to Forever. He very quickly became one of the greatest stars of jazz-rock, and developed in the 1980s a style which was more soul, with George Duke. Deeply imbued with bebop (he took Oscar Pettiford as his master) and Latin jazz, he was generally considered as the most complete virtuoso of the 'all round' bass players.

Michael Henderson (1951) beat the longevity record as a regular bass player for Miles Davis after Paul Chambers died.

From November 1969 to 1975, he contributed to the heavy and torrid climate of the trumpeter's 'psychedelic' period, with the sharp *soulful* sound he had retained from his experience with Stevie Wonder and Aretha Franklin. He later embarked on a soul singing career on the Buddah label.

Alphonso Johnson (1951) started with Horace Silver, then went to the Adderley brothers before replacing Miroslav Vitous in the group Weather Report. Having become a studio musician, he is very much in demand for jazz-rock recordings, to which he brings a unique funky tone.

Jaco Pastorius (1951–1988), who succeeded him in Weather Report in 1976, revealed his spectacular creativity in assuming a quadruple role in the band: a blues-like walking bass, a collective approach modelled on Scott LaFaro, funk rhythms, and solo — often solitary — performance, in which he surpassed all his rivals due to his exceptional charisma on stage, which did much to promote the group. Strongly influenced by Jimi Hendrix, he soon revealed his originality as a composer, with themes that include amazing figures of electronic counterpoint.

He was the first to play an electric bass without frets, thus bringing it closer to its ancestor, the double-bass. His fluidity, his vibrato, his very lyrical phrasing, his speed and his mastery of harmonics offered, in the face of Stanley Clarke's then predominant style, an alternative which fascinated a whole new generation. An ex-drummer like his father, but also a guitarist, pianist and saxophonist, as soon as he left Weather Report (1982), he started a big band, in which he provided the harmonic basis single-handed (bass and keyboard), playing essentially bebop and Latin jazz. Alcohol and drugs cut short his dazzling career.

Mark Egan (1951) came from a rhythm 'n'blues background, like Pastorius who, together with Dave Holland, was his mentor to some extent. He soon began to work in tandem with the drummer Dan Gottlieb, in Pat Metheny's group (1977–1980), and together they went on to form their own group Elements. With his metallic, syncopated and very recognizable style, he became a popular accompanist and played with Gil Evans, David Sanborn, John McLaughlin and many others.

Jamaaladeen Tacuma (1956), whose impressive size and energy are reminiscent of his favourite maestro, Stanley Clarke, joined Ornette Coleman's Prime Time Band in 1977, where his role became crucial to their explosive cocktail of free and funk. He proceeded to make the most of every opportunity to form countless groups and play with musicians as different as Max Roach, Santana, the guitarists James Blood Ulmer and Kazumi Watanabe, the singer Wilhelmina Fernandez, Kip Hanrahan or Bill Laswell. Such diversity culminated in the record *Music World* (1986), recorded in about ten different countries with local musicians. Tacuma is the supreme master of the Steinberger 'stick', which is simply a bass neck with a very biting sound.

Jonas Hellborg (1956) only plays basses that he makes himself. This Swedish virtuoso achieved an international audience through his association with John McLaughlin (1984). A disciple of Alphonso Johnson, he became a real stage animal, nicknamed 'Elegant Punk', and has developed a very original technique, playing everything in chords in such a 'pianistic' style that he manages to transpose entire Bill Evans or Herbie Hancock solos.

Bill Laswell (1956) is less a bass virtuoso than a brilliant producer who uses this instrument as a support. His informal group with a changing name (Material, Golden Palominos, Massacre, etc.), but with an unchanging keyboard specialist, Bernie Worrell, has included — if only for a single recording session — such different 'members' as Tacuma, Archie Shepp and Henry Threadgill, Whitney Houston, Peter Brotzmann and Sonny Sharrock. Laswell has produced many hit records, from Mick Jagger to Herbie Hancock, as well as Last Poets, Yoko Ono, Manu Dibango and Toure Kounda, Fela, and even the 'pope of the punks', Johnny Rotten. Like his friend Tacuma, he expresses perfectly the effervescence of New York in the 1980s, gleefully mixing jazz-rock, Free Jazz, funk, rap and all sorts of exotic influences. He is a member of the radical quartet Last Exit, with Brantzman, Sharrock and Ronald Shannon Jackson.

Marcus Miller (1960) is, like Laswell, a 'bassist producer', a man of many talents, similar in some ways to Prince or Hermeto Pascoal, playing at least twenty instruments. His impressive musical background covers the whole American heritage, from Charles Ives to rap! Studying the classical clarinet did not prevent him from developing a passion for the funk bass giant Larry Graham. Being Wynton Kelly's cousin, he discovered jazz and soon became fascinated by Jaco Pastorius. Playing at first with David Sanborn, with whom he made several albums, he quickly became a producer in his own right, in particular producing Roberta Flack and Aretha Franklin. In 1981 he was hired by Miles Davis, who never left him completely, letting him produce most of his records. His very percussive manner, based radically on the *slap*, relies on rhythmic effects in a sober, speedy but airy style.

Wind in the wings

The traditional trombone

Like the clarinet, the trombone has now become a relatively marginal instrument, but it occupied an essential place in the historic period of jazz, from New Orleans to bebop. The valve model had a few rare experts (Juan Tizol, Bob Brookmeyer and Mike Zwerin all played the 'bass trumpet'), but it is the tenor trombone with a slide which was almost always the one used by jazz players. At the start, it was the spectacular glissando effect obtained by a rapid manipulation of the slide which popularized the 'bone, as it was nicknamed. One of Charlie Chaplin's famous gags — in *A Day of Pleasure* — magnificently illustrated this tailgate style, so called because, in the parades and the band marches, the trombone players sat right at the back of the lorry, facing out, to play their instruments.

Following the example of the trumpeters, the trombone players also invented many different kinds of mutes, thanks to which the sound of the instrument evolved considerably in a very few years. It is a far cry from the *Dixieland* of Kid Ory or Honoré Dutrey to the wah wah of Sam Nanton in Ellington's band. Virtuosos filed past one after another in the 1920s and 1930s: Miff Mole, Jimmy Harrison, J.C. Higginbotham, Tommy Dorsey, Lawrence Brown, Benny Morton, and, above all, Jack Teagarden, who became Louis Armstrong's alter ego. Trummy Young, Dicky Wells and Vic Dickenson opened the way to the boppers J.J. Johnson, Kai Winding, Al Grey, Slide Hampton and Frank Rosolino; henceforth, it was complexity of phrasing which took precedence over richness of tone. The latter recovers all its bright and even clashing colours in the playing of today's virtuosos: Roswell Rudd, Bill Watrous, George Lewis, Albert Mangelsdorff, Steve Turre. The trombone has even fanfared its way into funk with Joe Bowie and Ray Anderson. Archaic but arrogant, sliding with the fashions, it defiantly keeps up with modern music.

From marching bands to music stands

The main attraction in the New Orleans parades, the trombone player gives depth to the jazz band.

Kid Ory (1886–1973), born in Louisiana, typical New Orleans style (*tailgate*) trombone player, was also one of the first poly-instrumentalists, singers and composers in jazz ('Muskrat Ramble'). In 1922 he formed Kid Ory's Sunshine Orchestra, the first black group from Louisiana to be recorded. He later played with Louis Armstrong's Hot Five and Jelly Roll Morton's Red Hot Peppers. He stopped playing for about ten years, but took an active part in the New Orleans Revival from 1942.

With **Jimmy Harrison** (1900–1931) the trombone ceased to be a backing instrument, and became a fully fledged solo instrument. Harrison showed all his melodic creativity with the bands of Fletcher Henderson, Ellington, and finally Chick Webb, towards the end of his life.

J.C. Higginbotham (1906–1973) was to follow in his footsteps, with a more technical approach and extra speed. With his fiery, powerful attacks he was a forerunner of Swing, playing with the best bands in the 1930s and with Louis Armstrong from 1937 to 1940.

Dicky Wells (1907–1985), a remarkable technician, 'a musician with a romantic imagination' (André Hodeir), was one of the great soloists of the swing era, a model of balance and rigour. He is remembered especially for his part in the bands of Teddy Hill (1934–1938) and Count Basie (1938–1946 and 1947–1950). His Paris recordings on the Swing label are remarkable.

An accomplished stylist, Louis Armstrong's favourite trombonist, who seems to have given of his best with him between 1946 and 1951, the Texan **Jack Teagarden** (1905–1964), a remarkable

bluesman, was a great figure of classic jazz. His easy, natural, warm and rounded tone was admired by all his more modern colleagues, for whom he became a model. With his warm nonchalant voice 'Mr T' would sing responses in joyful duos with Louis Armstrong.

Vic Dickenson (1906–1984) and **Trummy Young** (1912–1984) were musicians of the transition between swing and bebop; the former often playing in different contexts, while the latter played mainly with Jimmy Lunceford's band alongside Parker and Gillespie, and then joined Louis Armstrong's All Stars where he replaced Jack Teagarden from 1952 to 1964.

The Ellingtonians

The styles and voices of the trombonists connected with Duke Ellington's band were very different.

Joe 'Tricky Sam' Nanton (1906–1946), a master of the growl, the wah-wah mute, and 'jungle' expressionism, joined the band in 1926 and stayed there until his death.

Lawrence Brown (1905–1988), who was never very popular with the critics, stayed with the Duke for nearly forty years. With his mellow tone and fluid articulation, he could swing as hard as he could sing a melodic line.

The Puerto Rican **Juan Tizol** (1900–1984), a specialist in the valve trombone, whose sound was similar to a cello, brought Latin colour to the band with compositions like 'Caravan' and 'Conga Brava'. He kept his place in the trombone section from 1929 to 1944 and again from 1951 to 1960.

Bebop and free 'bones'

Essential as a second instrument in modern jazz, the solo trombone became a 'challenger' to the trumpet

Bebop: notes come first

It was in Woody Herman's first Herd that **Bill Harris** (1916–1973) became famous due to his solo in 'Bijou', a real jewel of lyricism played with a slightly affected elegance. His sense of humour, his vibratoed tremolos and his incongruous glissandos were not appreciated by all, but he was admired and respected by his fellow musicians of the bebop generation, in which he exerted a considerable influence.

A pure bopper who liked taking risks, **Frank Rosolino** (1926–1978) shares the double heritage of the great classics and of Harris. Technically brilliant, with a deliberately exuberant style, he developed a vibrato with the lips instead of with the slide.

The left-hander **Slide Hampton** (1932), who is adventurous with his phrasing and his harmonies, sometimes using a beret as a mute to soften his tone, is capable of arrangements that can make a small group sound like a big band. In 1979 he recorded *World Trombone* (nine trombonists, including the excellent Curtis Fuller), after having spent several years in Paris and in Germany.

Bill Watrous (1939) is a hyper-gifted technician, with perfect pitch, and a specialist in high notes. His long, flexibly structured phrases contain passages played at impressive speed.

Starting as a pianist, valve trombone specialist **Bob Brookmeyer** (1929) is an original soloist, skilled in the art of counterpoint. He replaced Chet Baker in the Gerry Mulligan Quartet from 1954 to 1957. As a very gifted composer-arranger, he wrote pieces for the Thad Jones-Mel Lewis orchestra and for the American Jazz Orchestra (1986).

Steve Turre (1948), whose playing is firmly anchored in tradition, is modern in his approach, constantly reviewing and linking episodes of trombone history, and incorporating African and Latin American elements.

Free: sound is all

From the beginning of the 1960s, **Roswell Rudd** (1935) offered a new treatment of the instrument, whole-heartedly embracing the Free movement while constantly referring, with a distinct preference for vocalizations and deep sensuality, to the New Orleans tradition. He played with Archie Shepp from 1966 to 1968, composed for the Jazz Composer's Orchestra, and joined Charlie Haden's Liberation Music Orchestra, playing also with Carla Bley's ensembles. He is the composer of an opera, *Taki*, inspired by a famous New York graffiti artist.

Both born in 1952, **Ray Anderson** and **George Lewis** are interested in contemporary improvisation, establishing new limits for the instrument in all fields of music. Another point they have in common is that both worked with Anthony Braxton at different times, between 1976 and 1977. Anderson, who was fascinated by Lawrence Brown and Roswell Rudd, created the free-jazz-funk group the Slickaphonics in 1980 with Allan Jaffe, and went on to discover bebop a few years later. Lewis joined the A.A.C.M. in 1971, played with the best Free Jazz musicians, composed a piece for four trombones, explored electronic music, and has continuously widened his range of musical associations and collaborations, which include Gil Evans, Steve Lacy, Michel Portal, and Joachim Kuhn.

Albert Mangelsdorff (1928) displays a multiphonic technique (notes being sung and blown simultaneously) and makes constant use of harmonics, at the threshold of a great freedom of expression.

An extremely rare example of a star soloist whose jazz career ended at the age of 46, **J.J. Johnson** *could not resist the attractions of Hollywood.*

J.J. Johnson

1924, Indianapolis

The Maestro of the staccato

His three 'J's rejuvenated the trombone by getting rid of excessive glissando and integrating it in the bop virtuoso approach

Two major retreats have punctuated the career of this father of the modern jazz trombone. The first was between 1952 and 1954 when he became a quality controller in a gyroscope factory (!), and the second lasted from 1970 to 1987, during which time, apart from a few recordings, he dedicated himself entirely to writing and arranging for cinema and television (*Starsky & Hutch*). Nearly twenty years' absence from the jazz scene for the man who invented bebop trombone playing, by transposing Charlie Parker's legato cadences and Dizzy Gillespie's staccato phrasing and who was known as the best trombonist of the young generation, consistently taking first place in popularity polls.

In J.J. Johnson's own words:
'Fats Navarro and I were crazy about Lester Young and Roy Eldridge and we would listen to them in concert or on disc as often as possible. I can say that those two names were as important as the names of any trombonists in the forming of my style. After all Lester was the great pioneer of linear improvisation . . .'
(*Jazz-Hot*, interview with Mike Hennessey December 1980-January 1981).

He was first a pianist, then a baritone saxophonist. It was the Kansas City trombonist Fred Beckett who first influenced him. He was also influenced by Dicky Wells and Trummy Young, as well as his older partner in Snookum Russell's band which he joined in 1942, Fats Navarro. J.J. went on to play with the Benny Carter and Count Basie big bands (1942–1946), and with Jazz at the Philharmonic. He was a regular in the 52nd Street clubs where he met and played with the boppers, thus developing his famous style. Leaving Basie, he played with various groups, including Illinois Jacquet's, recorded with Sonny Stitt and Bud Powell and played with the Woody Herman and Dizzy Gillespie bands before going on tour with Oscar Pettiford, and interrupting his musical activities.

When he went back to playing his instrument (1954), he formed a trombone duo with **Kai Winding** (1922–1983) which was to go down in the history of jazz. Their harmony of tones (though J.J.'s is more velvety) and nearly identical styles gave the combo they formed in 1956 an enthusiastic acclaim; they came together three more times for recording sessions and in 1982 for a tour in Japan. Winding went on to organize several small trombone ensembles with as many as four trombones, and played duo with Curtis Fuller in *Giant Bones* in 1979. Johnson turned to writing and arranging, working with Miles Davis (1961–1962) and Bobby Jaspar before setting off for Hollywood.

He went on a few tours and made several recordings before returning to the stage in 1987. Let us hope that this giant of the trombone will not disappear in the wings too soon again.

Eric Dolphy *Paris (1964)*.

Tongue-tip jazzmen

The delicate flute

Too faint to battle with the brasses without amplification, the flute was virtually non-existent in jazz until the 1950s. It was then that some saxophonists adopted it as a second instrument. With Bud Shank, Buddy Collette (in Chico Hamilton's group) and Jimmy Giuffre, it became a characteristic element of Cool style and the California sound. It was also gradually integrated in big band arrangements, in small doses to begin with by Count Basie, Quincy Jones and Dizzy Gillespie, then more systematically by Mingus, Gil Evans and Sun Ra. In the 1960s, the classic European technique was enriched by the coloured jazzmen who introduced unusual effects and contrasts. James Moody, Yusef Lateef, Charles Lloyd, Prince Lasha, Sam Rivers and above all Eric Dolphy made the most of the expressionist potential of this instrument. Others — Joe Farrell, Sam Rivers, George Adams, Pharaoh Sanders, Chico Freeman — also began using traditional African and Oriental techniques like dissonance, continuous breathing, and breathy tones. Some real specialists emerged and, with their recordings, managed to convince the wider public that the flute is a fully fledged jazz instrument. Herbie Mann became the most popular, Hubert Laws and Jeremy Steig impressed with their virtuosity; James Newton, under the simultaneous influence of his master Buddy Collette, the Debussy tradition and the Japanese shakuhashi, became one of the main exponents of the avant-garde in the 1970s. In Europe, too, the flute found some talented players among the saxophonists — Bobby Jaspar, Jacques Pelzer, Michel Roques, and more occasionally, Francois Jeanneau, Jean-Louis Chautemps and André Jaume, but more recently real specialists are appearing, like Michel Edelin.

Eric Dolphy

1928, Los Angeles — Berlin, 1964

The nearest to a bird

Fluttering endlessly from one instrument and one register to another, his improvisation became a dazzling bird song.

A great solitary and eccentric jazz personality, who from the early 1950s, together with Ornette Coleman, provoked and instigated jazz to become free, Dolphy embodies the 'exaltation and anxieties of a jazz explorer', according to Alain Gerber, who says he is between bop and 'New Thing'. As a nonconformist, he broke away from the pattern set by Charlie Parker and his followers, developing a personal style in which he remained faithful to the melodic line while constantly breaking it up and remaking a newer and better one: angular or winding phrases, bouncing in surprising zigzags, distortions and extentions which sometimes resembled the human voice or cry, harmonic liberties, rhythmic breaks,

In Eric Dolphy's own words:

'You tell me that my whinnying is anti-musical and that my flights into squeaks hurt the ears. O.K., but still if everyone disappeared as soon as I put my lips to one of my three instruments, if no firm agreed to record me and if I had to die of starvation in order to play what I feel — it's just that, what I feel — well I would continue to play, against the wind and the tide. I feel it's the only way I can project my personality and reach some kind of maturity. Of course, if people listen to my playing, it's encouraging'. (*Jazz-Hot*, November 1974).

but all within an internal logic, all this *is* Dolphy's music, which is also deeply rooted in the great Afro-American tradition.

As a player of the alto sax and the bass clarinet (which like Michel Portal and André Jaume after him, he turned into a jazz instrument) and a flautist, Dolphy adapted these three techniques and sounds perfectly to his universe. We feel that it was on the flute that he best conveyed his insolent spirit of freedom, spotted and striped, jagged and deliriously airy, wild escapades, dizzy heights (listen to 'Gazelloni' on the record *Out to Lunch*, February 1964).

Engaged by Chico Hamilton in 1958 on Buddy Collette's recommendation, Dolphy joined Charles Mingus's Workshop, and caused a certain upheaval among the spectators at the Antibes Festival in 1960, the year he played in Ornette Coleman's double quartet for the record *Free Jazz*. He worked with Oliver Nelson and George Russell, played at John Coltrane's side (1961–1962), and could be heard at the *Five Spot* in the company of Booker Little, Mal Waldron, Richard Davis and Ed Blackwell. He travelled to Europe in 1961, played in Paris with Donald Byrd and in Stockholm with Coltrane, then led various groups. In 1964 he recorded *Out to Lunch*, and went on a new tour in Europe with Charles Mingus, the faithful Dannie Richmond, pianist Jaki Byard, saxophonist Clifford Jordan and trumpeter Johnny Coles. Eric decided to spend some time on the Old Continent, and played in the Netherlands and in Berlin, where he died of a heart attack following neglect of the diabetes he suffered from. Thus passed away the man who used to say that on the flute, he so much loved 'to imitate the singing of little birds'.

The flights of the flute

The flute made a late and timid entrance on the jazz scene; it wasn't until the 1950s that it awakened the interest of jazz players since most of the flautists were first and foremost saxophonists. Musicians included under this heading chose to express themselves primarily on this instrument which still lingers on the fringe of jazz.

Herbie Mann (1930), saxophonist and flautist, devoted himself to the flute in 1953 in the quintet of the accordion player Mat Matthews. After forming a flute duo with Sam Most, he went on to form groups in which he incorporated the musical elements of other continents. He occupied first place in the *Down Beat* poll from 1957 to 1970.

The career of **Hubert Laws** (1939) oscillated between jazz (the Jazz Crusaders to Fusion Super Jam) and classical music (with the Metropolitan Opera Orchestra and the New York Philharmonic), not to mention various musical encounters from Chick Corea to Gil Evans, from Paul Simon and Astrud Gilberto to Ron Carter. His classical technique enabled him to play everything on his 'C' flute as well as on altos and piccolos. His jazz adaptations of pieces by Bach, Mozart, Debussy, and Stravinsky crowned him with success.

Jeremy Steig (1942) relied on a wide range of flutes from various places to produce his multi-faceted music. He structurally incorporated sound effects, the clapping of keys, finger and breathing sounds, simultaneous voice (humming) and blowing combined with electronic effects. He recorded mainly with the Bill Evans Trio (1969), and in 1973 took part in a Flute Summit' with his fellow flute players Chris Hinze (Dutch), James Moody and Sahib Shihab. He particularly likes playing in a duo (with the Dutch drummer Pierre Courbois or the double bass player Eddie Gomez) and often enters into dialogue with himself, by means of re-recording.

James Newton (1953), who had a classical training and was a pupil of Buddy Collette, possesses an amazing technical capacity which he dedicates to his music, which is at the same time elaborate and open, and popular with the black jazz musicians of the 1970s and 1980s. As is borne out by his collaboration with the pianist Anthony Davis, contemporary music flirts outrageously with jazz (the complicated structures leave a lot of space for improvisation).

Michel Roques (1936), also a composer, and a player of various types of saxophones, is a generous musician when he plays the flute, overflowing with a sunny lyricism in his ballads — which earned him praise in the magazine *Down Beat*.

Michel Edelin (1941), composer and an expert in musical education, is the only French jazz player who plays the flute alone. He joined in the creation of the group Triode and then created the group Flute Rencontres (with the flautist-saxophonist Denis Barbier). Surrounding himself with highly qualified partners (his old accomplice, the double-bass player François Méchali), his music synthesized the moods of cool, West Coast and Free Jazz.

Chromatic harmonica genius: **Toots Thielemans** *Antibes (1987)*.

The 'bizarre brigade'

Instruments on the fringe

The French horn

From his professional debut (1943), **Julius Watkins** (1921–1977) persevered in his career as a jazz player (working all the while in classical music ensembles and Broadway bands), contributing, in spite of the rarity of his appearances, to giving the French horn a solo role. He played with the boppers, to whom he felt close (Kenny Clarke, Oscar Pettiford), he shared leadership of Jazz Modes with Charlie Rouse, and played with Charles Mingus, after recording with John Coltrane (*Africa/Brass*) and participating in the records of the Miles Davis-Gil Evans association.

West Coast musicians were interested by the taste for form and sound shown by **John Graas** (1924–1962), and by his lightness and mobility. Thus Stan Kenton, Shorty Rogers, Jimmy Giuffre, Bud Shank were all influenced by him. Like his fellow horn player, Gunther Schuller, he was interested in closing the gap between the Afro-American art and that of the Western tradition, and he adapted Bach and Mozart and composed several pieces, including a symphony in which he proved his mastery of counterpoint.

Bagpipes

Fascinated by the performance of the Black Watch Bagpipe Band at President Kennedy's funeral, the saxophonist, flautist and oboe player **Rufus Harley** (1936) became interested in the bagpipes, and was the only musician to adapt them to jazz. He used a Coltranian approach impregnated with blues, as far as the instrument would allow. He played with Sonny Rollins at the Montreux Festival in 1974 (the record *Cutting Edge*).

Oboe and Bassoon

Apart from Illinois Jacquet and Bob Cooper (already mentioned), the tenor sax player and flautist William Evans, who became **Yusef Lateef** (1921) after his conversion to Islam, was an expert in both these instruments seldom used in jazz. With the desire to extend jazz to other musical horizons, he showed his attraction for the music of the Middle East and the instruments generally used (wooden flutes, and the argol, a sort of Syrian oboe). Playing the tenor sax, he stayed faithful in his approach to bebop, and played notably with Cannonball Adderley's sextet between 1962 and 1964. Henceforth, he was to devote a lot of time to teaching, continuing in the meantime to play what he called an 'auto-physio-psychic' kind of music.

Mandolin

David Grisman (whose records are numerous) adapted the instrument from bluegrass to jazz, from funk to Latin American. Stephane Grappelli and Eddie Gomez played with him in the record *Hot Dawg* in 1979, and the violinist joined his quintet in 1981 for a live recording.

Tuba

The tuba, the wind equivalent of a double-bass, was initially limited to regimental bands, and was played in jazz bands during the 1920s. Most tuba players switched to the stringed double-bass in the following decade. Among the first virtuosos in the depths of the bands, we must mention John Kirby (who played in Fletcher Henderson's band) and Red

Callender, who after becoming a double-bass player, sometimes reverted to the instrument of his youth with Stan Kenton and Charles Mingus, in the 1960s.

Ray Draper (1940–1982), the first tuba soloist in modern jazz, played in the company of Jackie McLean, John Coltrane and Max Roach at the start of his career (1956). He then diversified, composing (*Fugue for Brass*), forming a rock group, accompanying Archie Shepp and Don Cherry, and recording with Mick Jagger and Eric Clapton.

Howard Johnson (1941) a poly-instrumentalist (baritone saxophone, bass clarinet) and a versatile musician, was from 1963 the first great tuba virtuoso in jazz, to be joined by **Bob Stewart** (1945) in the 1970s. Both were capable of an agility, a lightness and a speed similar to that of a trumpeter, while they could guarantee a dynamic rhythmic bass. They crop up constantly in different contexts, always in the vanguard of modern trends. Howard Johnson played with Charles Mingus, Archie Shepp, Charlie Haden's Liberation Music Orchestra, Michel Portal, and was also the leader of Gravity, a group including several tubas. Bob Stewart played notably with Arthur Blythe, in Carla Bley's band, and Lester Bowie's Brass Fantasy, and he also shared the direction of a quartet with the horn player John Clark.

In France the trio of tubas plus drums, Tubapack, and the octet Elephant Tuba-horde led by Marc Steckar with Michel Godard, revived the spirit of the brass bands with a music which is resolutely open and lively.

Cello

Fred Katz (1919), also a pianist, was the first to adapt the classical technique and tone of the instrument to the characteristics of jazz. His collaboration with the groups of

Chico Hamilton (1955–1959) is particularly memorable, notably for a tribute to Duke Ellington, the record *Ellington Suite* with Jim Hall (guitar) and Buddy Collette (alto sax, tenor sax).

Jean-Charles Capon (1936), won first prize at the Conservatoire, and was a pupil of Paul Tortelier. In 1962 he created a quintet under the double ensign of chamber music and jazz. He then formed a duo with the guitarist Christian Escoudé and a trio with the accordionist Richard Galliano and the vibraphone player Philippe Macé or the drummer Gilles Perrin. He was a member of the Swing Strings System, the group of double-bass player Didier Levallet.

Another musician to express himself uniquely on the instrument, **Abdul Wadud** (1947) played jazz from the age of fourteen, performing in a trio with Anthony Davis and James Newton, and until 1985, with the Black Swan Quartet.

Sitar and Tabla

Collin Walcott (1945–1984) displayed his talents on these instruments in the group Oregon, together with guitarist and pianist Ralph Towner, double-bass player Glen Moore, and oboe and horn player Paul McCandless.

Steel drums

Othello Molineaux and **Andy Narell** are included in the ranks of those jazz musicians who specialize in playing the steel drums. This instrument is made from salvaged metal containers, and is the invention of poor countries. Molineaux played in the big band of Jaco Pastorius and Narell with his own groups.

Toots Thielemans

1922, Brussels

The harmonic heart

From the most childish of instruments, he made a sort of 'trumpet-organ' through which modern harmony really 'breathes'.

Jean-Baptiste Thielemans was always fascinated by harmony. A child accordionist, he was converted to the guitar by the discovery of his compatriot Django Reinhardt — whom he followed step by step through the streets of Brussels — and to the harmonica by listening to the records of Django with Larry Adler, and Max Gueldray with Ray Ventura. After the Liberation, the revelation of bebop gave him wings, but teased by European jazz fans, for a long time he shunned the harmonica in public. Invited by an American uncle, he played in *Birdland*, notably with the Charlie Parker All Stars. He was hired for a tour by Benny Goodman and then by Dinah Washington, and in the 1950s he became the guitarist in George Shearing's prestigious quintet. Thus he found himself propelled into the jazz 'aristocracy', touring with Lester Young, Count Basie, Stan Getz and Sarah Vaughan. The British pianist also introduced him to Bill Evans, with whom he recorded one of his most

'**Jazz** is like a shower . . . there are notes which flow and then others which stick, which cling to the skin' (interview with Gérald Arnaud, 1980).

beautiful records, *Affinity* (1978). In the 1960s, he lived for a time in Sweden, where he played regularly with Svend Asmussen and N.H.Ø.P. He began to whistle while he played the guitar, which brought him a huge success with one of his rare compositions 'Bluesette' (1963), a 'Bluesy' waltz improvised one evening with Stephane Grappelli, remembering one of Cannonball Adderley's choruses.

A little later, Thielemans began to play with Quincy Jones, whose favourite soloist he became, and played in a lot of film themes, (*Midnight Cowboy, Salut l'Artiste . . .*) and on television for the ABC Channel. His life then became a series of perpetual comings and goings between the United States and Belgium, between pop and jazz. He accompanied Paul Simon and Peggy Lee, recorded with Dizzy Gillespie, Oscar Peterson, Joe Pass, Zoot Sims, J.J. Johnson, Philip Catherine, and the Brazilian accordionist, Sivuca. 1979 saw the start of a prolific friendship with Jaco Pastorius, then he played more and more with his own quartet.

A debonair character with youthful enthusiasm, and a collector of dirty stories, he had a passionate lust for life and for music, and even more for the harmonica. Toots is without doubt the most 'transatlantic' of jazz musicians, effortlessly translating his Belgian cheekiness into New Yorkian jive. Born the same day (but twenty three years later) as Duke Ellington, he was just as able to magnificently transpose his whole band to the guitar. An unrivalled master of the chromatic harmonica, as such he had very few real disciples, (apart from the Brazilian Mauricio Einhorn).

Accordion swing

For a long time, the odour of sanctity did not belong to the 'free reeds' in the jazz world, some critics going as far as to describe the accordion as 'anti-jazz!'

Nonetheless, from the beginning of the century, Pietro Deiro was a remarkable ragtimer, and in 1930, 'Accordion Joe' Cornell Smelser, let the instrument in to jazz by the front door, recording with Duke Ellington. In the same epoch, Django Reinhardt made his debut, accompanying accordionists (Jean Vaissade, Louis Vola, who became the double-bass player of the Hot-Club in France) and certain harmonic features invented by the brilliant guitarist owe a great deal to listening to them, as did the much later innovations of Joe Zawinul, who himself had been an accordionist in his youth. The 'poor man's piano' inspired other instrumentalists as well (Charley Bazin, Buster Moten, George Shearing, Fred Van Hove, Bernard Lubat, Emmanuel Bex and the Sardinian Antonello Salis), but it still remains a specialist's instrument.

Art Van Damme (1920) made his career in Chicago, as the 'shark' of the N.B.C. Studios. Under the influence of Benny Goodman, he adapted the aesthetic of swing to the accordion, and his quintet won remarkable success in the 1940s and 1950s.

Tommy Gumina is his only rival in this respect, due to his regular collaboration with the clarinettist Buddy DeFranco. He is also one of the greatest technical innovators on the accordion.

Gustave Viseur (1916–1974), known as 'Gus' or 'Tatave', is the great pioneer of the 'jazz-musette' style. A talented composer — 'Jeannette', 'Flambée montalbanaise' — he leaves us the memory of a great improviser on a par with Django or the Ferret brothers.

Tony Murena (1917–1971), linked like Viseur to Django and to the Hot-Club of France, also had an influence on the whole

of the following generation, which discovered through his records that 'the bellows' could swing' . . .

Jo Privat (1919) is the permanent support of the *Batalajo*, the famous Parisian cabaret of Rue Lappe. He knows better than anyone how to slide unobserved from 3/4 time to 4/4 time, and he also likes to surround himself with 'manouche' guitarists.

Clifton Chénier (1925–1987) is the great master of *zydeco* (from 'haricot', the music of the Cajun balls of Louisana, derived from the French quadrille, in its closest form to blues). Influenced by the great master **Amédée Ardoin** (1900–1930), but also by blues players like Lowell Fulson, he spread this kind of very unusual music throughout the U.S., and also, towards the end of his life, in French-speaking countries.

Marcel Azzola (1927), the accompanist of Montand, Greco and Brel (amongst others), is one of the greatest virtuosos of the instrument (Oscar in 1962). This Italian from the Pantin quarter of Paris contributed a great deal to jazz rather late in his life, notably by his association with Martial Solal and his records with the Caratini and Fosset duo.

Richard Galliano (1950), another Paris Italian, accompanied Claude Nougaro for a long time, before he founded his own group, brilliantly adapting for the accordion the entire harmonic language of contemporary jazz, as well as certain electronic effects.

Francis Varis, member of the Corde and Lames quartet, which recorded especially with Lee Konitz, claims in his repertoire, which reaches from Ellington to Monk, that the accordion is the greatest jazz instrument.

Jazz goes electric
Sophistication and synthesizers

The arrival in force of electrified instruments in the 1950s, then above all the wave of electronic instruments in the 1970s and musical computer technology in the 1980s, is certainly the greatest challenge jazz has had to accept since its origins. There are three reasons. First, the word 'jazz' has been linked since the start, in the collective imagination, to the specific sound of an acoustic ensemble where pianos, wind instruments, plucked strings and percussion predominate. Then, amplification in an early period guaranteed the success of singers regardless of their real musical sense, and later, the instrumentalists who were the most 'effective' in keeping strict time. Finally, the take-off of electronic stringed instruments forces us to reconsider the human factor in the spontaneity required by improvised music.

All this explains the reticence and even the resistance — evidently in vain — with which jazz players and their habitual public for a long time opposed the first great revolution in musical history. It was only timidly, and twenty years after their commercialization, that jazz really adopted the guitar without a drum and the electric double-bass and piano, and ten years later, the synthesizer. It is also true that the cost of the equipment is more difficult to meet for jazz musicians who generally have a lower standard of living than their rock counterparts.

Nevertheless, there have been electronic pioneers in jazz. An ingenious handyman, Sun Ra used synthesizers from the end of the 1950s, well before rock and pop took off. Paul Bley and Bill Evans very soon, although very seldom, used the Fender piano. Some musicians, like Oscar Peterson or Jean-Louis Chautemps, were very keen on the new technology without using it on the jazz scene.

At the end of the 1980s, a distinction could be made between six categories of material available:

– electro-mechanical instruments: the sound is produced physically (electric guitar and bass, electric piano with dynamic keys, lyricon, etc.), then transformed and in particular amplified electronically, revealing inaudible frequencies and harmonics at a low volume;

– sound 'effects' (echo, distortion, reverberation, etc.) generally activated by pedals, which could be adapted to all instruments;

– synthesizers: sound is programmed electronically from basic parameters. First monophonic, they were to become polyphonic and numerical from the 1970s. Thanks to the standard 'MIDI' system they could be linked to instruments and accessories of all makes;

– *Samplers* made it possible to memorize and re-use any sound at will. It is possible, for example, to get Ray Charles's 'voice' from a piano, or Miles Davis's 'sound' from a guitar. Brass instruments themselves did not escape this revolution, since several saxophonists like Mike Brecker immediately experimented successfully with the Steinerphone EWI, a real 'sax-synthesizer' commercialized by Akai;

– Sequencers: they recorded a series of notes (percussive sounds for rhythm boxes or *drum machines*), which could be treated by a sampler; sequences programmed in this way could be replayed on the synthesizer.

Finally, micro-computers made a dazzling appearance in jazz player's homes, if not on their stages: all the great names — Macintosh, Atari, Amstrad — have software which makes it possible to compose and to play complex orchestral parts in real time, to edit scores, and to make multi-track recordings, etc. A real Rolls-Royce in the fabrication of electronic stringed instruments, the Synclavier — and its rivals Fairlight or Kurzweil — combines the functions of a keyboard synthesizer (which produces an excellent piano-like tone), with that of sampler, computer and mobile sound studio.

The studio itself has become the most sophisticated of instruments, which should suffice to calm those jazz players who remained fiercely opposed to anything electronic. Indeed, if at the start musical electronics has been satisfied with producing rather 'vulgar' sounds, today it has assumed quite another dimension. Thanks to the magic of programming, the improviser has available not only a choice of notes limited by the register, the tone and the fingering of his instrument, but an infinity of sounds and rhythms which he can summon at will in real time.

Completely acoustic music retains its champions, notably Wynton Marsalis and Keith Jarrett, a trend it would be stupid to consider as reactionary. The traditional fabrication of stringed instruments is thriving, and continues to reveal new virtuosos. Some musicians, finally, will combine traditional instruments and the very latest technology on the same stage: this is the case with Miles Davis, Herbie Hancock or Chick Corea.

Just as in the so-called 'cultured' contemporary music a Dusapin and a Pierre Henry can co-exist, an Arvo Part and a Boulez, jazz will henceforth have two universes at its finger-tips, which are moreover not separated by being in airtight compartments.

Jimi Hendrix

1942, Seattle — London, 1970

The blues and 'flash'

The ephemeral hero of a generation ready for all experiences, he developed a symphonic concept of the electric guitar.

Hendrix also gave a universal dimension to wild and provocative behaviour among rhythm'n'blues musicians. He began with the best among them: Solomon Burke, Wilson Pickett, Curtis Knight, B.B. King, Ike and Tina Turner, and above all Little Richard, his main model. His sexual freedom and his immoderate taste for hard drugs too often led people to forget that he was the greatest guitarist of the 1960s, and the most inventive since Django and Charlie Christian.

He was left-handed, but nevertheless played a right-handed guitar with an unorthodox technique. As a child he learned to play the blues from listening to Robert Johnson, B.B. King and Muddy Waters. He settled in New York in 1965, and was encouraged by Bob Dylan and John Hammond Jr., but his success never exceeded the boundaries of Greenwich Village. However, the bass player Chas Chandler took him to London where he had instant success. He founded a trio, the Jimi Hendrix Experience, with Noel Redding (bass) and Mitch Mitchell (drums). A regular performer at *Ronnie Scott's Jazz Club*, it was there he met Roland Kirk who became his favourite musician. His first 33 rpm recordings — *Are you Experienced?*, *Axis — Bold as Love* and, above all, *Electric Ladyland* — were the most successful 'concept-albums' of the time, as were his concerts with their incomparable ritual of ecstatic improvisation. In 1969, the trio separated, and apart from his brief episode with the Band of Gypsies — with Billy Cox (bass) and Buddy Miles (drums) — Hendrix's life became more and more chaotic, divided between his triumphs at important festivals (Monterey, Woodstock and the Isle of Wight) and his mad solitary research in his New York studio. He drew closer to jazz, re-doubled his jam-sessions, (with Larry Young, Dave Holland, John McLaughlin and with the musicians of the Art Ensemble). He made friends with Miles Davis, and Gil Evans invited him to record. Too late: he died aged 28, from a mixture of alcohol and barbiturates.

A treasure-trove of posthumous records confirms that no-one had better mastery of the polyphonic resources of recording and expressive effects of the Fender Stratocaster guitar, on which he remains the unrivalled champion, like feedback, wah-wah or reverberation. Practically all the guitarists of contemporary rock and jazz are his disciples. A sometimes shattering blues singer — even if his ethereal voice is not always in tune — he was also a real poet, worthy to figure in an anthology of the 'post-beat generation'.

The story of Jesus is so simple:
When they crucified him, a woman cried his
   name (. . .)
As men,
We cannot explain
Why a woman is always at stake . . .
When we die (. . .)
The story of Jesus
Is yours and mine
It's not worth fearing solitude,
You and me, in search of freedom.
The story of life?
Shorter
Than the bat of an eyelid . . .
The story of love?
Hello and goodbye,
Until we meet again!'

unpublished poem by Jimi Hendrix, written
on the eve of his death).

Weather Report

1970 — 1985

An electronic group of genius

Breathing in all the scents of the air of the times, this evolutionary but coherent band embodied a sort of traditional futurism.

Few groups in the history of jazz have so fully reflected the spirit of an epoch, or rather a generation. In the beginning, they had the impulse of Miles Davis who from 1969 paved the way to a 'fusion' which was to burst into a violent but short-lived eruption, ending in the tragic withdrawal of the trumpeter through exhaustion in 1975.

The saxophonist **Wayne Shorter** left the Miles Davis group in 1970. He then participated in the first phase of this alchemical experience, where an alloy was forged of hard bop, funk, Hendrixian romanticism, and a certain taste for free-jazz inspired atonality, Coltrane-style hyper-modulation and various exotic influences — Caribbean, Hindustani,

African, and (what impressed Shorter the most) Brazilian. With another former member of Miles's group, the saxophonist was to attempt to continue an already substantial achievement.

Joe Zawinul (1932) played a number of instruments since childhood, including the accordion. As well as being the arranger for Friedrich Gulda, he was the pianist of Dinah Washington (1960), then Cannonball Adderley (1961–1969), before spending a year with Miles, for whom he wrote a portion of the decisive albums *Bitches Brew* and *Live-Evil*. After a few lessons from Roger Powell, the maker of ARP synthesizers, he became their best user, and with a greatly advanced technology, he recorded a first album, called simply *Weather Report*. It is freely improvised, highly spiced with rhythm'n'blues and his inimitable sound is already recognisable. As the name of the group indicates its purpose was to reveal, month by month the musical climate of the environment.

In 1976, the weather changed brutally with the arrival of a hurricane called Jaco Pastorius, who amplified the motor role of the double-bass, then the use of a synthesizer brought a real rainbow of polyphonic sounds. Weather Report henceforth blended an ensemble of richer and richer riffs in the manner of Duke Ellington (some of whose themes have been borrowed), of voice, sounds and instrumental tones whose succession evokes a world tour at the speed of sound. In this unheard of proliferation Shorter's presence seems to be gradually extinguished, and the group ended by disbanding in 1985. The new bands of Zawinul — Zawinul Syndicate — and Shorter continued to prolong the electronic dialogue, but they never recovered its evocative powers.

The main sidemen of Weather Report
(with the date that they joined)

Bass: Miroslav Vitous (1970), Alphonso Johnson (1974), Jaco Pastorius (1976), Victor Bailey (1982).

Drums: Alphonse Mouzon (1970), Eric Gravatt (1972), Chester Thompson (1976), Peter Erskine (1978), Omar Hakim (1982).

Percussion: Airto Moreira (1970), Dom Um Romao (1971) Alex Acuna (1976), Manolo Badrena (1977), Robert Thomas Jr. (1982), Jose Rossy (1983), Mino Cinelu (1984).

Swing Machines
Big band music

If 'big band' were to be translated as 'large group', the term would lose all its sound effect without gaining anything in clarity! In fact it is not so much its size — the number of its members — which decides whether or not a jazz band is a big band: it is a definite style relying on its division into sections (reed and woodwind, trumpets, trombones, rhythm section), rather than on the use of orchestration (so called arrangements or scores) more or less pre-written and complex.

In the 1920s, in order to progress beyond the basically orderless polyphony issuing from New Orleans, big band music was born as a response to the challenge of 'symphonic jazz'. The radio, at the peak of its development at the time, played a decisive role; on its wavelengths, which were still unsteady, brass sounded better than strings, and offered a seductive contrast between the mellow sound of the saxophones and the stridence of the mouthpieces. This is how in the 1930s and 1940s, the big band became the most widespread jazz formation. In these times of struggle against the Depression, it represented a luxury within everybody's reach, a marvellous accompaniment for dancing and a spectacular solution to the unemployment of musicians! In the 1950s, the reversal of the trend had a brutal effect on these *swing machines*: numerous clever arrangers had learned how to make small groups 'make a big sound' through the artifices of writing and the combination of sections. It was nothing but profitable for the promoters and the record companies! Even Basie had to give up his big ideas for a while.

But the big band has since resumed its dynamic role in the life of jazz. Not a single American university is without one of its own, following the example of the French National jazz band 'Orchestre National de Jazz', a repertory orchestra and a real living school for musicians of any age or style.

Duke Ellington Orchestra

1923–1974

From the jungle to the garden

The greatest of the Afro-American composers wrote only what was necessary to express his people's genius: the memories of a band leader, through fifty years of masterpieces.

In 1923, when Ellington returned to Harlem where he already had his place among the disciples of James P. Johnson, Fats Waller and Willie Smith, the neighbourhood was immersed in the *Harlem Renaissance*. The existence of this widespread movement of artists and intellectuals was due to the fact that the black bourgeoisie was was very rapidly replacing the German, Irish, Italian and Jewish immigrants from central Europe. This new Harlem was not yet a ghetto, and every evening all Manhattan surged into numerous theatres, cinemas, music-halls and night clubs, which rivalled those on Broadway. To accompany the singer Bricktop, then star at *Barron's*, Duke got his first band together (which he baptized The Washingtonians), with his childhood friend, drummer Sonny Greer, saxophonist Otto Hardwicke, banjo player Elmer Snowden and trumpeter Arthur Whetsol. The following year, Duke took over effective leadership of the group, engaged the dynamic Irving Mills as manager, and recruited the musicians who were going to contribute the most to the definition of the Ellingtonian 'range', due to the ingenious use of mutes: trombone player Charles Irvis (replaced two years later by 'Tricky' Sam Nanton), and trumpeter Bubber Miley.

From that time, and for half a century, the Duke Ellington band was to impose the

'Harlem sound' on the whole world. In 1927, Duke was engaged by the Cotton Club, the most luxurious of the Harlem cabarets. He performed there regularly until 1938. This was the *jungle* period, when the group, already a big band, accompanied the sumptous pseudo-African reviews which would send shivers down the spines of a *white only* public (whose conscience was not always as light as its colour!), and where he integrated his greatest soloists (Barney Bigard, Harry Carney, Johnny Hodges, Cootie Williams, Lawrence Brown, Rex Stewart) and his most beautiful voices (Adelaide Hall, Ivie Anderson). His 'successes succeeded one another': 'Black and Tan Fantasy' and 'East Saint Louis Toodle-Oo' (1927) 'Creole Love Call' and 'Black Beauty' (1928), 'The Mooche' (1929), 'Rockin' in Rhythm' and 'Mood Indigo' (1931), 'I Don't Mean a Thing if it Ain't Got That Swing' (1932), which became the most convincing definition of jazz, 'Sophisticated Lady' (1933, the year of a triumphant European tour), 'Solitude' (1934), 'In a Sentimental Mood' (1935), 'Echoes of Harlem' (1936). With 'Caravan' (1937) the Puerto Rican Juan Tizol co-wrote, with Duke, the first of a series of titles which are the ancestors of Latin jazz and salsa. In all Ellington wrote, alone or in collaboration, a good thousand themes which in quantity as much as in quality, make him the greatest composer in the history of jazz.

The 'Ellingtonian system' consists of writing pieces which, generally on the same harmonic scale, each include several motifs whose rhythmic and melodic structures are expressly conceived to highlight the performance of a specific musician. The latter 'rebounds' as it were on this basis, to further diversify his improvisation. Duke was also an absolutely unequalled master of orchestration; he never ceased to invent new combinations of sound which we infinitely varied because of his intensive use of mutes, including the famous plunger mute, his most obvious 'invention'.

In 1939, all these qualities were somehow enhanced by the arrival of Billy Strayhorn, a pianist and composer more Ellingtonian than Ellington himself, who until his death in 1967 was Duke's alter ego. The band was to live a second golden age with the arrival of Jimmy Blanton and Ben Webster, and several new masterpieces whose effect was proved on the vast stages of the enormous concert halls for which Duke had by now forsaken the cabarets: 'Concerto for Cootie' and 'Ko-Ko' (1939), 'In a Mellowtone' and 'Cotton Tail' (1940) 'Warm Valley' and 'I Got it Bad' (1941), 'C-Jam Blues', 'Diminuendo & Crescendo in Blues' (1942), which in the middle of the 1950s, thanks to the tenor Paul Gonsalves, became the old favourite of their marathon concerts. Composed for a Carnegie Hall concert with Mahalia Jackson as a soloist, 'Black, Brown and Beige' (1943) was the first of these 'suites', which were to become Duke's favourite form.

Friendly with world celebrities, and considered throughout the world as the most prestigious ambassador of the American melting-pot, Ellington nonetheless kept his feet on the ground. His slightly shabby elegance and his rather aloof courtesy never permitted him to prefer the aristocracy to the eternal caste of troubadours (of which he was one of the last). Spangled with decorations, regularly received at the White House and at the court of Britain, welcomed as a head of State in Africa, in Asia and in South America, he absorbed musical impressions everywhere he went, which immediately became the ingredients for new masterpieces: 'Far East Suite' (1964), 'Virgin Islands Suite' (1965), 'La Plus Belle Africaine' (1967). These 'suites' succeeded each other without ever having any similarities, other than that of the sovereign personality of the leader and the musicians he promoted. Nagged by his nostalgia for original jazz — 'New Orleans Suite' (1971) — or motivated by a spiritual quest which gradually tore him from his legendary hedonism, — the three 'Sacred Concerts' — Duke Ellington wrote an opus in the margin of jazz history, which magnifies his ephemeral charm all the more, Above all, his discography was to be the most wonderful tribute that a musician ever paid to other musicians, those of a band which was simultaneously his work, his studio and the artist himself.

The main soloists and their dates with the Ellington band:

Cat Anderson [trumpet] (1944–47, 1950–59, 1961–71); Harold Baker [trumpet] (1942–44, 1946–52, 1957–63); Louie Bellson [drums] (1951–53, 1965–66); Barney Bigard [clarinet, tenor sax] (1927–42); Jimmy Blanton [bass] (1939–41); Wellman Braud [bass] (1927–35, 1944, 1961); Lawrence Brown [trombone] (1932–51, 1960–70); Harry Carney [baritone sax, clarinet, etc] (1927–74); Wild Bill Davis [organ] (1969–74); Mercer Ellington [trumpet] (1964–); Paul Gonsalves [tenor sax] (1950–74); Sonny Greer [drums] (1920–51); Fred Guy [banjo, guitar] (1925–49); Jimmy Hamilton [clarinet, tenor sax] (1943–68); Johnny Hodges [alto sax, clarinet] (1928–51, 1955–70); Wendell Marshall [bass] (1948–54); Ray Nance [trumpet, violin] (1940–44, 1945–63, 1965–71); Joe 'Tricky Sam' Nanton [trombone] (1926–46); Oscar Pettiford [bass] (1945–48); Russell Procope [clarinet, alto sax] (1946–74); Al Sears [tenor sax] (1944–49, 1950–51); Rex Stewart [trumpet] (1934–45); Billy Strayhorn [piano, arranger] (1939–67); Billy Taylor [bass] (1935–40); Juan Tizol [trumpet] (1929–44, 1951–53, 1960); Ben Webster [tenor sax] (1935–36, 1940–43, 1948–49); Cootie Williams [trumpet] (1929–40, 1962–74); Sam Woodyard [drums] (1955–65).

Fletcher Henderson

1898, Cuthbert — New York, 1952

A formidable head hunter

Leaving baseball for music, he managed to include almost all the pre-war stars in his team.

As a pianist, Fletcher Henderson first accompanied singers, Ethel Waters (1921–1922), Bessie Smith, and Ma Rainey, then he directed a small dance band, playing a passably commercial brand of music. It was at the *Roseland Ballroom* in New York, in 1924, that everything was to change. There he got his first jazz band together, which included two trumpets, one trombone, three reeds, and a rhythm section. Towards 1927, he decided on the division of the band into the following instrumental sections: three trumpets, two trombones, three saxophones, one piano, one double-bass and a percussion section. The big band had just been born. The formation was hardly to vary even to the present day.

Served by talented arrangers (Don Redman, also a saxophonist, Benny Carter, his brother Horace, a pianist and also a band leader like him, Coleman Hawkins), and an arranger himself from the beginning of the 1930s, Henderson brought the technique of writing for separate sections to the highest degree of perfection, invented riffs and background music destined to support, re-launch, or to surround the soloist's intervention.

From autumn 1924 to summer 1925, Louis Armstrong arrived from Chicago on Fletcher's invitation, and occupied a decisive place among the ranks of the band, as well as Coleman Hawkins, who established himself until his departure in 1934 as the main soloist. The frequent changes in musicians never changed the quality of the ensembles, indeed far from it, since each new soloist brought his own contribution, and the arrangements were organized around the personality of each (Rex Stewart, Cootie Williams, Dicky Wells, Buster Bailey).

After the space of a year, Fletcher formed another band, playing alternately with the bands of Count Basie and Earl Hines, at the *Grand Terrace Café* of Chicago. But in 1939 all kinds of problems forced him to dissolve the band again; he joined Benny Goodman's band as a pianist and arranger. He had already supplied the clarinettist with an impressive series of successes since 1935, contributing to launch a band other than his, to a glory he himself never attained ('King Porter Stomp', 'Blue Skies').

Henderson reduced his activities in 1940. He again worked for Goodman in 1945, once again accompanied Ethel Water (1948–1949), and was the leader of a sextet when he was struck by partial paralysis. H was hospitalized for a long period, and die two years later. In the history of jazz, the young pianist of the 1920s remains the firs great architect of the big band.

The swing era (1935–1945)

1935: America recovered from the depression — it was swing time, and the big bands were at their peak, for the pleasure of the dancers who invaded the ballrooms of the big hotels as well as the Cotton Club, Small's Paradise, *the* Apollo *and especially the* Savoy *in Harlem, baptized the 'House of joyful feet', the kingdom of the* Savoy's Sultans *of Al Cooper and Chick Webb. It was the epoch of the 'battles' of bands and new fashions in dance: Big Apple, Black Bottom, Suzy 'Q' and the famous Lindy-hop.*

Benny Carter (born in 1907), an elegant, refined, eclectic musician, a composer, and an inventive arranger whose broad range of sound is associated with an extremely free swing, led several bands from 1928 to 1945. His contribution was most important in the evolution of the orchestral composition of jazz, from classical to modern.

Andy Kirk and his Clouds of Joy was one of the bands who were triumphant in New York (*Apollo, Savoy*) in the 1930s, with the music of Kansas City, of which he was one of the experts. Under the musical direction of the pianist and arranger Mary Lou Williams, the group discovered its true identity.

Lucky Millinder (1900–1966), first 'master of ceremonies' in the Chicago clubs, directed the Mills Blue Rhythm Band from 1934 to 1938, and the Bill Doggett Band, before founding his own band (1940–1952), which welcomed in particular the trumpeters Henry 'Red' Allen, Charlie Shavers and Dizzy Gillespie.

After forming with his brother Jimmy (saxophonist and clarinettist) the Dorsey Brothers Orchestra in 1928, **Tommy Dorsey** (1905–1956), the 'sentimental gentleman of the trombone' who had a formidable technique, a fluent legato and a silky tone, directed one of the best and most popular swing bands from 1935 to 1953. The choice of arrangers like Benny Carter, Deane Kincaide, Sy Oliver, and the presence of excellent musicians such as Bunny Berigan, Ziggy Elman, Bud Freeman, Dave Tough, and a singer making his debut, Frank Sinatra, is certainly not surprising. Reconciled with his brother, they joined forces again in 1953 until Tommy's death.

The saxophonist **Charlie Barnet** (1913), whose constant preoccupation was to produce the maximum swing, created his very Ellingtonian first band in 1933. The following year, he performed at the *Apollo*, the first white group engaged in this sacred place of Harlem. He very soon integrated black musicians like Roy Eldridge, Oscar Pettiford and Trummy Young. His signature tunes 'Cherokee' (1939) and 'Skyliner' (1944) were a great popular success.

One of the favourite bands of the habitués of the Savoy was that of **Erskine Hawkins** (1914), nicknamed the '20th century Gabriel'. A trumpeter specializing in the high register, he surrounded himself with the best arrangers (Jimmy Mundy) and soloists. 'Tuxedo Junction' is a perfect example of the style of this champion of swing.

Among the approximately three hundred bands submitted for appreciation to the readers of the magazine *Metronome* between 1937 and 1940, our attention is focused on some of the most typical of this period which is now past.

Jimmie Lunceford

1902, Fulton — Seaside, 1947

A joyful perfectionist

Assisted by Sy Oliver, he made his band a miracle of wisely controlled rigour and surprises.

When Jimmie Lunceford died during a session autographing records, a page in the history of big bands was brutally turned. To tell the truth, it had already been gradually crumpled by the departure in 1939 of Sy Oliver (1910–1988), trumpeter, singer, but above all a great arranger to whom Lunceford owes his style, and by the mobilization of several of his best players in 1942. From its peak as a serious rival of the bands of Basie and Ellington, the band continued to decline until the death of its leader. A salvage operation was attempted under the lead of faithful friends, but it had no future.

A saxophonist, Lunceford played in various bands, before teaching music in Memphis, where he formed a big band with his pupils, the Chickasaw Syncopaters (1926). Three pillars of the band soon joined them: drummer James Crawford, saxophonist Willie Smith, and pianist and arranger Edwin Wilcox.

Its rise: from 1930 to 1933, the formation

trained in Buffalo under the iron baton in the velvet glove of an exacting boss who strengthened his team of arrangers by engaging Oliver. The band became famous in just a few weeks thanks to its success in the *Cotton Club* in Harlem, where it replaced that of Cab Calloway (January 1934).

Its peak: 1935–1940. 'Rhythm is our business' proclaimed the whole of that lovely world whose motto is 'For dancers only'. Under the leadership of Oliver, the band found the Lunceford tempo and style: all the different sections blended harmoniously, answering each other song-after-song, that of the saxophones with a powerful volume, that of the trombones with broad and supple glissandos, of the trumpets with Paul Webster's flights into the highest register, and that famous two-beat based on the nonchalant stress of two-time, that elastic balance which, played at medium tempo, gave birth to the bounce style.

In the midst of these disciplined ranks, which was animated by a rare team spirit, the saxophonists Willie Smith (alto) and Joe Thomas (tenor), and the trombonists Trummy Young and Eddie Durham distinguished themselves, as did guitarist Al Norris. Drummer James Crawford galvanized the ensemble (a flexibly emphasized off-beat rhythm), and the band had an excellent vocal trio. They performed in ballrooms, especially at the *Savoy*, where the dancers particularly appreciated the tempo.

Its decline: Sy Oliver left, the great team crumbled, Lunceford joined the saxes, the band tried desperately to survive, but there was no longer any heart in it, and Jimmie gave up.

Count Basie

1904, Red Bank — Hollywood (Florida), 1984

The swing in . . .

Returning to the crystalline simplicity of the blues, he invented a mechanism of precision which punctuated the tempo with memorable riffs.

The 'Red Bank Kid', fascinated in his youth by Fats Waller — who initiated him to the organ — and by the stride pianists, the accompanist of singers, a pianist at travelling shows, found himself out of work in Kansas City.

The capital of Missouri was a real laboratory hatching black music, where a

In Count Basie's own words

'I got everything I wanted. When I was young in Kansas City, I knew nothing about Frank Sinatra, Billy Eckstine, Ella Fitzgerald, of all those concert halls, of all those countries. I did not know what it was like to direct a band . . . All I wanted was to be big, to be in show-business and to travel . . . and that's what I've been doing all my life'.

In the words of the pianist George Shearing:

'One simply could not tire of this machine in the end — clink, clink, clink, — one could never leave it . . .'

Basie's Piano

In Count Basie's own words: 'I was never a very good pianist, I was always content with playing a few little pieces at the beginning to set the band going, and sometimes to fiddle around in the middle of a piece.'

lot of clubs welcomed musicians on tour, and where they met for interminable jam sessions. Gradually, a style emerged, based on blues, which was to influence the course of jazz with its use of riffs and *four-beat* time. Enthusiastic about the music by the Blue Devils, directed by the double-bass player Walter Page, a respresentative of this trend with the band of Bennie Moten, William 'Bill' Basie, who was then an accompanist for the silent movies, wrote to Page. In 1928 he became the band's pianist, then, a year later, the pianist in Bennie Moten's band, until Moten died in 1935.

After some hesitation, Basie ended by joining with the saxophonist Buster Smith, to lead the Buster Smith and Basie Barons of Rhythm in the *Club Reno* in Kansas City. It was during a repeat broadcast on the radio that a speaker attributed the title of 'Count' to Basie, and the critic John Hammond 'discovered' him: 'I could not believe my ears . . . Basie had developed an extraordinarily economic style. In a few notes, he said everything that Waller and Hines could say on the piano, using a perfect punctuation — a harmony, a note — capable of stimulating the wind players and making them reach peaks which had so far been inaccessible. Between 1932 and 1936, Basie had discovered the efficiency of simplicity.' Among the musicians could be found notably the trumpeter Buck Clayton, Lester Young, Walter Page and Jo Jones.

Hammond helped Basie to strengthen his band, got him engagements at the *Grand Terrace Café* in Chicago and in the *Roseland Ballroom* in New York, and to record, in October 1936, a session which included Carl Smith (trumpet), Lester Young (for his first recording), the Count, Walter Page, Jo Jones and, for two songs, the singer Jimmy Rushing, with whom Basie had made friends, in the Blue Devils.

In 1937, Basie engaged the guitarist Freddie Green (1911–1987), who stayed for fifty years, and was THE guitarist of the band, forming the All American Rhythm Section with Page and Jones. The formidable Swing Machine had been set going, and at the height of the swing era, it made a place for itself next to the bands of Ellington, Benny Goodman and Tommy Dorsey.

Between 1936 and the beginning of the war, the team was relatively stable, and an impressive number of masterpieces were recorded. Let us mention the greatest soloists of this first period: Buck Clayton, Harry Edison (trumpet), Benny Morton, Dicky Wells (trombone); the formidable reed section: Chu Berry, Hershel Evans, Buddy Tate, Earl Warren, Lester Young,

the singers Billie Holiday and Helen Humes; and let us evoke a few titles: 'Jumpin' at the Woodside', 'One O'Clock Jump', 'Every Tub', as well as the arrangers Eddie Durham, Jimmy Mundy, Buster Harding.

The departure of Lester Young, in December 1940, and of the musicians who were conscripted, created a space in the band, which Basie dissolved in 1950. After directing a small group, he started again in 1952, with new musicians and arrangers: Thad Jones, Joe Newman (trumpet), Eddie Davis, Frank Foster, Frank Wess, Ernie Wilkins (reeds), Sonny Payne (drums), Neal Hefti (arranger) The popularity of 'Every Day' (sung by Joe Williams) and of the record *The Atomic Mr. Basie* put the band back on the top of the list: world tours, accompanying 'stars' (Ella Fitzgerald, Sarah Vaughan, Frank Sinatra); many guests (Roy Eldridge, Dizzy Gillespie, Milt Jackson), festivals (Antibes, Montreux); the engagement of young musicians and arrangers (Eric Dixon, Oliver Nelson, Chico O'Farrill, Sam Nestico); piano duets with Oscar Peterson. Alongside Ellington's the band become a real institution and continued to swing like it did when it began, until the death of its leader and even afterwards, since Frank Foster perpetuated the tradition of this ensemble as the best carrier of pure swing whose name resounds like a symbol COUNT BASIE.

> **In the words of the guitarist Freddie Green:**
>
> 'Basie's piano contributes, without any doubt, to the beat of the band. He stopped the gaps. I feel very at ease when I play with him, for he always seems to know what to play, from the point of view of rhythm. Count is also the best pianist I know for warming up an orchestra, and accompanying soloists. I am thinking of the way he prepares the entrance of each soloist, even at the end of his own solos. He opens the door for you.'

Facing page:
In the 1950s
above:
Count Basie's big band

below:
Duke Ellington's big band

Bop big bands . . .

*In dizzy glissandos and devastating riffs, the history of the great band of modern
jazz is written in the career of its greatest exponent, John Birks 'Dizzy' Gillespie.*

All these dashing young men who were to
revolutionize jazz around the middle of the
1940s belonged to some of the big bands in
which they could only rarely express their
new ideas fully (a few brief solos). For
many of them this stage, usually imposed
by the need to eat, proved rich in
experiences in the first three bands
mentioned below; for these bands, the
arrival of young recruits pawing the
ground, could only be a source of
rejuvenation, at the time when the great
bands of the Swing Era were shortly to
decline.

The band of **Teddy Hill** (1909–1978)
numbered several brilliant soloists among
its ranks, including Dizzy Gillespie; he was
engaged in 1937 for a tour which took him
to Paris for the first time with the *Cotton Club*
Review at the *Moulin Rouge*. In 1940, Hill
became the director/master of ceremonies
of *Minton's Playhouse* where one young bop
'wolf' succeeded another.

Cab Calloway (1907) renewed the
members of his famous *Cotton Club* band
around the end of the 1930s. As Frank
Ténot has stressed, 'the verbal and musical
audacity of the leader helped to encourage
classical jazz in the direction of the riffs and
explosions of bop'. In 1939, he engaged
Dizzy Gillespie, the author of several
arrangements, and fired him in 1941. Why?
Because he flicked little paper balls on to
the stage while his leader was singing(!)

Earl Hines, was the mainstay of the
Grand Terrace Café in Chicago from 1927 to
1948. He was responsible for the evolution
of his various groups from a style imbued
when they began with the aesthetics of the
Chicago bands of the 1920s, to the first
upheavals of bebop. This advance was due

to an adventurous leader, and arrangers
such as Jimmy Mundy and Budd Johnson.
Dizzy Gillespie and Charlie Parker tried
out some of their most fruitful ideas in
Hines's band, in 1942; the singer, Billy
Eckstine, had the young Sarah Vaughan
hired (she had to understudy the leader at
the piano).

After leaving Hines, **Billy Eckstine**,
'Mr. B' (1914), a ballad singer with a
beautiful baritone voice, created his own
group (from 1944 to 1947), competing with
his arranger, Budd Johnson. The masters of
bop could express themselves solo, or be
challenged in duels (chase): Dizzy Gillespie
(always him), Miles Davis, Fats Navarro,
Dexter Gordon, Wardell Gray, Art Blakey
and . . . Sarah Vaughan.

Dizzy Gillespie set up his first permanent band in 1946, a lovely chance for him
to extend his melodic harmonic and rhythmic discoveries within the framework of a
big band. As the main soloist, he surrounded himself with imaginative arrangers like
Walter Gil Fuller, George Russell, and
Tadd Dameron, as well as a whole range of
future stars: Monk, John Lewis, Ray
Brown, Kenny Clarke, Milt Jackson, John
Coltrane in 1949, and introduced Afro-
Cuban contributions with his percussion
player, Chano Pozo (1915–1948). After
1946, the band, explosive, scintillating,
burning furiously, was spangled with
success everywhere it went in the United
States and Europe, but it was dissolved in
1950 for financial reaons. It was to be re-
established for a tour (Middle East, South
America), in 1956–1957, under the musical
direction of Quincy Jones, subsidized by
the Department of State.

. . . and cool big bands

At the same time there is a growing trend among 'white' jazz musicians to attempt to give their ensembles the size, discipline and concert quality of symphony orchestras.

The orchestra of the pianist and arranger **Claude Thornhill** (1909–1965) was completely dedicated to Cool jazz by 1941, thanks to the arranger Gil Evans. By including initially two horns for harmony, and then a tuba (1946), he established that mellow, velvety tone colour, that feeling of immobility ('the band was like afraid to move, making as little noise as possible, all in order to get the "sound"' ... 'that sound was like a cloud sitting above us', admitted Evans later), a style which was a forerunner of Miles Davis's Nonet, as in the album *The Birth of the Cool* in which Evans participated. In 1947 Lee Konitz joined the band (it was practically his first job) and met Gerry Mulligan; in 1951 the latter wrote several arrangements for this band, which was to remain one of the most underrated in the history of jazz.

Woody Herman (1913–1987), a saxophonist, clarinettist, singer and composer, seems to have had a single passion in his career as a musician: to be a band leader, which he became in 1937, and remained until his death. From The Band that Plays the Blues (very successful in 1939 with 'Woodchopper's Ball') to his latest Herds, the musicians were very varied, but the boss kept his band going for nearly fifty years, with only seven months of inactivity. The first Herd, formed in 1943, with exceptional vitality, quickly became famous; Igor Stravinsky was impressed, and composed *Ebony Concerto* for him, which was performed at the Carnegie Hall in 1946. In 1947 Woody led his second Herd, which included the fabulous reed section that became known as the 'Four Brothers'

(Herbie Steward, Stan Getz, Zoot Sims, Serge Chaloff), after the Jimmy Giuffre composition of that name recorded in December 1947. One year later the band recorded 'Early Autumn' (on a Ralph Burns arrangement), in which Stan Getz's legendary solo was to influence a whole generation of tenor saxes. Thus the second Herd found its place in jazz history as a forerunner of cool jazz, alongside Lennie Tristano, the Claude Thornhill band and Miles Davis's Nonet.

The pianist, composer and arranger **Stan Kenton** (1912–1979) led several bands from 1941. His taste for adventure, his temptations and attempts in the field of 'progressive jazz', for the renewal of music as a whole, although his *Innovations in Modern Music*, with 43 musicians, were not universally appreciated, especially after his Swing beginnings with Lunceford, Pete Rugolo's arrangements, so full of 'effects', were to a large extent responsible for this reaction. The period that followed (from 1952) brought unanimous approval, as the band included all the great cool musicians: Lee Konitz, Zoot Sims, Art Pepper, Shorty Rogers, as well as arrangers such as Gerry Mulligan and Bill Holman. Today the waters have been calmed and certain judgments corrected, and one must recognize the important role this band has played in jazz 'with its polymorphous opus which often includes the joy of playing, a taste for challenges, a perverse liking for paradoxical cocktails and a tremendous thrust of innovation . . .', as Alain Tercinet relevantly puts it.

The big machines

Having become an American cultural institution on university campuses, in hotel lounges, and in army messes, the big band was the musical symbol of a dream of unity, freedom and power.

Paul Whiteman doesn't deserve the excesses of praise and criticism that were directed at his 'symphonic jazz', a trifle pompous and not very swinging, between 1919 and 1942. Excited by the possibilities for innovation, and seduced by the notion of a synthesis of musical genres, he commissioned from George Gershwin his famous *Rhapsody in Blue* (February 1924, with the composer at the piano), and created his *Concerto in F*. His band featured several great white jazzmen: Bix Beiderbecke (from 1927 to 1929), the Dorsey brothers, Frankie Trumbauer, Jack Teagarden , and the singer Mildred Bailey.

The drummers **Buddy Rich** (1917–1987) and **Louie Bellson** (1924), fine virtuosi on their instruments, were quick to start up their own large swing outfits, Rich starting in 1946, and Bellson off and on from 1953. Both leaders directed their bands with their hands and with their sticks, without, however, exploiting them as showcases for the instrumental prowess (showy solos) that their audiences expected. Both were able to gather around them talented arrangers: Benny Carter, Tadd Dameron, Oliver Nelson, and remarkable soloists: Harry Edison, Terry Gibbs, Steve Marcus in the case of Rich, and Conte Candoli, Blue Mitchell, Don Menza in the case of Bellson. In the 1970s and 1980s, they were not slow to call on the talents of graduates of the Berklee School of Music in particular.

Faster and faster, higher and higher — that seems to have been the motto of the trumpet-player **Maynard Ferguson** (1928), who drew attention to himself in Stan Kenton's 1950 band with his stratospheric acrobatics. From 1956 to 1964 he was at the head of a super-outfit, the Birdland Dream Band (soloists: Clifford Brown, Al Cohn, Hank Jones; arrangers: Manny Albam, Jimmy Giuffre, Johnny

Mandel, Marty Paich), but after that he turned towards a jazzy variety of commercial jazz-rock, and at the beginning of the 1980s led High Voltage, an 'electronic fusion' septet.

The trumpeter **Don Ellis** (1934–1979), working both in jazz and in contemporary music, started from 1963 on renewing the conventional orchestral language (time signatures from 5/4 to 19/4, incorporation of vocal or string quartets into the ensemble, experiments with oriental instruments and compositions, quartertone trumpets, trombones combining slides with valves). This music, full of virtuosity, collages, and free improvisation, is poorly represented on disc.

Bringing together the traditions inherited from Basie and Ellington with more advanced ideas, the big band formed by the trumpeter **Thad Jones** (1923–1986) and the drummer **Mel Lewis** (1929), and set up in 1965, first performed at the Village Vanguard and soon came to be considered 'the best thing to have come along in the big band world for the past twenty years'. Some new young talents were featured: Larry Schneider, Eddie Daniels, Billy Harper, the singer Dee Dee Bridgewater. From 1979 onwards, the band played under the leadership of the drummer only, with Bob Brookmeyer as official arranger.

An original trumpet player with a style that combined traditional and modern styles, an incomparable technician who specialized in the technique of half-valving, and a humorous vocalist, **Clark Terry** (1920) spent several periods with big bands (Hampton, Basie, Ellington, Quincy Jones, Gerry Mulligan) before forming in the 1970s a joyful and, alas, short-lived 'Big Bad Band' whose arrangements were penned by Jimmy Heath, Frank Wess, Ernie Wilkins and Phil Woods.

Gil Evans

1912, Toronto — Cuernavaca, Mexico, 1988

The disruptive arranger

The New York cool guns would have made the big bands into an ideal setting for the biggest contemporary soloists and composers.

The young, self-taught arranger who introduced French horns and tubas into the Claude Thornhill band was not only to disturb the classic make-up of the big band by using unusual instruments, but also to overturn the traditional cleavage of the orchestra into sections. Evans was the author of a music in perpetual motion, and an indefatigable leader of often short-lived bands. What counted for him was tone colour rather than swing, and timbre rather than mass effect, in an impressionist style (influenced by Debussy, Ravel, de Falla, Albaniz, whom he listened to in the 1930s) of great harmonic sophistication.

Another characteristic, and not the least important, was the freedom that reigned in the performance of his compositions, and the freedom accorded the soloists from the 1970s onwards, when Gil, appropriating electronics and two-beat rhythms, proposed a superior brand of 'fusion' between jazz and rock.

The majority of jazz lovers discovered Gil Evans through his collaborations with Miles Davis; he contributed to the key album *The Birth of the Cool*, for which he wrote two masterpieces, 'Boplicity' and 'Moon Dreams'. Six years later, Miles called upon him for five more indispensable albums: *Miles Ahead* (1957), *Porgy and Bess* (1958), *Sketches of Spain* (1959, which included the famous 'Concierto de Aranjuez'), *At Carnegie Hall* (1961) and *Quiet Nights* (1962). Gil did not perform very often throughout the 1950s and 1960s, but carried on working as an arranger. He recorded a few albums under his own name, such as *Out of the Cool* in 1960, and worked with Steve Lacy, Lee Konitz and Cannonball Adderley.

His first 'electric' album, *Svengali* (1973), stirred up a lot of polemic. Surrounded by young musicians (George Adams, David Sanborn and Hamiet Bluiett on reeds, Jon Faddis, Lew Soloff and Hannibal Marvin Peterson on trumpet, and Warren Smith on percussion), Gil offered a music that espoused rock, free and funk, and which blended Charlie Parker with Jimi Hendrix, some of whose compositions he recorded in 1974. He gained a certain international reputation; he collaborated on Miles Davis's *Star People* album, played New York's Sweet Basil club every Monday, recorded with Helen Merrill, then in France with Laurent Cugny's big band, *Lumière*, and in a piano-soprano sax duet with Steve Lacy.

It's all in the arranging . . .

From the origins of jazz, arranging has played a part in collective improvisation (particularly in brass bands and ragtime and novelty groups). During the generation of the New Orleans pioneers, Jelly Roll Morton was an authentic 'arranger', even though he worked by explaining things verbally to his musicians (head arrangement). But it was only with the Swing Era that writing scores became a real profession.

Big band leaders, even when they themselves signed orchestrations, began to fight over scores arranged by the real specialists, often based on the latest hit song. Thus the great big bands owed a great deal to musicians whom the general public have never heard of: Don Redman, Charlie Dixon, Horace Henderson, and above all Benny Carter with Fletcher Henderson and the McKinney's Cotton Pickers (both these bands being managed by the enterprising Jean Goldkette, who was himself a talented arranger); Eddie Durham with Basie and Lunceford; Jimmy Mundy with Basie and Goodman; Sy Oliver with Lunceford and Dorsey; Edgar Sampson with Chick Webb. Neal Hefti, Frank Foster and Quincy Jones were responsible for the 'resurrection' of the Count Basie Orchestra in the 1950s and 1960s.

In modern jazz, following the example of the pioneer John Kirby, small ensembles gave the same importance to arrangements as did the big bands. With the latter on the way out, the arranger's skill was in producing a 'big sound' with a modest group. The use of classic techniques (fugues, counterpoint), unusual combinations of timbre, frequent breaks in tempo, all such 'tricks' made up the trade of a musician, just as much as his themes or his instrumental style. Indeed jazz had a development similar to that of the cinema, in that the director or author (in this case the arranger) ended up competing with the producer (the leader in the traditional sense, more of a business man than an artist) and with the actors (the musicians). From the bebop period, and especially in the West Coast Cool movement, the definition of a distinct group sound, of an identifiable style, became vital to musi-

cians, even if individual mastery of their instrument was sufficient to ensure their success. Many great soloists of contemporary jazz are in fact also great arrangers: Dizzy Gillespie, Charles Mingus, Jimmy Giuffre, Gerry Mulligan, J.J. Johnson, Slide Hampton, Shorty Rogers or Bob Brookmeyer, to name but a few. The following are therefore arrangers 'par excellence' who have not been mentioned elsewhere for other reasons.

Don Redman (1900–1964) was the first star in this field. A child prodigy who, at the age of twelve, could play all the wind instruments, he joined Fletcher Henderson in 1924 and wrote several scores for him that laid the foundations of what was to become the big band style until the 1950s: scores for the different sections, breaks, ad lib codas, chases between soloists, etc. Making magnificent use of Louis Armstrong's genius for improvisation, he orchestrated his famous 1928 concerts. He then became the musical director of McKinney's Cotton Pickers, before forming his own band in the 1930s. From then on he wrote for all the big bands of the swing era, from Paul Whiteman and Jimmy Dorsey to Cab Calloway as well as Basie and Lunceford.

Horace Henderson (1904), the pianist, was the other great arranger, discovered by his brother Fletcher, who collaborated with Redman in the Dixie Stompers. He was the author of many Henderson hits — 'Nagasaki', 'Big John's Special', 'Christopher Columbus' — and later arranged 'Dear Old Southland' for Benny Goodman and 'Indiana' for Earl Hines, as well as many other masterpieces of characteristic efficient simplicity.

Eddie Durham (1906–1987), a trombonist and also a pioneer on the electric guitar, which he introduced to Floyd Smith and Charlie Christian, was a member of the famous Kansas City Six with Lester Young (1938), but also applied his talents to writing, including many real hits for Glenn Miller ('Slip Horn Jive', 'Wham'), Lunceford ('Pigeon Walk', 'Lunceford Special') and Basie ('Topsy', 'Time Out'). His brilliant and wilfully humorous style was of great service to these three prestigious 'clients'.

Sy Oliver (1910–1988), a trumpeter and singer, replaced Durham in the Lunceford band — giving it its definitive style — before going on to become Tommy Dorsey's official arranger. He vied with Redman and Benny Carter in the use of the reed section, which he frequently had playing as a unit in dazzling glissandos. He was fond of 2/4 time (two beat) and piano/forte contrasts.

Edgar Sampson (1907–1973), a saxophonist and a violinist who learned a lot from playing with Fletcher Henderson (1931), before becoming Chick Webb's 'ghost', also wrote for Benny Goodman, Artie Shaw and Teddy Hill. With a preference for clarity and swing he was the author of many swing hits: 'Stomping at the Savoy', 'Blue Lou', 'Don't Be That Way', 'If Dreams Come True', etc. In the 1950s he was the author of many arrangements for Tito Puente and other Latin jazz bands.

Jimmy Mundy (1907–1983), a saxophonist and violinist like Sampson, also gave Goodman several hits — 'Sing, Sing, Sing', 'Solo Flight', 'Madhouse', 'Airmail Special' — after working with Claude Hopkins and Earl Hines. But it was Basie who made the best use of his incomparable way with the trumpet section in brief and powerful sequences, producing masterpieces like 'John's Idea', 'Cherokee', 'Shorty George' or 'Super Chief'.

Glenn Miller (1904–1944), a trombonist, had a career as an arranger and musical director well before he started his own big dance band (only seven years before his plane crashed in the Channel), which earned him immense popularity, especially in Europe. The very particular sound he managed to produce with his rather massive big band, doubling the lead tenor with a clarinet, has remained a symbol of a certain way of life in the dark years of the war. His two hits, 'In the Mood' and 'Moonlight Serenade', stayed in the memory of all those who could only hear them through the cracklings of Nazi jamming!

Billy May (1916), a trumpeter, wrote many arrangements for Charlie Barnet and Glenn Miller before becoming one of the most famous orchestrators of the Californian scene, particularly for his use of spectacular glissandos of saxes in unison. Working with the Capitol label, he arranged many records on the fringe between jazz and crooning, including some of Sinatra's masterpieces.

Tadd Dameron (1917–1965), a pianist, was the first great composer-arranger of modern jazz, the immortal author of themes which were played by Parker and above all Gillespie and became the prototypes of bebop: 'Hot House' (1945), 'Good Bait', 'Our Delight', 'Cool Breeze'). Before that he had already done some writing for Lunceford, Basie and Bill Eckstine, and had brilliantly absorbed the influence of Sy Oliver and Ellington. After the war, he formed a quintet with James Moody and Fats Navarro, then with Miles Davis (whom he brought to Paris in 1949), and finally a nonet with Clifford Brown and Benny Golson. He exerted a decisive influence on all of these, as well as on the drummer Philly Joe Jones, who dedicated one of his albums to him. But it was his ability to give bebop its perfect expression in big band music that made him the key musician of this period, especially with the success of the Dizzy Gillespie big band.

John Lewis (1920), a pianist, is another of Gillespie's great arrangers, hired at Kenny Clarke's suggestion to replace Thelonious Monk in 1946, whom he celebrated with a splendid version of 'Round Midnight'. Dizzy also plays his 'Toccata for a Trumpet', which shows the influence Bach had on him. This was to be a determining influence in Lewis's work: as is confirmed by his part in *The Birth of the Cool* sessions with Miles Davis ('Move', 'Rouge', 1949) and even more in his founding of the Modern Jazz Quartet. The fugue and counterpoint are the main skills of this infinitely subtle 'orchestra player'.

205

Gil Fuller (1920) is the third person of the Gillespian 'trinity': blending with ironic humour blues, scat and Afro-Cuban rhythms, he was the arranger of Dizzy's greatest hits — 'Manteca', 'One Bass Hit', 'Things to Come', 'Ray's Idea'. Later he was cleverly hired by Stan Kenton, as well as by Machito and by Tito Puente.

John Carisi (1922), is a trumpeter whose creativity is much greater than the number of his works would indicate. Having been a pupil of the composer Stefan Wolpe, he managed to integrate the blues in arrangements crammed with ultra-chromatic effects, to the point of sounding atonal. The most famous example is 'Israel' recorded by Miles Davis in 1949, for which many consider him the real father of cool jazz. Gil Evans and Bill Evans were later to be his best interpreters.

Bill Holman (1927), a saxophonist, expresses Californian mellowness perfectly, but is also capable of striking contrasts, both with Kenton and with his own groups. As well as accompanying some of the greatest singers (Sarah Vaughan, Ella Fitzgerald, Anita O'Day), he has polished countless scores eliminating every trace of bad taste. One of his remarkable orchestrations is a late Basie album, *I Told You So*.

Shorty Rogers (1924), is a trumpeter with a New York background, but he became the personification of West Coast jazz in the 1950s. He wrote some of the best scores for Woody Herman, Stan Kenton, Terry Gibbs and Gerry Mulligan's Concert Jazz Band. But he is at his best with small groups (with his friends Shelly Manne, Jimmy Giuffre, Howard Rumsey, Bud Shank, Art Pepper, or playing his own music) where he excels in pitting soloists against their ensembles in a splendid balance of swing, with a taste for unusual combinations, clearly inspired by Miles Davis's nonet.

Marty Paich (1925), a pianist, is another of those subtle musicians who illustrate the amazing emulation which existed between arrangers on the West Coast, largely due to the difficult working conditions in the Hollywood studios. As a pupil of the composer Castelnuovo-Tedesco, he was able to reconcile his solid classical base with his passion for Lunceford's style. He specialized in orchestrations for singers (from Sarah Vaughan to Astrud Gilberto, but also Ray Charles), and he had a group of his own, of variable size, in which nearly all the great Californian soloists played to his arrangements.

Gary McFarland (1933–1971), a vibraphone player, went the other way, from the West Coast to New York, with a spell at the Berklee School in Boston. As arranger for Getz, Mulligan, Anita O'Day and Bill Evans, he managed to incorporate elements from Debussy and Ravel in jazz, and developed a passion for the bossa nova.

Oliver Nelson (1932–1975), a saxophonist and clarinettist, started in rhythm' n'blues, with Louis Jordan in particular, and was a jack of all trades (chauffeur, enbalmer) before devoting himself fully to arranging in the 1960s. He soon asserted his originality (progressions in fourths, poly-rhythmics using an odd number of bars) without, however, frightening his audience. He was both avant-garde and popular and in less than five years made an impressive series of records with Eric Dolphy and Bill Evans (*The Blues and the Abstract Truth*), with Rollins (*Alfie*), Monk (*Monk's Blues*), Jimmy Smith and Wes Montgomery (*The Dynamic Duo*).

Producer by profession

Without going as far as to compare this profession to its equivalent in the cinema, it is nonetheless important enough in jazz for some producers to be considered great 'creators'.

The first name that springs to mind is that of **John Hammond** (1910–1987). This New York patrician, who was the heir to an enormous fortune, devoted his whole life to the blues and to jazz from the early 1930s. As Fletcher Henderson's mentor, he 'invented' live broadcasting at concerts and became primarily a tremendous talent spotter, working closely with CBS. Without him, given the toughness of the competition on the American market, one might never have heard of Billie Holiday, Count Basie, Charlie Christian, Teddy Wilson, Aretha Franklin, George Benson, Bob Dylan or Bruce Springsteen! Later, most great producers were the proprietors of independent labels. These include: the Berliners Alfred Lion and Francis Wolff, who founded Blue Note Records in 1939; Lester Koenig, the creator of Contemporary; the Turkish brothers Ahmet and Nesuhi Ertegun, who created the Atlantic label in 1947. Two years later, Bob Weinstock launched New Jazz and then Prestige, and in 1954 hired the man who was to become the greatest sound engineer of jazz, Rudy Van Gelder, who also went on to work for Blue Note and other labels.

Teo Macero (1925), together with Quincy Jones, was one of the rare producers who were also musicians. An original saxophonist and composer, he was in charge at Columbia (from 1959 to 1975) of all the Mingus, Monk and Miles recordings (one can sometimes hear the latter groan at the end of a piece 'O.K. Teo?'!).

Norman Granz (1918) is without a doubt the 'biggest', if not the greatest, jazz producer. This clever Californian first created the travelling jam sessions known as Jazz at the Philharmonic in 1944, which had an enormous success, and brought together all the big names of mainstream jazz. Two years later he founded the Clef label, which later became Verve, Norgran and finally Pablo, with a logo by Picasso. Continuing John Hammond's work, he rejected racial segregation at the concerts he organized.

Quincy Jones (1933), a trumpeter, is undoubtedly the most famous jazz producer and arranger. He got started in the big bands of Hampton and Gillespie, before settling in Paris at the end of the 1950s. He studied under Nadia Boulanger, became the arranger for the Barclay label, orchestrating the first record of Mimi Perrin's Double Six (1959). As musical director of Mercury Records, he composed for Sarah Vaughan, Billy Eckstine, Sinatra, Basie, Ray Charles. As an intimate friend of the latter, he veered gradually from jazz to soul music, and his name became a guarantee of success on record sleeves, featuring under such names as Roberta Flack, Aretha Franklin, Al Jarreau, and above all Michael Jackson, whose mentor he became. Jones soon became a symbol of the quiet revolution that was taking place in popular music: electronics were submerging acoustics, the studio was becoming more important than the band, and the arranger's job was merging with the producer's, a mixture which in fact enabled him to cook up some of his most original albums, with ingredients ranging from the purest gospel to the most baroque violin pieces.

A few club owners can also be included in the list of great producers, the most famous of all being, of course, **Max Gordon** (1902– 1989), who in 1936 started the perennial Village Vanguard in a Greenwich Village cellar, which is the only one of the 'historic' New York clubs to have survived (Birdland, Half-Note, Minton's and Five Spot all having been 'gobbled up' by the greedy 'Big Apple' promoters).

The 'third stream'

Apart from the mainstream, with its rapid flow, taking jazz through a variety of changing landscapes, but also avoiding the torrents and whirlpools of the avant-garde, there is also a capricious 'third stream' based on arranged improvisation and themes inherited from the European tradition.

The expression 'Third Stream' only appeared at the end of the 1950s and, rather than defining a 'school', was the official recognition of a trend common to all great jazz musicians, the desire to go beyond the conventional framework generally associated with the word 'jazz', but without relinquishing the two essential elements, swing and improvisation. This organic osmosis between written and spontaneous music goes far beyond the scope of symphonic jazz, which, from Paul Whiteman to Ornette Coleman ('Skies of America') not to mention Stan Kenton and Ellington, did nothing more than dress up a highly predetermined style.

The **Modern Jazz Quartet**, founded in 1951, is the main ensemble of 'third stream' jazz. One of their albums is in fact called *Third Stream Music* (1959). The following year they recorded the 'Concertino for Jazz Quartet' with a symphonic orchestra. John Lewis (see p. 160 and 205) relies greatly on fugue and counterpoint techniques, with reference to Bach.

Gunther Schuller (1925), a friend of John Lewis who often worked as conductor with the M.J.Q., is the undisputed leader of the third stream, to the point of actually holding a chair in 'Third Stream' at the New England Conservatory! As a horn player in Miles Davis's Nonet in 1949, he participated in *The Birth of the Cool*, before becoming radically eclectic, confronting tonal, polytonal and serial composition with free improvisation. As founder of the U.S.A. Orchestra and the Jazz Repertory Orchestra, he acquired a reputation for modern orchestrations of big band classics.

George Russell (1923), a pianist and percussionist, started as a drummer but soon became fascinated by Debussy and Stravinsky, and gradually stopped playing the drums to devote himself to composition and musicology. In 1953 he published the fruit of his research on the 'lydian concept of tonal organization'. His theory contributed greatly to the adaptation of a modal approach in jazz treatments, particularly in the works of Miles Davis, Bill Evans and Coltrane. The latter two, as well as Paul Bley, Phil Woods, Art Farmer, Max Roach, etc., were, in fact also to interpret his compositions, which are some of the most original works in modern jazz, including 'Ezz-thetics' (played solo by Eric Dolphy), 'Stratus-funk', as well as 'Outer Thoughts'. Unanimously respected and admired by the musicians of the orchestras he conducts (sextets or big bands), he subtly integrates electronics and percussion in a language which is at the same time complex and logical, futuristic and deeply rooted.

Dave Brubeck (1920) is undoubtedly the most famous musician of the third stream. The pupil of Schoenberg and especially of Milhaud, he is himself an excellent composer ('The Duke', 'In Your Own Sweet Way', 'Unsquare Dance'), even if 'Take Five' the tune which made him so popular, is in fact a theme created by the saxophonist Paul Desmond. The latter was a co-founder of the Dave Brubeck Quartet in 1951, and was replaced in 1978 by Gerry Mulligan, who quickly left his place to the very original clarinettist Bill Smith. Strongly influenced in his piano playing by Ellington, and much less 'rigid' than is generally thought, Dave Brubeck is fond of odd rhythms, the rondo form, sudden changes of tempo, fugue-like passages, all subtleties that he ably integrates into clear and communicative treatments.

Carla Bley

1938, Oakland

A fairy with a wand

The most famous 'jazz-woman' manages to imbue marvellously clear scores with her orchestral humour.

In fact her story began like a modern fairy tale, retold by Tex Avery. At eighteen, Carla Borg was not a shepherdess but a cigarette girl at Birdland, the most famous of the New York clubs in the 1950s. That was where she met her first prince charming, the pianist Paul Bley, whom she married in 1957. Two years later in California, where they settled, she started composing for his trio and for his friends, Art Farmer, Jimmy Giuffre and George Russell, who recognized her talent as a melody maker.

To tell the truth Carla had not turned up in Birdland just by chance. Her mother was an organist who had taught her to play hymns on the piano at the age of three; by sixteen she was playing fugues, playing in piano bars, accompanying a folk singer and getting interested in jazz. Then, like Parker, who washed dishes in order to hear Tatum free, she found a way of being paid

---

In Carla Bley's own words:

'I come from a comic strip culture, and I think my compositions are rather singular because of my unconventional background, I have managed to preserve my ignorance. And that is a quality that you can never recover once you have lost it!'

---

to listen to Miles Davis, Coltrane, or The Jazz Messengers every night! But there is no trace of these models in her own first compositions, which were astonishingly original: 'Ida Lupina', 'Sing Me Softly of the Blues', for example are a strange mixture of bebop and folk which immediately attracted the young Keith Jarrett.

Living in New York in the early 1960s, Carla Bley joined the Jazz Composer's Guild, and together with the trumpeter Michael Mantler — whom she later married — became the co-president of the Jazz Composer's Orchestra Association. She wrote one of Gary Burton's masterpieces, 'A Genuine Tong Funeral' (1967), and then took part in the founding of Charlie Haden's Liberation Music Orchestra in 1969. In 1972 she composed a surrealist opera on a libretto by the poet Paul Haines, *Escalator Over The Hill*. Two years later she wrote '3/4' for Keith Jarrett and a chamber orchestra.

With her own band — which gives top priority to low brasses, horn and the tuba — and her own record company Watt, (which entered into a partnership with the German firm E.C.M.), Carla Bley developed a music full of parody and colour, mostly reminiscent of Charles Ives, Kurt Weill, Nino Rota or the 'musiques d'ameublement' by Erik Satie. Then, together with the bassist Steve Swallow, she returned to a less cluttered style, a sort of 'elegant rhythm'n'blues'.

She is a sober soloist but with great presence on the keyboards, who has created a universe comparable to the paintings of Douanier Rousseau, where improvisors feel at the same time directed and free to explore all sorts of unbeaten tracks.

The women in jazz

While female singers, who enjoyed both prestige and long-standing second class status, have had a leading role in the history of jazz (and are often amazing pianists), pure women instrumentalists are rare, which may be explained by the male chauvinism prevalent in marginal urban societies. Being closer to traditional music, where women rarely participate (except in the East), jazz has taken some time to accept them. And yet, as early as the 1920s, there was a proliferation of female jazz bands, in Harlem (eg The Twelve Vampires) and especially in Chicago.

In the 'Windy City' the pianist Cora Calhoun, known as Lovie Austin, for a long time led the Blues Serenaders, which accompanied all the great blues singers and vaudeville shows.

Lil Hardin (1898–1971) also played in Chicago in that period. She had been the pianist of the original Creole Jazz Band, first with Freddie Keppard and then with King Oliver, and it was there she met Louis Armstrong, whom she married in 1924. She played in his Hot Five and Hot Seven, while prudently creating her own band, which after her divorce in 1931 became 100 per cent female. After the war she pursued her own career as a soloist.

Mary Lou Williams (1910–1981) became, before she was twenty, the first great lady of jazz. As a child prodigy, she performed under the name of the Little Piano Girl in Pittsburgh vaudeville shows. At sixteen she married the saxophonist John Williams, with whom (in 1929) she joined Andy Kirk's Twelve Clouds of Joy, for which she made the best arrangements until, in 1942, she decided to form her own band. She also composed for Armstrong, Ellington, Hines, Lunceford, Dorsey and Goodman. At the end of the 1940s, she became a friend of Monk's and Bud Powell's, and composed for Gillespie and Dameron. She also composed some religious pieces and played them in incongruous contexts (duo with Cecil Taylor in 1977), with her versatile style, where the grit of stride and blues are combined in fertile modernist experiences.

Melba Liston (1926) started her career as a trombonist in the big bands (Gerald Wilson, Basie, Gillespie), and accompanying Billie Holiday, before starting an original female band in 1956, and revealing her talents for composition and orchestration in a wide range of different contexts (from Ray Charles to Bob Marley, including M.L. Williams, the Double Six, Milt Jackson, Art Blakey and even Archie Shepp).

Toshiko Akiyoshi (1929) is a powerful and lyrical pianist, strongly influenced by Bud Powell. With her husband, the fiery sax and flute player Lew Tabackin, she leads a very bright and colourful big band which sometimes plays in a way reminiscent of Japanese music.

Emily Remler (1957–1990), a disciple of Wes Montgomery revived the intimate and impetuous language of bebop guitar.

Jane Ira Bloom (1955) is undoubtedly one of the most brilliant saxophonists (and flautists) alive today. A virtuoso on the soprano, often playing with the vibraphone player David Friedman, she has an airy sensual style which owes more to the influence of singers than to that of other saxophonists.

Finally it should be mentioned that more and more young ladies are attracted by so-called 'macho' instruments. The 1980s thus revealed some excellent bassists (like Joelle Léandre and Hélène Labarrière in France), percussionists (the Dane Marilyn Mazur, who has played with Miles Davis), and even drummers. The most famous of these is already Terri Lyne Carrington (1965) who, starting at the Berklee School at twelve, has shot to an impressive career.

Free sound and freedom

Reflecting both an aesthetic and a political rebellion, going way beyond its musical scope, Free Jazz got its official name after a record was issued bearing this title: Ornette Coleman's Free Jazz, *recorded in 1960. But the attraction of improvisation completely emancipated from the trammels of harmony and bars was already inherent in jazz from its beginnings: blue notes, for instance, cannot be precisely written in a score.*

Without going back to the flood of notes that poured from the New Orleans *honky-tonks*, we shall simply mention a few of the forerunners, such as Jimmy Giuffre, Mingus, Sun Ra, Coltrane, Rollins, and before them Lennie Tristano ('Digression', 1949 and 'Descent to the Maelstrom' (1953)).

A radical literary and poetic movement, the musical expression of the Black Power movement, but also the rediscovery of the purely playful meaning of the word 'to play', Free Jazz was all of these at once. At the end of the 1960s, jazz 'returned to order', like many other things. Many of its initiatives disappeared prematurely, and most of the others reverted to a more controlled form of expression.

Albert Ayler (1936–1970) was, in less than ten years, the most heartrending and shattering voice of this trend. Deeply marked by the gospel and the religious bands of his youth, he made his real debut as a sax player aged sixteen, with the great blues harmonica player Little Walter. He joined Cecil Taylor, then Coltrane, and recorded with Don Cherry, Gary Peacock, etc. His full-bodied vibrato, his apparently incongruous quotes (hymns, rhymes, Mexican tunes) and even more his demonstrative religiosity, disconcerted the American public and critics. His music contains a boundless sincerity, and rather than naivety, it should be qualified as raw art. To his contemporaries, it even appeared brutal, in so much as it resembled the arid slopes of a peak, whose other side was occupied by Jimi Hendrix. Both were to suffer a similar fate: a few months after his last major concert (at the Maeght Foundation), Ayler's corpse was found in East River, on November 25, 1970.

Bill Dixon (1925), ascetic improviser and trumpeter with a limited register, was a sort of patriarch of Free Jazz, the founder in 1964 of the legendary Jazz Composers' Guild of New York. A partner of Cecil Taylor and Archie Shepp (with whom he created the New Contemporary Five, before being replaced by Don Cherry), he recorded little in his own name, but his pedagogical role seems to be eminent.

Sam Rivers (1930) represented the harmonious transition to Free Jazz from a career which was already very full when he became the saxophonist of the Cecil Taylor Unit in 1968. Previously he had accompanied Billie Holiday as well as Jaki Byard, Wilson Pickett, B.B. King and T-Bone Walker, and even toured with Miles Davis (1964). His records for Blue Note revealed a composer with great polytonal daring who was at the same time very romantic. The founder of the Studio Rivbea in 1971, he thus started the *lofts* movement, where all the new avant-garde jazz of New York originated. A voluble and sensual saxophonist, an impulsive flautist and a sober but incisive pianist, he generally played in a quartet, but also as sideman in Dizzy Gillespie's big band.

The pianist **'Muhal' Richard Abrams** (1930) was, with Cecil Taylor, the reference point of Free Jazz. With a sweeping range from ragtime to the most radical atonality, he was first the accompanist of all the greats of bebop when they visited Chicago. It was here that, in 1965, he founded the A.A.C.M. — the Association for the Advancement of Creative Musicians — to which soon almost all the artists engaged in the 'Windy City' were to belong, musicians but also poets, singers and dancers.

The **Art Ensemble of Chicago** is the most famous of many bands formed by or around the A.A.C.M. In its definitive form it is a quintet, all of whose members are multi-instrumentalists and participated in working out a repertoire which referred to *Great Black Music* in all its forms, from the blues to the most unstructured expression, including gospel, pygmy polyphonies and reggae. Each concert of the Art Ensemble is a real stage creation, where costumes, make-up gestures and decor were inseparable from sound. When it was founded (1967), the group was only a quartet led by the trumpeter **Lester Bowie** (1941). He arrived from the Chicago blues scene, which at the time (the 1960s) was going strong, as a counter coup to the British revival. His membership of the A.A.C.M. plunged him into the heart of a much more 'permissive' world where he could give free reign to his truculent verve and his taste for experimenting with unheard of sounds. His tone, alternately blaring and velvety, strident and secretive, is among the 'great signatures' of his generation. Besides the Art Ensemble, Lester Bowie played in Jack DeJohnette's Special Edition, The Leaders sextet, and directs his Brass Fantasy, a very unusual group of nine brass instruments, acompanied by a drummer, whose repertoire owed a lot to gospel.

Roscoe Mitchell (1940) became the Art Ensemble's main composer, playing a very wide range of reed instruments. From a very busy life outside the group, he introduced into all contexts a most personal expressivity, rich in contrasts and tinted with irony, which he pulled together in his formula 'a collage of sounds'.

Joseph Jarman (1937) was the second saxophonist and the most unnerving soloist of the Art Ensemble. His performances often had the character of a challenge, if not a provocation. The other members of this band that is always so inventive, and which recently integrated electronic music, are the double-bass player Malachi Favors and the percussionist Don Moye.

Perhaps **Anthony Braxton** (1945) came from this nursery, 'the second school of Chicago', and is the best known of these musicians in Europe, where he has often performed. Playing the whole range of saxophones and clarinets, he considers himself above all a composer, and indeed, his writing eventually overtook his improvisation at the end of the 1970s. His music makes him a sort of 'link' with 'third stream'. If his approach remained imbued with jazz influences — from ragtime to Eric Dolphy, including Charlie Parker and Paul Desmond — his writing has many relations, ranging from Bartók, the Vienna School, even to Cage or Stockhausen.

Henry Threadgill (1944) started with Muhal Abrams and the members of the Art Ensemble, all the while earning his living in gospel and rhythm'n'blues, before founding the most seductive trio, Air, in the 1970s, with the bass player Fred Hopkins and the drummer Steve McCall. Familiar with all the reeds, but also flute and percussion, he attracted attention by his compositions with a most original instrumentation (quartet for double-bass and reeds together) and developed music elaborated with Air in a sextet, and later a big band.

John Zorn (1953) was converted to jazz by listening to Braxton, after he had listened to the music of the less conformist composers (Ives, Cage, Kagel, Stockhausen). Alto saxophonist, the author of a thesis on music for cartoons, he quite naturally became the leader of *noise music*, succeeding Free Jazz in the form of a varied collage of the most unexpected sounds: blue phrases and bebop, electronic rumblings, noises, deformed voice, etc. Often associated with the bass player/producer Bill Laswell, and with the guitarist Arto Lindsay, he seems to be evolving towards an art based on the use of quotes and references, which owes a lot to the creative use of multi-track recording studios.

Carla Bley *(1979)*

Sun Ra and his 'Arkestra', *Germany 1980*

Sun Ra

1914, Birmingham (USA)

The extraterrestrial of jazz

Son of the Sun and the Heavenly Twins, the most enigmatic of jazz players was also to be one of the most prophetic.

What does it matter if his true name on Earth was Herman Blount or Sonny Lee, and whether he was born in 1914 or 1915, according to the presumptuous researchers who have tried in vain to demystify him. What is important is that this intergalactic poet should have permitted himself to land beside Birmingham and for a long time hesitated to show his godlike genius to the humble mortals that we are, since almost nothing certain is known about him before the 1950s.

Some people affirm that they saw him in Chicago in the 1930s (he is supposed to have accompanied Coleman Hawkins). Around 1947, his band is also supposed to have played at the *Cotton DeLisa*, alternating with that of Fletcher Henderson, for whom he apparently wrote some arrangements. His first recognized 'appearance'

took place the following year, when he played the piano at a recording session of the Dukes of Swing. In the early 1950s, he performed in a trio on an electric instrument, a keyboard which he himself had put together, and which recalled the Ondes Martenot.

It was then that the true career of Sun Ra, pioneer of electronic music but also of associative music, began in earnest. His Arkestra functioned from the start as a co-operative, a system which spread among musicians in the 1960s. As with Duke Ellington, people found him a 'hard nut', virtually immovable: John Gilmore, Marshall Allen, Pat Patrick (saxophone) and Ronnie Boykins (bass), as well as 'long term visitors' such as Charles Davis (saxophone), Julian Priester (trombone) Wilbur Ware (bass) and Clifford Jarvis (drums). Directed by a hand of iron clad in a velvet glove, the Arkestra ingeniously combined the great tradition of big bands of the swing era and the rhythmic suppleness of bop, the wealth of Ellingtonian range and an unlimited freedom in collective improvisation, alternating with very elaborate riffs. Thus Sun Ra exercised a considerable influence on all the avantgarde, and he took part in the Jazz Composers' Guild and the Newport Festival. Settled in Philadelphia since 1970 (not far from the Egyptian Museum, where he rubbed shoulders with some of his pharaoh cousins!), he continued to tour the whole world, constantly renewing his repertoire. The classics of Jelly Roll Morton, Fletcher Henderson or Duke Ellington were themselves metamorphosed into the *joyful noise* which this militant pacifist wanted to impose over the entire planet, in a debauchery of pseudo-ritual dances, make up and costumes which could be described as 'Afro-Martian'.

> **In Sun Ra's own words:**
> 'As soon as I started to play, I dedicated my music not to man but to the Creator of the Universe, in order to show him that on this planet full of death and destruction, someone understands everything beautiful that he made (. . .) I hope also to teach what the black race was able to produce: something other than religious ideas and politics, and all the usual futilities . . .'

Into the melting-pot
Fusions of ethnic music

'Impure' by nature, jazz has always been able to assimilate the best of all the music with which it has come into contact. The fact that it was born in New Orleans has enabled it to crystallize an extraordinary wealth of rhythms which allowed it to become the first truly universal art form: the 'Cité du Croissant' was in fact the American outlet to the whole of the Caribbean and Atlantic (thus African) and Latin-American worlds, and at the same time the terminus of a great variety of immigrants of European origin (Spanish, Italian, Greek, Dutch, Irish and, of course, French and Cajun) and the favourite town of the freed slaves and 'coloured Creoles'. Through its port it brought exchanges with Cuba, flourishing since the Hispanic-American war (1891). Moreover with Cuban and Puerto Rican music, jazz achieved its first true 'fusion' half a century later, while throughout the Caribbean world musical styles developed which showed the existence of an aesthetic Afro-American heritage. With Brazil, it was a true gentle shock which happened at the end of the 1950s, when avant-garde jazz advocated an enlivening tour to 'Mother Africa'. Then it was the Orient which paid its tribute to a music which had become global. While Japan became the greatest consumer of jazz and began to produce several original stylists, India fascinated all those who sought a metaphysical game in improvisation, and communion with the nature of sounds. At the end of the century, jazz had become a Tower of Babel, where an impressive quantity of idioms melted into one common language. It retained the impurity of its origins more ferociously than ever.

Return trip to Africa

Certain musicologists (Sam Charters, Paul Oliver) were able to show all that blues and jazz owe to their African origins, and more precisely, West African. Through an inevitable return, jazz was transplanted to the Atlantic coast of Mother Africa from 1920, immediately awakening hybrid forms where European influences — military bands, religious choirs, accordion, etc. — vied with those of ancestral music.

In Ghana the high-life fashion was born (whose great creator was the multi-instrumentalist E.T. Mensah), which soon became very popular over the whole continent — with numerous local variations — after 1945. Its instrumentation is that of the jazz combos, but the guitar assumes greater importance, replacing brass — in marvellous exchanges with the 'talking-drums' — in ju-ju from the 1960s (three names should be remembered: I.K. Dairo, Ebenezer Obey, Sunny Ade).

In central Africa, the music of the colonial work camps (sanza and guitar) evolved at the time of independence, to the Congolese soukous and rumba (Kalle, Franco TPOK Jazz, Tabu Ley). As its name indicates, the Afro-Cuban influence is considerable, as much in the Senegalese mbalax (Xalam, Youssou N'Dour, Super Diamono, Ismael Lo) or in the great 'mandingo' bands of Mali (Ambassadeurs, Rail Band, Super Biton) and of Guinea (Bembeya jazz). In the South African townships the mbaqanga and the jive developed in the 1930s. Here, as the name also shows, swing was the main reference. It is found in Zimbabwe in bands like the Devera Ngwena Jazz Band.

Taking into account the diversity and the distance (geographic as well as historic) between the African and Afro-American musicians, it is easy to contest the expression 'African jazz'. Nonetheless, this music is generally closer to American jazz than certain types of music identified as 'European jazz'. They have the place and the function in common with jazz: clubs, hotels, dances and conviviality, but also in some countries a militant, anti-colonial and pan-African attitude. When the American musicians discover it, they are amazed.

From the 1950s, for the great creators of all generations, from Armstrong to Archie Shepp, from Ellington (who composed the 'Liberian Suite' and 'La Plus Belle Africaine' and launched Dollar Brand) to Art Blakey, (West) Africa became a centre for pilgrimages, or rather family reunions. The exchanges which resulted were to integrate some of the great African creator in jazz life.

Manu Dibango (1933) was born in th Cameroons, and if it was in France and Belgium that he made his debut in the jaz clubs (he founded one in Douala), he soo gravitated to the African Jazz of the Zairian singer Kabasele, called 'Le Gran Kalle', and later directed the big band the Ivory Coast radio. In the meantime, h forged an original style for himsel blending the traditional Cameroon-styl makossa, hard bop and Afro-Cuban, to en in *Soul Makossa*, a form which revealed hi to the whole world. He kept a very stror link with jazz, including recording wit Herbie Hancock. A feverish, voluptuou saxophonist, he mixed very different influences, from Earl Bostic to Rollin including King Curtis and Cannonba Adderley. He also used the vibraphone an the piano to develop traditional Africa melodies.

Abdullah Ibrahim (Dollar Bran (1934) started as a pianist in the Cap clubs. Ellington helped him make his fir record in Paris in 1963, and even chose hi as 'substitute' in his orchestra in 1966. Th he became the wandering ambassador South African artists in exile, playing numerous compositions with the best Sou Africans — Dudu Pukwana and Ba Coetzee (saxophone), Johnny Dyani (ba — and American — Max Roach, Elv

Jones, Hamiett Bluiett, Don Cherry, Harold Land, Cecil McBee, Carlos Ward — jazz players. A lyrical soloist, a powerful and willingly repetitive pianist, he also plays reed instruments and flute, and always seems to be on a quest for a new form of trance.

Chris McGregor (1936–1990), another native of South Africa, was one of the first white musicians to defy Apartheid, forming the Blue Notes in 1962, with Pukwana, Dyani, and the trombone player Mongezi Feza. Exiled, together they were to form the core of the big band Brotherhood of Breath, created in 1969 with the best London jazz players to freely perpetuate the torrid jazz of the townships. A crude but efficient pianist, McGregor lived near Agen from 1974 until his death.

Fela Anikulapo Kuti (1938), known as a candidate for the presidency of Nigeria, for his denunciation of corruption and for the co-operative autonomy of his neighbourhood in Lagos, Kalakuta, for which he paid by several years in prison, has caused more ink to flow for his polygamy and his political attitude than for his extraordinary musical charisma. At the head of his big band Afrika 70, then Egypt 80, based in his own club, the *Shrine*, in his imperious voice and his furious style on the tenor sax, he expressed joyful indignation on a continental scale. From the 'boppy' high-life of his youth he developed towards an 'Afrobeat' marked by the impact of the triumphant tours of James Brown, whose gift of exciting his audience only he could rival.

Hugh Masekela (1939) from Johannesburg, was converted to the trumpet by listening to Bix Beiderbecke, before attempting a fusion between bebop and the mbaqanga, in the Merrymakers of Spring. Exiled at the same time as Dollar Brand and Miriam Makeba (who was his wife), he made a career in the United States, making many records with Mercury and M.G.M, notably with the Jazz Crusaders, before promoting studios for South African musicians in Zimbabwe and Botswana.

Certain American musicians made the trip the other way round, back to their African roots. There were two particularly notable cases. Both musicians were born in Brooklyn one year apart.

Randy Weston (1926) is a pianist of Jamaican origin, who made his debut in rhythm'n'blues, before immersing himself in the boppers environment, and being strongly influenced by Monk and, through him, Ellington. Then, introduced by Melba Liston to African music, he travelled to Nigeria in the 1960s, and ended by settling in Tangier. A frequently played composer — 'Hi Fly', 'Little Niles' — he is also the author of 'Ellingtonian' suites such as 'Uhuru Africa' and 'Three African Queens'.

Ahmed Abdul-Malik (1927), of Sudanese origins, started under the protection of Art Blakey. Then the neighbour and also the bass player of Weston, he travelled like him in Africa in the 1960s. Almost all his recordings (under his own name or the names of Monk, Herbie Mann or Jutta Hipp, the pianist) bear the mark of his rise, and his passion for pentatonic scales and oriental modes. He also played the oud (the Arab lute).

Finally, some excellent African Jazz players live in France, like Adolf Winkler, from Togo, a hearty trombonist trained in the high-life bands of Ghana, or Tchangodei, the pianist from Benin, who lives in Lyon, and who has made many solo recordings, but also in a duo with Mal Waldron, Steve Lacy and Archie Shepp.

Afro-Cubop

Contrary to their brothers in North America, the transplanted Africans in the Caribbean (as in Brazil and Venezuela) were able to preserve some of their rites and rhythms, songs and ancestral instruments. This partly explains the fascination they exercise on numerous jazz players, and their considerable influence on a modern jazz that is most energetic in claiming its 'negritude'.

After the First World War, the United States welcomed many Cuban immigrants, then Puerto Ricans, armed with their U.S. passports. At first, few musicians emerged from anonymity. We should mention as pioneers the Cubans Rod Rodriguez, Benny Carter's pianist, then Don Redman at the end of the 1920s, and Alberto Socarras, one of the first flautists of jazz in the 1920s, without forgetting, of course, the Puerto Rican Juan Tizol, the valve trombone player with Ellington from 1929, whose compositions 'Caravan' (1936), 'Conga Brava' (1940) and 'Perdido' (1942) were the first models of 'Afro-Cuban jazz'. Right away an explosive combination of new bebop and Cuban polyrhythms came into existence. It was integrated in the playing of the drummers, but it also made the use of *hand drums* more widespread, and drums like congas and bongos. This is how what later became 'Latin-jazz' was born, with its brilliance and innovation, its fireworks and its damp squibs.

Mario Bauza (1911), trumpeter and arranger, left Havana for New York in 1930, playing at Noble Sissle's, before he became the musical director of Chick Webb (1933–1938), then of Cab Calloway (1939–1941), where he engaged and 'initiated' the young and turbulent Dizzy Gillespie, and finally Machito, for whom until 1976 he was lead trumpet, arranger and brother-in-law!

Machito (1912), whose real name was Raul Grillo, sang and played the maracas in the prestigious Sexteto Nacional de Havana, before settling in New York in 1927, where three years later he founded what became the best of the Afro-Cuban jazz groups. In thirty-five years, the Machito Orchestra hosted the greatest soloists as *guest stars*, from Parker to Cannonball Adderley, including Dexter Gordon, Johnny Griffin and of course Gillespie. His influence on the latter (as well as on Stan Kenton) was decisive.

Chano Pozo (1915–1948) has, according to Dizzy, 'contributed as much to modern jazz as he himself or Charlie

---

Jazz and tango

Emerging from the brothels to invest in dancing, then concerts, a product of the black 'candomble' of the carnivals of Montevideo and Buenos Aires, the tango is a cousin of jazz with which many great creators have been involved.

Gato Barbieri (1934), Argentinian saxophonist, made his debut playing the requinto (clarinet) in the 'milonga' bands, before imposing his own inimitable tone on the tenor sax in various contexts, from Free Jazz to Latin. Lyrical and out-spoken, he was on the fringe of the avant-garde in the 1960s (Don Cherry, Carla Bley, Charlie Haden) before he became the tenor player of tropical alcoves and clubs.

Astor Piazzola (1921) is the grand contemporary master of the bandoneon, but also a remarkable composer and arranger who has been involved with many jazz players. Besides his own albums of 'neo-tango', his performances with the likes of Gerry Mulligan, Gary Burton and Kip Hanrahan have alrady become classics.

Among the Argentinian musicians on the borderline between tango and jazz, mention must be made of the pianist Horacio Salgan, the guitarist Osvaldo de Lio and the bandoneonist Juan Jose Mosalini, who was inspired by the double-bass player Patrice Caratini.

Parker', a forceful statement alluding to the unforgettable months this devilish percussion player spent in his big band. Pozo was instructed in the African rites of Lucumi and Abakwa in Havana, and was a member of the Nanigo sect. From September 1947 to December 1948 (the date of his mysterious assassination in Harlem's *Rio Café*), Chano (not to be confused with his cousin Chino, another percussion player), worked out in this ideal framework, the definitive model for Afro-Cuban drumming, alternately imperious and voluptuous, velvety and explosive. He also wrote the the famous 'Tin Tin Deo'.

Chico O'Farrill (1921), Cuban trumpeter, in the 1950s became the favourite composer-arranger of the big bands, to which he added an inimitable 'Latin' touch: Benny Goodman, Count Basie, Stan Kenton, Dizzy Gillespie, Clark Terry and many others have called upon his highly colourful writing.

Mongo Santamaria (1922), disciple of Chano Pozo, is like him a virtuoso of the congas and bongos, initiated into the ancestral rites in the Cuban capital. Leaving the *Tropicana* in Havana in 1948 or that of New York, he played for a long period as sideman (in particular with Perez Prado, Tito Puente and Cal Tjader), before forming his own group in the 1960s. Incorporating African and Brazilian rhythms in an original 'Afro-Cuban hard bop' style, he recorded with numerous jazz players Chick Corea, Hubert Laws, Toots Thielemans, Nat Adderley, Dizzy Gillespie) and scored a hit with Herbie Hancock's 'Watermelon Man'.

Tito Puente (1923), born in the 'barrio' of New York, never set foot in Cuba, but is nevertheless the unrivalled master of its kettledrums. He was also an excellent vibraphone player, and above all an incomparable leader who succeeded, at the lead of a more or less regular big band since the 1950s, in galvanizing numerous guest soloists, whom he accompanied and with whom he recorded, including virtually all the great figures of salsa, but also jazz players like George Shearing or Cal Tjader. His repertoire includes numerous jazz classics.

Ray Barretto (1929) came from a Puerto Rican family in Brooklyn, and was a self-taught percussion player who, like a number of his colleagues (Candido, Willie Bobo, etc.), was perfectly able to integrate himself in modern jazz, accompanying Parker, Gillespie, Max Roach, Wes Montgomery and many others, before playing with Tito Puente, and finally founding his own band.

Perez Prado (1918–1983), a pianist, organist and conductor of Cuban origin, and a most inventive disciple of Machito, incarnated, popularized and brought to its highest level (at least during his best period) the mambo style, incorporating in it certain influences from Mexico, where he worked for a time.

Charlie (1927) and **Eddie Palmieri** (1936), originally from New York, are two brothers, both pianists who each in his own way, transplanted in the dance music of the *latinos*, the repertoire and 'chorus' form which came from jazz, abandoning the strings of the traditional charanga for wind instruments, which they were able to combine in unheard of, subtle ways. Eddie, the more futurist, developed a piano style which was both ultra-lyrical and syncopated which recalls (at the same time!) Monk, Bill Evans and McCoy Tyner.

Paquito D'Rivera (1948) was the principal saxophonist from Cuba, which he left in preference for a European tour with the famous group Irakere, in 1980. He settled in New York, and accompanied Dizzy Gillespie, then McCoy Tyner, before he created his own group. A clarinettist who is deeply influenced by Benny Goodman (in jazz as in classical music) in his alto style he combines Parker's spirit and the suavity of a Paul Desmond, albeit with a marked tendency to exaggeration!

Arturo Sandoval (1949) was also a great star, and the co-founder (in 1973) of Irakere, a virtuoso big band directed by the pianist Chucho Valdes, in Havana. A highly gifted multi-instrumentalist (keyboard instruments, percussion, brass and others), he was one of the great technical virtuosos of the trumpet, demonstrated in his epic jousts with his friend Dizzy Gillespie, with whom he made the film *A Night in Havana*, in Cuba.

Bossa-nova and the jazz-samba

Jazz in Brazil was in fashion from the 1930s and gave rise to local variations, notably, the gafiera, whose great modern specialist was the clarinettist-saxophonist Paulo Mouro. It was only really at the end of the 1940s, however, that musicians began to integrate it consciously in the intimate music of the town clubs, very influenced by the samba.

It was at its height as much in the seasonal framework of carnivals as in the individual form of samba-cancao. Although its ultra-syncopated form reminds us that the word probably comes from the Angolan *semba*, one finds above all in this rhythm composed of many elements, traces of the polka and the Cuban habanera. Certain samba players, like the multi-instrumentalist **Pixinginhas** (1898–1973) developed since the 1920s from the chorro (the Brazilian blues) a refined instrumental music , full of improvisation and 'swing' like jazz. But it was in the clubs in Rio, at the end of the 1940s, that the history of the jazz-samba really took off.

Johnny Alf (1929) is considered as the inventor of what was not yet called (in 1949) the 'bossa-nova'. This transposition of bebop harmony, then Cool, on the lightly unaccented samba rhythm, was to mature slowly under the fingers of this discreet pianist of the boates of Copacabana.

Antonio Carlos 'Tom' Jobim (1937), also a pianist, gave the bossa-nova (the expression means 'new-machine') its classical form with his *Sinfonia de Rio de Janeiro* (1955). He was soon famous in the United States, where he recorded with Sinatra and Ella Fitzgerald, and some of his compositions like 'Wave' became the classics of modern jazz.

Joao Gilberto (1931) originally from Bahia, is by far the greatest interpreter of Jobim, and of the bossa in general. A singer and guitarist, he is better than anyone at making voice and instrument dance together, according to the batida, which is the Brazilian form of swing, nonchalant but irresistible. In 1963, Stan Getz recorded the album *The Girl from Ipanema* with him and his wife, the singer Astrud Gilberto, thanks to which the bossa immediately spread round the world.

Airto Moreira (1941) settled in New York in 1970, was immediately hired by Miles Davis, and subsequently became (together with his compatriot Paulinho da Costa) the most sought after percussion player in all jazz styles, accompanying Weather Report and Chick Corea just as well as Lee Morgan, Paul Desmond, Keith Jarrett, Kenny Burrell, Gato Barbieri or McCoy Tyner. He formed his own group in 1986.

Hermeto Pascoal (1936) is the most astonishing of all the Brazilian musicians linked to contemporary jazz. Exceptionally talented, he started as an accordionist in the Recife region, before founding in 1964, with Airto Moreira, the legendary Quarteto Novo, which was dedicated to a traditional North Eastern repertoire. In New York in 1970, at the same time as Airto, he met Miles Davis, who, fascinated, recorded with him one of his compositions ('Nem Um Talvez' on *Live Evil*). Living in Rio from 1971, he regularly toured the world with a repertoire to which he contributed all possible sounds imaginable, natural or electronic.

Finally, it should be mentioned that in the relative decline of popular Brazilian music — which became very sensitive to the sirens of world 'pop' — some musicians continued to elaborate an ambitious jazz which lacked neither humour nor lyricism for example, the pianists Cesar Camargo Mariano and Wagner Tiso, the guitaris and composer Toninho Horta (sometime associated with Pat Metheny), the singe Milton Nascimento (who recorded with Wayne Shorter), the composers Arrige Barnabé and Itamar Asumpcao.

Blues with ultramarine reflections

From the near Antilles (the West Indies) and far off India, exotic currents flowed into jazz.

Caribbean connection

Curiously absent from most of the works (it is not an exaggeration to speak of ostracism) the 'Petites Antilles' (as well as the other greater ones such as Cuba and Puerto Rico) have given jazz a number of excellent soloists, while musical forms developed there which are the closest ancestors of original jazz. 'Ancestors' and not 'cousins', because it must be recognized that they came first: the 'biguine' from Guadeloupe seems to have landed in New Orleans in about 1890, with its characteristic instrumentation (clarinet, trombone and banjo); as for the calypso from Trinidad, the term only appeared in 1900, but the first evidence (as also of the Cuban rumba) dates back to the 18th century, while the first records date from 1912, before jazz was recorded.

There is no attempt here to describe in detail the complex interpenetration of jazz by these types of music, which are as numerous and varied as the islands themselves. Nevertheless, it should be remembered that as from the 1940s, the radio (American but also French and Haitian) increased the influence of jazz enfold, and especially of rhythm'n'blues. Furthermore, musicians from the Antilles played an essential role in the European cities. In London, sax players of Jamaican origin — Joe Harriot (in the 1950s and 1960s) and later Courtney Pine, were active on the jazz scene; in Paris, the colonial exhibition in 1931 attracted some of the best musicians from Guadeloupe and Martinique. Very soon, clubs like *La Cigale*, *a Canne à Sucre* and *Le Bal Blomet* became the hottest places of the capital. The most remarkable clarinettists and saxophonists powered there: Stellio, Ernest Léardé, Sam astendet and the Coppet brothers for the pre-war generation; then Robert Mavounzy and Emilien Antile, both excellent disciples of Charlie Parker, and

finally Lucien Joly. Moreover, bebop was assimilated amazingly easily in the Antilles, and it was the trombonist Al Lirvat's intelligent fusion with his own rhythmic tradition that became the *biguine wabap*.

On the fringes of contemporary jazz there are also some talented saxophonists like Gaston Lindor from Guyanne and Bib Monville from Martinique, who formed the excellent jazz fusion group, Fal Frett. Guitarists are less numerous, but they include Henri Salvador from Guyana, who was a 100 per cent jazzplayer when he began, and above all the remarkable bopper from Guadeloupe, André Condouant. Other musicians to be mentioned are the drummer-percussionists Henri Guédon, Jean-Claude Montredon and Charlie Lamotte, the bass player Michel Alibo, and the flautists Dédé Saint-Prix and Eugène Mona.

Sonny Rollins, by the way, is from the Virgin Islands, and no one can beat him playing the calypso; Luther François, from Saint-Lucia, is another musician who is expert in this style.

Jamaica, particularly at the time of the *ska* (the original and specifically instrumental form of reggae), also produced some excellent musicians, playing both jazz and this local variety of rhythm'n' blues: the saxophonists Roland Alphonso and Tommy McCook, the trombone players Don Drummond and Rico Rodriguez, and the pianist Gladstone Anderson, who recorded the best records of this style under the name of The Skatalites. Some became, in the States or in Europe, remarkable bebop or hard bop jazz musicians: the guitarist Ernest Ranglin, the saxophonists Harold McNair and Wilton 'Bogey' Gaynair, the trumpeters Dizzy Reece and Sonny Grey.

Finally we shall linger over a number of pianists who form an actual school of Caribbean keyboard specialists.

Ram Ramirez (1913), a Puerto Rican, accompanied Rex Stewart, Ella Fitzgerald, Charlie Barnet and John Kirby, before setting up on his own. A dazzling performer of blues and stride, a disciple of Waller and Tatum, he is also the author of one of the jazz classics, 'Lover Man'.

Michel Sardaby (1935), a Martinican based in Paris from 1957, where he played at the Cigale, was a virtuoso with a classical training, and a great piano teacher. Amenable to all jazz styles, he was able through a positively 'Petersonian' profileration, to reconcile the meaning of blues and a certain nostalgia for the Antilles. He recorded in particular with Richard Davis and Ron Carter, Billy Cobham and Ray Barretto, as well as with his Jamaican 'twin', Monty Alexander.

Marius Cultier (1942–1985) was the first great jazz pianist who was active in his native Martinique, before he emigrated to Canada and the United States, where he was noticed by Stevie Wonder and Miles Davis. Back in Fort-de-France in 1973, he was the centre of jazz activity until his premature death. An eclectic and educated musician, for the French-speaking Antilles he was a sort of equivalent to Eddie Palmieri or Chucho Valdes, reconciling the most pointed harmony with the traditional rhythms and styles of his island.

Monty Alexander (1944) grew up to the sound of the calypso and ska, in Kingston where he was born, before developing a passion for jazz under the influence of King Cole, George Shearing and above all Wynton Kelly. Emigrating to the United States, he became there a sort of 'godson' to Oscar Peterson, some of whose former accompanists he recruited for his trios and quartets (Ray Brown, Herb Ellis, Milt Jackson, Ed Thigpen). Brilliant and swinging, he sought less for fusion than a discreet Caribbean imprint on the already rich palette of the jazz virtuoso.

Alain Jean-Marie (1945), who came from a family of well-known musicians in Guadeloupe, settled in Paris in the 1970s, where he became one of the pianists most in demand as accompanist, all the while recording in his own name delicious albums mostly devoted to the biguine. An excellent 'post-bopper', he was able to dominate the influences of Bud Powell and Wynton Kelly, and to play chords with a very personal touch. He mainly played and recorded with NHØP, Dee Dee Bridgewater and Barney Wilen.

India songs

The inevitable encounter between the most classical of improvised music (the interpretation of ragas) and jazz, was long expected. At first it was reduced to superficially exotic titles, such as 'The Snake Charmer', 'Sweet Indian Princess' or 'Taj Mahal' by Michel Warlop and Django — who firmly claimed the Indian origin of Tziganes.

It was only from the 1950s that it became the fashion for the rhythmic formulas (*talas*), then instruments from India, to make timid appearances in the style of certain compositions. The first seems to be 'Bohemia after Dark' (1955) by Oscar Pettiford, who toured the Far East several years earlier. Shortly afterwards, the multi-instrumentalist Yusef Lateef integrated in his panoply the shenai (Northern Indian oboe), and recorded some clearly Hindu-type themes, notably 'Before Dawn' (1957) and 'India' (1964). During the same period the first encounters beween jazz players and Indian virtuosos took place: Ravi Shankar with Bud Shank (1961), then Paul Horn; Dave Brubeck with the great percussion player from Madras, Palghat Raghu (1967).

But it was John Coltrane who from the end of the 1950s, incarnated at his highest level, the fascination that India then exercised on a growing number of great artists from the West. Like Stockhausen, he was less interested in the musical system (which he studied nonetheless) than in the instruments (he adopted in the soprano sound inspired by the shenai) and above all in the spirituality, and the 'rhythmic prayer' which soon pervaded in all his music: from *India* (1961) to *Meditation* (1965).

In this he was copied by numerous disciples: Pharaoh Sanders (*Karma*, 1969) and above all Don Cherry, who without doubt was the first to make a decisive step in studying with the Dagar brothers the *drupad* (the most complex and the mo 'noble' of the styles of northern Indian singing). The trumpeter (who also played various Indian flutes) recorded with the tabla player Latif Khan and formed his trio Codona (in 1980) with the Brazilian Nana Vasconcelos and the New Yorker Collin Walcott.

Collin Walcott (1945–1984) was the first tabla and sitar virtuoso from the West. As well as Codona, he was also part of the famous Oregon quartet, with Ralph Towner (guitar), Glen Moore (bass) and Paul McCandless (reeds). His whole group was in a coach accident which cost him his life, and he was replaced by the percussionist and drummer from Bombay, **Trilok Gurtu** (1951). Since the 1970s, Gurtu has been one of the protagonists of this 'Indo-jazz' which was emerging: in 1987 he became a member of the John McLaughlin trio, and also enlivened his own group with his mother, the traditional singer Shoba Gurtu, the Danish trumpeter Palle Mikkelborg, the Swedish bass player Jonas Hellborg and the pianist Daniel Goyane, who was the pioneer in France of the 'fusion' style. Gurtu also took part in many sessions with Terje Rypdal, Barre Phillips, John Tchicai and Charlie Mariano.

Charlie Mariano (1923), a remarkable alto, soprano and flute virtuoso, was at the start one of the most brilliant disciples of Charlie Parker, and one of the great figures of Cool jazz and West Coast. But the discovery of the East has profoundly changed his life and his music: married at the time to the pianist Toshiko Akiyoshi, he travelled to Japan in 1961 and learned the shakuhachi flute. Then, as conductor of the orchestra of Radio Malaysia (1966–1967) he discovered the nagaswaram (oboe of South India, where he later lived) and

increased his musical meetings, which ended in the 1980s with his regular participation at Karnataka College of Percussion, Los Angeles.

The **Shakti** group of 'Mahavishnu' John McLaughlin represents today the most accomplished form of Indian jazz, but has also provided the first formal meeting of great musicians from the south (the violinist L. Shankar and the mridangam player Raghavan) and from the north of India (the extraordinary tabla player Zakir Hussain). McLaughlin has also recorded with the greatest living north Indian flautist, Hariprasad Chaurasia.

We must also mention the sitar and tablas (Badal Roy) used by Miles Davis in the 1970s; the recordings of the saxophonist John Handy with the great southern violinist Subramaniam (the brother of L. Shankar), and the genius of the sarod (the great northern lute), Ali Akbar Khan; the trumpeter Don Ellis's Hindustani Jazz Sextet in the 1960s; the recordings of the sax/flautist Paul Horn, especially with Ravi Shankar; and the work of John Mayer's Indo-Jazz Fusion group in London.

In Europe, the record *Jazz Meets India* (M.P.S. 1967) signalled the departure on 'the road to Calcutta', along which many jazzmen have occasionally met Indian musicians. These have included the pianists Irène Schweitzer, Jasper Van t'hof, Joachim Kühn, Wolfgang Dauner; the saxophonists Joe Harriott, Barney Wilen; the trumpeter Manfred Schoof; the trombonist Albert Mangelsdorff. As for the saxophonist Richard Raux, whose group Hamsa Music is distinctly 'oriental'; he dedicated a beautiful composition to the great shenai player Bismillah Khan, one of John Coltrane's idols.

From rhythm'n'blues to rock'n'roll

The real 'hidden face' of jazz, and most popular with the Afro-American public, rhythm'n'blues was officially born on 25 June 1949, when Billboard, the main show-biz magazine, substituted this expression for 'race records', which was something of a caricature. Dance music with pervasive riffs and a binary rhythm, like the urban blues, boogie-woogie, and the profane derivatives of religious music (doo-wop), rhythm'n'blues evolved in the 1950s in contact with 'Country & Western', to become in turn — a long time after jazz — interracial music: rock'n'roll.

From 1939, **Louis Jordan** (1908–1975), alto sax player and singer with his Tympany Five, typified the fashion for the 'jump band' which replaced the big bands in the dance halls. Star of numerous film clips, record millionaire with 'G.I. Jive' and 'Choo Choo Ch'Boogie', vehement improviser and remarkable swing player, he was without a doubt the most 'jazzy' of the forerunners of rock'n'roll, and his numerous recordings on Decca-MCA (with Ella Fitzgerald as well as others) can be rated among the classics of their kind.

Jack McVea (1914), tenor saxophonist, left Lionel Hampton in 1943 to form his own combo in Los Angeles. A real hyphen between swing, bop (he recorded with Slim Gaillard, Parker and Gillespie) and jump-jive, he won world success with his *Open the Door, Richard*, translated into every language.

Charles Brown (1920), singer and pianist, contributed to the evolution of the Texan blues under the influence of Nat King Cole, to become the great maestro of the 'blues ballad'.

Dave Bartholomew (1920), trumpeter, singer and above all producer based in New Orleans, was largely responsible for the 'boom' of rhythm'n'blues at the beginning of the 1950s. A most enlightened animator of the labels Aladdin, Deluxe, Specialty and especially Imperial, we owe to him the discovery of . . .

Fats Domino (1928), pianist and singer

in the great New Orleans tradition. French by birth, he won his first success in 1949 with 'Hey La Bas'. Then followed 'The Fat Man', 'Goin' Home', 'I'm Walkin' '. Like all pioneers of rock'n'roll, he gradually slipped (for a few dollars more) into the crooner style, which earned him world glory with 'Blueberry Hill' (1950).

Chuck Berry (1926), Californian guitarist and singer, made his debut in Saint Louis with the pianist Johnnie Johnson, before being 'launched' in Chicago by Muddy Waters and his label Chess. An incomparable 'theatre animal', he exploded at about 19 years old, with 'Maybellene' and 'Wee Wee Hours' followed by 'Roll Over Beethoven', 'Too Much Monkey Business', 'Schoolday' 'Rock'n'Roll Music', 'Sweet Little Sixteen', 'Johnny B Goode' and 'Carol', a profusion of immortal hits which made him the archetype of the genuine rocker.

Bo Diddley (1928), guitarist and singer trained in the school of gospel, Chicago blues, and Louis Jordan, was from the middle of the 1950s, the other great star of the Chess label, and his corrosive humour had a considerable influence on most of the rockers.

Little Richard (1935), pianist and singer from Georgia, in 1955 with his 'Tutti Frutti', then 'Long Tall Sally', 'Rip it Up' and 'Lucille', inaugurated the frenetic style of which he is the best exponent, and went on to devote himself mainly to gospel.

Jazz and 'classical': a reciprocal but equivocal fascination

Improvisation, which was still very much part of the world of romantic music, practically disappeared in cultured European music at the very time when jazz was born. This original paradox was kindled by a complicated relationship where curiosity vied with mistrust, naïvety with clairvoyance, admiration with scorn, and where of course, racism was not always lacking.

On the one hand, jazz players, who more often than is generally believed have a solid training in the rudiments of music and harmony right from the start, aspire to the recognition of their music as a publishable, lasting work. But, for the 'classics,' the attitude differs a lot according to the function: the composers very quickly perceived the nobility and the magic of jazz, but without always clearly distinguishing the good from the bad, and often going no further than the analysis of transcriptions which never give more than their palest reflection. As for the musicians themselves, the best have always been fascinated by jazz.

Social issues evidently play a decisive role in this ambiguous relationship: jazz was still, not so long ago, considered as an interloper, even subversive, and generally not allowed to exist in our music schools. Recognized by the media, and to a certain extent adopted by cultural organizations and the intelligentsia, it acquired a sort of sulphurous halo. More than one maestro, more than one opera star dreamed of mixing with the riff-raff, at least for the length of a TV programme, with their 'somewhat neglected, but so charming' counterparts, some of whom 'even know how to read music'!

The impossible written jazz

The historical attitude of European or American composers can be described thematically in three stages. Until the 1930s, there was a widespread craze for syncopation, a 'brassy' sound and a

predominance of percussion in jazz. Then, in the 1940s and 1950s, the disillusion was just as general. Failures were numerous among works inspired by jazz; on the other hand, the sudden mutation represented by bebop disconcerted some composers, who ceased to follow the evolution of Afro-American music. On its side, the avant-garde entirely converted to 12-tone music, considered jazz as henceforth archaic, as with any other sort of tonal music. Finally, from the 1960s, a new convergence emerged through efforts to write 'random' music, where improvisation regained a certain place in the interstices of rigorous and complex writing.

We are only discussing here composers who were, in their sometimes clumsy way, 'creators' of jazz.

Anton Dvorak, during a trip to New York, composed his *Ninth Symphony* (known as the *New World Symphony*) in 1892–1893, and chose for the theme of the second movement, the negro spiritual 'Goin' Home'.

Claude Debussy wrote the 'Golliwog's Cake Walk' in 1908 which is included in his *Children's Corner* for piano; then in 1910, his 'Minstrels' close the procession of the first book of *Preludes*.

Erik Satie was one of the first to discover and to play in public the music of Scott Joplin, which led him to include in his extraordinary ballet *Parade* (1917) a 'Ragtime du Paquebot' inspired by 'Mysterious Rag'.

Maurice Ravel who, like Debussy, exercised a considerable influence on the pianists of modern jazz, was himself immediately won over. In 1919, he made the cup and the tea-pot in *L'Enfant et les sortilèges* dance a fox-trot. An habitué of the Parisian jazz cabarets, in 1923 he composed the magnificent *blues* which served as the second movement of his *Sonata for piano and violin*. Finally, in his two *Concertos for piano* of 1931 (especially the one in G), jazz became the object of a delicate but perfectly successful graft.

Igor Stravinsky had a captivating relationship with jazz. In Paris in 1918 he crossed the threshold: wild about Scott Joplin's pieces that Ernest Ansermet brought him from New York, they inspired him to write *Ragtime for eleven instruments* and especially *L'Histoire du soldat*. Next came the *Concertino* (1920), *Prélude pour ensemble de jazz* (1937), *Tango* (1940) and of course, *Ebony Concerto*, created for Woody Herman in 1946.

Darius Milhaud only had a very superficial knowledge of jazz when he composed *Le Boeuf sur le Toit* (1920). But he already had a passion for Billy Arnold and, two years later, he went to New York, where he ignored Broadway and preferred Harlem. From this 'coup de foudre' *La Création du Monde* (1923) was born. That was the great period for 'concerts-salades', in which jazz and classical music were mixed, organized by Jean Wiener, who with Clément Doucet formed the piano duo in the famous 'Boeuf sur le Toit', the temple of jazz 'à la française' where great musicians from all over the world would meet for one for the road.

In the musical avant-garde of the 1920s and 1930s nearly everybody tried to write 'scores that swing'. In Germany **Paul Hindemith** was probably the first to acknowledge jazz with his foxtrot *Finale 1921*.

In Vienna, **Ernst Krenek** composed a jazz opera, *Johnny leads the dance* (1927).

Kurt Weill, then in Berlin, was close on his heels with *Mahagony* (1927) and the *Threepenny Opera* (1928), many of whose songs entered the jazz repertory.

Bohuslav Martinu wrote two pieces of symphonic jazz, *Half Time* and *The Jazz*.

In the U.S.S.R., **Dimitri Shostakovitch** composed a *Suite for jazz orchestra* in 1934.

George Auric, who was the honorary president of the Jazz Academy until his death, often mixed the influences of jazz

and folklore. **Francis Poulenc** was practically born from jazz, since his first work was his *Rhapsodie nègre* (1918). In Europe **Bela Bartók** must certainly be mentioned, for his *Contrastes* (which he composed with Benny Goodman in 1940).

George Gershwin was of course the greatest of all these composers of 'symphonic jazz' — *Rhapsody in Blue, An American in Paris*, 1924), *Concerto for piano* (1925) — and jazz opera with the incomparable *Porgy and Bess* (1935). We can also thank him for *Jazz Preludes* for piano, and above all for numerous songs which jazz players know by heart.

We shall also mention the *Concerto fo clarinet* by **Aaron Copland** (created for Benny Goodman in 1950) and especially the most strange *Imaginary Landscape no. 5* b **John Cage**, a 'collage' made from 42 jazz records (1952).

In fact, since the second World War, jazz rarely served as an explicit reference in written music. Nevertheless, we must mention the superb *Concerto no. 2* for trumpet b **André Jolivet** (1954). On the other hand various composers included in their music improvised sequences in a spirit close t contemporay jazz: this is especially the cas with Lutoslawski, Kagel ('Blues Blue') Stockhausen (whose son is a jazz trumpeter), Globokar (founder with Michel Portal of the New Phonic Art), and Pendecki, who recorded Action in 1971 with the trumpeter Don Cherry.

When the interpreter improvises (and vice-versa)

It is not surprising that much passion for jazz was aroused among the classical virtuosos by listening to Art Tatum. The most dazzling of the great improvisers had himself made the first step, including in his themes pieces by Dvorak, Schumann and Liszt in particular.

André Prévin (1929) thus became remarkable West Coast jazz pianist whose style shows the influence of Art Tatum and Bud Powell, often playing with Shelly Manne, Shorty Rogers and Red Mitchell This has not prevented him from becoming one of the greatest conductors of h generation, directing the London Symphony Orchestra and composing symphonies and concertos in his own right. He notably managed to convince the great violinist **Itzhak Perlman** to join him in recording two jazz albums, together with Jim Hall and Red Mitchell.

Frederich Gulda (1930) is both one of the best contemporary interpreters of Beethoven and Mozart and a brilliant jazz pianist in the Tatum and Bud Powell tradition. In 1960 he started the Eurojazz Orchestra, he also plays the flute and the baritone sax and likes to play in duo with his friend Chick Corea.

There are many classical virtuosos who, like **Vladimir Horowitz** and **Samson François**, demonstrate their passion for jazz by regularly frequenting jazz clubs. Since the 1970s many have overcome a certain endemic shyness to 'cross swords' with jazzmen: **Jean-Pierre Rampal** with Claude Bolling, **Yehudi Menuhin** with Stéphane Grappelli, **Katia Labèque** with François Jeanneau and John McLaughlin, **Maurice André** with Dizzy Gillespie and Arturo Sandoval.

For their part, many jazzmen are sufficiently skilled with their instrument to tackle the most difficult pieces of classical or contemporary music, and frequently do so: **Keith Jarrett** has already recorded Bach's *The Well Tempered Clavier* and *Goldberg Variations*. Chick Corea has composed his own *Piano Concerto* and recorded Mozart's *Concerto for two pianos*. Playing in duo with Herbie Hancock, they enjoy slipping pieces by Bartók or Stravinsky into their concerts. **Siegfried Kessler** prefers the romantics. **Martial Solal**, who is seriously working on Bartók's compositions, has also composed a *Concerto for jazz trio and orchestra* and created works for Marius Constant and André Hodeir. The trumpeter Jean-Lou Longnon is the composer of a remarkable symphonic suite *L'Ours* (The bear). Finally, it should be added that a growing number of contemporary jazzmen are also by training and by profession virtuoso interpreters, like the bassist **Jean-François Jenny-Clark**, the pianist **Simon Nabatov** and, of course, the trumpeter **Wynton Marsalis**, whose recordings of Haydn or Leopold Mozart actually sell better than his jazz records!

Chick Corea and **Friedrich Gulda** *(seated)*

Michel Portal

1935, Bayonne

With a firm base of perfect instrumental skill, he never hesitates to carry improvisation to the threshold of the unpredictable.

He is the first to note with amazement that he is the only major 'classical' soloist to devote at least half his life to improvised music. It is true that there is an element of schizophrenia in this, as he reserves the clarinet for the playing of Mozart, Brahms, Schubert, Berg or Boulez (whose *Domaines* he has recorded), and plays his jazz on other instruments: soprano, alto and tenor saxes, bass clarinet, bandoneon, etc.

From his childhood in the Basque country, Michel Portal has kept a taste for a lively, deeply rooted, but also flowery popular music, and a distinct preference for live concert performances rather than recording sessions. The first music he

played consisted of fandangos, waltzes and tangos, then the mambo with Benny Bennett and Perez Prado. His attraction to jazz was gradual; listening to the clarinettists — Bigard, Noone, Giuffre; the shock of Dizzy Gillespie's big band, then of Coltrane and Dolphy. This musician who won the first prize at the Conservatoire was among the pioneers of Free Jazz in France, with Bernard Vitet, François Tusques, Beb Guérin and Sunny Murray. At the same time, he participated in the experience of the New Phonic Art (with Vinko Globokar, Carlos Alsina and Jean-Pierre Drouet), who played 'improvised contemporary chamber music'. In 1971, he founded his Unit, an open, informal (and eternal) group, which welcomed dozens of European or American guests. Often associated with Henri Texier, Jean-François Jenny-Clark, Joachim Kuhn, Aldo Romano, Daniel Humair, François Jeanneau and Bernard Lubat, he played more rarely with Steve Lacy, Martial Solal, Pierre Favre, Gérard Marais, Claude Barthélemy, Dave Liebman, Jack DeJohnette. His concerts brought some unexpected moments in festivals, 'happenings' where his versatile and introverted personality was revealed. He was also one of the best French authors of film music (*La Cecilia, France Société anonyme, l'Ombre rouge*).

It would be in vain to try to define the 'style' of an artist who incarnated an arrogant freedom which did not exclude provocation and the inevitable shock of conflicting with personalities as strong as his own. Fascinated by Spain — but not that of the 'espagnolades' — by Oriental modes and by the multi-rhythms of Africa, he was able to suit his passions to the conscious expression of a romantic lyricism which he never found the opportunity to express in the repertoire of contemporary European music.

Jazz and other art forms

The silver screen

This episodic relationship began with a double paradox. The first film 'with sound and talking' was *The Jazz Singer* (1927), a musical comedy by the obscure Alan Crosland. Nevertheless, it was not really jazz but vaudeville, and the hero — the singer Al Jolson — is a white in blackface, as can be seen on the tins of shoe-polish of the time! Three years later *The King of Jazz* was released, whose hero was obviously not Armstrong — who had the role of a cannibal chasing after Betty Boop in cartoons (which were in fact hilarious) by the Fleischer Brothers — but the pale Paul Whiteman. It was not until the most beautiful *Hallelujah* (1931), directed by King Vidor, the first good quality talking film, that Afro-American music (blues, honky-tonk and gospel above all, with a superb score by Irving Berlin) was treated with respect, even if the characters embody rather heavy clichés. But henceforth, jazz became unavoidable from both sides of the camera, as soon as it was a question of illustrating a fragment of American night life. It played a very distinct role, both in front of the camera and behind it.

Swing sequence

It should first be emphasized that jazz invaded the cinema well before the voice: just before the 1920s, it was the basic material for pianists, organists and orchestras to fill the silences, and the dark halls, where many made their debut, from Fats Waller to Stephane Grappelli, offered a large part of their resources to jazz musicians. Naturally, little was known of their 'furniture music', whose witnesses agreed in their recognition of its extreme wealth and incomparable spontaneity. It was necessary to improvise 'in real time' in accordance with the action of films which succeeded each other day after day and night after night, and the musicians who most recently tried their hand at this little game (like Martial Solal with the L'Herbier films) are still in a cold sweat! In the silent cinema, jazz was also represented in a thousand burlesque sequences — notably in Charlie Chaplin's films like *A day's pleasure*.

From the beginning of the 1930s, jazz was to be frequently filmed, either (rarely before 1945) by amateurs or in the form of 'clips', which had great success during the many intervals while the spool was being changed. Armstrong, Fats Waller, the Mills Brothers, most of the big bands and singers thus made thousands of short films which have since become like 'the early printed books' of collectors, and are little by little coming out on video. Décors and costumes inspired by the 'black reviews', dance numbers (Bill Robinson, the Nicks Brothers, Sammy Davis Jr.), sketches (Fats Waller), mini-melodramas (Duke Ellington, Bessie Smith, Billie Holiday) and even already, a mixture of real images and cartoons beside which Roger Rabbit would pale (Cab Calloway in *Minnie the Moocher*, for example); the imagination of these first little masters of the video clip seemed inexhaustable.

Soon, (in the 1940s) more ambitious films appeared, including *Jammin' the Blues* (1944, with Lester Young), made by **Gjon Mili** which has remained an unequalled masterpiece: here there is no décor other than the night and smoke, no action other than the suspense of the chorus, even the cameraman seems to film by snapping his fingers! Then television imposed its own aesthetics (different enough it is true) on the 'jazz film', which became reportage rather than entertainment. In the same period, brief sequences of 'atmosphere' shot in jazz clubs, multiplied in the comedy of manners — *Rendez-vous de juillet* by Jacques Becker (1949) — and above all of the gangster type — the *Johnny Stacatto* series by the young Cassavetes, and *The Sweet Smell* *of Success* by McKendrick reveal the best of West Coast jazz at the end of the 1950s. If many musical comedies are sprinkled with jazz, — *Artists and Models* by *Walsh* (1937), *Cabins in the Sky* by Minnelli (1942) — few of them gave it a good part: **Andrew Stone**'s *Stormy Weather* was the archetype of the kind, definitely more convincing than **Arthur Lubin**'s *New Orleans* (1947) and comparable at a distance to the screamingly funny *Blues Brothers* by **Jon Landis** (1980).

The 'romantic biography' type also had few successes: *Young Man with a Horn* (1949) rather flatly relates the life of Bix Beiderbecke; the success of *The Glenn Miller Story* by **Anthony Mann** (1953) is held together mainly by the combination of James Stewart and June Allyson; Diana Ross is not a very convincing Billie Holiday in *Lady sings the Blues* made by **Sidney Fury** (1973). On the other hand, Dexter Gordon magnificently portrays the hybrid of Lester Young and Bud Powell in the very musical but somewhat tame *Round Midnight* by **Tavernier**. Of course, the presence *in vivo* of Armstrong and Ellington in *Paris Blues* by **Martin Ritt** (1961) conceals all its defects, while the absence of the real Charlie Parker weighs cruelly on **Clint Eastwood**'s beautiful *Bird*. In the 'luxury' bracket, one should not forget the dull but spell-binding *Cotton Club* by **Coppola** (1985).

At the two opposite poles of these Hollywood sagas, the 1970s and 1980s saw a new style bloom, which was on the borderline between cinema and television: the 'jazz documentary', generally conceived as a commentary on a cross between the elaboration of the music, an autobiography of the musician, the life of the band, and the social environment (*Too Late Blues* by Cassavetes), ethnic and even political or financial. In France, the bass player Frank Casenti is a specialist in this delicate style (Sun Ra, Archie Shepp, Michel Petrucciani), magnificently illustrated in the United States by Robert Mugge (Sonny Rollins, Gil Scott-Heron, Al Green, Sun Ra). It should be noted that the blues is fairly neglected, which increased the interest of Les Blank's magnificent documentaries.

Finally, a few rare feature films were concerned with the daily life of the musicians and their environment: after the masterly *The Man with the Golden Arm* by **Otto Preminger** (1955) — with a spell-binding Frank Sinatra — *The Connection* by **Shirley Clarke** (1960) deals in an original way with a subject which is less interesting, drugs and jazz; *Jazz Band* (1980) tells the epic story of a group of Soviet jazz players in the 1920s; *Sven Klang's Quintet* by the Swede **Stefan Olsson** describes the daily problems of unknown musicians, like the mediocre *Saxo* by Ariel Zeitoun, saved by the blowing of Archie Shepp.

'Big band sounds'

Jazz has had its greatest effect on the cinema through background music. Chance led to the most successful arrangements between fiction and jazz: **Louis Malle** was seeking a band for his already edited *Ascenseur pour l'échafaud* (1957), when his friend Marcel Romano let him know that he was organizing a European tour for Miles Davis. In a few hours, the trumpeter, surrounded by the best jazz players of Saint-Germain-des-Prés, was improvising some of the most beautiful film music ever. Godard did not even know the name of Martial Solal when **Jean-Pierre Melville** recommended him for *A bout de souffle* (1960): this cult film of the Nouvelle Vague owes just as much to the pianist as to the director, or the Belmondo/Seberg couple. Just as in *Anatomy of a Murder* by Preminger (1959), the terrifying silence which weighs on the final trial is still Duke Ellington's! Innumerable films since the 1950s have marked this 'other look', which is that of a great jazz musician: *Sait-on jamais?* by **Vadim** (1957, John Lewis); *Des femmes disparaissent* by **Molinaro** (1959, Art Blakey); *Un témoin dans la ville* by Molinaro (1959, Barney Wilen); *Shadows* by **Cassavetes** (1961, Charlie Mingus); *Repulsion* by **Polanski** (1965, Chico Hamilton); *Alfie* by **Lewis Gilbert** (1966, Sonny Rollins); *Blow Up* by **Antonioni** (1967, Herbie Hancock, who also wrote the score of *Round Midnight*); *Last Tango in Paris* by **Bertolucci** (1972,

Gato Barbieri); *Les valseuses*, by **Bertrand Blier** (1974, Stephane Grappelli); *L'Ombre rouge* by **Comolli** (1982, Michel Portal); *Mortelle Randonée* by **Claude Miller** (1982, Carla Bley); *Siesta* by **Mary Lambert** (1987, Marcus Miller and Miles Davis).

Cartoons have always been a privileged medium for jazz since Walt Disney's *Silly Symphonies* (Paul Whiteman at his peak) and the marvels of Dave Fleischer (Cab Calloway, Armstrong, etc.). Finally, throughout the history of the cinema, jazz is never more present than when one is the least expecting it, around an image. One thinks, for example, of Henry Mancini's music for *Touch of Evil* by Orson Welles, who joined moreover in the 1940s with Ellington on a project dealing with the history of jazz — unfortunately abortive due to the lack of funds — or of the disturbing Patrick Deweare listening obsessionally to Ellington's *Moonlight Fiesta* on his mini-K7 in *Séri noire* by Alain Corneau (1979), who was himself a jazz drummer before exchanging his drumsticks for the camera.

Jazz and fashion: from the 'zazous' to Yves Saint-Laurent

Because jazz embodied all the Afro-American cultural features and their progressive assimilation into the Western way of life, it was seen right away as a social phenomenon which exceeded its musical expression by far. To a greater or lesser extent, later generations were to assume jazz players' behaviour, their way of speaking (jive), walking, dressing, living and thinking. In the 1920s, the exuberant image of **Josephine Baker** served as an example to a great many elegant eccentrics. In the 1930s, the fashion for swing took off, then Cab Calloway imposed his extravagant *zoot suites* and onomatopeas on the 'hepcats'. In France, their atypical appearance and their hermetic slang were to be a *soft* form of resistance to the deprivation and discipline imposed by the occupation and the 'national revolution'. Bebop topped off this panoply of marginality in delirium: crumpled, loose clothes, striped or flowered ties and bow-ties, goatees, and berets like **Dizzy Gillespie**, plus brilliantined hair were to be the attributes of the *hipster*. Being *hip*, (later 'in' was to be 'cool', neither the dupe of social convention nor of the meaning of words — was the triumph of the *double talk* of the black ghettos, with asystematic double meaning. Assimilated in the night life of the existentialists of Saint-Germain-des-Prés, jazz became, in the image it was given by its heralds Boris Vian or Norman Mailer, a peaceful form of dandyism.

In the United States, towards the end of the 1950s, the *hipsters* quite naturally took over the *beatnik* movement: the beat generation was the generation of a single beat, a single rhythm, jazz, which gradually abandoned the parody of the bourgeoisie's flashy rags (threadbare suits, battered hats) for exotic paraphernalia such as Hawaiian shirts, or a mass of hair. The hippies succeeded the hipsters and relegated jazz to the background for a long time, behind the front ranks of rock and pop which were emerging. At the same time, Free Jazz triumphantly harboured the streaky magnificence of Africa and the Orient. But it was necessary to wait for the 1980s for the jazz fashion to return. Certain pop stars (Van Morrison, Tom Waits, Elvis Costello, John Lurie, Sade, Carmel, Rickie Lee Jones) contributed largely to its return. Mondino's video clips, films like *Absolute Beginners* and of course, *Round Midnight, Bird,* and *Mo' Better Blues* enhanced the jazz aesthetic from the 1950s to the 1960s. Advertising cashed in: the café played the black card, perfume hinted at Daddy's jazz (Yves Saint-Laurent) and on the billboards, dreamlike creatures blew absent mindedly into their upside-down saxophones!

Jazz in comics: a nightlife mythology

It was not until the 1980s that comic strip illustrators got involved with the wild scene they associate with jazz, and the saxophone became the symbol of any slightly shady environment

The models of the genre are still *Joe's Bar* by the Argentinians **Munos** and **Sampayo** (Pub. Casterman) and especially *The man from Harlem* by the Italian **Guido Crepax** (Pub. Dargaud). Their influence is present in the dark intrigues by the Belgian **Louis Joos**, a specialist in bluesy comics with his *Ostende-Miami, Saxo-Cool and Night Music* (Pub. Futuropolis). Another Belgian, **Ever Meulen** has not published books but strips, posters and record sleeves which have been brought together in an anthology published by Futuropolis. With *Blues in the night*, **Filips** provides a very colourful pastiche of the song *La Boite de Jazz* (Pub. Art Moderne).

On the French side, **Fernandez**, the illustrator of *Jazz Hot*, has published *Nostalgia in Times Square* with **Raynal** (Futuropolis), while **Loustal** and **Paringaux** were inspired by the life of Barney Wilen in *Barney et la Note bleue* (Casterman), which comes with an original tape by the musician! In the **Götting** collection *Détours* (Futuropolis) the hero of 'Carnegie Lune' is (again !) a jazz saxophonist. As for the Italian Liberatore, he is the author of 'Sax Blues' in the album *Musicomix* (Pub. Artefact).

Finally it is **Crumb**, the star of American underground comics, who best expresses the genuine spirit of the blues, in black and white, of course . . .

The Man from Harlem by Guido Crepax.
copyright Ed. CEPIM, Milano (1976), copyright Editions Dargaud, Paris (1979)

Rhythm and the plastic arts

As early as 1910 a strange romance started between jazz and painting, both increasingly attracted by rhythm and spontaneous improvisation. Their adventure was full of repercussions with more to it than just the anecdotes of the frequent meetings between jazzmen and painters.

Indeed, there was much more than the constant interest the great artists of the time demonstrated in the 'painters of the night', as Cocteau called them, in the common approach which united music and painting around the beginning of the 20th century, for both began seeking the same freedom of expression and establishing new rules that were far from being academic.

'Coloured rhythms', 'freedom of instrumental movement', 'expressionism', 'harmonic palette': it was not by chance that these expressions became common usage with artists and jazz musicians alike. One could speak of jazz entirely in painting terminology: from the polyphonic 'tachisme' of New Orleans to the 'lyrical abstraction' of Free Jazz, not to mention the expressionism of big bands and the futurism of bebop!

One can identify several ways in which exchanges between jazz and painting occurred:

— from the 1910s many painters portrayed jazzmen, especially black Americans;

— from the 1930s certain trends in abstract painting were inspired by the swing and improvisation inherent in jazz;

— from the 1940s certain painters tried to paint works in real time collaboration with musicians improvising simultaneously;

— from the 1950s, with the appearance of LPs, record covers became a support for some of the most creative contemporary artists;

— finally certain jazzmen, and among them some of the greatest, devoted part of their lives to painting; and some painters play jazz.

Jazz in the museum!

The following is a brief chronology of the relationship between jazz and 20th century painting.

1913: upon his arrival in New York, after hearing some blues musicians, Francis Picabia painted *Chanson nègre*. The same year, Sonia Delaunay (whose son Charles was to start the magazine *Jazz-Hot* in 1935) painted *Le Bal Bullier* and four other canvasses inspired by the foxtrot and the tango.

1915: Albert Gleizes — who sent Cocteau some ragtime scores from New York — painted several canvasses inspired by the nights he spent with Duchamp and Picabia in the first Harlem jazz clubs.

1918: in New York, Fernand Léger exhibited *Les Disques*, a painting which so enthralled a group of jazz musicians and dancers that the painter offered them a gouache on the same theme, which they assured him they would use as inspiration for their improvisations. Marcel Janco painted *Jazz 333*.

1923: Picasso's *Three Musicians* (one of whom was a saxophonist) were clearly jazzmen. Léger designed the sets and costumes for Darius Milhaud's 'ballet nègre' *La Création du Monde*, inspired by African art and jazz.

1925: Yves Tanguy exhibited silhouettes of jazzmen at the 'Salon de l'Araignée'. At the Bauhaus Kandinsky painted a series of canvasses under the title *Swinging*. Henri Laurens painted a portrait of Josephine Baker.

1926: Frank Kupka painted his first jazz canvasses, including *Le Jazz-band machiniste*.

1927: Paul Colin designed the posters for the *Revue Nègre*.

1927–1928: jazz featured in German expressionism, particularly in canvasses by Beckmann and Otto Dix.

1935: Kupka painted a new series entitled *Jazz Hot*.

1942–1943: Matisse made his collage album entitled *Jazz*.

1943: Félix Labisse painted *Tiger Rag*.

1943–1944: New York, last works painted by Mondrian: *Broadway Boogie Woogie* and *Victory Boogie Woogie*.

1948: allegorical portrait of Thelonious Monk painted by the surrealist Victor Brauner.

1948–1951: painters of the Cobra experimental group (Appel, Constant, Corneille, Doucet, Alechinsky, Jorn) sought direct inspiration from jazz in their work and often referred to it explicitly: *Hommage à Armstrong* and *Bal nègre Rue Blomet* (Jacques Doucet), *Bird* and *L'Orchestre bebop* (Corneille), etc.

1953: inspired by a Sidney Bechet concert at Antibes, Nicolas de Stael painted his last monumental canvas, *Les Musiciens*.

1957: settling in New York, where he lived in the company of jazz musicians, Karel Appel painted portraits of Count Basie, Miles Davis and Charlie Mingus and 'performed' with Dizzy Gillespie.

1967: 'L'Age du Jazz' exhibition of 100 painters at the Galliera museum.

1976: Magritte painted his *Hommage à Armstrong*.

Jazz painting: U.S.A.

It was the American painter Gerald Murphy who, settling on the Côte d'Azur, introduced jazz in the region by organizing sumptuous evenings and creating what was probably the first important record collection in Europe. In 1919, Man Ray gave the title *Jazz* to one of the first works done with an air brush.

Stuart Davis chose jazz in the 1930s as his main source of inspiration. An adept of Greenwich Village night life, Davis put Mondrian on the right track for his ultimate masterpieces with a series of canvasses he called *Pads*, where he tried to translate jazz syncopation in coloured surfaces. Throughout the 1940s and 1950s he continued to pay tribute to jazzmen: *Tropes de Teens* (1956) even includes some verses by Duke Ellington.

While all the masters of lyrical abstraction and *action painting* in the 1940s and 1950s were more or less deeply involved in jazz, Franz Kline above all turned it into his main theme, from his 1940 mural *Hot Jazz* to his *King Oliver* (1958). It turns up in more subtle ways in many works by Pollock, De Kooning and most of all Sam Francis and Romare Bearden (*A Blue Note*, 1946).

From the 1950s certain painters systematically paid homage to jazzmen in their work, like J.F. Koenig (*Requiem for Sidney Bechet*, *Blues for Charlie Parker*) or James Pichette.

Finally there exists a specifically Afro-American school of painting where blues, gospel and soul are favourite themes. Linked to the typically New Yorkian movements of New Figuration and graffiti painting, and therefore to the rap trend, it is nonetheless full of allusions to jazz itself. An example is *Tribute to Gillespie* by Jean-Michel Basquiat.

Jazzmen and painters

There are many jazzmen who have also wielded the paint brush: Django Reinhardt and his 'neo-primitive nudes', Charlie Parker and his moving family portraits, Miles Davis and his female monsters made of colourful arabesques, Marion Brown and his portraits of musicians. Ornette Coleman, Don Cherry, Paul Bley and a few others have tried to convey the spirit of Free Jazz in paintings.

There are also a few rare artists who divide their time more or less equally between jazz and painting: the first was undoubtedly the saxophonist Larry Rivers. In Europe, the Swiss drummer Daniel Humair puts transparence and mystery first in his luminous and voluptuous acrylics. For his part, the famous East German painter and sculptor A.R. Penck, a drummer and founder of the Dresden Jazz-Club, has introduced the gestures of jazzmen in his neo-primitive works, and has designed some splendid record sleeves.

Painters and jazz

The record — and its sleeve — is the obvious place for jazz and painting to meet. This gives rise sometimes only to intelligent approximations: De Chirico illustrates Monk's *Misterioso* perfectly, just as Ornette Coleman's *Free-Jazz* is to be recognized in Pollock's canvas which it reveals. There are many artists — generally graphic designers rather than painters — who have expressed themselves in this field: David Stone-Martin and Raymond Moretti for Verve, Andy Warhol for Blue Note, and even Picasso, whose drawing is the logo of the label which bears his name, Pablo.

Finally some artists like to paint with music, accompanied by jazzmen: Jean Berthier seems to have been, with the bassist Henri Texier in 1966, the pioneer of this form of exchange, which has also been tried since by George Mathieu (with Kenny Clarke), James Pichette and quite a few others. A number of painters of the New Figuration movement even became jazz specialists — Rancillac — while others (Keith Haring, Alechinsky) are involved with it through concert and festival posters.

Jazz and dance: somersaults and tip-tap

Putting those two words together seems tautological, because so much bodily expression has been inherent in jazz since the legendary 'Congo Square' exhibitions in New Orleans. Yet the term 'jazz dance' used by teachers and choreographers has absolutely nothing to do with the Afro-American tradition. Only cinema archives can give an idea of this rich art that went into decline as from 1945: from then on jazz became the music of concerts and crowded clubs, where dancing was literally out of place, finding an outlet only in the ever freer gesticulations of the drummers. Until then the temples of swing had been the ballrooms whose names have remained legendary: *Savoy Ballroom, Roseland Ballroom, Apollo,* etc.

Acrobatic and fantastically diversified, this 'lost art', which can be seen in dozens of films, almost archeological treasures, include, as Charles Delaunay says, 'like jazz music, an incredible diversity of figures, routines, techniques and styles . . .'

The best known form (and the least forgotten) is the *tap dance* of the *hoofers,* who go back to the minstrel shows, where *sand dancers* produced a regular rhythm by dragging their feet in sand. Great stars of shows like the *Cotton Club*'s, the hoofers rightly considered themselves as proper musicians, avidly following the instrumental development of jazz, which they in turn influenced: thus, Armstrong always quoted as his model the great **Bill 'Bojangles' Robinson**, who can be seen in *Stormy Weather,* to whom Ellington dedicated his composition *Bojangles* and to whom Fred Astaire — who claimed he owed him everything he knew — paid homage in *Swingtime.* Others to be mentioned are Bunny Briggs, Leon James, 'Slide' Rochester Anderson, Al Minns, Buck and Bubbles, the Nicholas Brothers, 'Taps' Miller, 'Rubber Legs' Williams (also a singer) who recorded with Dizzy Gillespie and Parker, Baby Lawrence and Jimmy Slyde, who, having settled in France, brilliantly continue the tradition. Some contemporary dancers, like **Gregory Hines** (the hero of Coppola's *Cotton Club* and more recently of *Tap Dance*), form a bridge between the hoofers and contemporary dance, which in fact is not closed to jazz. Since the innovations of the great New York choreographer Martha Graham in the 1940s, many troupes have sought a great deal of their inspiration in jazz (Alvin Ailey, Pilobolus, etc.). The dancer-choreographer **Carolyn Carlson** makes regular use of jazz musicians like John Surman and Barre Phillips. But the true heirs of the hoofers are probably the thousands of rappers, who from the streets of New York, have spread *breakdancing* worldwide.

Jazz 'in print'

One can never sufficiently stress how much Afro-American music owes to the 'word', to the whole oral tradition of the blues, work songs, dirty-dozens, spirituals and gospel songs, the clever appropriation of 'lyrics' from the standard repertory, and even more to the witty diction, the ghetto verve that starts with the jive and ends up in the modern rap. Since the 1920s many works of literature have tried to capture the spirit of jazz in many different forms: poems, short stories, novels, plays, essays, autobiographies and portraits of musicians, as well as a considerable part of what has become a genre in its own right, jazz criticism.

The syncopated muse

The 'Harlem Renaissance' of the 1920s revealed a remarkable generation of poets whose main inspiration came from the popular form of the spiritual, and even more from the blues and the work song. A community with a lot of solidarity had much in common with the two great theorists of 'the back to Africa' movement (Marcus Garvey and W.E.B. Dubois), but in preference to the political debate chose a more lyrical expression, where jazz is often present. This was the case with Claude McKay, a New Yorker of Jamaican origin (1860–1947) and the author of *Banjo* (1928), with Sterling Brown (1901), Countee Cullen (1903) and above all with **Langston Hugues** (1902–1967), a globe-trotter constantly accompanied by his gramophone and his Louis Armstrong records, the author of 150 blues, most of which have been set to music. This tradition was radically prolonged after 1945, notably in the texts — usually designed for reading in public — of a **Leroi Jones** (Amiri Baraka) or a **Ted Joans**.

In Europe, and strangely, in France, certain poets immediately felt that jazz was blowing in their time like a breath of fresh air. Even though most of the surrealists were treading in the footsteps of Breton who poured scorn on all music, **Philippe Soupault** nevertheless wrote his superb *Ragtime* in 1917. Included in the collection called *La Rose des vents*, the poem is dedicated to **Pierre Reverdy** who twenty years later, recorded his own *Fonds secrets*

with the trumpeter Philippe Brun. As for **Cocteau** — who played the drums at the Boeuf sur le toit! — he was the pioneer of these 'jazzified poetry readings', recording with the orchestra of Dan Parrish from 1929 on. In the same period, **Michel Leiris** wrote a column on Ellington's records for George-Henri Rivière's review, *Documents*. The Belgian Robert Goffin, author of the *Jazz-band* series (in 1922), and the Swiss Charles-Albert Cingria, were deeply interested in the contribution of swing to modern poetry, while Garcia Lorca gave free reign to his enthusiasm in his *The Poet in New York* (1929).

After 1945, the number of poems directly inspired by jazz increased: we mention *Carte noir* by François Balorbe (1953), *Les Chasseurs* and *Lourdes, lentes* by André Hardellet (1969), as well as the works of the piquant Jacques Rèda, *L'Improviste* (1980) and *Jouer le jeu* (1985).

An entire essential range of French songs was built on the foundations of jazz, from Charles Trénet to Michel Jonasz, not to mention the unforgettable pair Boris Vian and Henri Salvador, the young Serge Gainsbourg and naturally, Claude Nougaro.

In the United States, outside Afro-American poetry, there was of course the *beat generation* of the 1950s and 1960s, which produced the most beautiful jazz poems: the two hundred and forty-two choruses of *Mexico City Blues* by **Jack Kerouac** (1955): under their influence the New Orleans writer, Bob Kaufman, dedicated the best part of his work to jazz.

The great pages of swing

A universe so naturally romantic could not fail to have an effect on the masters of contemporary fiction. Authors in Europe were the first to penetrate it, although it is true that jazz only served as 'background music' to the famous *Tales of the Jazz Age* ('The Children of Jazz', 1925) by **Scott Fitzgerald**. The German **Hermann Hesse** cut a figure as a pioneer with his very autobiographical novel *Steppenwolf* (1927) whose hero, Haller, has a dark and complex feeling about jazz. **Paul Morand** follows close on his heels with *Magie noire* (1928), then *New York* (1930). It is impossible not to mention the extraordinary 'descente aux enfers' by Céline, plunging into the cabaret of *Guignol's Band* (1944). In 1938 *The Young Man with a Horn* by Dorothy Baker appeared. It was a romanticized biography of Bix Beiderbecke, which was translated by **Boris Vian**, who was obviously one of the great 'romancers' of jazz, above all with his book *Ecume des jours* in which the hero, Colin, quenches his thirst with Ellington's chords transformed into cocktails. **Jack Kerouac**, whose cult novel *On the Road*, written between 1948 and 1956, became a real bible for the 1960s generation; the tales of his wanderings are told in the language of bebop.

Curiously, a certain number of writers were amateur drummers, from Cocteau to Milan Kundera, and including **Alain Gerber**, whose novels *La couleur orange*, *Une sorte de bleu*, *Jours de vin et de roses* express the communicative passion of jazz even in their titles.

As for short stories, our approval extends to the admirable *Saxophone-basse* (1967) by the Czech writer Joseph Skvorecky — whose first autobiographical novel, *Les Laches* (1958), forbidden for 'cynicism', already exalted the jazz craze — and of course also to *L'Homme à l'affut* (1959) by the Argentinian **Julio Cortazar** inspired by the life of Charlie Parker; by the same author, two books, more important and punctuated by allusions to jazz, should not be missed: *A Day in Eighty Worlds* (1967), which contains articles on Louis Armstrong and Thelonious Monk, and his extraordinary multi-layered charade, *Marelle*, a book of a complexity akin to

James Joyce in his *Finnegan's Wake*.

In the 'young authors' category, two names should be mentioned: Dany Laferrière, a Canadian of Haitian origin, whose hilarious *How to make love with a negro without really trying* (1987) is sprinkled with particularly useful discographic references; and Marc-Edouard Nabe, the son of the saxophonist Marcel Zanini, author of a very beautiful posthumous declaration of love, *L'âme de Billie Holiday* (1986) and of *La Marseillaise by Albert Ayler* (1989).

Jazz and crime stories

The two are such a perfect match that there is even a festival, at Bourg-la-Reine in France, to celebrate their encounter! In fact it would probably be quicker to make a survey of the crime stories that do not in some way feature a saxophonist. To begin with there are the masterpieces of **Chester Himes** (1909–1984), in which one could say that the (many) allusions to jazz are superfluous given that his writing and his favourite setting (Harlem) are the breath of jazz itself: *The Real Cool Killers*, *All Shot Up*, *Cotton Comes to Harlem*, *The Heat's On*, etc. Himes wrote crime stories just for subsistance, and his rather 'ethno-sociological' major novels: *If he hollers let him go* (1945) and *The Primitive* (1955) are his best works.

Himes's Harlem is clearly inspired by the Watts ghetto in Los Angeles where he lived, and which is the setting of Malcolm Braly's remarkable *La neige était noire*. Others to be mentioned are *Jazz Gang* by Paul Jeffers, *L'ange du jazz* by Paul Pines, *Le Petit Bleu de la West Coast* by the French author **Jean-Patrick Manchette**, and finally *The Jazz Makers* by the great journalist Nat Hentoff (a member of the editorial staff of the New York magazine *Village Voice*).

Criticism and biographies

Certain authors are not satisified using jazz as a literary ingredient, they have also gone to the very core of the subject. In fact, criticism of jazz has often been by inclination the work of the essayist, the poet or the humorist. If the first work which appeared was the remarkable *Le Jazz* by the ethnologist/musicologist André Schaeffer (1926), the second is the work of the Belgian poet Robert Goffin, *Au frontières du jazz* (1932). Numerous articles preceded them: the first was the fascinating chronicle of the *Revue Romande* (1919), in which the leader of the band, Ernest Ansermet, was inflamed with enthusiasm for Sidney Bechet's genius, until then unknown in Europe.

If the pen of the first specialized critics — John Hammond, Leonard Feather, Dan Morgenstern, Barry Ulanov, Stanley Dance in the United States; Hugues Panassié and Charles Delaunay, who founded the review *Jazz-Hot* in Paris — was not very 'colourful', it nevertheless deserves the credit for having succeeded in convincing the public of the high artistic value of jazz. After 1945, musicians like André Hodeir, Jacques B. Hess or Gunther Schuller were to add their indispensable musicological rigour. At the antipodes by his humour and detachment, (some said his casualness), the most famous of these 'historic' critics was evidently **Boris Vian**, whose columns in *Jazz-Hot* and *Combat* still have an astonishing freshness. The autobiography, another literary form favoured by jazz lovers, was certainly not the most successful. We shall remember for their quality as 'open-hearted-confessions', the memoirs of Billie Holiday (*Lady Sings the Blues*), of Mezz Mezzrow (*Really the Blues*), of Charles Mingus (*Beneath the Underdog*), of Art Pepper (*Straight Life*) and of Hampton Hawes (*Raise Up Off Me*), and for their great documentary value, those of Duke Ellington (*Music is My Mistress*), and of Dizzy Gillespie (*To Be or Not to Bop*).

Jazz and photography: capturing the instant of an ephemeral art

The great visual testimonies of our century have curiously neglected jazz: apart from several prints by Roy Avery, Robert Frank and Weegee, the photos of Robert Diosneau of the clubs of Saint-Germain, or the portraits of Miles Davis by Irving Penn, the jazz photograph has always been essentially the business of the expert.

In the United States, the Frank Driggs collection and the archives of Duncan P. Schiedt offer an irreplaceable iconography of the period before 1945. Otto Hess printed the portrait of the stars of Dixieland, Swing and boogie, William Claxton took portraits of everybody, from the young Sidney Bechet to Coltrane in his last years. As for Herman Leonard, and his assistant Charles 'Chuck' Stewart, they provided thousands of sublime images in the wings, and in the studios of New York. We must not forget to mention Bill Gottlieb, or Veryl Oakland, the privileged witness of the great Californian festivals since the 1960s.

Japan, thanks to its sumptuous specialized magazines, has become a paradise for jazz photographers: Yukio Ichikawa, Katsuji Abe, Tadayuki Naito and Yuzo Sato.

In Europe, the Italian **Giuseppe Pino** is without doubt, with the Frenchman **Guy Le Querrec**, the most original of the 'backstage' portrait photographers. In Paris, **Jean-Pierre Leloir** since the 1950s, and **Horace** since the 1960s, have built up magnificent archives of concerts and festivals. The Englishwoman Valerie Wilmer, since the early 1970s, has been making an effort to reveal the 'hidden face' of the life of jazz players on tour.

Relief has been brilliantly assured, notably in France, by excellent technicians who also have the gift of being everywhere at once. This is the case with the photographers of the specialized agency **Mephisto** (Yves Carrère and Didier Ferry), Jean-Marc Birraux, Philippe Cibille and Christian Rose, or all-round reporters with a passion for jazz like Philippe Etheldrède. It should be noted that jazz photos are more frequently being reproduced in the popular press (and therefore in colour) which makes the correspondence between jazz and black and white photos obsolete.

Index

Note: Entries in **bold type** refer to articles headed with the name shown.

Louis Armstrong *in 1958*

Ella Fitzgerald *and*
Duke Ellington *at the Birdland
in 1950.*